AF409613

Stress, Emotions and Health

The Manual for Integrative Professionals

Intervening on all body-mind levels in a scientific and multi-disciplinary approach

Science, methods and tools to work on connections between emotions, posture, brain, metabolism, immunity and all the processes at the heart of health and development

Authors: Fabio Sinibaldi and Sara Achilli

INDEX

Foreword   12

Part 1 - The need for an integrated care and change approach   18

Introduction   19

Complexity today: from daily life to disease   19
Interoceptive test 1   23
The important resources offered by modern science   27
How the right tools can get you anywhere   35
Looking at people and really seeing the whole person   37
References   42

Stress: an updated scientific reworking   43

Axis 1 - Sympathetic   45
Axis 2 - The HPA axis   51
Cortisol, more than just 'the stress hormone'   55
Axis 3- Neurogenic Inflammation (or NNA)   56
Even more axes   57
References   59

Emotions: an updated scientific review   60

A change of perspective to avoid reductionism   60
Adaptation and/or Emotions?   61
One brain or three brains?   64
The vagus nerve and emotions (and more)   65
Emotions, Networks and Experience   68
The Higher-Order Theories of Emotions   70
Practical implications for application   72
References   74

Planning and promoting care and change processes   **75**

Doing your job well   75
Who are care and change professionals and what do they do   76
An overarching work method   77

PART 2 - Mechanisms, Processes, Patterns and Methods of intervention   **91**

Integrative Functional Patterns   **93**

Keeping everything under control with timing   93
Behaviour: its origins, use and ending   96
3 Macro-areas of Integrative Functional Patterns   97
THE 8 PHASES OF THE IFP   98
The start of everything: from detection to evaluation   *98*
The importance of what happens first: Predictions and Preconditions   *100*
Moving on to action: from reflexes to full control   *103*
From rest to added value: adaptation, recovery and development   *105*

Change Switches - Introduction   **108**

What are switches and what is their source?   108

Switch Group n. 1 CORE - Greasing the cogs   **113**

Plasticity, Energy and Mind Metabolism, Epigenetics, Circadian Rhythms   113
Assessment: what to observe and what to work on   115
Importance of the 'micro' level   118
3 levels of neural plasticity for change, learning and flexibility   121
The intracellular level: a powerhouse at our disposal   *123*
Epigenetics: the roots of change   124
How to intervene on these processes in a practical way   *125*
HISP Exercises: High Intensity for Short Periods   128
Inter-cellular level: learning and flexibility   *131*
Favouring Learning   133
Extra-cellular level: a powerful ally   *137*
Body and Mind Energy, Efficiency and Physiology   140
The metabolism viewpoint   *140*
The role of oxygen   *145*
A First integrative technique: Crossed Cycles Breathing   147

It's a matter of (circadian) rhythm   151
  Frame the problem   *151*
  Several practical solutions   *153*
References   157

Switch Group n. 2 SYSTEM REGULATION – The art of daring and rebalancing   **159**

Homeostasis, Allostasis, Abuse of function, Inflammation (body, mind, brain)   159
Assessment: what to observe and evaluate   162
The stress limit: where flexibility ends and you begin to pay the price   163
  Rethinking homeostasis and allostasis   *163*
  The Principle of Minimum Free Energy   *165*
Psychosomatic Release Techniques   166
  Allostatic overload   *170*
Technique: The Emotional Buffer   173
Technique: Vagal RESET   176
Posture, Muscles and Allostatic Load   178
  Where to start: what to pay attention to – 2 practical modes   *179*
Psychosomatic Stretching Technique   180
  Different degrees and levels of physical and mental suffering   *183*
Mind and Body joined in inflammation   184
  What is inflammation?   *186*
  What activates or amplifies inflammation   *188*
  The second brain: the gut and the immune system   *189*
  Food and Inflammation: What to eat and what to avoid   *193*
The power of the Microbiome on Mood, Behaviour and Health   195
  The emotions–trauma–inflammation connection   *196*
  Depression or sickness behaviour?   *198*
References   201

Switch Group n. 3 ADAPTATION - Radar and Computer to manage complexity   **203**

Networks & Hubs: control centres for emotions and behaviour   203
Assessment: what to consider and evaluate   205
The crucial role of cerebral networks   206
It all starts with perception… which is often wrong   210
  The complexity of feeling and perceiving correctly   *213*
Avoid unnecessary triggers   216

From Allostasis to Predictions   219
Prediction-adjustment loops   222
Interoception   224
Interoceptive tests 2   227
Feeling the boundaries of perception   229
The practical benefits of thinking in terms of networks   231
The radar-switch that analyses dangers and resources   233
Resource Balance techniques + Reconsolidation   239
Taste as a way to heal and grow   242
Uncertainty: life is unpredictable. Problems and solutions   244
    A generational reading: Predictability, age, and mastery   247
The switch-manager analyses the environment, resources, goals, and action plans   248
Reboot Techniques   252
Modular Thinking Technique   254
The Pre-Solution Technique   256
Possible Scenarios Technique   258
References   260

Switches Group 4 SOCIAL – Man: the lost animal   **261**

Evolutionary Relationships, Primary Social and Interpersonal Systems   261
Assessment: what to observe and evaluate   263
Social interaction and relationships from an ethological perspective   264
Attachment and other inter-connected areas   265
    Attachment... or Contact?   270
    Changing perspective: Detachment   273
Technique - Parallel Worlds   274
    The power of synchrony and context in emotional-interpersonal dynamics   275
Facing Technique: Knowing how to face things   281
Tolerance towards ambiguity and social engagement skills   285
Rethinking Aggressiveness   286
    The different paths of aggression   288
Emotion Modulation technique: anger and aggression   292
    Incorporating relevant factors   295
Ancestral Needs   296
    The 6 Ancestral Needs in summary   298
    The Importance of Nurturing Ancestral Needs   304
References   309

Switch GROUP no. 5 - FLOWS – Harmonies and rhythms of life   **310**

Natural Flows: autonomous, interdependent, and integrative pathways for ideas, thoughts, movements, posture, language, etc.   310

Assessment: what to observe and evaluate   313

(No longer) Natural flows   313

Framing the different flows   314

Observing flows   320

Technique - MAD Mapping of Dysfunctional Automatisms   327

Reaction questions   329

Ideative flows: schemas and rhythms   332

Thought: in-between language learning and culture   334

Mind O'Clock & Turn your Mind Techniques   337

Method - Ideographic thinking   339

Achieving self-assessment and improvement   344

Method - The camera's objective eye   345

Knowing how to change your mind   346

When we tell stories about ourselves and tell ourselves stories   348

Focusing other people's emotions   350

From trauma to flow obstruction and release   351

Inverse Physiological Replay + Obstruction Release Techniques   352

Points of contact between creative, postural and motor flows   354

Schema Inversion Technique   355

Movement and postural flows   358

The structure of movement, stress and emotions   359

Freedom of movement = emotional and mental freedom   360

Isometric Emotions technique   361

Interpersonal Accommodation Technique   365

The physiology of emotional movement: the devil is in the detail   368

Balance and fluidity of control   371

Even more flows   372

2 Communicative-Interpersonal techniques   373

References   376

FOREWORD

Stress and emotions are a key part of human life and play a central role in every daily experience as well as in shaping health or disease. At work, in our interests, love lives and friendships, stress and emotions are always at play. In fact, these are the two fundamental adaptation and development mechanisms as they allow us to face any challenge – from the traffic we encounter when driving to the realisation of a large project – and they represent a fundamental engine for our motivations and for reaching the objectives we set ourselves every day. Stress responses and emotions take shape through complex mechanisms, which involve the whole body. Starting from the metabolism and epigenetics of each cell, activating brain areas and networks, interacting with the immune system and manifesting themselves in thoughts, postures, relational behaviours and every other way in which we live our lives. These are very complex processes, which influence each other and interact – in a more or less favourable way – with our physical and mental health. Because they are sophisticated mechanisms, they offer numerous possibilities for flexible adaptation, to live intensely and to evolve. If we think about it, every great invention is born to remove a stress factor or to complete the evolutionary sense of an emotion. This is true for the discovery and use of fire (to protect us from other animals and feed us more effectively) and the construction of a musical instrument, which – once made – will serve to give a constructive expression to passions, desires or disappointments. Between these two extreme examples lie all other human activities in which, in one way or another, stress responses and emotional reactions are a central component.

In shaping stress responses and emotions, for each possible benefit there are just as many processes that can lead to problematic alterations or dysfunctions. For example, a stress response that does not end when it should, keeps neurotransmitter levels high over time, affecting memory skills (adrenaline and cortisol, which in addition to being known as 'stress hormones', play a fundamental role in the processes of memorization), but also making long term changes to the contraction of some muscles which, in turn, alter body maps and identity. We have just seen a short introductory example, but there are multiple aspects to consider. It is, however, already clear that in order to restore overall balance and well-being consistently, it is essential to understand and know how to act on all the factors involved.

In this book we take all the main adaptation and development mechanisms that revolve around stress and emotions into consideration, so that we can understand and act on the processes underlying physical and mental health in their entirety. We will see that there are different stress axes and how they interact with the immune system, in order to understand in a scientific and concrete way, how and why, among other things, so-called psychosomatic disorders take shape. We will delve into the mutual influence between emotions, stress, language, posture, mental patterns, nutrition and every other aspect of regulation of human life. We will analyse how these processes can impede each other, or how flow and act in synergy. We will tackle the multi-directional connections between physical and mental pain, anxiety, body activation, epigenetics, circadian rhythms, neurobiology, physical activity and numerous other fields and disciplines from a practical perspective.

In this text we share all the studies and research we have carried out over the past 20 years. We offer a special thank you to the members of the Association for Integrative Sciences who have enthusiastically adhered to this approach and actively taken part in various research initiatives, helping us to carry out increasingly broader evaluations and research with multidisciplinary feedback. In fact, we will provide insight on the connections between different fields and disciplines, in order to gain the widest possible vision of the person we wish to help at 360° over their care, well-being or development journey.

It is now well established by numerous researches in different fields that it is impossible to fully understand emotional and mental dynamics without considering the body and, vice versa, it is not possible to act effectively and permanently even on the most (apparently) "banal" dislocation of an ankle without considering thoughts, identity, stress and emotional experiences. For example, consider an anxious teenager who locks himself in the house for fear of challenges at school and who constantly focuses exclusively on these perceived dangers. It seems a fairly clear and limited issue, yet to resolve it we need to analyse and act on other levels in addition to the mind. One of the many key factors could be the fact that his brain networks are continually under pressure, 'bombarded' on multiple levels: on the one hand, from the stimuli of social networks that overexcite the amygdala and other key areas for self-regulation; on the other hand, from the lack of certain and predictable perspectives, which do not fall within logical plans but in the non-conscious predicting system, which is not reactive to talking-therapy and logical reasoning (we will see several modes of intervention in the course of the text). Even a blocked body is more often a cause than a consequence of these situations and we will be able to act on many practical aspects that include daily habits, posture, type of nutrition, physical exercises, mind-body exercises, metabolism of mental processes and more. This is just a brief teaser; in the book we will look at all these aspects and a series of other insights organized into structural and functional models. One of these models, the main one that also shapes this whole book, is organized in *Switch areas*, or metaphorically the different levers on which it is possible to act – in the right sequence and/or in synergy – to activate change or to put a body-mental mechanism back into physiological state.

Taking into consideration the other example we had introduced, that of the sprained ankle, someone might object *"but if a young boy heals his ankle and starts playing sports again, what's the point of looking at everything else (epigenetics, emotionality, immune system, etc.)?"*. In fact, if everything had gone smoothly in that boy's life, it wouldn't make much sense. Yet, very often, that sprained ankle is linked to some relevant emotional, if not downright traumatic event. Maybe in the short term the boy resumes playing sports, but the emotional memory remains active in the background and then it will drive the next accident to happen. Or, during the forced resting phase required by rehabilitation, negative brooding about the fact that he is missing the competitive season, or simply not having fun with friends, will cause his new body map and motor patterns to be altered and form new connections to these negative assessments, damaging sports performance, as well as walking in everyday life. Another interesting aspect is that chronic stress (even outside sports, perhaps at school or with a girlfriend) as well as nutrition, lifestyle and possible drug abuse, can modify immune response, increasing tissue rigidity (thus making it less elastic and at greater risk of injury), as well as amplifying pain responses.

We will see in subsequent chapters how emotional memory, body maps and motor patterns are connected to each other, they influence each other and also interact with thought flows, sleep-wake rhythms, neural plasticity, epigenetics, hormones and the immune system in relation to these two examples. Knowing these mechanisms, it will be possible to act on them in our current professional setting (we will also look at various practical techniques and application strategies) and also in what ways they can be applied at home.

This book is for those who have understood that it is necessary to take a broad perspective and a multi-disciplinary approach in order to best help people in different critical situations: illnesses that persist, situations of serious suffering, physical and emotional trauma, in case of chronic stress, complex psychosomatic disorders, stunted growth or development processes. Those who have gained this awareness have usually faced these situations first-hand. To do this, they have already studied and investigated a number of aspects and have noticed directly the significant difference that an integrated and integrative approach can have. It has been the same for us and, over time, it has become an exciting path of personal and professional passion in synergy and in continuous evolution.

This volume is, first of all, for care and change professionals who have realized that more can be done and who wish to expand their range of action, both in terms of conceptualization and understanding of the situation, and in terms of potential and intervention tools. Since it is an integrated and multi-disciplinary approach, we have tried to explain everything so that it can be clearly understood independently of one's previous knowledge. We think that this book, like the courses we have been running for years, can be used well by both experienced professionals and by students and postgraduates who want to go a step further right away. Even a non-professional reader will be able to encounter interesting concepts to better understand their situation and find useful practical ideas to help themselves and be helped in the best possible way.

Reading this book from start to finish is the ideal order. However, you can also read it in no particular order, according to your interests. For those approaching an integrated multi-disciplinary science for the first time and are not used to the concept of acting on the more 'biological' aspects, the chapters dedicated to the first two Switches may seem less attractive. On the other hand, it is precisely these parts of the text that are most useful in debunking the knowledge previously acquired with respect to the processes that generate and sustain various pathologies, physical and mental dysfunctions. On the other hand, you can also start from switch 5 and go backwards, if this makes you feel comfortable. It depends on your style with respect to novelties. In any case, there are many connections and links between the different areas, so it will be useful to reread everything a second time. In fact, regardless of specific order, each chapter will be clearer in light of the knowledge developed throughout the book. In this way, moreover, it is possible to integrate and consolidate one's learning and develop an all-encompassing overview.

A stylistic note: to ensure maximum usability of the text, we kept a single narrating voice, that of Fabio Sinibaldi. The parts edited by Sara Achilli can be found above all where we talk about metabolism and nutrition, but her hand is present in other parts of the text too, precisely with a view to maximum integration.

Throughout the book we will analyse a series of themes and we will look at some illustrative cases. Each case, although described in detail as a single person, is a synthesis of typical cases that we have encountered in professional practice and supervision. This mode guarantees the reader maximum usability and, on the other hand, maximizes the privacy of real patients. Following the same logic, the photographs shown are not of patients, but have been taken with subjects who have applied all the techniques and strategies exactly, in order to be realistic and reliable, but always respecting effectiveness and privacy.

These cases help us to understand how many other levels of reading we have available when we are in front of a person and on how many aspects we can intervene to foster change and optimize the care processes, as well as potentially introducing new ones. Most of the cases will be developed over various chapters, in order to identify the different perspectives for in-depth analysis and synergistic interventions.

This book, although delving in detail into the scientific foundations of the various mechanisms taken into consideration, is intended to be a pragmatic applicative manual. Therefore it is full of practical ideas and operational indications. Most of them are shown graphically in the following ways.

INSIGHT OR TECHNIQUE EXAMPLE

Insight or technique text

🔍 Sample case

💡 Application idea

🤲 Practical pointers

PART 1 –
THE NEED FOR AN INTEGRATED CARE AND CHANGE APPROACH

INTRODUCTION

COMPLEXITY TODAY: FROM DAILY LIFE TO DISEASE

When a person says "*I have a problem*" referring to their daily life or to their health, what are they really talking about? What is really hiding behind a misunderstanding with a colleague, a frustration towards something we can't achieve, a disabling anxiety or chronic pain? Over the years there have been many enlightening theories that have helped us reveal the 'real cause' behind a problem: a person was aggressive with their partner not because of a relationship problem, but because of their personal disappointments; a knee hurt because the opposite shoulder was stuck; a child's asthma was due to separation anxiety from their mother and, conversely, an emotional trauma would not resolve because physical aspects had not been considered; and so on.

Looking for new explanations is crucial. Personally, I love doing it, but it's often not enough. Almost always there are various explanations to consider at the same time. The first is found almost immediately, another emerges with the new studies and insights. We also often find a third and fourth reason. Sometimes there are causal factors that triggered that mechanism, in other cases we may find contributing factors or elements that occurred later, but which prevent its resolution. There may be significant influences between apparently unrelated areas, as in the case of Jack, who was afflicted by forward hunching in the shoulders which he had tried to correct through various sports, developing significant muscle mass, but without being able to open up his chest area. This created emotional pain for him because he was the first to not accept himself like that and, moreover, the other kids at school made fun of him. As we will see in the course of the text, in addition to mental processes, this type of posture also supports a type of biofeedback (which here we can literally consider 'a message that goes from the body to the brain') that promotes conditions of insecurity and low self-confidence at a biological level. In cases like this it is essential to identify the various mechanisms at play and act on them in a targeted manner. For example, Jack's posture was influenced by excessive diaphragm contraction due to the chronic stress he was subjected to (also due to congenital factors independent of his experiences with respect to his body) and which biomechanically influenced the kyphosis curves of the upper back and cervical lordosis.

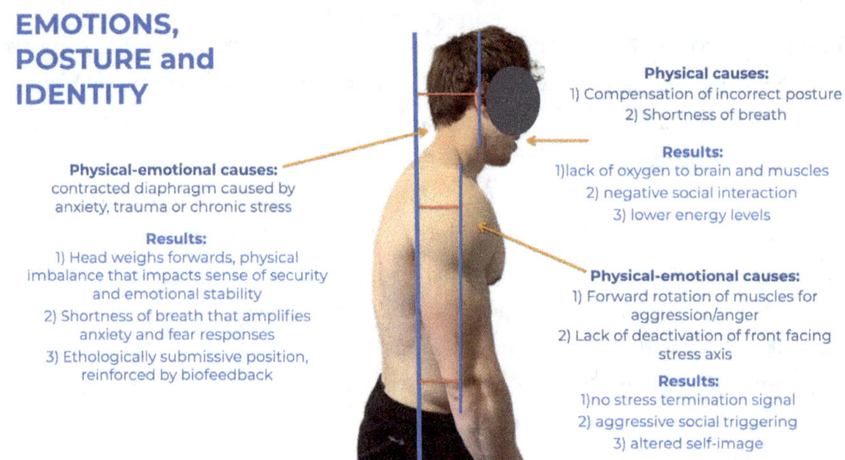

Fig. - Some mutual influence dynamics between emotions and posture in cases like Jack's. Only some of the possible causes and implications are noted, by way of example.

On the other hand, anger at an injustice suffered a few years earlier created strong tension that drove to the clamping of his mouth muscles, leading to grinding his teeth at night and generated a 'turtleneck' posture. Jack could not stand how he looked and was unbalanced forward, also creating a sense of poor and cascading physical-emotional stability. All this was supported and amplified by his diet and the use of pro-inflammatory supplements, which helped him to develop the desired muscle mass, but at the expense of an increasingly hyper-reactive nervous system. In light of all these observations, we worked with Jack with mental, bodily, mind-body integration techniques, self-image representation and through the review of the nutritional style (all described later in the book), obtaining the desired results in about 3 months, but above all achieving overall physical and mental well-being.

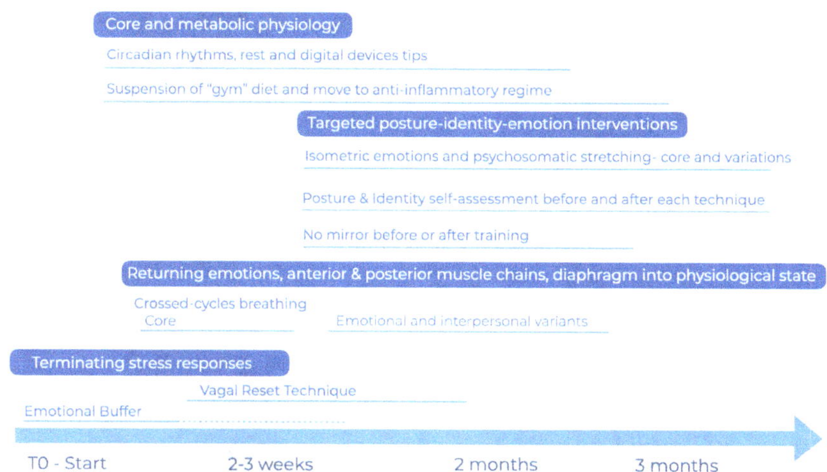

Fig. - The integrated therapeutic project proposed for Jack. The techniques and strategies mentioned will be covered in later chapters of the book

A theme that I enjoyed very much in my research and in-depth studies is that of resistance to change. When a therapy – physical or mental – did not work, we initially thought of mental resistance by the patient who didn't want to cooperate for transparent (for example *"if I recover I have to go back to work"*) or subconscious reasons (for example *"I cannot have a child, otherwise I would be a bad parent, just like my father"*). Today we have seen that this type of resistance can be combined with more complex and hidden factors in other levels too. For example, immune system inflammation makes psychotherapy for depression less effective[1], just as excessive cortisol for prolonged stress responses makes the flu vaccine ineffective[2]. These are just two introductory examples; we will analyse many other reciprocal and multi-dimensional phenomena that we group under the name of Influencing Hierarchies.

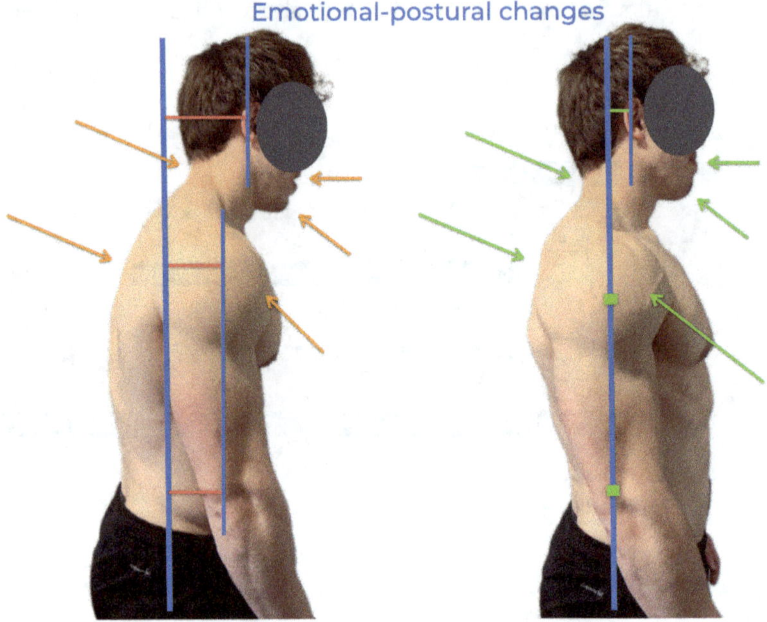

Fig. - After an integrated intervention on several levels it is possible to obtain a natural change of posture and its emotional correlations (both in cause and in effect). These photos are about four months away from each other. As you can see, in addition to the postural-emotional changes, the quality of the tissues also changes (less fluid retention and skin irritation, both signs of overcoming systemic inflammation, with overall benefits to physical and emotional health).

In addition to analysing this type of mechanism, in this book you will find many practical box-outs, such as the following one on interoceptive tests. Their purpose is to provide tools (tests, techniques, methodologies) that can be used in different moments and with specific purposes. A distinctive feature of the Integrative Sciences, just as the term 'integrative' and not just 'integrated' underlines, is how dynamic the approach is. A test like the following one, in fact, can be used during the very first meeting, even after just twenty minutes of talking to give a first practical tool and show an active approach. This does not mean that it is 'tiring' for the patient, but rather that it is an approach that involves and motivates them in the process. A test like this can be used to provide a first concrete example of what we are doing, to begin to explain while at the same time gathering information (the working method in its entirety will be analysed in depth in a specific chapter).

INTEROCEPTIVE TEST 1

The connection between different systems and domains can be easily demonstrated. I typically propose some tests to give substance to the explanations of the mechanisms that I am illustrating; this significantly helps my audience - whether it is an individual session, a consultancy or a group in training - to feel the value of what is being discussed on their own skin. Furthermore, these small experiential tests almost always open associative links that help to understand how these aspects specifically concern them, as well as impact many other aspects of daily life.

One of these tests (we will see others in different chapters of the book) consists in asking you to slowly turn your head, first to the right and then to the left, paying close attention to the physical sensations, but also to what happens on a physical and mental level. After the first test, you are asked to do the same exercise again, only this time clenching your teeth. Many people immediately notice that there is a smaller range of motion, which is quite normal from a purely mechanical-anatomical point of view. What they are amazed by is that they realize that much more has happened: they realize that their heart rate increases, that sensory perception in the mouth and neck increases, that they feel even the slightest pain and that when you can combine different emotional experiences (a sense of helplessness, limitation, frustration, of "being at risk" even though fully aware that it is irrational in that context, etc.) to all these sensations, thoughts of self-criticism (*"I am unwell"*, *"I should take care of my neck"*, *"I'm really old"*, etc.) or negative thoughts towards the external environment (*"why is it making me feel pain?"*, *"it's work's fault that I don't have time to exercise"*, etc.) can be triggered. By reading these examples you have probably already tried to take the test. In any case, I recommend that you try it first-hand and then also propose it in your professional practice. Some people immediately notice multiple aspects, others need to redo the two variants (natural and with gritted teeth) 3-4 times and to be invited to do them very slowly, to perceive the changes well.

It is also possible to add a third variant, in order to further increase perceptions. You can make the head move holding the mouth open passively, or relaxing facial muscles, perhaps facilitating relaxation with a light massage on the temples and masseters.

An important point to underline during the discussion is that everything that is experienced happens because of very small intentional variations. In everyday life this type of change often occurs without our being aware of it, and yet they still initiate a series of behaviours, emotions and experiences that we attribute to something else. On the other hand, you may note that it takes very little to bring the situation back to neutrality, with the related benefits.

This first interoceptive test is deliberately introductory and simplified, in the next chapters we will develop further insights and application subtleties.

It is safe to say that today all cases are complex and based on multiple factors and, in one way or another, they can be defined as psychosomatic and resistant to change. This can also be sensed by looking at things from a different perspective: that of resolution. Many cases are successful, but just as many people do not heal or change, despite their and the therapists' efforts. Sometimes there are improvements, but in the long run we often see relapses or other setbacks. A few years ago, in psychotherapy, the saying was that if you do not work on the deeper cause, the symptom could reappear again, sometimes under a different form; a dog phobia could disappear and then recur as dermatitis, for example. This intuition remains valid in part, but needs to be revised and expanded on the other hand. The basic problem must be solved, it's true, even if it is not necessarily an unconscious conflict. That could be the central element, but it could also be a chronic activation of the stress axis (or better 'of the stress axes', as we will see later), or the result of a habit, lifestyle, mindset, belief and conviction, of nutrition, inflammation, of epigenetic marking, allostatic load or more. In most cases it will be a combination of these factors, almost always in interaction with each other. For us, going through the different chapters of this book, it will be important to get to know all these factors and to find a method to analyse and manage them in an organized way, each within our own profession.

In all this rich complexity, it is also important to look outside the individual and consider them as a complex system that lives and is part of several other complex systems. Man's life is increasingly against nature; the cultural and physical environments in which we live are as stimulating as they are hostile to our well-being and physiological development.

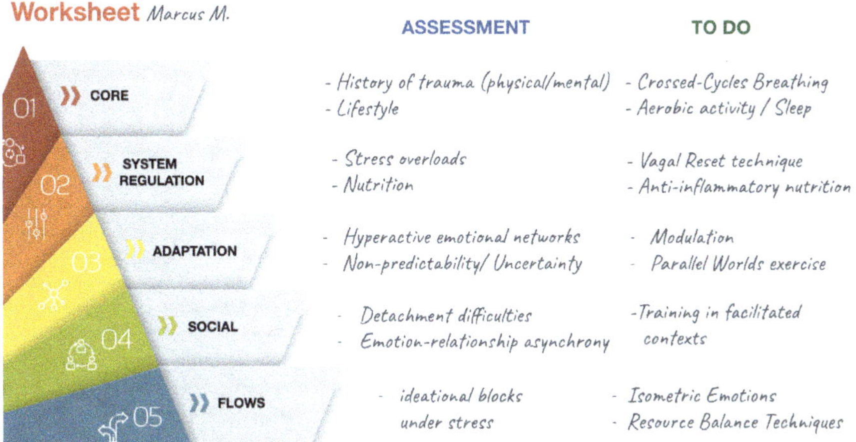

Fig. -A worksheet based on the Switch model (which we will explain later in the book). It is a practical way to actively involve the patient or client in the cognitive process, give him a sense of guidance and orientation among the many aspects at play and reveal the mutual influences between the different factors. Furthermore, the approach that seeks practical solutions for the different aspects identified is thus immediately visually evident. This worksheet, like those of other models and techniques that we will see in the text, can therefore be used to explain and interact with your audience. In addition, it can also represent a tool for autonomous self-exploration between one meeting and another.

Nowadays most people live tiring and stressful lives on several levels: they are deprived of sleep; they frequent an environment in which people are proud to work too much, often to the detriment of other interests and relationships; people are subjected to constant challenges at work and socially to which they have to adapt with high performances; they are bombarded with stimuli from social networks and technology; they live in unnatural environments; eat junk food that alters metabolism and offers little energy; they do little or no physical activity and, if they do, it is often for competition and not pleasure; and so on. These ways of life are not neurobiologically sustainable and do not even make sense for our development.

Graphic representation – not only through diagrams and tables, but also through visual representation of thought – can greatly help people understand all the mechanisms and systemic implications underlying their physical and mental health. Furthermore, it allows us to clearly emphasize that a behaviour, an emotional reaction or a way of thinking can be the result of many different mechanisms.

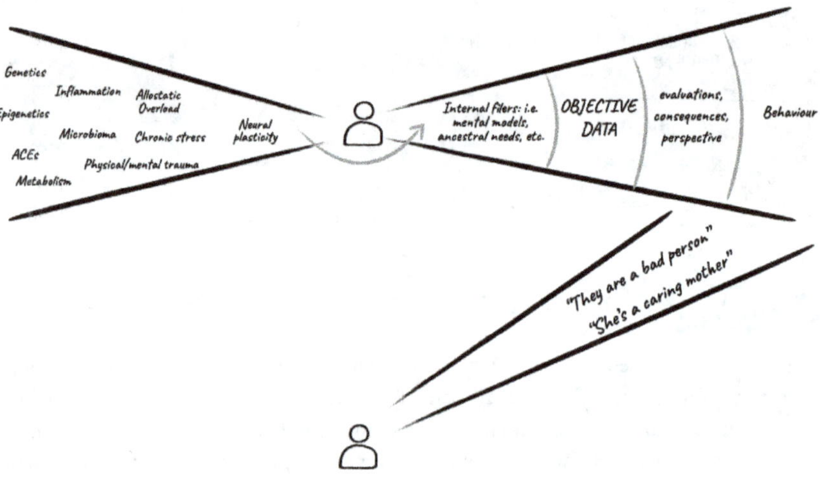

Fig. – A scheme created with the Spotlight technique (one of the different applications of Ideographic Thinking, which we will explore further on) that can guide data collection by making us immediately understand the importance of looking at factors from the past as well as the present and the future. Furthermore, in this way it is easy to make a person understand that their judgment on themselves or on another person is based on little data and, consequently, is reductive and can lead to incorrect assessments and choices.

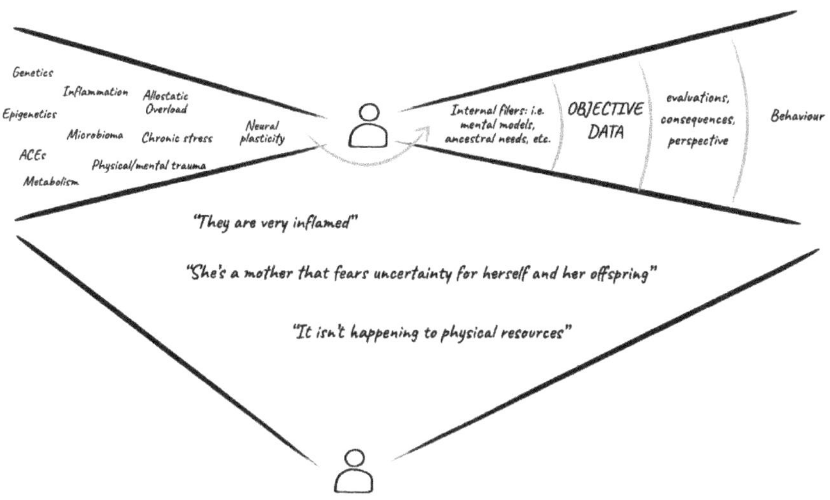

Fig. - By broadening perspective it is easier to identify the mechanisms that generate those behaviours, thus helping to better understand real motivations, empathising and applying healthy compassion and, based on the role played in that relationship, improve it in the best way.

THE IMPORTANT RESOURCES OFFERED BY MODERN SCIENCE

Reality is complex, just like people and their lives and problems. Fortunately, science is also constantly evolving and offers us more and more tools to understand and act effectively. We could say that the sciences themselves constitute a complex system and their integration generates added value, which exceeds the sum of the parts. In fact, this is one of the reasons why we have developed the Integrative Sciences over time: as a framework to grasp the added value that arises from the synergy of different sciences. This is why we describe them not as 'statically' *integrated*, but *integrative*, with reference to their dynamic interaction and evolution over time.

The people we help, whether over the course of therapy or on a path of change or development, need and rely on us. It is our responsibility to have the clearest picture possible and to have a broad set of effective tools in order to accompany them along the path that is most useful for them, one that makes them feel fully understood in their entirety. They quickly need all the relief possible (respecting the physiological processes of the mechanisms involved, but without colluding with the request for 'magical' and unsustainable solutions) and, at the same time, we must know how to identify the most suitable mechanisms and ways to set a treatment or change project with broad perspectives and with significant and lasting effects over time.

We are now used to complexity, it is an integral part of our life. Every day, we think in terms of: complex systems, multi-factorial, multi-disciplinary, neural networks, networks, synergies, systemic vision, sometimes we even come to mention entanglement and other concepts derived from quantum physics. In most cases, however, these are words used to refer to complexity, but without necessarily having understood it. Indeed, unfortunately we often witness a manipulative phenomenon in which a complex concept is used to justify a pseudo-magical solution. There are slogans like *"with the power of the quantum mind you will find happiness"* around for example. If the promoters of these solutions are asked about the postulates of quantum physics, they usually do not know them and clearly have no idea what they are (I, at least, have not met anyone who was able to so far). This does not mean that we all need to gain any complex knowledge, but that it is certainly necessary to know some key concepts related to our field of action. What we have been trying to do for years with Integrative Sciences is precisely this: to study, understand, select and make these concepts clear and shareable and, as a fundamental final step, make them practically applicable to those who have to work in the field every day.

In fact, practical application is the fundamental point of arrival, the concrete and effective fallout that gives meaning to theoretical study. This concept is now so clear that even the didactic planning for elementary school children outlines that they will acquire skills for the management of projects, of course gradually and in a manner proportionate to their age. This approach might seem precocious and excessive, but if you look at the many daily problems each person faces, from children to adults, from work-related issues to the number of daily environmental and social stimuli and demands, it's clear that this is a skill that must be nurtured from an early age.

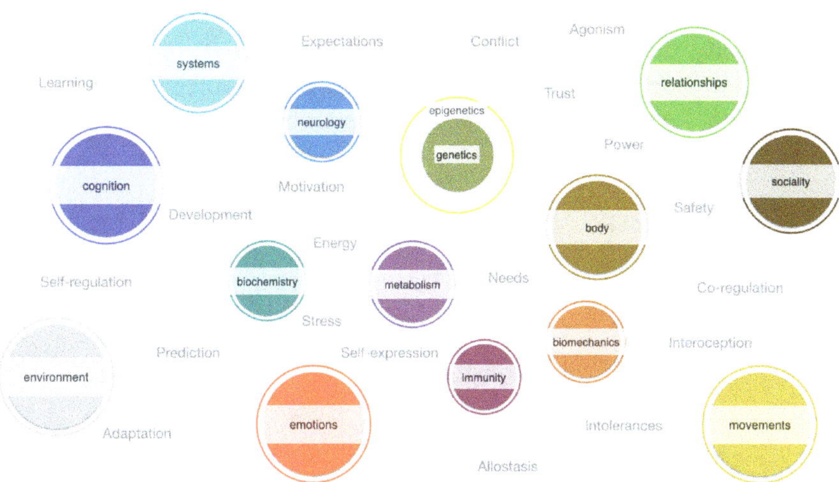

Fig. - A graphic representation of how different elements of daily life can be explored by specific fields of study, disciplines and sciences that revolve around common themes that, only through an overall and synergistic vision, can be fully understood.

Thinking in flexible modular projects and systems not only allows you to move with awareness and calm through complexity and in ambiguous and unpredictable conditions, but it also creates the basis for a healthy taking on of responsibility, without feeling overwhelmed or inadequate due to external pressures.

To further explore these aspects, let's now consider a transversal theme for health and well-being such as the relationship between posture, stress and emotions. Let's focus for a moment exclusively on the first aspect: posture. It is a complex subject, that should be analysed from different perspectives: we can and must study the muscles that govern it, as well as their relationship with the bones on which they are articulated; anatomy, together with evolutionism and neuro-anthropology, highlights the interesting fact that the bones of the arms and legs are not straight, but rotated on their central axis; the study of the engineering of human body movement, taking into account forces and vectors, highlights that in order to follow the functional anatomy of muscle chains and to develop maximum power – with its implications for the feeling of self-efficacy and mastery – there must always be a rotational component to the limbs. There are also other aspects that we will pick up in the course of this text. Furthermore, all this is fully in line with what has been observed for centuries by disciplines that are attentive to the physiology of movement such as yoga, tai chi and various martial arts.

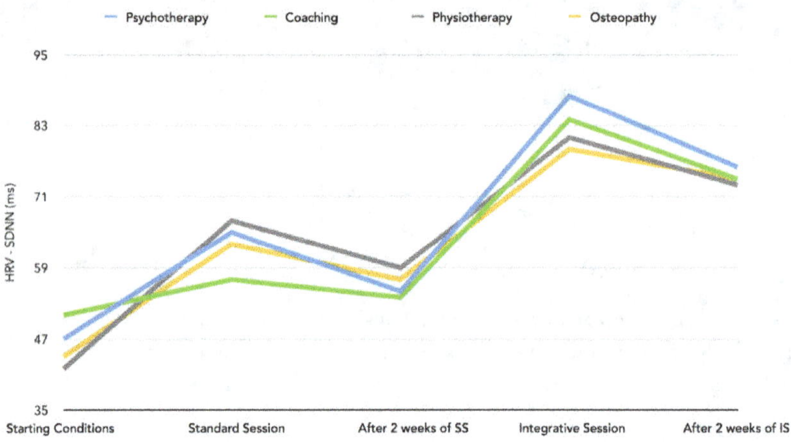

Fig. - In this research, carried out thanks to the contribution of various professional members of the Association for Integrative Sciences (psychotherapists, coaches, physiotherapists and osteopaths), we noted cardiac variance (HRV) from two different groups: one group was treated with the classic approach (Standard Session) others with an approach in which concepts and techniques of Integrative Sciences were introduced (Integrative Session). For each subject, the cardiac variance was detected at the time of arrival, during anamnesis (starting situation), during the active part of the session (in the Standard or Supplementary version) and two weeks after the first treatment in normal living conditions, that is, not during a session. As you can see at a glance, the use of an integrative approach that takes care of the person as a whole favours more effective results both in the session itself and in terms of maintaining the benefits over time.

To understand what we are talking about in practical terms, try putting your hands in the typical push-up position or when you push a barbell forward in the gym to train the pectoral muscles. Try to bring your hands forward in a perfectly linear motion. Now try to repeat the same movement but this time rotate your hands slightly inwards as they advance. The sensation is more fluid and natural this time. If this movement occurs with contrast (for example, pushing against the edge of a table, a wall, a bar), when even a slight rotation is applied, the thrust is more effective, powerful and connected to much more positive emotions regarding the situation and with respect to self-image. This ease and naturalness shape the feeling of mastery and effectiveness. In the event that these movements take place in an interpersonal relationship, they allow you to take control and have a tangible effect on the other person, even if it's only a delicate movement as you make room for yourself moving through a crowd without feeling overwhelmed. As we will see, these considerations can have different practical implications in the realization and improvement of different techniques across multiple disciplines: pain management, body psychotherapy, manipulative techniques, emotional-somatic exercises, mind-body integration, awareness, sports or work performance, etc.

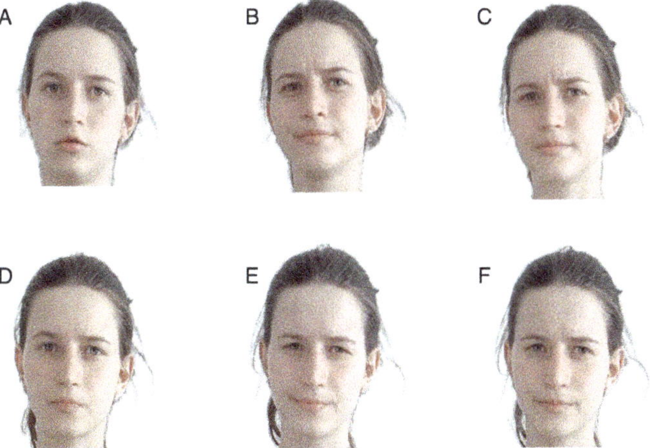

Fig. -. Look at the six images and try to imagine what difference there is in the situations that the girl is experiencing and in what could cause her expressions. In the next image you will find the explanations.

Fig. - These are the full-length photos of which you only saw the face previously. The situations are very similar, but the resulting changes in expression are significant. In all three images (A, B, C) the girl is thinking about a person she experienced as invasive (it could be an attacker, a stalker, an abusive parent, a manipulative boyfriend, etc.) and she is imagining that she is pushing them away. In image A the girl assumes this pose, but without intentionality, in order to control bodily activation regardless of her emotional one (B, C). The difference between B and C is the fact that the arm movement is not just linear, but also rotational. From the photos, as well as from the subsequent verbalizations, it is clear that the experience of power, a sense of control, security and other positive emotions are much more relevant in the second mode (C).

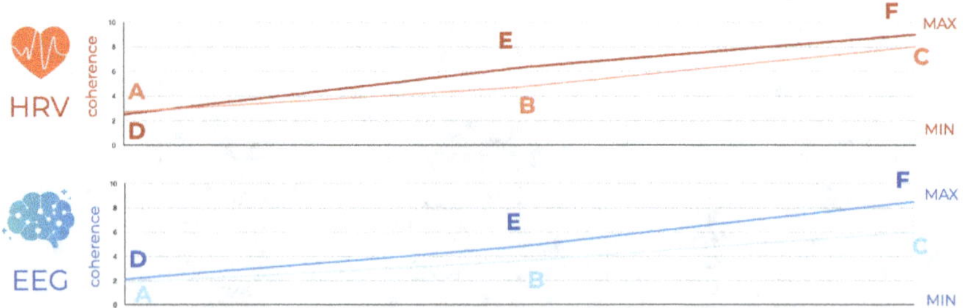

Fig. - The difference between the thrust (A, B, C) and the traction (D, E, F) modes is also noticeable through biological parameters such as cardiac variance and brain waves.

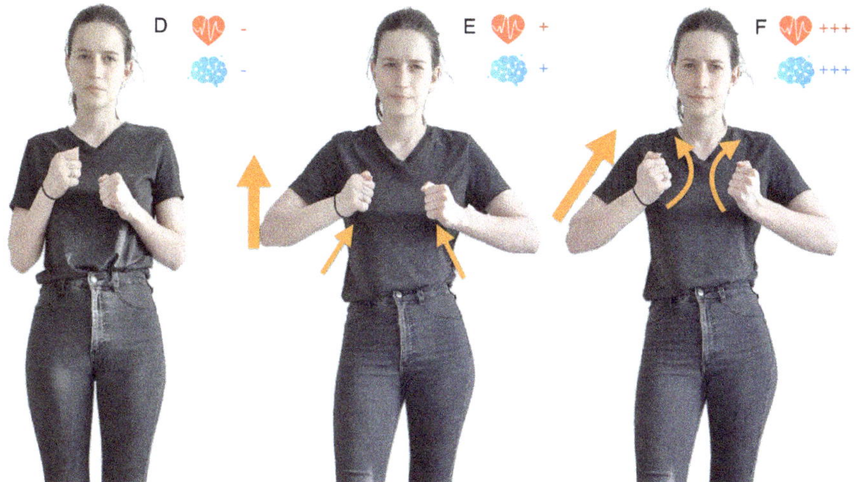

Fig. - In this second variant, the only difference from the previous one is that, instead of pushing the person away, the girl imagines pulling them. It might seem counterintuitive, but as we will see in the switches in area 5, the motor engram of approach and submission is natural and instinctive for humans, as for other mammals. Conversely, pushing away is not an innate but learned mechanism, so it acts on less profound brain circuits and also concretely offers less control and security (the enemy is far away but could get closer, whereas in submission there is direct control and we wait for the other party's surrender to clearly end the exchange). Again, the difference between the two images (E and F) is in the physiological rotational movement of the arms which involves the whole body.

We have only highlighted a few elements of the posture-emotions relationship, focusing on one important biofeedback mechanism at the basis of self-regulation, safety and development of self-image. Let's now briefly look at some other important factors at play to further broaden our perspective. In the coming parts of the book, we will take up all these aspects in a systematic and in-depth way.

Posture can be better understood thanks to disciplines that do not originate from care and health. Cartoonists and animators, for example, have been studying the connection between posture and emotions for some time. If we think about it, this is an extreme approach and, for this very reason, interesting: since the character of the drawing or cartoon does not have a biology, an embodied emotional story or thoughts that interfere with the realization of that posture, studying this perspective offers us clear insights into how an emotion is perceived and how it influences the observer. These approaches, together with neuroscience studies applied to the expression of emotions, for example, have made it possible to significantly revise many of the previous beliefs regarding non-verbal communication. Later we will further explore these aspects and those of emotions and stress, proposing an updated and scientifically based vision of these issues. This way it will be possible to understand that so-called *psychosomatic mechanisms* require the analysis of several factors at the same time. For example, to understand how a certain type of back pain is linked to stress and emotions – and above all what can be done to facilitate the situation – you must consider all the elements described above, but also how much the myofascial tissue is inflamed by dysfunctions (e.g. stress overload and incorrect posture maintained due to failure to terminate adaptation processes) but also due to an incorrect diet, altered sleep-wake rhythms, not giving space to one's needs (even regardless of stress factors), and many other possible and contributing causes.

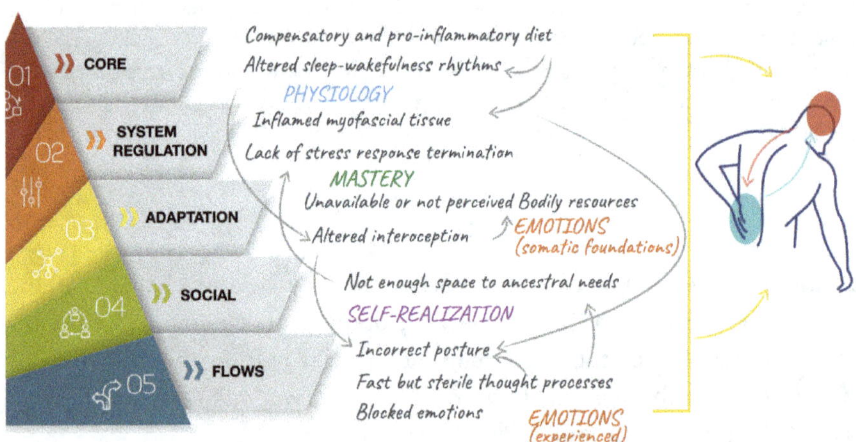

Fig. - The worksheet we used to identify the various factors involved in a case of back pain and, in particular, the connections with emotions and other important experiences, such as a sense of mastery and self-realization.

In the light of these examples, it becomes clear why among the Integrative Sciences we do not only find disciplines that are traditionally relevant to health (biology, metabolism, epigenetics, neuroscience, anthropology,

PNEI, etc.), but also different disciplines such as game theory (which despite its name is a complex mathematical theory, very useful among other things for understanding the irrational part of the decision-making processes), various sports (fundamental for understanding physiology, the physical roots of safety and mastery, motivation, etc.), music (which allows us to study the effects of self-regulation and co-regulation through the voice from a new and measurable perspective, but also to identify the mechanisms that activate and develop certain neural networks in a unique way), expression (using communicative force and the expression of the visual arts for the benefit of mind and brain) among others.

HOW THE RIGHT TOOLS CAN GET YOU ANYWHERE

Try to imagine this: you wake up tomorrow morning and your bed is in the middle of the jungle, you don't know where you are, you have nothing available. You feel disorientation and terror. Ok, it was just a nightmare.

Now imagine this: you wake up tomorrow morning and you are in a hut. You remember that you arrived there by your own volition because you wanted to take an explorer course. There are maps, compasses, tools, enough food and a guide at your disposal. You feel enthusiasm and curiosity. The adventure begins!

The difference between these two scenarios makes us practically perceive that, with the right mindset and tools at your disposal, you can do anything. Don't be overwhelmed or frightened by the complexity and volume of information in different areas that we haven't dealt with before; instead, it is a fascinating situation, which offers clarity to us and security to the people we work with. On the other hand, we are naturally curious individuals: we like to find out more about cooking, even if we are not professional cooks; we are curious about the sports that friends or children play, even if it seems impossible for us to carry it out personally; we look with curiosity at the 'behind the scenes' of how films and special effects were made, even if it is not our job. These are ideas that we understand and quickly enter our knowledge base. Of course, becoming an expert is different and requires practice and application. Precisely for this reason we have made the utmost effort to create a book full of explanations, examples and techniques that you can try first-hand even before applying them to patients or clients. Furthermore, precisely because we have to try to find our way among so much information, explore it together with the patient and evaluate how to intervene, we have developed many schemes over time; these are modular models and tools to help manage all this knowledge and make it applicable and manageable. Being oriented and organized makes everything easier both for us and for the people we work with. We don't have to know everything by heart and understand everything in no time at all; this is a skill that will develop over time. Once we have confidence in the information and the tools, everything becomes simpler and can take shape gradually. This begins a process of discovery and experimentation to be done with one's patient or client. He/she will also be able to do some helpful work independently at home with different types of exercises and worksheets. This way complex and multi-factor cases, such as typically psychosomatic ones (from intolerances and dermatitis right up to degenerative diseases), anxious or depressive pathologies, chronic pain and headaches, can be addressed in their various components methodically, ensuring more consistent and lasting results over time.

When moving through a new and large territory, even if you are an expert, it is normal to use a map, compass or a more modern GPS. What we want to share is a smarter way of working, where a lot can be achieved with little effort. We will outline an entire working method, plus a series of insights, with related models, cards, exercises and techniques. Some aspects will be immediately understood, others will become clearer as you go along. We will see many cases, examples and analogies to make everything as easy and practical as possible. As they say in IT, and beyond, when you have to learn a new program – eg. you leave the old program to manage and retouch photos and use another one – *"the learning curve is quite steep"* (usually parabolic): after a short initial phase, you enter the right mindset, the pieces begin to fit together and everything goes well. That's exactly how it works, I've seen it happen many times during courses, masters and supervisions.

LOOKING AT PEOPLE AND REALLY SEEING THE WHOLE PERSON

When we look at the way that a person 'works' – their reactions, their modes of being, their more or less effective ways of adapting to reach their objectives – we are actually only observing the end result of a complex system of processes and phenomena taking place inside them. Different processes occur simultaneously: some sequentially, others simultaneously. Some steps affect those that come directly after, and often there is a system of retro-feedback which allows the re-evaluation of what is happening so as to respond more flexibly to a change in the environment, in other people, or even in the resolution of the initial situation.

Understanding the hierarchies and the ways that these systems and processes influence each other is very useful to help design a therapeutic or educational strategy that respects and follows these patterns. It also provides a way to help understand resistance to change: if you are trying to change downstream or somewhere along the route, you need to look to the source first.

We often focus on psychological resistance to change such as 'secondary advantage' or as a 'mental or emotional dependence on others'. We will see later on that there can also be resistance with indirect psychological roots (such as an unpredictable environment which boycotts brain networks related to long term investment and impact motivation to change). There are also types of resistance to change that we can describe as 'psychosomatic', such as an inflammatory state of the immune system which can alter neural plasticity and the state of alarm. As a result, we could also say that there are no 'difficult patients', but only patients that need to be tackled in their full complexity.

This type of information becomes strategic to solving problems such as chronic pain, psychosomatic issues, mood disorders, stress-related pathologies, PTSD and more, in which the correlation between mental and emotional processes is in a two-way relationship with inflammatory states (see the first three switch levels and in particular those belonging to group 2, a little further on in this book).

The hierarchies with which adaptation and development systems are activated and take shape are thus fundamental not only in pathology, but also in various areas of daily life. There are also different aspects of daily life in which behavioural hierarchies are critical. It has been amply proven, for example, that regular physical activity improves mood, health and motivation (we will analyse the details relating to the various anti-inflammatory, neural regulation and dopamine circuit processes – as well as many more – that are involved in these processes in the coming paragraphs). It has, however, also been proven that physical activity that is carried out unwillingly (for example at externally imposed times and rhythms) increases stress levels in a way that is both measurable emotionally and traceable in serum biomarkers[3]. This phenomenon is explained by a metabolic process, known as insulin resistance (see group 1 switches), which affects both resistance to change and homeostatic and allostatic mechanisms (as we will see in group 2 switches).

An important fact, when dealing with interconnected systems and influencing hierarchies, is that insulin resistance can also be detected at neuron level and is at the heart of various neurodegenerative diseases (in fact we now refer to type 3 diabetes to describe cerebral insulin resistance in Parkinson's disease, Alzheimer's disease and various other diseases)[4].

Looking at things from yet another perspective, there are also interesting priming phenomena (such as the seemingly irrelevant information that we are exposed to when we overhear a conversation over a cup of coffee, or the colour of the walls in a particular shop) which can influence behaviour and decisions in apparently unrelated areas. These could be our ability to solve a maths problem, our choice of food or level of irritability. Various studies have been carried out and it has emerged that priming can significantly impact outcomes such as exam results or shop revenues[5].

External elements interact directly and indirectly with various internal elements such as self-image and the need for social acceptance, right through to the awareness of available physical resources that have a relevant physical origin (processed by the insula in the earliest phase of risk-assessment as shown in the section analysing the Salience Network as part of the third group of switches, but also addressed from another perspective, in the earliest phases of the Integrative Functional Patterns, as we will see in the following chapters).

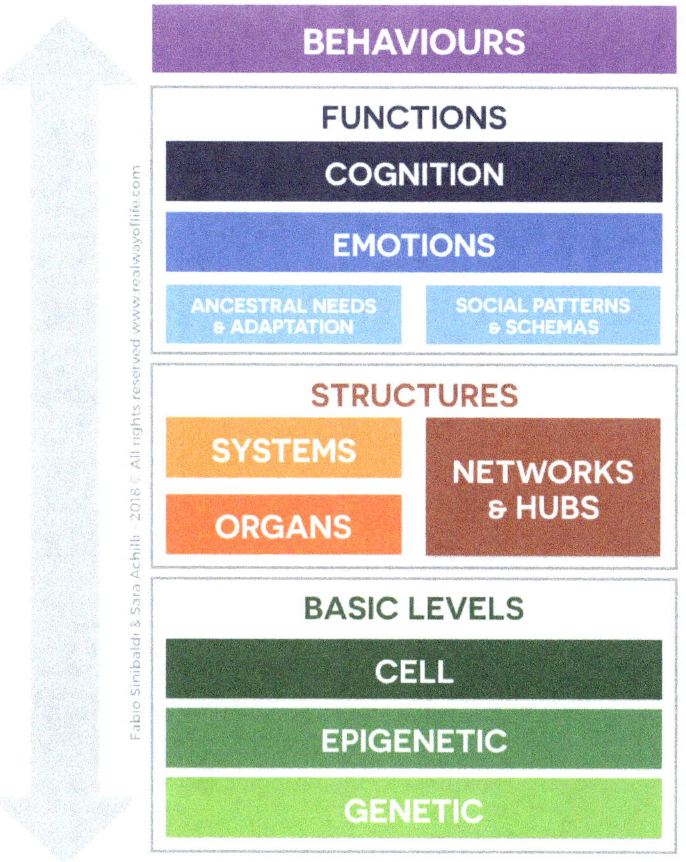

Fig. – Breakdown of all Interconnected Levels with heterarchical links (non-linear hierarchies) at the core of any behaviour and mind-body process.

We have looked at a series of examples focusing on some of the main functions and processes taking place. We have purposely used fairly neutral terms that are not connected to any particular theoretical system so as to highlight that these phenomena are always present regardless of how we choose to conceptualise them.

To fully understand these mechanisms, it is useful to go and look at the underlying structures and systems that support them. We will see that there are various *Interconnected Levels*[6], that provide meaning and enable targeted and methodical intervention on self-regulation processes, decisions, behaviour, safety, adaptation, development etc.

The concepts of *Interconnected Levels*, *Integrative Functional Patterns* and *Change Switches* can therefore support a methodical approach that evaluates all processes of interconnected influence by identifying synergies (or antagonisms) and developing a veritable map of the elements at play. It is thus possible to take a targeted decision with a clear strategy on:

- what requires immediate intervention;
- which elements are key but can cause resistance to change if not duly taken into account;
- what intervention is necessary to achieve the prerequisites for change;
- what strategies are useful to provide an experiential, open and constructive experience of new modes of adaptation;
- what criteria enable the consolidation of these new modes of being;
- which elements drive motivation;
- and so forth.

The professional's ability to heal and change boils down to how these mechanisms are managed: whether they are activated in the right sequence favouring physiological processes and tackling dysfunctional processes and the systems that fuel them in a multi-pronged approach that uses different tools.

To fully understand these processes and intervene in a targeted way, we will analyse all the governing factors in detail. Once we understand the different factors at play and the mechanisms that regulate them, we will look at how to keep all these elements under control and how to apply an integrated and structured intervention method.

Consistent with what we have seen so far, it is important to remember that two fundamental phenomena of life such as stress and emotions are themselves complex and multi-factorial. These are elaborate processes, in which different aspects of the mind-body dynamics are in continuous interaction with each other, affecting all the domains of human life: epigenetics, memories, learning, experiences, thinking, identity, physical activity, metabolism, nutrition, etc.

These are key phenomena to human experience which are – by their intrinsic nature – adaptation and development processes that interact with the spheres of action of all the different care and change professions reviewing them from a scientifically updated and multi-disciplinary perspective.

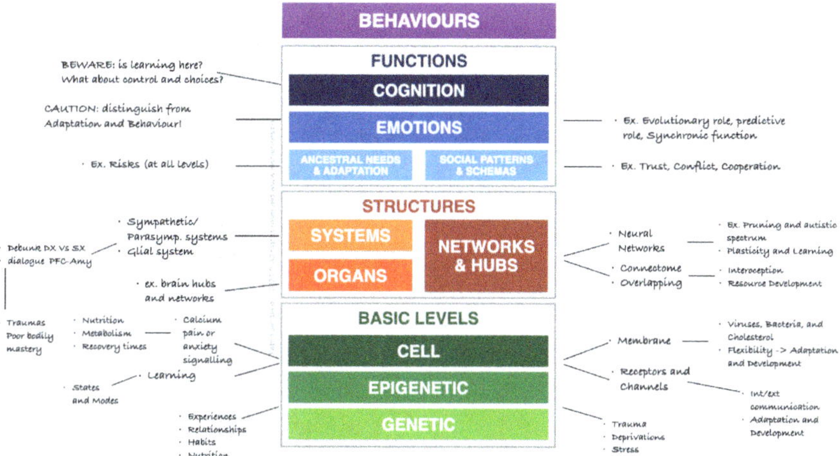

Fig. - With the Interconnected Levels map, you have a guide to help you explore various aspects that may be involved in, for example, in a diagnosis of ADHD, attention deficit in adults or children, learning disabilities.

In this first part of the text, we will look at some interesting mechanisms and their impact on daily life. In the second part we will pick up all these mechanisms and the processes that regulate them in a more operational way to understand them even better and, above all, to see all the ways in which every professional can intervene on them in their work-life to achieve an even more integrated approach and help the person as a whole.

References

[1] Danese, A., C.M. Pariante, A. Caspi et al. 2007. Childhood maltreatment predicts adult inflammation in a life-course study. Proc Natl Acad Sci USA. 104: 1319–24.

[2] Madison, A. A., Shrout, M. R., Renna, M. E., & Kiecolt-Glaser, J. K. (2021). Psychological and Behavioral Predictors of Vaccine Efficacy: Considerations for COVID-19. Perspectives on psychological science : a journal of the Association for Psychological Science, 16(2), 191–203.

[3] Sasaki, H., Hattori, Y., Ikeda, Y., Kamagata, M., Iwami, S., Yasuda, S., Tahara, Y., Shibata, S. (2016). Forced rather than voluntary exercise entrains peripheral clocks via a corticosterone/noradrenaline increase in PER2::LUC mice. Scientific reports, 6, 27607.

[4] Mittal, K., Mani, R. J., & Katare, D. P. (2016). Type 3 Diabetes: Cross Talk between Differentially Regulated Proteins of Type 2 Diabetes Mellitus and Alzheimer's Disease. Scientific reports, 6, 25589.

[5] Langer, E. (2009). Counterclockwise: Mindful health and the power of possibilities. NY: Ballatine Books.

[6] Sinibaldi F., e Bartozzi R. (2017), The stabilization phase: bottom-up techniques and the use of the body for somatic resources in: From bottom to top (and back...). New bottom-up approaches: cognitive psychotherapy, body EMDR. (Onofri A, La Rosa C).

STRESS: AN UPDATED SCIENTIFIC REWORKING

There is a lot of talk about stress, both on a personal level, as a problem that almost everyone experiences, and in the various scientific communities. In fact, the stress response (or rather 'responses', as we will shortly see) is closely woven into the fabric of life and affects everyone all the time. Modern life often pushes us to the limit, towards wanting to achieve more in our studies, at work or in our other areas of interest.

Fig. - The two main and best known stress axes have direct implications on the respiratory, circulatory, and digestive systems. In this simplified representation we can see some of the more direct activation pathways that come into play if stress becomes chronic and there are no recovery or compensation measures. Stress can, in fact, lead to various 'stress disorders', typically including heart attacks, colitis, dysbiosis, ulcers, etc. We will see that there are also numerous other ways in which the stress axes alter our physiology and create various dysfunctions.

We're pushed to never stop (*"just one more..."* is the typical mantra when we're watching a TV series that fascinates us, or opting for another chocolate, a caress and other things we like), but often the consequences of this behaviour are much more damaging in the long term than they are beneficial in the short term.

From a scientific perspective, it is a good thing that stress is studied by several disciplines because it is a phenomenon that affects the whole being and that moves on emotional, mental and physical levels driving constant reciprocal influences. Thanks to targeted investigations, it has been possible to discover that there are multiple stress axes (and not, as it was previously taught, a single axis) and to clearly understand the scientific foundations of typical psychosomatic disorders. It is now in fact possible to clearly understand how stress can generate stomach pain, dermatitis, physical or emotional suffering, depression and even serious degenerative diseases. At the same time, the inverse mechanisms, whereby certain bodily conditions can alter mental state and cause emotional distress, are also well understood.

Recently, research has revealed a close interaction between the nervous and immune systems in the regulation of inflammation that links psychological and social stress with chronic somatic diseases and vice versa. In the short term, stress can save our lives, allow us to adapt, help us overcome new challenges and learn new skills. It is also the basis of various motivational and hedonistic processes: just think of any game or sport and you will find they have all these typical elements in common. In the long run, however, when stress becomes chronic, when we cannot see escape routes or alternatives, there are no opportunities to fight or to reinvent ourselves because we have run out of resources (from the most concrete ones to emotional and social ones) then health pays a price.

To understand these processes and to shed some light on them, let's take a look at the main stress axes. Once these aspects are understood (it is not necessary to know and remember every feature in detail, but it is enough to grasp the general mechanism), the need for an integrated approach immediately becomes clear. We will illustrate the various practical applications that derive from it throughout the book.

The axes described below are not independent, but act both in parallel and in synergy with each other, exerting reciprocal influence. A clear distinction, however, helps us identify all the different processes that compose them more clearly.

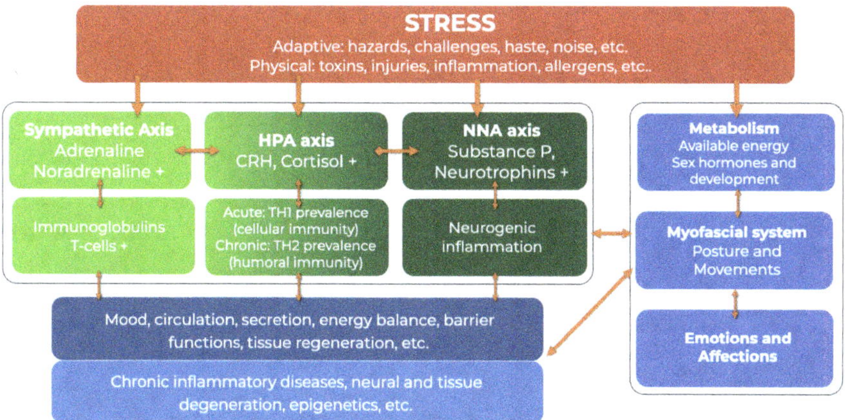

Fig. - The 3 main stress axes with their interactions and implications in all areas of human life (thoughts, emotions, movement, posture, pathogenesis, etc.).

AXIS 1 – SYMPATHETIC

In chronological order, the earliest known stress axis is the Sympathetic. Walter Cannon Bradford, with the discovery of norepinephrine in peripheral nerve fibres and of adrenaline derived from the adrenal gland, identified the so-called fight-or-flight response. This nervous system axis triggers the orthosympathetic system (in instances of activation) or, vice versa, makes room for the parasympathetic one (in deactivation instances). Contrary to teaching up to now, the sympathetic and parasympathetic systems are not opposites and antagonists (an accelerator and a brake) but work in synergy (we will return to this aspect later in the book).

This axis starts at the hypothalamus, passes through the Locus Caeruleus and works through other organs up to the adrenal glands, in particular the medulla, where it produces adrenaline and noradrenaline (called catecholamines).

It is a well-known fact that the hypothalamus plays a key role in stress responses, integrative processes and numerous self-regulation activities.

Although less widespread, the notion that the locus caeruleus also plays a central role on several fronts is also common. In fact, it centrally controls activity and connectivity of all brain areas both directly and indirectly, especially when it comes to the regulation of the prefrontal, motor and sensory areas as well as the limbic cortex. This helps us see clearly that stress responses are all-round reactions on a physical, motor, emotional and mental level. Furthermore, counter-evidence shows that dysfunctions in the connection between the LC and the previously mentioned areas are detectable in any psychiatric or motor disorder.

Noradrenaline, which activates us in the short term, can increase IgE (E immunoglobulin) levels in the long run. These are antibodies that are produced in response to the presence of a stimulus perceived as a potential threat. If the stress reaction is prolonged and not terminated, these excess immunoglobulins give rise to the typical symptoms of sinusitis, asthma, dermatitis, etc. In the long run, an excess in norepinephrine drives neurons to induce mast cells to degranulate histamines, thus favouring allergic reactions.

Peter is 6 years old and was sent to therapy on the recommendation of his teachers who see him as a worked-up and restless child. His mother confesses that he *"is so worked-up that he can't tolerate anything; sometimes he scratches his arms until they bleed"*. Peter also has some allergies and intolerances, but his mother doesn't see this as a problem; she says: *"nowadays it's a very common issues, in fact, who doesn't have allergies?!"*. Unfortunately, the mother is right on this last point: far too many people have immune problems that manifest through allergies and intolerances. Excessive levels of stress, which are now common in our culture, are one of the primary reasons. There are of course also other environmental aspects (pollution and endocrine disruptors), drug abuse, pro-inflammatory nutrition and other elements that we will see in due course. Accepting that it is *normal* to have problems with intolerances and allergies just because it is widespread is a serious mistake. Let us remember that the norm (hence 'normal') is a statistical criterion for the frequency of an event, it does not mean that *it is okay*.

In Peter's specific case, it is enough to observe him while he plays in the waiting room and to talk to him about his interests to see that there are no negative thoughts or worries in his mind. He is a child whose face and words exude serenity. But he seems to be in a body that fits him too tight, like an old outfit: he constantly fidgets, tugs at the neck of his shirt and, at a certain point, begins to scratch himself energetically. I ask him why he does it and he replies that it itches so much, that scratching gives him relief, so much so that he goes on, even though he hurts himself and he knows that his mother and father will scold him for it.

It doesn't take an expert dermatologist to immediately notice that his skin is extremely dry on his arms, but also a little dry on the rest of the body. Precisely because I am not a dermatologist, I know that plan B, after the necessary tests and checks, is to send him to a specialist. But plan A is as follows: first of all, try to verify or falsify my hypothesis. I explain to Peter and his mother that maybe he is not anxious, but he really does feel a great urge to itch, so they should try applying a common moisturizer (so long as of good quality) over the next few days and see if itching improves and, consequently, reduces the nervousness induced by the itching, pain and a sense of helplessness towards this symptom. This makes Peter immediately feel understood; someone finally offers him an explanation and does not tell him that "*he has a problem*". Also, he now knows that he doesn't have to feel guilty about his parents, and this removes an additional source of stress.

As we noted earlier, chronic stress releases histamines and promotes allergic reactions. If this is Peter's case (we are only making a hypothesis, but we can verify it in a simple way), by reducing stress and reducing histamine-rich foods (cured meats, canned foods, strawberries, etc.), we would expect a reduction in symptoms. To temporarily reduce stress, by talking to mum, we decide to suspend violin lessons for a week (which he does not like very much, but his parents push him to attend), to avoid football training (which he does like, but where he is sometimes teased badly).

Four days later, the mother writes to me announcing a miracle: she says that Peter is now a peaceful child and that he no longer scratches himself. Obviously, no miracle has occurred, but we have identified a fundamental element relating to the start of the problem. As a result, using further anti-inflammatory (switch 2) and metabolic (switch 1) measures, we have helped Peter find a balance between duties and pleasures in relation with his parents' wishes (the violin but not just that, switch 4) and to help manage the kids who made fun of him (both on a communicative-relational level, and working on his confidence at a mental and physical level Switch 3).

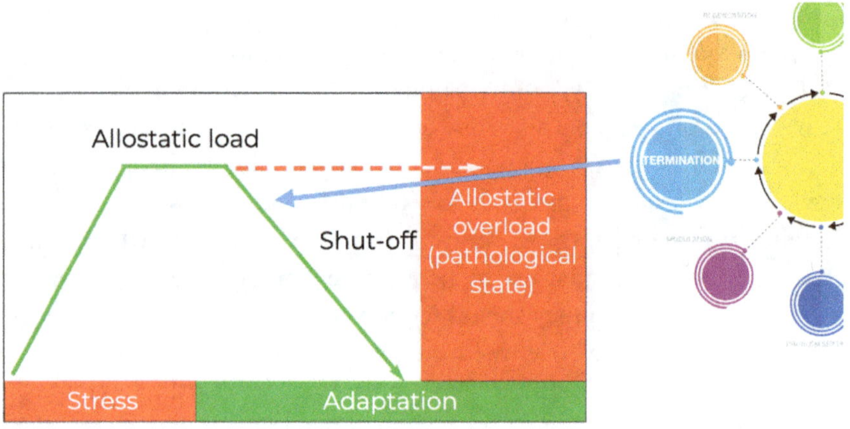

Fig. - The Termination of an adaptation cycle allows you not to go into hyper-adaptation or into a chronic state, avoiding having to pay a price at psychosomatic level.

A key concept, which will accompany us right across this text, is that of Termination (the concept will be explored further in the chapter on Integrative Functional Schemas), or the importance of completing stress responses, precisely to prevent the consequences their prolonged activation leads to as described above and many others that we are about to analyse.

Another critical aspect concerns the great variety of possible stress reaction triggers and the reasons why they may not go to termination. This axis, as already intuited by Cannon, is linked to the attack-flight dynamic. This means that in us humans, as in any mammal, the axis may be activated whenever there is a vital risk (even of emotional, affective or identity survival), or the threat of some form of predation. We will rarely meet a natural predator, such as a tiger that wants to eat us, but our life is dotted with other types of predators: aggressive people, conflicts, colleagues competing for a rise or a promotion, rivals in sports or in affections, a child or colleague who asks us for help just when we were about to relax, activities that rob us of energy and time. Even the car in front of us that 'steals' the last free parking space may trigger this type of response.

Continuous stimulation of this type, without the right *recovery* times and adequate time spent in a *state of safety*, can significantly alter our body, leading us to pay a significant psychosomatic price.

The mediators of the Sympathetic Nerve Axis are, among other things, responsible for the rapid redistribution of immune system cells in the target organs following the acute activation of stress. This stress reaction is also linked to survival behaviours (fight or flight) at the local immune defence level and promotes the rapid elimination of microbes or tumour cells on site. This is further promoted by the activation of natural killer cells and the differentiation of Th1 cells (the immune group that protects against viruses and bacteria), but at the expense of the Th2 response that protects body tissues. If we think of animals or the life of our ancestors in more natural environments, these mechanisms have a clear evolutionary significance: we are likely to get scratched, infected, or break bones or body tissue in our fight or flight, and these may come into contact with microbes and bacteria from our opponent. For this reason, the immune response is associated with the acute stress response, it allows us to avoid the damage that could typically follow a fight or flight response. There are people who, despite being fairly balanced and aware, often experience acute stress: these may be high-level professionals in challenging contexts (important financial responsibilities, involvement in the life or death of others, ethical dilemmas with repercussions on entire communities, etc.), performers, professionals on construction sites and in high-risk laboratories. We will see that it is essential to understand the different mechanisms underlying their stress responses, how they connect with their basic physiology, their deepest needs, the mental, postural and motor flows that distinguish them.

On the other hand, if the stress response becomes chronic, the situation is reversed: the sympathetic-spleen innervation (the spleen has a crucial role in monitoring the type of stress response connected to stress) is altered, as is the apoptosis of immune cells and the reduction of TNFα and interferon gamma (IFNγ) and, consequently, a systemic shift towards the Th2 response occurs. The Th2 response protects human body tissues, but at the expense of the Th1 response, which fights viruses and bacteria.

For this reason, when stress becomes chronic, it is easier to catch a cold or other viral or bacterial diseases.

Unfortunately, today it is very easy for the stress response to become chronic. This often initially happens at a sub-clinical level, doing little visible damage, but creating a series of problems that are not understood or attributed to anything else. The classic stressed professional (who today represents more than half of workers) switches incessantly from one activity to another at work and, often, in their private life too. They then begin to feel pain, for example, in the lower back, which they often fail to treat thinking: "I don't have the time to deal with this too", or try to manage passively, with a drug or targeted manipulative intervention (physiotherapy, osteopathy, etc.). In the latter case, if they do not meet an integrated professional, they often feel slight relief, perhaps the symptom passes, but after a few days a stomach-ache emerges, then a headache, and so on.

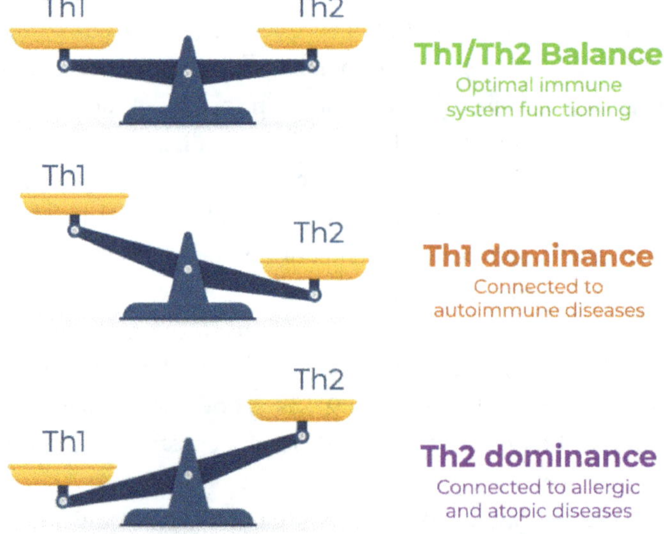

Fig. Any type of stress (emotional, affective, environmental, physical, etc.) can lead to an imbalance in the immune system with consequent physical pathologies.

The core problem remains unsolved: the stress response is always active. Furthermore, attempts at solutions often create more stress: money spent, time wasted, a sense of inadequacy, a deteriorating self-image. Not to mention any drugs that, to treat a symptom, generate a greater dysfunction, such as the various drugs that have a systemic pro-inflammatory action, destroying the intestinal microbiome or worse.

As we have already introduced, and as we will analyse in more detail in different parts of the book, stress and inflammation are two sides of the same coin and can both be the cause and effect of different problems. For example, a child may have a chronic inflammatory state sustained both by their diet and by irregular sleep rhythms, because their parents have a restaurant and therefore food is always accessible while sleep-wakefulness schedules are always altered (or there may be a thousand other reasons that lead to these irregularities). In addition to this, the child may have had to take antibiotics, but their intestinal microbiome was never brought back into physiological state (the microbiome, among other things, regulates the immune system and produces various neurotransmitters that are essential for the regulation of emotions and for learning) and so on. All this alters their emotional state and mood and does not provide the child with the resources required to stay focused, because the body spends all its energy managing this inflammation.

Immune system T cells have, among other things, the function of 'telling' the brain that if there is an immune response, an ill mental attitude must be maintained. This is functional in the short term, because it focuses all the body's resources where they are needed. The problem is that, if the situation continues, this mental attitude becomes a normal part of life and merges with everyday reality and identity. From the opposite perspective, a difficult childhood, with trauma or adverse events of various types, creates mental patterns, emotional learning and relational dynamics that support a continuous stress response with all its implications at the physical level. Intervening on several of these aspects simultaneously allows us to see faster improvements and more lasting change over time.

AXIS 2 – THE HPA AXIS

In the 1950s a second axis, the best known today and often identified as the "stress axis" par excellence, was identified. The term 'stress' itself in its current meaning was coined by Hans Seyle to describe the functioning of the hypothalamus-pituitary-adrenal axis (HPA).

This axis starts from the hypothalamus, which is a hub that receives information on vital status and survival issues (hunger, hydration, danger, etc.), but also information on body states in general such as emotional condition and higher needs (i.e. those not directly related to survival).

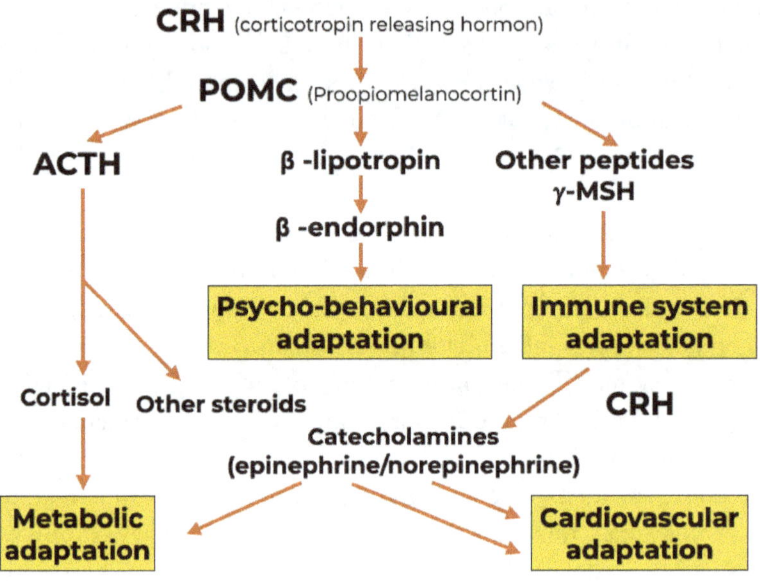

Fig. - The stress response leads to adaptations on several levels, as shown in the boxes. Beta-endorphins are endogenous opioids, for example, that are typically associated with a positive surge when exercising.

The hypothalamus produces CRH, the corticotropin-releasing hormone, which reaches the pituitary gland. The pituitary, also known as "the mother endocrine gland", produces many hormones that go to different glands (to regulate the activity of the thyroid, gonads, etc.). In particular, it produces ACTH which goes to the adrenal cortex, which in turn produces cortisol. CRH not only kickstarts this stress axis but affects every domain of life.

Even cortisol, known as the 'stress hormone', actually has many other functions and triggers: cold, lack of sleep, toxins, physical exercise, pain, hypoglycaemia, trauma, emotions and many others (see the specific box for more detail later on).

To try to cure her headache, Alice tried everything: acupuncture,  meditation, osteopathy, two different types of psychotherapy, hormonal treatments, and much more, but nothing worked. Some activities have given marginal benefit, others nothing at all. Analysing Alice's current life and past, it was immediately evident that the continuous activation of the HPA axis was a common factor. All the techniques and therapies she had undergone tried to modulate the stress response, but none alone had been sufficient. In fact, it often happens that although the right therapies and activities are chosen to solve one's problem, the desired results are not obtained precisely because the specific condition requires stronger signals across more areas. In this case it was essential to intervene on several levels simultaneously: 1- making life choices to reduce certain stresses a priori (from her way of going about shopping to temporarily suspending an English language certification course); 2- dealing with a trauma from the past that recurred daily, continuously reactivating the stress axis through targeted psychotherapy; 3- Use techniques of self-perception and release of muscular tension that are typical of the HPA axis, so that the body could give the correct biofeedback to reduce the hyper-adaptation response and recover a postural physiology that does not compress nerves and others tissues capable of triggering headaches; 4- working on nutrition and physical activity to reduce a generalized inflammatory state and to improve the quality of the connective tissue which mechanically created tension and stiffness with physical (crushing) and neurobiological actions (neurotransmitters that amplify pain); 5- mental strategies to recontextualize the meaning of the headache and the real impact on her life; 6- acting on sensory perceptive processes, so that they were not excessive (hyper-stimulating and therefore amplifying the pain of the headache) and more 'straightforward' (i.e. perceived more objectively and not deformed by negative expectations). There were many aspects to consider, and, in other cases, there may be even more. Throughout the book we will look at all these aspects, their foundations and how it is possible to intervene on them in various ways with advice, explanations, techniques, tricks to integrate into existing work practices. There are interesting boundary areas where every professional can extend his or her interventions: for example, a psychotherapist can put simple physical exercises into practice with important results, just as a physiotherapist can give initial indications and concrete suggestions to offer relief in moments of stress or anxiety. It is not a question of trespassing into professional territories that are not one's own, but of extending the effectiveness and boundaries of one's own sphere, creating a favourable ground to then continue, if necessary, with an effective and targeted session with a specific professional. Furthermore, thanks to the schemes and models that we have developed, we will always have navigation maps that are both a reminder of what to investigate and what to intervene on, to explain to the patient how it works and why this activity is synergistic and integrated.

Cortisol plays a central role in this axis. If everything is in physiological state and proceeding correctly, its production peaks just after waking up and drops to its minimum around midnight. For this reason, it may be called the *day* or *wakefulness hormone*. Cortisol quantity and cycles are based on external stimuli (such as activation or deactivation), but also on some daily rhythms, such as exposure to light, time of rest, timing and content of meals and other factors. There are sophisticated feedback systems of self-regulation (e.g., checking how much cortisol is already present in certain areas of the body) and systemic regulation. The problem is that often our compensatory behaviour in the face of stress – eating to release tension, going to bed late to carve out a rewarding moment, etc. – offers short term relief and alters cortisol production and basic cycles in the long run.

Increasingly common dysfunctional behaviours nowadays are binge-watching or binge-gaming, the compulsion to watch continuous episodes of online TV series and to play video games non-stop. The magical world these activities lead us into is in itself useful, we all need to disconnect from our problems, but the fact that these are mostly carried out at night leads to circadian rhythms being overturned, altering a series of neurotransmitters.

Melatonin is a circadian rhythm opposite to cortisol and regulates its effects. It promotes, for example, the Th1 immune response (whereas cortisol promotes Th2). If we upset day-night rhythms, melatonin levels are also altered, thus increasing the negative effects of cortisol, inhibiting the positive ones of its natural 'antidote'. Sleep is also a powerful antioxidant and vital regulator of the immune system. This is true for any sleep disruption, including that experienced by night shift workers, bar workers, as well as anxiety and post-traumatic stress disorder sufferers.

Sleep is not the only key factor. The list of neuroendocrine and immune activities of the HPA mediators is conspicuous and continuously updated. There are clear and important interactions at a motivational (dopamine and more), sexual (from menstrual pain, to both male and female fertility), gastrointestinal (from digestive problems to irritable bowel), osteo-muscular (pain, fibromyalgia, motor, etc.), cardiac, epidermal and practically every other level.

The fact that different symptoms and problems can be activated in each person depends on the different mix of characteristics: state of acute or chronic stress, type of stress, life cycle phase of the individual subject, their intestinal microbiome, neural structure, active or inactive epigenetic markers, previous and habitual physical activity, eating habits, mental patterns, neural plasticity and more. Similar observations can be made regarding the sympathetic axis that we have previously analysed. The operational consequences, fortunately, are similar and concrete: we will see that daily measures concerning lifestyle, sleep-wake rhythms, nutrition, but also the way in which digital devices are used (from the telephone to the computer and beyond), as well as a series of more targeted psycho-physical activities can easily restore the balance within the processes underlying this and other stress axes.

CORTISOL, MORE THAN JUST 'THE STRESS HORMONE'

Some of cortisol's main functions[1] that most significantly influence body and mind are:

• Increasing sodium and water retention, as well as the glomerular filtration of the kidneys;

• Increasing the absorption of food by the intestine, altering the intestinal barrier and increasing intestinal permeability, giving shape to the infamous leaky gut syndrome (leaky intestine);

• Stimulating microcirculation towards the tissues (muscles, brain, etc.);

• Stimulating protein catabolism and suppressing protein synthesis. In the right doses cortisol, therefore, develops the nervous system and strengthens muscles and bones, while – if it is in excess for a prolonged time – it leads to neural and muscular atrophy and fracture. This in turn leads to the body no longer developing some fundamental structures (muscles, neurons, etc.) in the long run;

• Influencing mood and behaviour, supporting anxiety and fear. In situations that have become chronically dysfunctional these responses are active even in the absence of valid triggering reasons;

• Stimulating hunger, reducing gastric secretion and causing insulin resistance, which in chronic cases favours the accumulation of fat in every area of the body;

• Increasing red blood cell mass and the proliferation of granulocytes (neutrophils, eosinophils and basophils). Both red and white blood cells (leukocytes) are found in tissues for immediate use when needed, highlighting another connection between emotions and immunity;

• Displacing leukocytes in peripheral tissues, stimulating Th2 humoral immunity (to the detriment of Th1 cellular immunity);

• It is anti-inflammatory in acute states, but inflammatory (stimulates cellular activation of NF-KB) in chronic states;

• Interfering with Treg immunity by altering cytokine production (Treg = regulatory immunity, i.e. creating balance between Th1 and Th2 and more).

AXIS 3– NEUROGENIC INFLAMMATION (OR NNA)

Since the 1970s, further mediators with an important role in orchestrating the stress response, to the point of postulating the existence of a third axis, have been identified. Peripheral nerve fibres, including sensory sub-population, contain neuropeptides with potent immunomodulatory activity and undergo neurotrophin-driven neuronal plasticity.

These neurotrophins activate neurogenic inflammation, which entails the release of neuropeptides such as substance P (SP) and subsequent degranulation of mast cells in organs that are more exposed to the environment such as skin, lungs or intestine, where typical symptoms become psychosomatic.

In more practical terms, the mind can influence the immune system so powerfully that it gives rise to a number of important reactions. These reactions are identified as neurogenic inflammation (to be understood as 'generated by the mind through the nervous system').

Neurotrophins represent the central element of the NNA axis (Neurotrophin Neuropeptide Stress Axis) and give it its name. They are an integrated network capable of significantly influencing physical and mental health. This axis acts in close interaction with the HPA axis. For this reason some prefer not to consider it a network in itself, but to focus on its mechanisms and effects (neurogenic inflammation), but it also has autonomous action.

Prolonged stress can chronically alter the HPA and NNA axes, resulting in various mental and physical disorders.

Neurotrophins such as NGF (Nerve Growth Factor, i.e. the initial stimulus for the development of the nervous system) and BDNF (Brain Derived Neurotrophic Factor, central to survival, development and neural plasticity) are also known for their contribution to endocrine regulation. Recent studies show that epigenetic alterations of the relationship between the HPA axis and neurotrophins play a key role in triggering various psychiatric disorders[2].

Neuropeptides W and B are two regulating peptides highly expressed in different brain regions and also in some peripheral tissues. Both take part in the central regulation processes of: the neuroendocrine axes, eating behaviours, energy homeostasis, cardiovascular functions, circadian rhythms, pain perception and modulation, emotion regulation. We are once more faced with further confirmation of the need for an integrated approach in which emotions, thoughts, the immune system, vital energy, rest, tolerance of physical and emotional pain must be seen and managed with an integrated approach.

EVEN MORE AXES

So far we have analysed the three main stress axes. However, the complete and definitive picture cannot yet be seen. For example, an additional axis defined as H-LC-mPFC[3] (hypothalamus, locus coeruleus, medial prefrontal cortex) which converts hypothalamic activation into a rapid enhancement of cortical excitability following acute stress has been identified. This process is initiated with the release of glutamate and, in cascade, other powerful neuroexciters.

Other axes have also been identified, such as the direct connection between the brain areas of motor activity (in the sense of pure movement and its definition) with the adrenal glands, further demonstrating that the stress response is embodied by nature and across multiple levels.

Understanding all these aspects is of fundamental importance to fully understand the systems that govern health and disease processes within both the mind and body, while also obtaining various operational clues on which to act concretely, as we will see in the following chapters of the text. We will learn how to move practically in this direction starting from the next chapter. Now let's consider a topic closely connected with stress and the mechanisms of adaptation and development: emotions.

References

[1] - Chiera M, et al. (2017), La PNEI e il Sistema Miofasciale: la struttura che connette, Milano, Edra.
- Picard et al. (2014), "Mitochondrial allostatic load puts the 'gluc' back into glucocorticoids", Nat Rev Endocrinol, 10(5), pp. 303-10.
- Lieberman & Marks (2013), Marks' Basic Medical Biochemistry. A Clinical Approach.
- Elenkov (2008), "Neurohormonal-cytokine interactions: implications for inflammation, common human diseases and well-being", Neurochem lnt, 52, pp.40-51.
[2] Kumar, A., Kumar, P., Pareek, V., Faiq, M. A., Narayan, R. K., Raza, K., Prasoon, P., & Sharma, V. K. (2019). Neurotrophin mediated HPA axis dysregulation in stress induced genesis of psychiatric disorders: Orchestration by epigenetic modifications. Journal of chemical neuroanatomy, 102, 101688.
[3] Pozzi D., & Matteoli M. (2018). The hypothalamic-LC-PFC axis: a new "ace" in the brain for fast-behavioral stress response. The EMBO journal, 37(21), e100702.

EMOTIONS: AN UPDATED SCIENTIFIC REVIEW

What exactly are emotions? How do they work? Over the years, many hypotheses have been made starting from many different perspectives. This often happens when a theme is complex and interpretations can become too simple or linear, espousing a cause-and-effect relationship.

Let us start from one of the most typical questions in traditional psychology, which in turn draws on a theme that has already been dealt with by the ancient Greeks: *"Do we cry because we are sad, or are we sad because we cry?"*

In line with the Integrative Sciences approach, in order to answer this question, we will have to draw on different scientific areas and disciplines, introducing new perspectives and some paradigm shifts. In fact, today, thanks to an interesting shift in perspective and to increasingly refined affective neuroscience techniques and emotional analysis, it is finally possible to reach a definitive answer with important implications.

A CHANGE OF PERSPECTIVE TO AVOID REDUCTIONISM

The first change of perspective to be made concerns the heuristic value of a model – i.e. how intuitive and convincing it is to use, even if this does not necessarily indicate its real effectiveness – and the language and dissemination of information, even among sector specialists[1].

Let's take an example: when we talk about emotions, we often refer to Paul Ekman's model, which was widely taken up in part due to the appeal of reading emotions via facial expressions. Here is the first communicative and heuristic risk: Paul Ekman's model is studied, it is found useful and interesting and then it becomes easy to make the transition to saying and thinking that *"there are 5 fundamental emotions that are independent of each other"*. The sentence that is typically reported usually ends here. There is a major problem with this summary, which is that we are leaving out the specification element where we add: "*…according to Paul Ekman, regarding the expression of emotions through the face*". Without this specification an opinion that, however authoritative, is limited to a specific aspect, is applied as a certainty to a wider issue.

On the other hand, affective and behavioural neuroscience, but also comparative ethology, have long proven that the transition from one emotion to another is fluid and modulable, that there are mechanisms and processes that integrate and influence each other. So, the 5 emotions are not independent, but related in their processes and manifestations.

We are assessing the work of Paul Ekman and then we will also constructively discuss McLean's triune brain model and S. Porges' Polyvagal Theory. It is important to clarify that all these authors are to be considered great pioneers and all of modern science owes a debt of gratitude to their work. With gratitude and appreciation, our aim is to highlight some aspects of these theories that can be further expanded, or partially revised, thanks to new scientific discoveries and through a multi-disciplinary approach capable of providing new theoretical horizons and operating methods, so as to be even more effective in clinical practice.

Returning to the expression of emotions, as Lisa Barrett Feldman has well demonstrated, their expression is not universal and sharply divided as Ekman and other scholars had hypothesized. The author, like many other contemporary researchers, has developed research projects with a more structured methodology than her predecessors, realizing that – indirectly and unconsciously – in much earlier research the correct positive answers had been induced or at least facilitated. It emerged that emotions emerge from the sum of interoception, external perception, different brain circuits, concepts, social and psychological constructs. We will develop these aspects from a practical point of view especially in area 3 switches.

ADAPTATION AND/OR EMOTIONS?

Another important aspect to reconsider regards the commonly held idea that "*emotions are part of our adaptation system*". This statement is true but needs a more accurate definition. We have an adaptation system that is able to react, mainly automatically and that is unaware of common dangers, even the more basic ones such as: the risk of predation, lack of nutrients, dehydration, energy imbalances, etc.[2].

Even if they seem like extreme cases that only concern animals that live in the wild, they are actually mechanisms that are very much a part of human daily life, only that they are well masked.

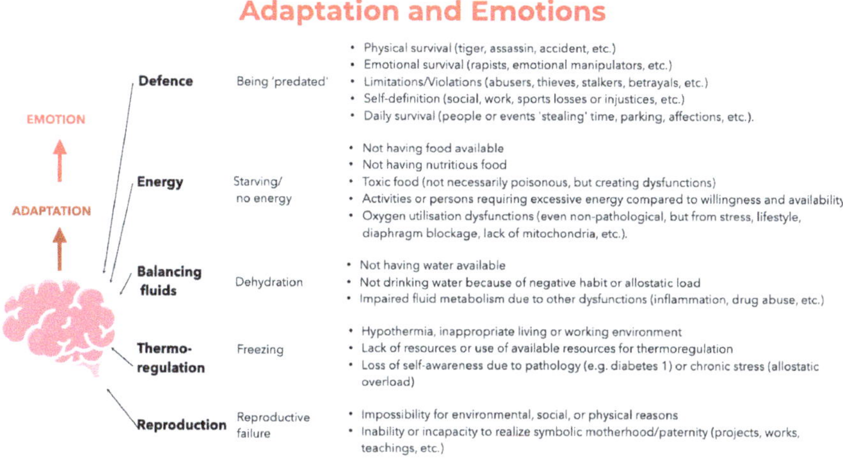

Fig. – A schematic representation of the main mechanisms that activate the adaptation responses which, in turn, give shape to emotional experiences. These mechanisms are not the only ones that shape emotions, but it is essential to take them into account, to come to a complete reading of all the factors (that patients are often not aware of and are not included in many professional approaches) that can have a central role in shaping emotions and affective experiences.

Predation is active every day: someone who steals our parking space, our merits at work, the increasingly precious time we have left, our hard-earned money, our sporting record and so on. In these cases the predator can be a well-known or passing person, but also an entirely different entity (work, competition). These mechanisms are active practically every day for most people and trigger adaptation processes and related emotions. There are also more serious levels of predators, such as stalkers, harassers and others equally harmful, albeit less explicit ones such as people with whom so-called 'toxic' relationships are created (for example, people who bring negativity to our lives, those that require an expenditure of energy without giving anything in return, those that manipulate others by leveraging their vulnerabilities, etc.).

Nowadays, with supermarkets and houses full of food, it might seem that lack of nutrients can never trigger adaptation processes. The problem, however, is not the quantity but the nutritional quality of these foods. The fact that they are rich in sugar does not mean that they are good for our adaptation mechanisms. In fact, to metabolize carbohydrates after an insulin peak, a collapse follows with the correlated activation of a state of alert. Industrial fructose (chemically produced from corn and used in practically every industrial product due to its cheapness) has the characteristic of not giving a satiety signal to the body which, once again, perceives a risk of adaptation and becomes active.

Despite all the comforts of modern life, actually paradoxically *because* of some of them, our adaptation system is activated much more often than it would be useful and necessary.

This primary coping system handles many behaviours, such as escapism, which is usually thought of as an emotional response. In reality, when the escape begins, the emotion has not yet taken shape.

Emotion builds by integrating the primary adaptive response with experiences, expectations, interaction with logical thinking, learned and now automatic behaviours, autonomic nervous system responses and hormonal levels. Recent methods of investigation and refined research projects have managed to isolate all these components, in order to demonstrate the solidity of this model which, as is now shown, is not a simple hypothetical abstraction, but represents precisely the different processes implemented during the responses to stressful, traumatic stimuli, but also business obstacles, challenges or games. For example, it is important to know that several researchers have managed to inhibit avoidance behaviour (for example in people with social phobia who manage not to run away from a party) while maintaining a high level of anxiety; vice versa, it was possible to modulate the sense of fear, while maintaining the behavioural or physiological responses high.

This research has had very important practical implications, highlighting all the levels on which it is possible and necessary to act to regulate emotions on a practical level. For example, it is possible to distinguish accurately between:
•triggering of the adaptation response;
•amplifying or inhibiting factors, interferences, learned patterns;
•the role of episodic and procedural memory, habits and response patterns;
•targeted biofeedback on specific motor and muscle patterns triggered in the various adaptive responses and - at a later stage - engaged by the emergence of emotion;
•aspects of social signalling and self and other people's learning (which is an innate part of the evolutionary value of emotions for the adaptation and development of the species);
•exploratory behaviours, curiosity and creativity as forms of adaptation;
•and more.

ONE BRAIN OR THREE BRAINS?

Another highly successful model is P. McLean's triune brain. This is an easy to understand representation of the dynamics at play between survival responses (that McLean identifies as *reptilian* brain), emotions (in the *mammalian* brain) and logical thinking (identified with the *neocortex*).

It represents the way we feel and behave very well, which is why it has had great success. It's easy to view our choices in ambivalent situations (e.g., "*Do I go to the gym or stay on the couch?*") as a struggle between the lazy crocodile and the sane, logical brain. Yet that's not how we work. Despite this, we must remember that this was a totally new model in the 1970s, the decade when he was born, but can now be enriched and developed in the wake of the latest neuroscientific discoveries. Today using the model of the triune brain and saying that the neocortex has an inhibitory function on emotional impulses, is somewhat simplistic. Rationality and emotion are not in constant conflict, on the contrary – as we will see – they are, and must be excellent allies[3]. Even from an anatomical point of view, they do not reside in different areas of the brain.

In fact, it has now been widely demonstrated that the PFC (prefrontal cortex) dialogues synergistically with the amygdala in the construction and modulation of emotions. It is not a push-and-pull relationship, rather a collaboration that can be supported at the level of neural plasticity (through nutrition, physical and cognitive activity) and through integrative activities between several different functions. Not only that, the prefrontal cortex (PFC) has extensive connections with the motor and sensory cortices, all of which play a central role in modulating both the unaware primary adaptive responses and emotions (as opposed to the idea that the PFC acts only at a rational and controlled level).

Let's take another example: the hypothalamus, thalamus and insula are today defined as integrative "hubs" with a central role in emotion regulation. In this perspective, it becomes interesting to use the 3-brain model as a starting point for a practical approach based on the neurosciences of emotions, to then move onto a more in-depth view of networks and hubs, capable of offering numerous practical and operational cues to improve their physiology and integration through different types of activities.

THE VAGUS NERVE AND EMOTIONS (AND MORE)

In recent years, the central role of the vagus nerve (NV) in self-regulatory and emotional processes has become increasingly known and widespread. This nerve, in fact, plays crucial and cross-cutting functions in various adaptation and developmental mechanisms of human life, and in particular all processes related to survival, motivation, and relationships. The VN has important functions ranging from regulating heartbeat to gathering information about the status of all vital organs, from digestion to immune system response, just to name a few examples.

In recent years, various theories and approaches have become popular to explain the functioning of the vagus nerve in physiology or in response to chronic stress or traumatic events. In order to develop an informed and maximally effective clinical practice, it becomes crucial today to know exactly why and how it is interesting to act on the vagus nerve according to a broad and integrated perspective. The continuation of this paragraph, due to the specificity of the topic discussed, is somewhat technical in nature and is primarily intended for those who like to know and delve into theoretical details. It is not necessary to go into them in depth and understand them thoroughly in order to then continue with the related practical applications found in the subsequent paragraphs of this chapter and in the rest of the text.

An initial clarification needed concerns theories on the vagus nerve. When a theoretical concept is spread primarily because of a single theory, in this case the Polyvagal Theory (PVT) by S. Porges, it often happens that the author's ideas are spread as the sole reference on the subject, especially if no prior information on the subject was possessed. We analyze below a summary of some important elements to consider, both for theoretical clarity and, more importantly, for their practical implications.

Comparative anatomy and functional anatomy studies go in a different direction than the proposed phylogenetic basis of PVT. It is undisputed that in mammals, myelinated cardioinhibitory axons are derived from the ambiguous nucleus. However, already in cartilaginous fishes (e.g., sharks), which have been existing now for 400 million years, cardioinhibitory neurons of the vagus are myelinated and operate at speeds between 7 and 35 m/s (corresponding to mammalian B-fibers). Moreover, their cell bodies are located in 2 different sites in the brainstem[4]. Therefore, in contrast to what Porges proposed, we could say that cartilaginous fish are already "polyvagal".

PVT categorizes the responses to perceived risks into three modes: 1) feeling safe, 2) being in danger, or 3) perceiving a vital threat. According to Porges, these categories follow each other in phylogeny and are related to adaptive social communication behaviours (facial expressions, speech, listening), which are hypothesized to be controlled by the ambiguous core. Defensive behaviour in terms of mobilization (fight, flight) and immobilization responses (vasovagal syncope, dissociation or emotional frozen state) are attributed to mediation by the dorsal vagal nucleus. Again, the proposed association of these behavioural phenomena with the older non-myelinated vagus nerve or the newer myelinated vagus nerve is incorrect. The mammalian ambiguous nucleus contains, in addition to cardioinhibitory neurons, mainly branchiomotor (special visceroefferent) neurons for the laryngeal, pharyngeal, and esophageal striated muscles[5], but it does not control facial expression (mimic muscles are innervated by the nucleus facialis) nor hearing through the middle ear muscles (tensor muscle, innervated by the motor branch of the trigeminal nerve, and stapedius muscle, innervated by the facial nerve) nor other muscles of the head and neck, as suggested by PVT. In contrast, the facial nucleus (nF) also does not affect the ambiguous nucleus.

Behaviours such as fight and flight, the state of immobilization or freezing, and risk assessment, along with associated motor, autonomic, and endocrine effects, are coordinated by the periaqueductal gray (PAG)[6]. The PAG is connected to the hypothalamus and limbic circuits (mainly the amygdala and prefrontal cortex)[7] as well as to various premotor and autonomic brainstem nuclei that coordinate breathing and the emotional motor system[8]. The PAG receives afferents from almost all sensory systems, not least the nociceptive system, and modulates their processing.

Unquestionably, the vagus nerve has a significant influence on emotions and various behavioural states because of its large afferent component. Vagal afferents, which constitute about 80% of its axons, are transmitted through the nucleus of the solitary tract to the PAG, hypothalamus, amygdala, and insular, cingulate, and prefrontal cortex, where they are integrated into emotional and cognitive processes[9]. Recent studies suggest that subdiaphragmatic vagal afferents influence innate fear, learned fear, and other behaviours[10]. In addition, vagal afferents modulate spinal nociceptive processes in different experimental models[11]. We can therefore conclude that it is not the ventral vagus complex, but the PAG in association with limbic networks (NB: for those who wish to elaborate, 'limbic circuits' do not exactly coincide with the so called 'limbic system') and other brainstem networks that are responsible as coordinators of these emotional-relational states and behaviours. In addition, numerous brain areas, if not the whole brain and the whole body – there are neurons in the skin called "peripersonal"[12] that can sense the presence of the other on a physical level even without contact – function as a social system.

Having clarified the underlying theoretical aspects, however, there remains no doubt that the vagus nerve plays a central role in self-regulatory processes, and trying to regulate it and bring it back into physiology is definitely an added value in therapeutic processes. For maximum clinical effectiveness, it is essential to have an expanded and multidisciplinary view, in which the vagus is considered as an integral part of other different systems (brain networks, gut-brain axis, myofascial system, interoceptive processes, allostatic mechanisms, etc.). Building on this awareness and knowledge it is possible – as we will see in different parts of the book – to structure different interventions, which can take the form of advice, information, special techniques, and targeted revisitations of tools and methods already in use in order to help people in a comprehensive way to recover physiology and resilience.

EMOTIONS, NETWORKS AND EXPERIENCE

As we have begun to see, today it is possible to identify the different networks that contribute to generating and sustaining an emotion: perception, attention, salience, motivation, interoception, self-regulation, different social networks and so on.

There is a fluid dynamic between these elements, which have different levels of power over action and hierarchies of influence. Furthermore, each of them is influenced by other different processes to which it is connected. It is thus possible to understand all the factors involved and to intervene in a targeted way through: the body, thought, goals, nutrition, movement, perceptive and sensory filters, predictions about oneself, the context and others, as well as any other relevant element.

These are factors and processes that are deeply rooted in our development and interconnected with each other. For example, the senses first of all have an important role for our survival and evolution. Being able to see or smell food or – by contrast – a predator, allowed us to increase our chances of survival. Only later did we develop the cultural or hedonistic value of these senses.

Pleasure originally arises in response to an event going as well or better than expected, sustaining positive emotions and reinforcing favourable behaviours in the future. Pleasure and positive emotions are intrinsically linked to learning and development, although for years mainstream culture has seen them as an interference ("*work then play*" has been the prevailing slogan for years).

Conversely, the emotional and physical reflexes of disgust save the lives of all mammals, including humans, by keeping them away from potential poisons. In humans, this mechanism has transformed as bitter foods (potentially toxic in nature) are included in our diet, the disgust response instead extends to 'toxic' entities at other levels, such as concepts, values, people, etc.

Fear and anger are intertwined with survival mechanisms and exploration (again in the broadest sense of the term). Likewise, the ability to move has been a great advantage for adaptation, so much so, that the nervous system has developed more and more in this direction. Reflecting on these aspects, we must not think only of movement as muscle coordination, but also as the functioning of the heart, the role of oxygenation, the activation of energy metabolism, and other factors that are fundamental to orchestrate for correct emotional responses that are both physiological and functional.

Another fundamental aspect is that of interoception, which allows us to organize these complex responses thanks to 'feeling from within'. Interoception, as we will see better in area 3 switches, not only *monitors*, but even *predicts* internal states, to optimize them and manage any request or challenge in daily life. From this perspective, we can say that the brain is a forecasting machine: both for external and internal senses, but also for behavioural effectiveness, evaluation of consequences, hypotheses about other people's intentions, relational choices, and more.

Let's see a brief explanatory example, the mechanisms of which will be taken up and explored throughout the rest of the text. A response that is referred to as 'fear' or as 'anxiety symptoms', does not start to take shape due to just a trigger factor (such as seeing a danger) as once thought. Our body, on the other hand, makes many more assessments, including: 1- the freedom of movement of our joints; 2- the number of mitochondria in the muscles and nervous system; 3- the level of acidity in different areas of the body; 4- how distant danger is (even if there is no real risk of physical aggression, our mind prefers to 'keep a distance', as they say): 5- configuration of the menacing face of the possible predator; 6- own and other's flexibility and muscle tone, 7- state of inflammation due to possible negative consequences during fight-flight; and so on. As we have mentioned, all these factors are not simply identified, but continuous predictions and adjustments are made (below our consciousness), influenced both by innate mechanisms and by one's own experience, but also by one's psychophysical and environmental conditions. For example, the threat of a face can be evaluated differently if an inflammatory state is underway in our body (even a simple cold), or during different moments of hormonal peaks, but also according to the state of the intestinal microbiota, based on room temperature, for cultural priming phenomena and many other aspects.

For all these reasons, once again, it becomes essential to know and be aware of the various factors involved and to introduce them into emotional regulation.

THE HIGHER-ORDER THEORIES OF EMOTIONS

The so-called *Higher-Order Theory of Emotional Consciousness*[13], that is, the more modern vision of understanding the functioning of emotions, consistently with what has been seen so far, highlight the need and the advantages of a multi-system approach, based on a networks and hubs model.

According to this constructivist view, emotions are not innate, fixed or in one-size-fits-all patterns. Emotions are elements embodied in the body, which the brain uses to make sense of the body's global physiological activations and environmental situations. Emotions are a process that relies on "higher-order states" embedded in cortical (conscious) brain circuits and emerge, but are not innately programmed, from the activity of subcortical (non-conscious) brain circuits.

In this perspective, asking ourselves *"what emotion am I feeling?"* to understand what is happening to us, can be a fallacious system. The reason is that what emerges to our awareness, what we "are feeling" represents a typical pattern, a configuration to which we have learned to give that meaning. Wondering what emotion we feel doesn't give us real information about our reaction to that specific event. In the light of these considerations, it becomes more useful to analyse all the factors involved (see diagram below) and ask yourself: 1- which predictions have been correct or not; 2- which adaptation mechanisms have been effective or not; 3- if the bodily activation was consistent with one's previous state and useful for adapting to environmental demands; 4- what interferences there have been; and so on. Changing perspective, a useful question could also be *"what emotion should I be feeling for this type of adaptation that I have implemented?"*. An additional, equally interesting question can be "How does it make me feel to have enacted that kind of response?" thus moving on to a meta-emotional level with respect to perceived efficacy and self-image.

In a nutshell, high-level theories of emotions identify basic adaptation mechanisms that activate survival-related responses rapidly and below the level of consciousness. As Joseph LeDoux [14] has well demonstrated, there are direct pathways which, from the perception of the sensory stimulus, separately activate: 1) the subcortical responses of the survival systems; 2) the perceptual processing cortices.

These two processes are then integrated with each other in a non-conscious area of *working memory*, where they are also processed together with memories, learned patterns, state of bodily and nervous system activation, body maps, etc. This first processing is integrated in the third instance with long-term memory. Together they provide the basis for emotional experience as we live it, which is processed in a consciously accessible area of working memory.

Taking this scheme into consideration we must also keep in mind a number of other aspects, including:
1) Both as initial inputs and as modifiers of the other mechanisms, interoceptive processes and contextual and interpersonal aspects have a central role (see switch 3);
2) All these mechanisms evolve and change continuously over time (see switch 4), they are dynamic and cannot be frozen in a static image;
3) All these aspects are subject to a fundamental functioning mechanism of the brain: continuous predictions and verification-adjustment cycles take place to optimize allostatic and homeostatic processes (as we will see in switch area 3).

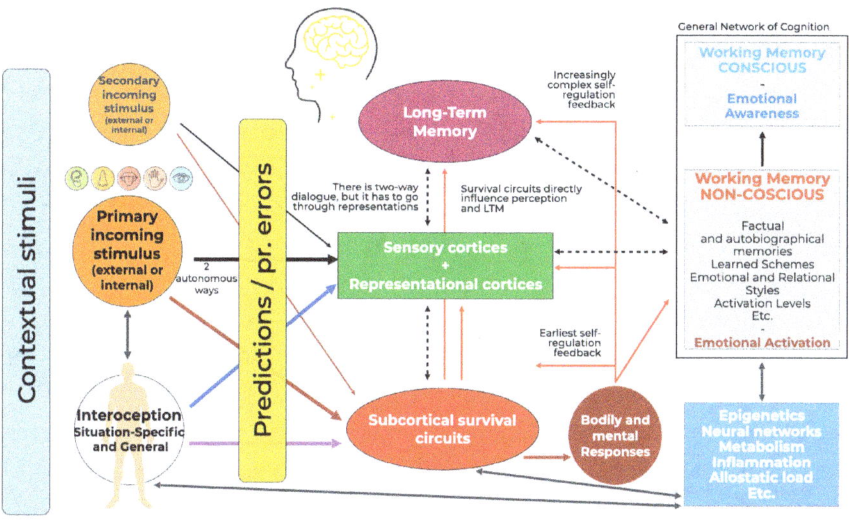

Fig. - A summary that extends the model proposed by J. LeDoux to clarify some elements and include others within an integrative perspective.

PRACTICAL IMPLICATIONS FOR APPLICATION

Understanding these mechanisms with respect to the functioning of emotions, together with the different neural pathways with specific priorities and action sequences (e.g. the survival circuits that manage to directly interact and modify long-term memory, while the latter must pass via the interaction with the perceptual system in order to influence the primary adaptation responses) allows us to develop targeted strategies that respect these same hierarchical processes.

Research on the processes of reconsolidation[15] also highlights that, like all learning – from studying to dysfunctional beliefs, up to memories following traumatic events –, this can be facilitated by some conditions. We begin by introducing three interesting aspects below. We will return in a practical way in the following chapters to these and other factors relevant to the processes of care and change.

A *first criterion* of effectiveness in change processes concerns the possibility of acting on non-conscious mechanisms (the sub-cortical ones of the functioning scheme of the *Higher-Order Theory of Emotional Consciousness*). To do this, it is possible to use masked stimuli, i.e., not perceived at a conscious level, but still capable of activating response mechanisms at a neurobiological level. We will look at how to use these in daily practice. A specific method, for those interested, can be carried out through a special software that we have made available free of charge to interested professionals (further information on www.insciences.co/repro).

The *second fundamental criterion* focuses on the need to pass from learned dysfunctional mechanisms to functional ones on all the mechanisms in place during these processes, for example by stimulating the mobilization of physical resources, body maps, monitoring switches of contextual and interpersonal clues and all the factors that we will see included from the first to the fifth switch area.

A *further criterion* of effectiveness concerns the relationship between the quality and quantity of stimuli (verbal, imaginative, the recovery of memories or experiences, the introduction of new evaluative or awareness elements, etc.) in relation to the time span between them. Taking care of these factors makes it possible to promote neural plasticity and – consequently – to increase the ease of abandoning old patterns learned in favour of new and more effective methods.

We will look at all these and other topics with techniques and methods presented in the following chapters in a practical and detailed way in the coming chapters.

REFERENCES

1 - LeDoux JE. Anxious: Using the Brain to Understand and Treat Fear and Anxiety. New York: Penguin Books; 2015.

- Barrett, L. F. (2017). The theory of constructed emotion: An active inference account of interoception and categorization. Social Cognitive and Affective Neuroscience 12 (1): 1-23.

2 LeDoux JE., Brown R. Emotions as higher-order states of consciousness. Proceedings of the National Academy of Sciences Mar 2017, 114 (10) E2016-E2025.

3 Pessoa L 2013. The cognitive-emotional brain: from interactions to integration. The MIT Press, Cambridge, MA.

4 Barrett Dl, Tayior EW. The location of cardiac vagal pregan glionicneurones in the brain stem of the dogfish Scyliorhinus canicula. J Exp Biol 1985; 117: 449-458.

5 Fritzsch B, Elliott KL, Clover JC. Caskell revisited: new insights into spinal autonomics necessitate a revised motor neuron nomenclature. Cell Tissue Res 2017; 370: 195-209.

6 Deng H, Xiao X, Wang Z. Periaqueductal gray neuronal activities underlie different aspects of defensive behaviors. J Neurosci 2016; 36 (29): 7580-7588.

7 Jänig W. The integrative action of the autonomic nervous system. Cambridge: Cambridge University Press; 2006.

8 Holstege C. The periaqueductal gray controls brainstem emotional motor systems including respiration. Prog Brain Res 2014; 209: 319-405.

9 Craig AD. 2002. How do you feel? Interoception: the sense of the physiological condition of the body. Nat. Rev. Neurosci. 3, 655–666.

10 Klarer M, Arno d M, Cünther L et al. Cut vagal afferents differentially modulate innate anxiety and learned fear. I Neurosci 2011: 34 (21): 1061 -1066.

11 Jänig W Creen P. Acute inflammation in the joint: its control by the sympathetic nervous system and neuroendocrine systems. Auton Neurosci 2014: 182: 42-54.

12 Graziano, M. S. A. (2018). The Spaces Between Us: A Story of Neuroscience, Evolution, and Human Nature . Oxford University Press.

13 Brown, R., Lau, H., & LeDoux, J. E. (2019). Understanding the Higher-Order Approach to Consciousness. Trends in cognitive sciences, 23(9), 754–768.

14 LeDoux, J. E., & Pine, D. S. (2016). Using Neuroscience to Help Understand Fear and Anxiety: A Two-System Framework. The American journal of psychiatry, 173(11), 1083–1093.

15 Ecker B, Ticic R, Hulley L. A primer on memory reconsolidation and its psychotherapeutic use as a core process of profound change. The Neuropsychotherapist. 2013;1:82-99.

PLANNING AND PROMOTING CARE AND CHANGE PROCESSES

DOING YOUR JOB WELL

When my son was small, we took him for an ultrasound check-up. A good friend recommended someone, saying: "*he is the best sonographer in Pavia*". That expression immediately made me smile. Even though I had heard it many times before applied to other professions, I had never had the same reaction. I had probably used that expression myself in the past, referring to people I respected. Yet, at that time, hearing that expression, my first thought was: "*but how do you identify the best sonographer? Do they have contests?!*". Despite the ironic tone, my curiosity was genuine. If I recommend the best pastry chef in town, it's clear that – at least in my opinion – they make the best cakes of all the ones I've tried in that area. The parameter is subjective, but it is certainly an opinion built over time and by making comparisons with similar products from other professionals (whether the cannoncino pastry is more or less crumbly, whether they use a crunchier or tastier chocolate, etc.). When we talk about care professions, how do we define which one is better? It's unlikely my friend had had ultrasound scans with all the professionals in the city.

This question, to which we will then seek a satisfactory answer, can also be broadened by considering a curious phenomenon: we often hear people say: "*Mark is a very good psychotherapist*" or "*Hanna is a brilliant osteopath*". The curious thing is that, usually, the person stating this is their apprentice or a person who has read their book, but not one who has been a patient, so they have no real data on which to base this assessment. Even more curious is the fact that, if you point this out to them, these people find themselves disoriented and unable to justify their belief. In fact, skill can only be evaluated on the basis of results and of the satisfaction of those who obtain them. These elements both need to be present, it doesn't always happen, but it should be this way. Being publicly recognized as good, brilliant or effective is only a question of public image, but this does not interest us. However, by working carefully and in a natural way on professional effectiveness, there will be a positive effect on public perception too.

WHO ARE CARE AND CHANGE PROFESSIONALS AND WHAT DO THEY DO

In light of all the elements we have seen so far – and which we will develop further on – we can ask ourselves: who is a care and change professional "with a capital P?". How should a professional think, organize and act if they wish to fully exploit all the potential of a multi-disciplinary, scientific and dynamic approach such as that of the Applied Integrative Sciences, or of a structured approach so as to intervene on several levels in synergy?

The answer to start from is: with a *plan*. A plan provides meaning to the whole; it helps look at interconnected elements and temporal perspectives without the risk of falling into limiting cause-effect models (that are easy to identify but are not effective or satisfying for the professional or their patients).

The change specialist can and should therefore be a designer, a fine architect who analyses different levels and processes, draws up a speculative plan, defines it and fine-tunes it with their 'client' (this can be a student, an apprentice, someone we coach or a patient, depending on context), and then actions it.

While the plan is taking shape the change specialist needs to position themselves on two parallel but interconnected planes:
- they need to remain *designers*, improving and refining the plan on the basis of new evidence and on contingent elements that emerge;
- at the same time, they need to take on the role of *trainer/coach*, ensuring that the alterations suggested take place and become actual transformative experiences.

In a nutshell, the change specialist plans, promotes and supports:
- **Knowledge** of the processes that govern change, adaptation and health (providing help to move from a passive to an active perspective, from improvising and attempting new solutions to studying to constantly improving understanding and planning).

- **Physiology and balance** between systems, networks, processes and functions (all the Switches and Functional Patterns we analyse in this book).
- **Transformative Experiences** in different environments (lifestyle changes, targeted stimulation using specific techniques) that respect the criteria for efficient change and learning, such as times, modes and structural foundations that can change neural networks, epigenetics and other elements – which we will tackle throughout the book – that support new modes of functioning.

These steps also promote **Autonomy**, making people capable of managing their own self-regulation and development personally and with good levels of mastery.

As we will soon see, all of this cannot be separated from an **assessment** of the current situation and past history. However, as often happens, it is not a question of a static evaluation, but of a dynamic method of gathering information and observations, in interaction with the patient and with constant updating, within each single session, as well as over time.

AN OVERARCHING WORK METHOD

In this book we will look at different models and working schemes that can be used in a targeted way or as part of a wider strategy. Let's now explore a transversal working method through which it is possible to apply and decline your work as a "designer" and "trainer" of care, change and development.

To work on Knowledge, Balance and Physiology, and Experiences, the *Designer-Trainer of Change* can articulate their work on the following areas.

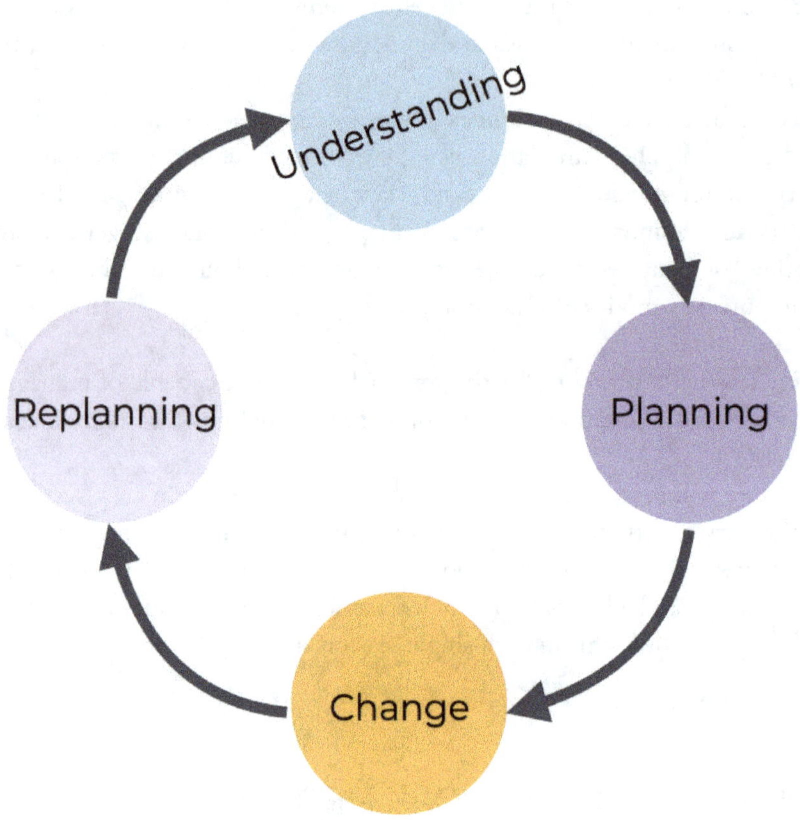

Fig. – The synthetic graphic is a representation (later we will look at the complete one) of the global method of application for the Applied Integrative Sciences. Each point must be *understood* by both the professional and the patient/client: both, each from their own point of view and in their own role, must understand (evaluate information, data, signs, symptoms, etc.), participate in the *planning* (and periodic *redesign* in fieri) of the customized and more effective treatment or change strategy, take action to favour *change* processes and/or recovery of physiology on several levels.

It is an application method that also lends itself very well to the integration of Integrative Sciences with the professional's existing way of working and professional baggage. Similarly, it can also take shape through the inclusion of Integrative Sciences tools, according to your own needs and preferences.

The phases do not follow on from each other rigidly but are always all present at different degrees. For example, in the first session the phases of the upper area will be dominant (*Understanding*: Assessment, Comprehending and Self-Observation), but feedback will start to be given on what is being observed and how you can work on certain aspects (central phase of *Planning* and subsequent re-planning), immediately offering some practical tips and initial tools with which to start activation (*Change* phase: Transformative Experiences, Global Changes and Lifestyle, Techniques and Targeted Interventions).

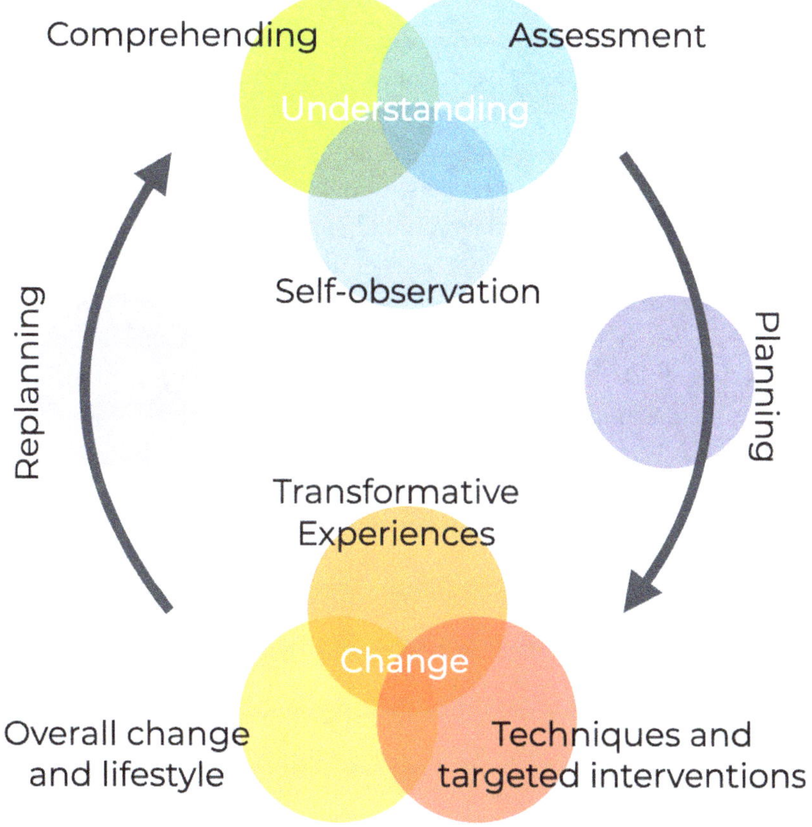

Fig. - Detail of the main factors included in the different areas of this working method.

At the end of the first or of the first two sessions, depending on the degree of confidence and the style of the specific professional, a structured *Plan* may be initiated to shape the most effective path in order to work on the therapeutic or change objectives identified can be laid out. From this moment on, the phases of the lower area (*Change*) will be dominant, but they will still include moments and activities that are typical of the first area (*Understanding*), in the form of insights into new topics, re-evaluation of data explored in the past but reviewed in light of new perspectives, learning new methods for self-evaluation.

AREA 1: ASSESSMENT, UNDERSTANDING, SELF-OBSERVATION

To give meaning to their work, the care and change designer must first of all analyse the specific reality experienced by their patient/client.

In this phase the professional observes and collects information (*Assessment*) and at the same time teaches the patient to observe themselves (*Self-observation*). It is a shared and collaborative process, that is supported by the multiple diagrams and tables offered by the Integrative Sciences, which can be printed out or viewed digitally on a screen together. By explaining these patterns and ways of gathering information, you begin to enter the Understanding phase, providing explanations on the functioning of the processes underlying physical and mental health. This way, the person is immediately involved and a new way of looking at themselves and at their way of knowing and caring for themselves is triggered, developing new self-observation skills. The term "self" should not lead you to think that the focus of interest is only the person themselves, new ways of looking at relational dynamics and contextual aspects of one's private and working life will also be learned. It is a broad, systemic and inclusive approach.

As for the external support used in this process, I personally recommend always leaving the cards and tables with the patient, perhaps first taking a photo as a reminder, inviting them to look at them again, and to add any other elements that come to mind after the session, so as to be able to review them together in the next meeting. This way, most people feel more in control of the situation (both in terms of the breadth of topics covered and in terms of professional trust), and become more active and involved in the therapeutic relationship.

This evaluation (*Assessment*) is not intended to provide a diagnosis, on the contrary, it is independent of any possible final label with respect to the type of problem. Our aim is to make an assessment of how things function to identify what is out of physiology and, therefore, what to do to recreate the optimal conditions (thus using *Planning* to shape *Change*). At the beginning of each chapter of the book dedicated to the various switch areas, you will find a section dedicated to assessment that gives a general overview of what can be a focal point in that thematic area. At various points throughout all the chapters you will find tests, cards and models to delve into specific topics.

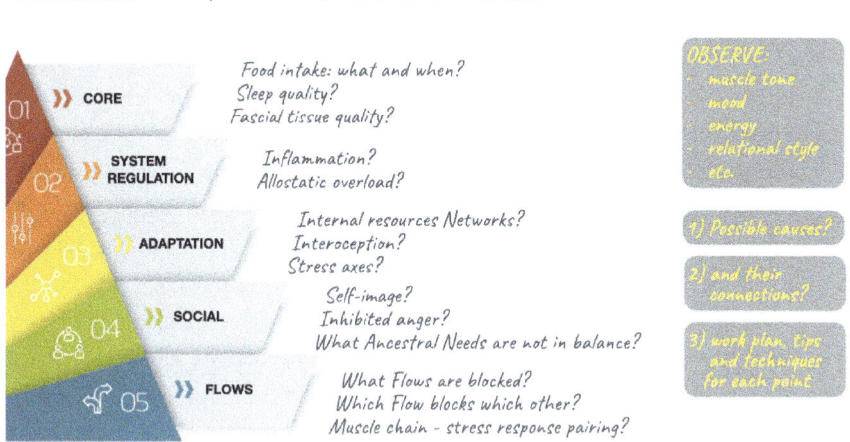

Fig. – Example worksheet a client can use to self-observe between appointments,

This analysis is not just a starting point, but must be continuously reviewed and updated, in order to identify the effectiveness of each single technique that has been carried out together, or at home both in the short term and over a longer period of time.

The change professional illustrates the basic Switches and Functional Schemes process in a way that is appropriate to the specific person (by age, interests, education, etc.) and functional to their purposes, so that they can:

- understand the causes and mechanisms of their own problems and difficulties first-hand (among other things, it is well demonstrated that knowing the precise mechanisms that modulate pain, without doing anything else, is enough to reduce - at least in part - the perception of pain);
- reduce erroneous attributions of guilt, sense of frustration or helplessness (e.g., thinking that they are distracted due to disinterest or lack of willpower, while their hormonal state, stress or other reasons influence their ability to pay attention);
- direct energies where it is possible and useful to implement change (e.g., avoiding persistence on aspects that are not important or that perhaps are, but can only be addressed after another aspect that functionally or structurally comes first has been resolved);
- find new ways of reading reality and their internal and relational world that are broad and flexible, supporting thoughts, emotional responses and behaviours that are more easily modulated on the basis of real circumstances.

Having clear ideas about the scientific processes underlying physical and mental health and disease helps both the end user and the professional. In fact, there are interpretative theoretical models, which, thanks to their simplistic reductionism, seem fascinating and obtain positive results. I have often heard people say: "This is typical of introverts like me", "I have a problem with power, it is typical of those with my physical shape", "this problem is due to my right hemisphere" and so on. Preferring to read a book over going to a party can certainly be consistent with a personality trait such as introversion, but we have to ask ourselves if it is simply a preference (and not a cause of that trait), or if – at least in part – it is not supported by having little energy due to metabolism, or by a protective mechanism of neural networks that either are subjected to too much stress every day, or behave in this way as a result of past trauma. Similarly, it is fascinating to hear: "*Your back is locked at this height; that is typical of someone who has suffered a betrayal of trust*". Most people over the age of 20 have both a blockage somewhere in their back and have had to deal with some betrayal, but that doesn't imply that they're connected. And even if they are, are we sure that blocked back will pass if we overcome the anger or disappointment at that betrayal? With our approach we evaluate possible connections on several levels, but above all we analyse all the aspects on which it may be useful to act to resolve both the back block and the pain of betrayal in each case, whether they are independent or related to each other. Once this assessment is made, it is possible to decide what to act on and in which order.

AREA 2: PLANNING AND MONITORING

In general, in this area our goal is to develop a broad and flexible treatment and/or change project, which takes into account multiple levels and systems, includes different perspectives, evaluates action and response times for each proposed intervention and includes several variables to identify which elements to leverage in a targeted way.

In order to develop a project of this magnitude, we have to take several aspects into account. A first aspect concerns the importance of connecting different systems and having clear mechanisms of mutual influence. In this, the Integrative Sciences – by definition – play a key role. In fact, they were born and developed specifically to understand the interaction between different systems (mind, neurobiology, physical and mental pain, posture, emotions, decision-making processes, relationships, etc.) and to identify the most effective ways to intervene. With this type of approach, a key factor to consider concerns the hierarchies of action which, if not respected, can generate resistance to treatment and change, mainly from a neurobiological and metabolic perspective (we will see other types later). A slogan to help us encapsulate the concept is: "the project works if the order is correct". It is therefore critical to identify the right intervention sequences, first creating the environment that allows the creation of adequate preconditions for the next phase to take place or, conversely, for deactivating the mechanisms that prevent the effectiveness of the proposed intervention. Metaphorically it is like saying that you can put a seed directly into the ground, but if you plough the soil before planting it, let it breathe for a few days and then fertilize it, once planted, the seed is more likely to grow and to do so faster and better. If the right conditions aren't there, even the most effective technique will yield disappointing results. If you have some experience with plants or in the kitchen, then you know that respecting the right sequences, even if it requires a little more planning and patience at the beginning, always saves time in the medium-long term and delivers better outcomes.

We will see that there may be different hierarchies to consider. For example, we may encounter protective conditions that are dysfunctional from a metabolic point of view, as in the – very widespread – cases in which there is little energy available due to incorrect nutrition, immune system inflammation caused by a pathology, stress, or other factors, which do not allow us to direct sufficient resources to cognitive, emotional and relational aspects (we will look at these aspects more closely in switch areas 1 and 2). Similarly, there may be energies that are blocked at a physical level (switch areas 3 and 5), that are there to preserve frozen postures caused by stress and emotional trauma that do not give space to any new mental motivational impulses (the classic *"I know I should do x but I can't"*).

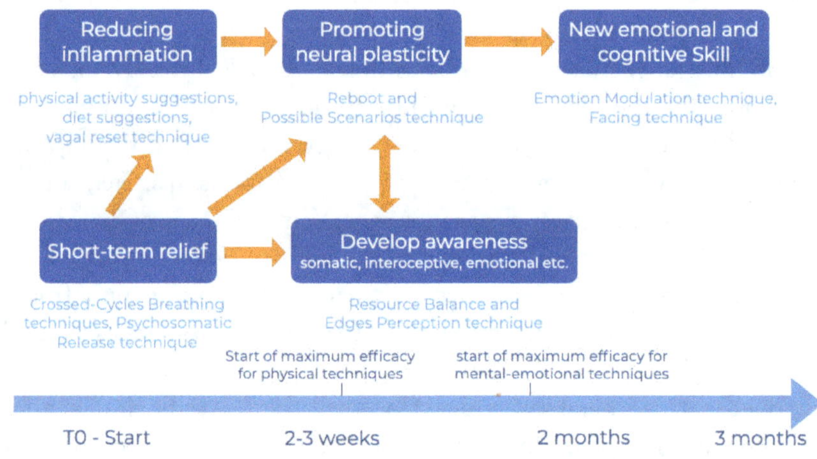

Fig. – In this example we see that the therapeutic project initially involves the reduction of inflammation, in order to create favourable conditions to then promote neural plasticity, which in turn represents the optimal basis on which to develop new emotional and cognitive skills. In the initial phase of the journey, it is also possible to offer immediate relief with specific techniques, which will then be expanded and used to develop somatic, interoceptive and emotional awareness, etc. Some techniques or methods (shown in blue) are typical of the Integrative Sciences and help achieve the objectives marked in the boxes. In this type of project, other techniques and the typical professional toolset also find space and can be used to create maximum synergy and effectiveness.

In these cases, it is not necessary to work on a cognitive level, but to remove excess of 'wasted' energy in maintaining protective postures or in ways of thinking that are quick but not decisive, which is typical of those who think anxiously about a problem, continually revisiting the problem but never solving it (we will see these processes in the switches 3 and 5 area).

As we will see, there are many processes like these even between domains that might seem separate: in order to develop emotional awareness it is useful to name emotions, but this cannot be done easily if bodily sensory awareness is not developed first. In turn, bodily sensory awareness (both exteroceptive and interoceptive) can be significantly improved through physical expedients and exercises (micro-movements, movements in negative phases, etc.) to which emotional awareness and cognitive reprocessing are added later.

You may encounter resistance to therapeutic expectations. Sometimes, despite the clarity and understanding of the explanations provided, we may get a more or less explicit response along the lines of: "*I came here for my pain (physical or emotional). I understand that physical activity and nutrition have something to do with it, but you have to make me feel as good as I expect (for example by talking/with bodily manipulations/with medication/ etc.)*". There are expectations about care professions and how change occurs that are very ingrained. If intercepted, it is usually better to immediately explain the various correlations that we have noticed, but to propose the supplementary initiatives gradually, so that the person can learn to trust them, feel the first improvements on their own skin and, consequently, be open to other suggestions.

Then there are also psycho-social and systemic resistances (in a more environmental and relational sense). Two very different situations, such as knee pain that does not go away and the fact of procrastinating the last university exams, can be due, in a non-conscious way, to the fear of responsibilities. For example, if the knee heals, one must admit that one has failed to become a professional sportsman, or that their desired self-image does not correspond to reality. Similarly, finishing university would mean having to work, detach yourself emotionally and financially from your parents, go and live with a partner you are unsure about and so on. These aspects must be taken into consideration when designing our care and change project as they can often make the difference.

Once all these factors have been considered, it is necessary to understand in which order to intervene to provide a different perspective, so that the patient can experience these aspects in a more natural and manageable way. Sometimes it is necessary to create a gradual strategy that is made up of intermediate steps that the body, mind and social environment can gradually accept and metabolize. We will therefore have to develop a project that is organized in flexible modules (in line with the way of thinking that we want to develop in the patients themselves, so much so, that we will find specific tools in the switches 4 and 5), so as to be able to reach the desired objectives with the right number of steps and with the flexibility to readjust the project according to individual, contextual and unforeseen factors.

An important criterion to consider therefore is that of *graduality and sustainability*. For example, you cannot suddenly stop intense daily sporting activity, both for metabolic and mental and emotional issues. If the person developed this process, it was their best solution to the problem. Stopping this activity could cause negative thoughts to emerge, impede the release of stress and anger and the disposal of excess neurotransmitters and hormones, not giving him/her the excuse to avoid staying at home or something else.

Similarly, it is often not possible to ask a person to go to sleep earlier than usual, suddenly going from 3 in the morning to 11 at night. Such a leap would create more anxiety than well-being, the body and mind would not be able to grasp the added value of the change. In both these cases, possible resistance to change on several levels, such as those mentioned above, must be considered and managed, but – even independently of them – a series of intermediate steps must be set up to make the change acceptable and usable by the body and the mind.

In this design, subjective preferences and organizational aspects must also be considered. For example, a patient may fully understand that circadian rhythms are critical to bringing physiology back into their stress response while improving anger outbursts, dermatitis, and back pain. On the other hand, if this person has a job with night shifts, or a job where they come back for dinner and have four 4 children they have to manage and want to enjoy, they will need practical support reorganizing various aspects (for example identifying with them which relatives to ask for help in managing their children). They should also immediately receive a bit of feedback and practical evidence of the possible advantages of our project, for example through exercises that require only 5-10 minutes a day to start releasing physical tension, zero cost changes (both financial and effort), like starting to sleep with the blinds partially raised (we'll see why in switch 1), etc. In this way, within a month, they will be able to recover some energy, be confident in the value of our proposal and have put into place the external conditions to give concrete form to even more substantial and, therefore, effective changes.

We focused on the design aspects, which are very important. As we have seen in the general model of our method, it's not just about developing an initial design, but the project must be constantly improved upon, on the basis of what happens, of the individual and environmental responses that emerge, considering how the various experiments proceed, the transformative experiences that we will have set up, the techniques, the reworkings and every possible variation.

During the journey there may be slowdowns, unforeseen events or unexpected instances. In any case, the correct mindset is one that does not see problems or failures, but only data to analyse and strategies to perfect.

With a calm and constructive approach, every aspect is analysed and the decision whether to change methods, introduce an intermediate step, implement a variation capable of isolating a specific behaviour or factor at play is made. Motivation, interpersonal relationships, trust and every other element must also be re-read according to switches and functional schemes: we need to ask ourselves what is out of place, and how we can put the various factors that support healthy, constructive and realistic motivation back in line through all switch levels.

AREA 3: TRANSFORMATIVE EXPERIENCES, GLOBAL CHANGES AND LIFESTYLE, TECHNIQUES AND TARGETED INTERVENTIONS

Thirdly, the change designer and trainer/coach provides practical indications and exercises, supporting and facilitating their implementation. They do it by making the most of their knowledge and on the basis of what has been analysed and set out in the previous two points.

The general and transversal objectives of this area are to recreate physiology in functioning and in the systems underlying the health and well-being of the person, in order to make the adaptation and development systems work better on several fronts: from having an immune system response that responds better if it encounters a virus to remaining lucid and effective under stress. In general, this means having a flexible and responsive body and mind that live in the present with an eye to the future, without getting stuck in the past (whether it's an incorrect posture due to work or trauma, a frozen emotion, a relational scheme activated some time ago but no longer effective today).

To move in this direction, initiatives that act on several fronts must be set up. Overall lifestyle changes will be required, because people often live in conditions that are unsustainable by our body due to how it has evolved over time, both because of cultural factors and as a result of deprivation, stress or trauma (we will examine several of these mechanisms transversally in all the switch areas).

The practical indications can sometimes be very simple suggestions, which the patient can decide to try out on the basis of understanding the explanations relating to area 1. To give a concrete example, the Switches of the second group and the *Preconditions* of the Integrative Functional Schemes, highlight how there can be a state of hyper-reactivity following various conditions (chronic stress, inflammatory diet, etc.). In light of these mechanisms, you may propose a reduction in the number of push notifications for a few hours a day (those that appear as soon as a message or email arrives, as well as from any other application or software). Reading the book from this point of view you will find many other ideas to implement.

At the same time, the use of targeted techniques is also key, because certain neurobiological mechanisms, mental, emotional, postural, motor and relational patterns are often 'crystallised' in dysfunctional configurations. With targeted stimuli, both in the session and then carried out independently, these mechanisms can be reversed or, at least, modified.

In this text you will find several specific techniques and exercises (for example *Psychosomatic Releases, Crossed-Cycles Breathing, Parallel Worlds, Emotions and Behaviour Modulation with Post-it, Isometric Emotions, Reboot Techniques, Interpersonal Accommodation, Resource Balance Techniques with or without Reconsolidation* and others) to intervene on the various elements of the Switches and Functional Schemes in a targeted way. In addition to these techniques and methods of intervention, other typical tools of one's profession or those learned in other courses can also be easily integrated in this phase, making them even more effective thanks to a global vision and synergistic action.

One very effective mode of intervention, which lies somewhere between life changes and targeted techniques, concerns the power of transformative experiences. The human being is an adaptive organism, specialized to adapt to the environment. It is probably the complex living being with the most flexibility in this regard. For this it will be essential to create the conditions to give shape to transformative experiences designed specifically for that person, so that they can experience situations that promote change in a more natural way. As we will see, this ability is based on the constitutive aspects of our organism, such as epigenetics, plasticity of neural networks, integrated and synergistic functioning of emotion, cognition and movement, and other factors that we will explore in this book. We have named the path through which to design and shape these experiences HXD, or *Human eXperience Design*.

The relationship with the care and development professional is also a transformative experience. We need to be aware of this aspect and find the right balance between a natural relationship (which is healthy, but also sets and example for our patient) and control over the responsibility of our role.

In shaping this phase it is important to remember that advice, techniques and strategies can be scientific and of proven effectiveness but, if you don't like them, the effects will be zero or almost nil. A lot of research has shown that meditation has positive effects, but if a person does it against their will or finds it excessively 'static' for them, it has no positive effects. On the other hand, the only effect is to lose trust and damage the therapeutic alliance with the professional that proposed it. Similarly, research has shown that certain types of physical activity are essential (we will see which ones in switches areas 1 and 3) only if carried out when desired. The best physical activity, done at the wrong time or with an inadequate mindset, increases stress hormones and inflammatory response instead.

When we take into account whether a certain type of physical activity, or other initiative may appeal, we must consider an important detail: some people are convinced that they do not like something, but in reality, it is a belief based on knowledge that is limited or biased. Sometimes the possibility of trying something new can be unlocked by the right knowledge or by taking an intermediate test. Other times, you get to try new behaviours or make new experiences gradually, guided in the development of curiosity and exploration. These are innate mechanisms that are limited by fear linked to a trauma or induced by education, or never correctly trained or supported, as we will see, for example, by addressing Ancestral Needs in switch 4 area.

PART 2 – MECHANISMS, PROCESSES, PATTERNS AND METHODS OF INTERVENTION

INTEGRATIVE FUNCTIONAL PATTERNS

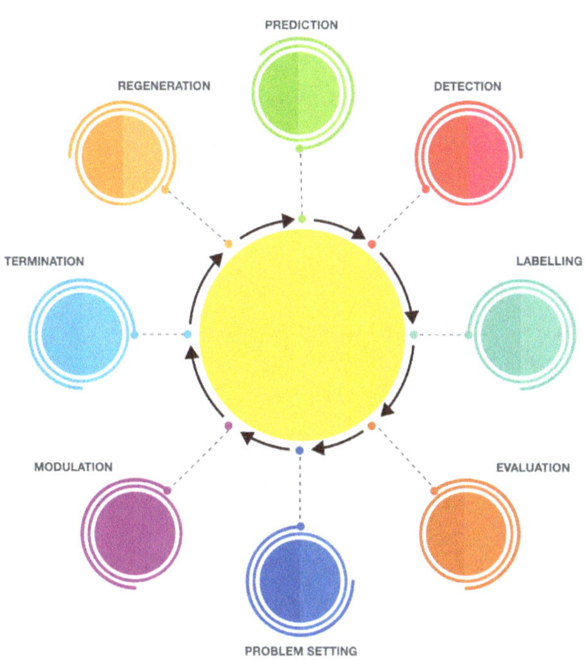

KEEPING EVERYTHING UNDER CONTROL WITH TIMING

Sequences of events occur within us that involve our entire body and interact with the external environment to carry out any behaviour, from simply lifting a pen to taking an important decision. Regulation processes, motivation, emotions, desires projected into the future, interpersonal relationships and many other aspects of our life take shape through these sequences of events. The *Integrative Functional Patterns* model focuses precisely on a time-based vision of what happens to shape our stress responses, behaviour and interpersonal dynamics. Understanding these sequences helps clarify how we arrive at an answer which, although rapid and sometimes automatic, is actually the composite result of several different steps. This way it is possible to identify where to intervene to change the process and – consequently – the final result, i.e. no longer feeling anxious, maintaining concentration, making less impulsive choices, perceiving less annoyance or pain, and so on.

In the following chapters, however, we will develop a process for more vertical structures thanks to the Switch model. These are two different approaches and perspectives, both are effective and complement and support each other.

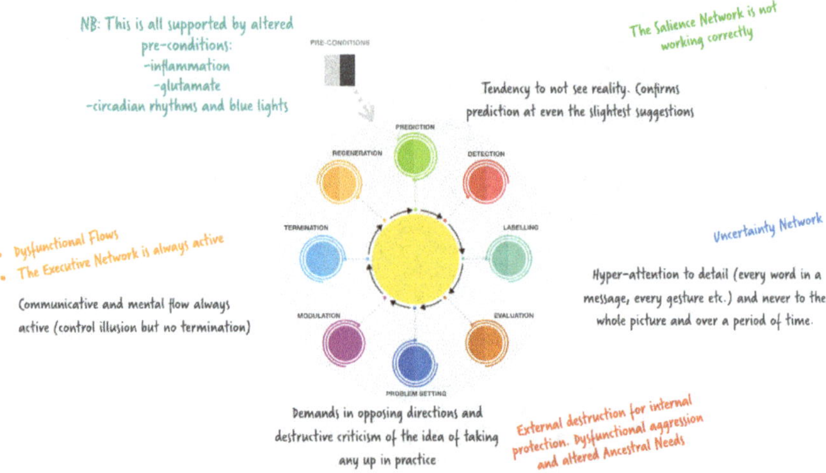

Fig. - In this image we see some points of convergence between the themes that we will explore with the change Switches, here as part of the Integrative Functional Schemes map.

Given that there are numerous factors that interact with each other to be managed, and given the importance of following the correct sequence of action, we have developed an integrative scheme over time to keep all these elements under control and introduce them into therapeutic or educational work according to a sequential perspective (*circular logic*).

These are the *Integrative Functional Patterns*. As the name suggests, they were developed to manage in a progressive and localized way all the elements at play (neural networks involved, the role of predictions, expectations, objectives, trust, the delicate balance between adaptation processes and emotional memories, interpersonal relations, but also environmental elements, nutritional elements and other aspects) with a significant focus on human behaviour in the widest sense of the term.

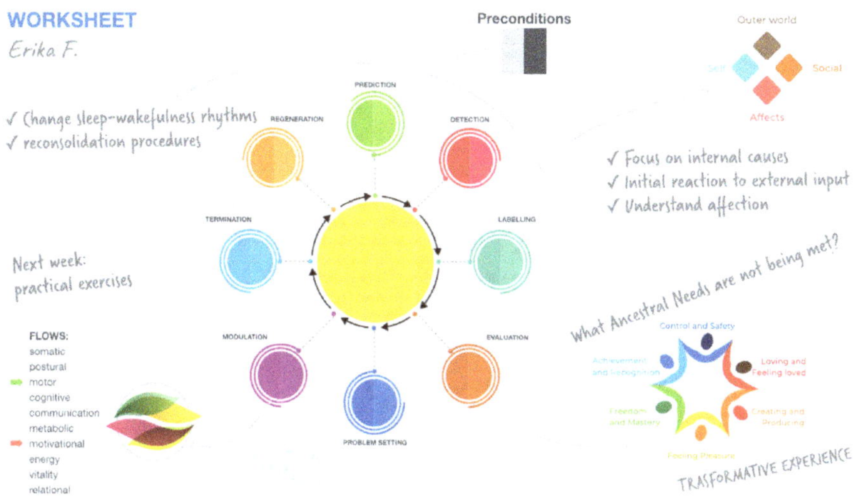

Fig. - This worksheet highlights some points in the Integrative Functional Patterns where it is possible to intervene in a targeted way, by considering, for example, the contribution of Ancestral Needs in the Evaluation phase (if they are balanced they can alter the way in which the gravity of a situation is perceived) or working on Flows to make the Modulation phase more effective and manageable.

Integrative Functional Patterns enable the pursuit of a logical and structured programme, acting on *Pre-existing conditions* (metabolic states, inflammation, first and second level switches etc.) that alter the early *Detection* stages of an internal or external stimulus, appropriate *Evaluation* (a multi-phase process including pre-logical and sensory phases as well as more structured and complex phases and the third level switches) including the deepest motivational elements in common to all mammals that cause psychosomatic damage in case of deprivation (*Ancestral Needs*). The later stages include elements of *self-monitoring* (metacognition), *planning* and *strategy*, right through to *physical and behavioural execution* (Flows from the fifth group of switches). The final phases are those of *Termination* and *Regeneration*, in which it is possible to respectively end the adaptation process, and bring the system back to physiological state, avoiding that conditions become chronic, and that hyper-arousal, traumatic memories and other dysfunctional elements are carried through from the adaptation process.

In this heterarchical (non-linear hierarchies) and circular perspective on the Adaptation-Development-Recovery process, each phase enables action that reinforces the abilities and capabilities that are a pre-requisite, or are fundamental to, the functioning of the subsequent phases such as the feeling of mastery and control, mental and physical flexibility, an increased degree of freedom of movement but also of behavioural choice, greater energy for movement and action initiation and to sustain motivational and creative impulses.

BEHAVIOUR: ITS ORIGINS, USE AND ENDING

Where does a specific behaviour start? How does it come into being? This looks like a simple question, but it really is not.

Whether it is the response to a potentially dangerous stimulus, what we say to someone to motivate them or to defend ourselves, or the result of a lengthy evaluation, it is basically always an action that is taken to alter the existing state of things.

This often coincides with solving a problem and/or adding value. As we know, however, this process is not always so straightforward. The routes and processes that follow on from each other are often very tortuous and not entirely conscious. We often act one way, when we had actually planned to behave differently.

In some instances, although the problem is solved and the possible action is terminated, thoughts still persist. This also takes place at a physical level: a state of physical activation remains over time even though it is no longer useful or required. It is easy to identify this phenomenon in relation to traumatic events, but it also takes place in many daily situations.

Let's take an example from everyday life that can happen to anyone: consider how many times after an argument is over, even conceding we were right, our body remains tense and active for hours later as though still prepared to face imminent danger. This does not just happen with arguments, but as a result of worries, danger and conflict of any type.

These examples have already highlighted three key elements relating to the issue we are analysing and to the Integrative Functional Patterns that we can put in place, that may be more or less effective. We will expand on these in the next paragraphs.

3 MACRO-AREAS OF INTEGRATIVE FUNCTIONAL PATTERNS

At the start of any behaviour there is an initial phase that is far more articulated and sophisticated than is usually expected.

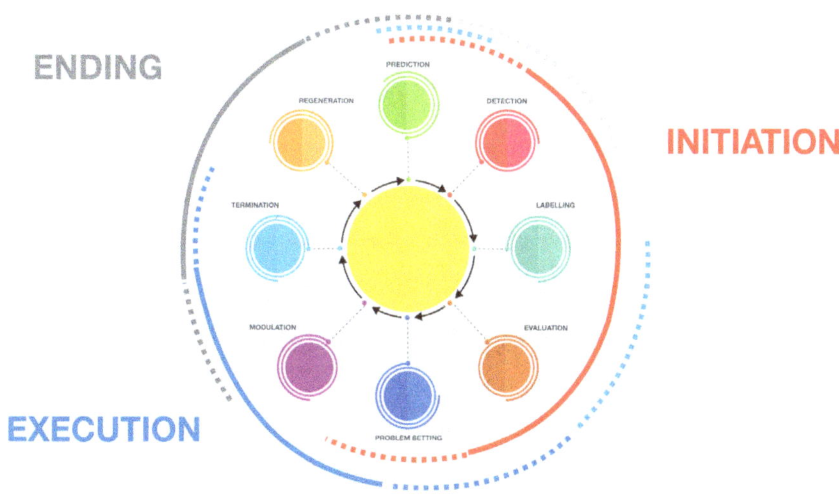

There is also a final phase in which various systems and processes should terminate to return to their physiological state or, if possible, to an added-value state. The situation is sophisticated in this latter instance too and needs deeper analysis. Please note that this is one of the critical stages in our system, one where there is direct contact between behaviour and self-image, between efficiency and psychosomatic cost. We will return to this numerous times to analyse it more in depth.

The central phase is related to the operational side of the resolution of a problem or to active change. Most people that come to us in private practice are very focused on this latter idea. Focus is usually directed to this area of Functional Patterns because it is the easiest to see as it concerns what is visible and within our field of awareness. It extends from logical planning to solve an issue right through to the practical execution of a behaviour.

The strength of Integrative Functional Patterns, on the other hand, lies in being able to see and actively manage all the different phases involved in every adaptation process whether it is a stress response, relationship dynamic or a type of behaviour with a specific objective.

THE 8 PHASES OF THE IFP

THE START OF EVERYTHING: FROM DETECTION TO EVALUATION

Even the simplest behaviour starts long before we see it in action. During this 'invisible' time many things take place that can influence whether the behaviour eventually takes place or not. In addition to this, these processes also affect the specific ways in which it will be shaped.

It all starts with the *detection* of an initial stimulus that can be external or internal. Seeing a menacing tiger, a missed call on the telephone from someone that we have a bad relationship with, or even noticing a memo that reminds us of a deadline, or the re-emergence of a negative memory in our mind are all instances that activate the system.

First of all, we carry out a *rapid evaluation.*

Various theories have enriched this aspect and highlighted the importance of different elements during this evaluation phase. If we consider all possible aspects and the latest findings, thanks to the contribution of neuroscience applied to change and of clinical practice – as well as other scientific disciplines –, some significant data emerges.

Firstly, this initial evaluation is a process that takes place over more than one stage. We can sum these up in two main phases each composed of numerous steps and processes.

The first of these two phases is extremely rapid and largely independent from conscious processes. It works a bit like *triage* in accident and emergency: a quick risk evaluation is provided factoring in, but not limited to, a range of different safety elements. As we will see, social and developmental aspects are also taken into consideration. This is why we call this the *Labelling* phase. This phase activates the very first physical responses and moves into the second phase of *Evaluation*, where the scenario of parameters taken into consideration expands significantly.

During the labelling phase the *Salience Network* plays a key role. As the name suggests, its role is that of a radar that perceives what is salient or 'relevant'. In case of a positive reaction, it activates adaptation processes, on the contrary, in case of a false alarm, it allows us to return to a state of calm.

As we will see in the third group of switches, the Salience Network is mainly based on physical data collected by the insular cortex and on the threat criteria evaluated by the amygdala and other brain regions. For this reason, in order to manage the very first emotional response and self-control, it is important to work on body maps, on mastery, on physiology and on the management of space and other environmental and physical elements. "Safety starts at the core", could be the slogan for this initial phase. At this first stage of our work a number of techniques and hacks can be used to provide immediate and practical self-control and awareness, allowing the subject to proceed effectively and serenely to the next phases.

Taking a step back though, it is important to remember that the Salience Network is already active during the *Detection* phase so these sensory elements can already be providing a filter – to our advantage or against – on the quantity and quality of what comes under our radar.

Let us take a day-to-day example: if we are in a negative frame of mind even a fly can set-off a negative reaction which can lead to so-called 'irritation' and eventually turn into stress, anger, impotence or aggressive responses.

By contrast, if we are in optimal conditions, we do not even notice that it has flown into the room. This means the filter has been useful right from the very start and the labelling phase has not taken place.

Regulating this stage provides a huge advantage: we can remain focused on what we are doing without even trying to control our thought processes, initiate self-control processes, or, more in general, we can avoid wasted energy and over-stimulation of systems that, evolutionally speaking, exist to help us respond to rare and occasional danger. Later we will look at how this relates to the *termination* phase from a different angle.

Let us briefly recap what we have covered so far: the process has been initiated and detection and labelling have ensued. We therefore have reached the proper Evaluation phase. In this phase the number of mechanisms involved increases and some of them are accessible – partially or entirely – to our consciousness (we will see that complete cognitive control starts with the following phase).

Somatic and procedural memories are involved during the Labelling phase and self-image is strictly physical and interoceptive. During the Evaluation phase we enter the reign of narrated memories, of experiences that are shaped by self-image and are linked to vitality and primary socialisation.

In the next phase, Problem Setting, the phase determining the most logical resolution of the issue, we see semantic memories enter the scene as well as conceptual schemas, cultural, contextual, ideal and value-based self-imagery.

THE IMPORTANCE OF WHAT HAPPENS FIRST: PREDICTIONS AND PRECONDITIONS

Does everything really begin when we perceive a starting point? No. Everything depends on two key elements.

The *first* relates to the conditions we are in just before detection activates, such as for example phenomena known as *hyper-* or *hypo-arousal*, or in other words conditions of chronic *activation* (excessive or insufficient) of the *sympathetic* or *parasympathetic* system, of certain *brain networks* or other interconnected systems between mind-brain-immune system-metabolism and many others. A person can find themselves in these conditions further to trauma, chronic stress, or other adverse states.

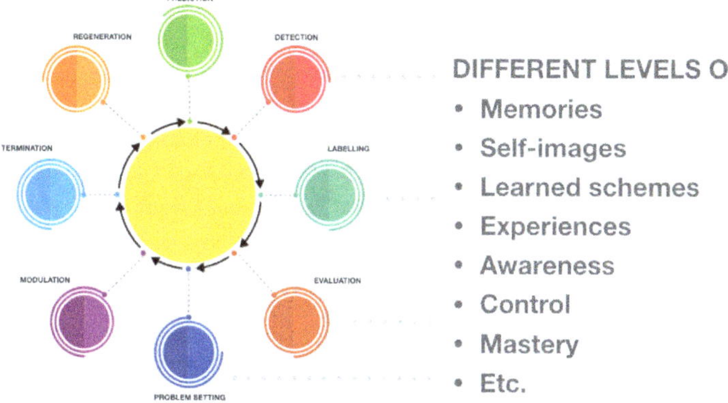

The physiological state, or lack of it, of the *first three groups of switches* plays a critical role here. In these instances, it is critical to act on core physiology even before acting on the response cycle, using techniques that are specifically targeted to act on these pre-conditions. Various practical suggestions that are easily applicable to real life (physical activity, nutrition, sleep-wakefulness rhythms etc.) are provided in the following part of this book.

On the other hand, it can be interesting to act in a controlled manner on certain phases of activation, to achieve a positive effect on core physiology. For example, the phases of Modulation and Termination play a key role in managing these states of hyper or hypo activation through practice and experience.

There are also some other *pre-conditions* that can influence the outcome of events: epigenetic mutations, inflammation due to bad nutrition habits and/or drug abuse, sleep-wakefulness cycles, and various other behavioural aspects.

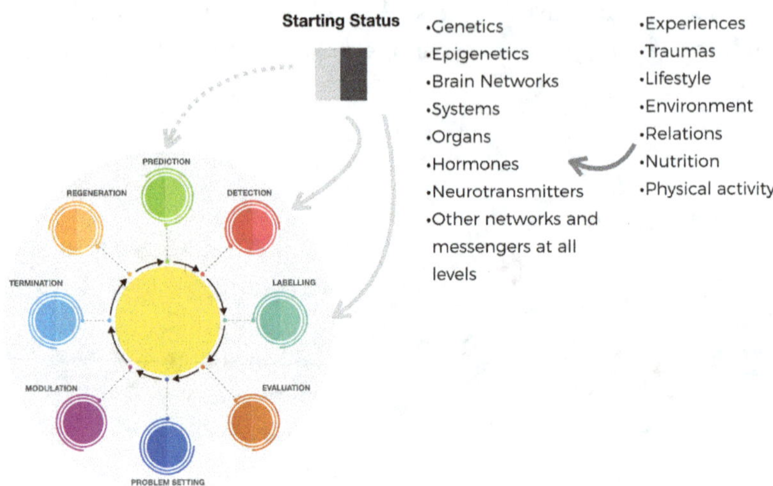

An integrated and integrative approach needs to consider all these elements to significantly improve later stage work. To think of this metaphorically: it is a process akin to preparing the soil to make it more fertile before planting a plant.

With this approach, people feel assisted and accepted all-round in every area of their daily life with an outlook that strategically encompasses the past, the present and the future.

The other element that plays a key role in the phase before reality takes shape is that of forecasting. Our brain is continuously making predictions; we do it to stay a step head and increase our safety, but there are also some interesting forecasting processes that relate to motivation, fulfilment and social interaction.

Our reaction often activates specific thoughts and emotions based more on forecasting than on actual perception. As shown by Lisa Barrett Feldman and other researchers, there is a neurological basis to this fact: the neural pathways that transmit predictions and pre-judgements (literally judgements made early) are faster and more powerful than those that carry internal and external sensory perception (you can find all the relevant scientific sources in the section devoted to ideative switches, in the fifth group). This has important repercussions on our reactions but also on the distortions with which we evaluate reality.

This is another instance where it is important to note some caveats: the forecasting involved in this phase is extremely rapid and often not conscious. Rational and pondered forecasts belong to the so-called *Problem Setting* phase. In the *Prediction* stage, there is a continuous system of anticipations that – if all is working correctly – should constantly be compared against reality in order to be as effective as possible. It is as though our mind is trying to stay a few seconds ahead of the present, in order to be prepared and help reality flow smoothly.

Issues arise when we try to impose our predictions on reality. People often superimpose the two levels: they focus on their forecasts, which they have forcibly confirmed, as though these were indeed reality. This mechanism is at the heart of numerous types of individual suffering and interpersonal misunderstandings that can result in exhausting conversations (during which each side tries to convince the other), or alternatively, in a frustrating sense of impotence in communicating.

It is not through logic or rhetoric that these forecasts can be altered. Rather, we need to act by changing the specific processes that are stopping the correct integration of data from reality and by restoring the functional system.

MOVING ON TO ACTION: FROM REFLEXES TO FULL CONTROL

Returning to our initial query: *"when does a type of behaviour start?"* we can now state that our system tries to adapt to a situation as soon as it is provided with a label. This happens shortly after the detection phase or after a potential prediction and is entirely influenced by pre-existing conditions.

The subsequent phases see evaluation and planning take shape and reach what represents – or at least should represent – the most structured type of human behaviour: the Modulation phase. This is where complex actions encompassing all elements and envisioning longer-spanning temporal outcomes can take place.

It is usually the quality of this middle phase that brings about satisfaction and fulfilment. It is often presumed that it is the termination phase that brings about fulfilment and finally determines the quality of an action allowing us to state: "I did it!". In reality, the termination of a type of behaviour often is not fulfilling at all. This is something you are bound to have experienced in more than one instance too.

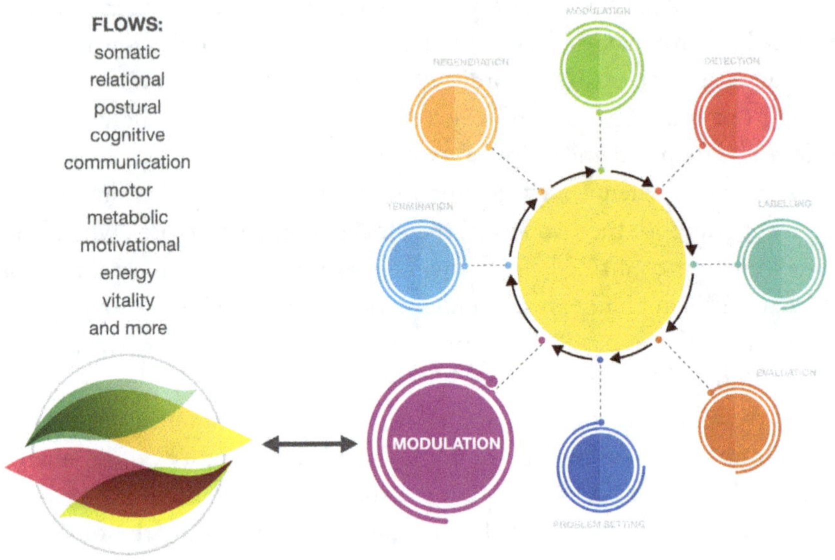

A useful system to understand Modulation and to act on it directly is that of Flows (Switch area n. 5), or in other words the ways our behaviour comes into actual being. There are somatic, relational, postural, motor, metabolic, motivational, energy and vitality Flow systems. These flows can be expressed automatically, if they are the result of habits consolidated over time, or they can be innate and express basic functions relating to key needs, or they can even be managed and controlled by changing habits and using retro-feedback on acquired patterns (altered to your own advantage) or even by acting at a relational systems level.

The Modulation phase also moves along circuits that have been forged by trust, values, cooperation relationships, evolutionary discovery, transformative experimentation and creativity. Experience is transformative at the deepest level: the epigenetic level. As acknowledged earlier this book, McEwen and other researchers have shown the criteria and effectiveness conditions at the heart of these processes.

FROM REST TO ADDED VALUE: ADAPTATION, RECOVERY AND DEVELOPMENT

Let us proceed with this run-down of all the elements involved in the process with which the behaviours we use every day take place: from single decisions to reactions to stress, right through to more complex experiences in our studies, or at work, or even in our personal relationships.

There is an issue we touched upon, but that needs to be expanded further and that is the fact that any behaviour needs to eventually come to an end. It is not a given. Does it end when we reach a vantage point or an objective? Because we give up? And on what basis? When observable behaviour ends, but we continue to think about it, what are we doing?

Here the edges between adaptation behaviour, self-realisation, motivation and psychosomatic conditions really blur. Just think of how, further to trauma or chronic stress, even though the problem has been overcome or resolved, the state of activation continues to function.

Termination phase disorders are easily found in daily life. One key example is that of people who cannot stop complaining; their difficulty in terminating a specific process highlights that the behaviour itself did not help solve the problem, so the subsequent behaviour of complaining is not effective – not even to blow off steam.

Another interesting instance is that of people who continue to insist in front of a clear negative or evident disinterest from the other party, or those that continue an argument started hours earlier with another person and in another setting, as though the issue is contemporary. In these instances too it may be that the termination signal is not strong enough or that the conditions for it to be accepted and included in the various adaptation phases are not present.

If we think about it, there are *termination* processes at many levels: from the nervous system to the immune system, the motor system to personal interactions, from stress to pain. These are all interconnected and put the bidirectional relationships of alteration of our behaviour at risk. These termination processes are mediated by various elements: the ability to understand interpersonal nurture relationships, those of trust or power; personal fulfilment, in the delicate balance between recovery, hedonism and motivation activities, by Ancestral Needs, which can be satisfied immediately or vicariously and much more (see the boxout in the fourth switches group).

The final phase to take into account is the so-called *Regeneration* phase which comes after termination. After an exertion it is normal to seek rest; sleep is the most intuitive way to achieve this, but there are also many others.

The key aspect to highlight is that this phase is not just one of recovery. Instead, it actually has *a significant development component*: muscles do not just rest, but become stronger, the nervous system is optimised, cells begin metabolic processes to improve energy deployment, but there is still more.

After stress there are *innate processes* that all mammals put into action to bring their bodies, and all the systems that were involved in the behaviour required to overcome danger, back to a physiological state. Horses run, bears and dogs shake, chimps groom after fighting. These phenomena are deeply rooted and bring various benefits.

From a neurobiological standpoint, there are important benefits: running and shaking are ways of expelling excess toxins produced by trauma and stress; while the oxytocin that is produced from grooming or physical containment combat the high cortisol levels.

From a functional perspective there are individual but also social benefits. These behaviours foster the need for freedom, self-mastery, they redefine physical limits, they consolidate trust and acceptance.

The regeneration phase therefore plays a central role in recovery, but also in development on many levels. It can be optimised naturally in every type of behaviour by following a few simple practical tips, but it can also be used in a targeted and specific way. It is, in fact, possible to develop a window of opportunity for consolidation at the end of therapy, coaching, training and study sessions during which via 10 minutes of regeneration specifically directed to follow certain criteria, it is possible to increase the effectiveness of the previous session very significantly.

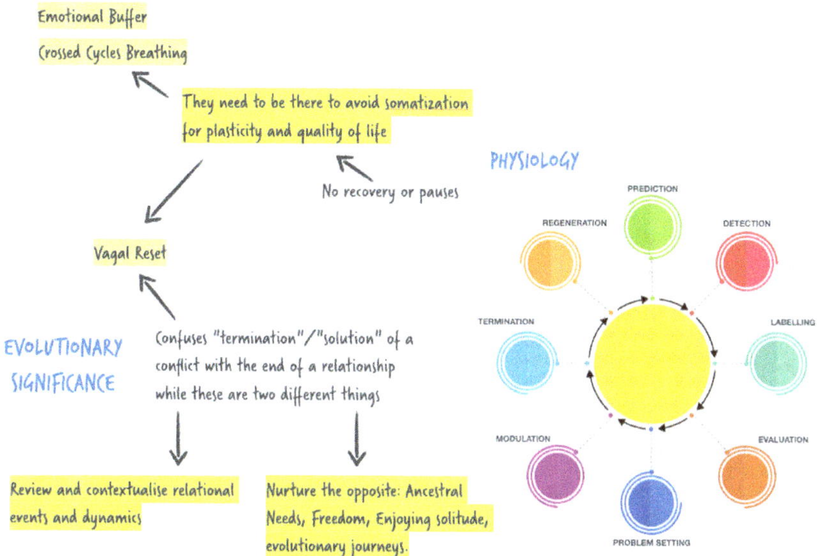

Fig. - Example of a worksheet shared with the patient: the problems identified and the techniques and strategies proposed are shown for the phases concerned.

CHANGE SWITCHES – INTRODUCTION

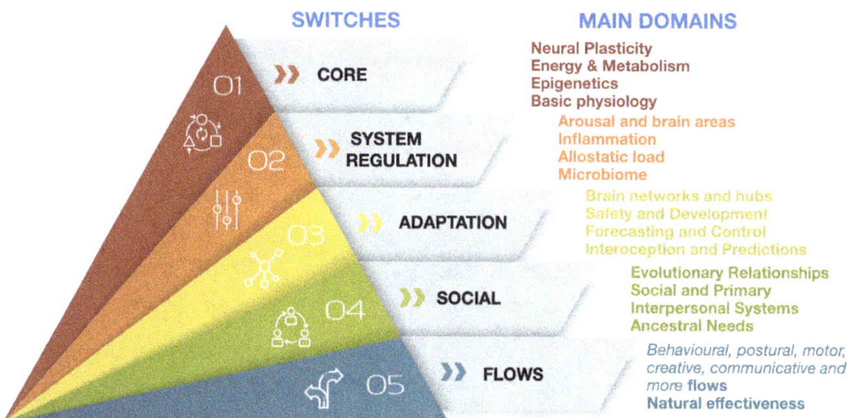

WHAT ARE SWITCHES AND WHAT IS THEIR SOURCE?

The Switch Model is the key tool for developing the integrated care and change approach that we present in this book. These are metaphorical switches that need to be "flicked" to promote flexible and evolutionary adaptation processes. These systems do not operate according to an on/off dichotomy but follow a series of gradual steps that can be worked on in a targeted way. The switch metaphor actually highlights the need to change state in order to activate the required change. In visual terms: to switch on a lightbulb you need to flick the switch up so as to drive electricity to it, but if electricity does not flow, or keeps coming and going, it will be difficult to do anything in that room (such as reading, playing or working) in an ongoing and satisfying way.

We have classified the different switches according to two criteria. The *first* type relies on reverse engineering by identifying what changes in people who have achieved a lasting and effective change. We have analysed various cases of effective change in different contexts (psychotherapy, physical pain, relationship problems, posture, medical conditions, etc.), and have identified the structures and neurobiological processes that were altered to enable change, both in terms of self-care, in adaptation processes, but also in terms of new abilities and skills acquired.

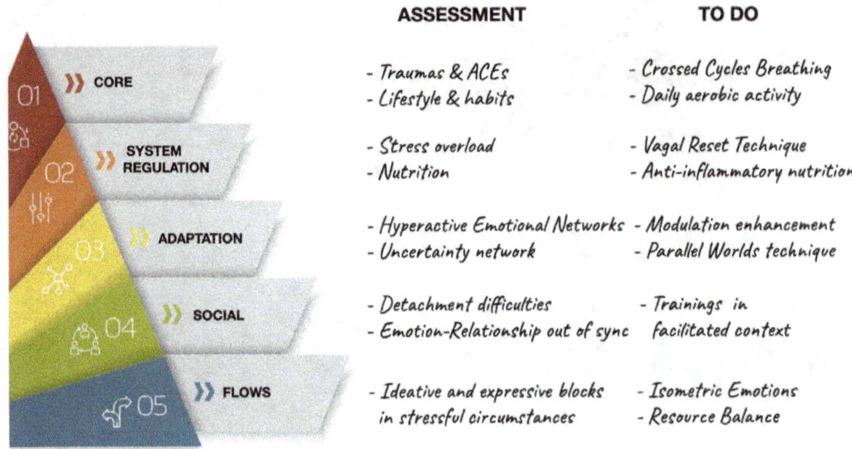

Fig. - Example of a worksheet from the Switch of Change model.

The *other* way is through a process of summarization and integration that draws efficient disciplines, approaches and methods that enable change, well-being and physiological states from different disciplines. We have also drawn from disciplines that are not usually connected to the study of the mind and of emotions, but that are actually very useful to help understand their physical side such as functional biomechanics for example. This is a science that enables us to delve deep into the feeling of mental impotence caused by the limited or constricted movement in trauma or other dysfunctional conditions.

From the opposite perspective, we have studied phenomena that are typically considered medical (e.g., diabetes or degenerative diseases) taking into account mental and emotional aspects, as well as neural networks and design-thinking.

Throughout the various phases of these processes we were supported by a network of global professionals belonging to the Association for Integrative Sciences and its HUB (training centre and inter-professional community). They contributed data from clinical activity and took part in forums and research groups online and in person. The primary focus has always been split between clinical evidence and ease of application in professional practice.

The 5 main groups of switches are:

→ 1. CORE

Neural Plasticity, Energy Metabolism and Epigenetics, Circadian Rhythms and other factors that represent the structural basis of health and change.

→ 2. SYSTEM REGULATION

The concepts and processes of scientific psychosomatics, including: Abuse of function, Inflammation, Allostatic Load and Overload, the Principle of Minimum Free Energy, and more.

→ 3. ADAPTATION

Networks & Hubs: i.e., the neurobiological centres of emotion and behaviour control that organize adaptation, stress and development responses through the perfect integration of body and mind.

→ 4. SOCIAL

Evolutionary Relationships, Primary Social and Interpersonal Systems to rethink Attachment and Detachment, Constructive Aggression, Ancestral Needs and other areas in which relationships are key.

→ 5. FLOWS

Natural Flows: autonomous, interdependent and integrative ways with which ideas, thoughts, movements, posture, language, etc. take shape and interact with each other.

In the next part of the book we analyse the 5 areas in which the switches have been grouped by type and by increasing level of functional interaction in greater depth. First level switches are the foundation of all level switches and each level also provides important retro feedback on earlier levels.

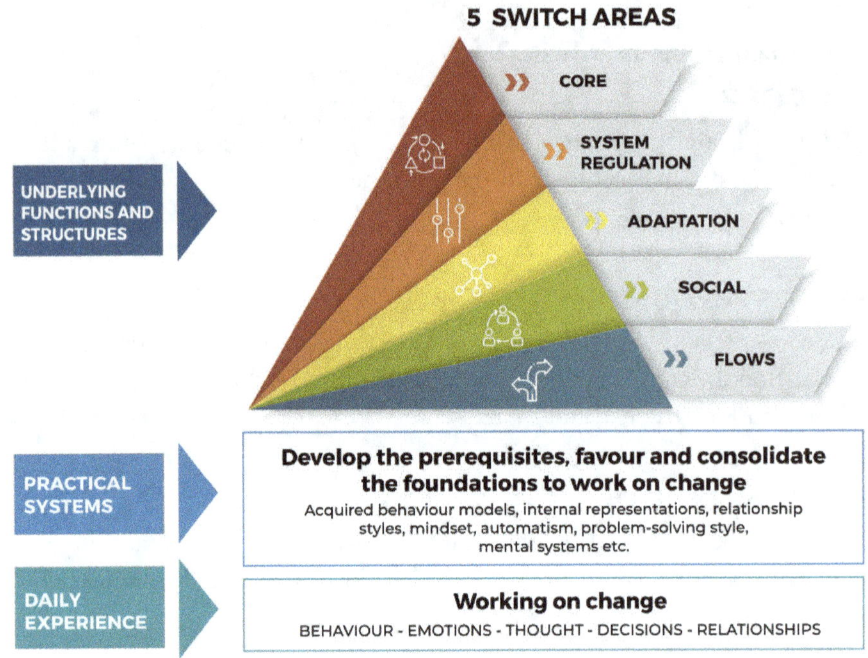

Fig. - The image highlights how switches can be acted on in various ways via the practical systems provided by different therapy and change disciplines (psychotherapy, counselling, coaching, training, education etc.). In this book we delve into the detail of these processes so that professionals can master the intervention modes or can perform a series of parallel interventions aimed directly at these different levels establishing the ideal prerequisites at the basis of therapy and transformation.

5 SWITCH AREAS	INTERVENTION AREAS	INTERACTIONS AREAS
CORE	· Energy metabolism · Neural plasticity · Integration · Epigenetics · Circadian rhythms	· Structural basis of change · Body-mind interaction · Flexibility of emotional and cognitive responses · Biological foundations of emotions, mood and motivation · Habits, lifestyle and basic regulation
SYSTEM REGULATION	· Arousal and brain areas · Inflammation · Allostatic load · Nutrition · Microbiome	· Inflammation, trauma, stress · Multilevel psychosomatic connections · Biological 'cost' of stress · Emotions, mood and immune system · Self-regulation and self-control
ADAPTATION	· Brain networks and hubs · Safety and development · Forecasting and control · Interoception and Predictions	· Stress response: all levels and systems · Adaptation systems and emotions · Danger, resources, forecasts, anticipation, clues · Contextual evidence, priming · Goals and Ideals
SOCIAL	· Evolutionary relationships · Social and primary interpersonal systems · Ancestral Needs	· Attachment and connected systems · Synchronised and unsynchronised social emotions · Social engagement abilities · The constructive side of aggression · Trust and its connection to relationships
FLOWS	· Behavioural, postural, motor, creative, communicative flows etc. · Natural effectiveness	· Objective self-evaluation and development · Awareness and mastery · Impact of posture and motion on emotions, stress and trauma · Creative and linguistic freedom · Subjective and interpretational power

SWITCH GROUP N. 1 CORE – GREASING THE COGS

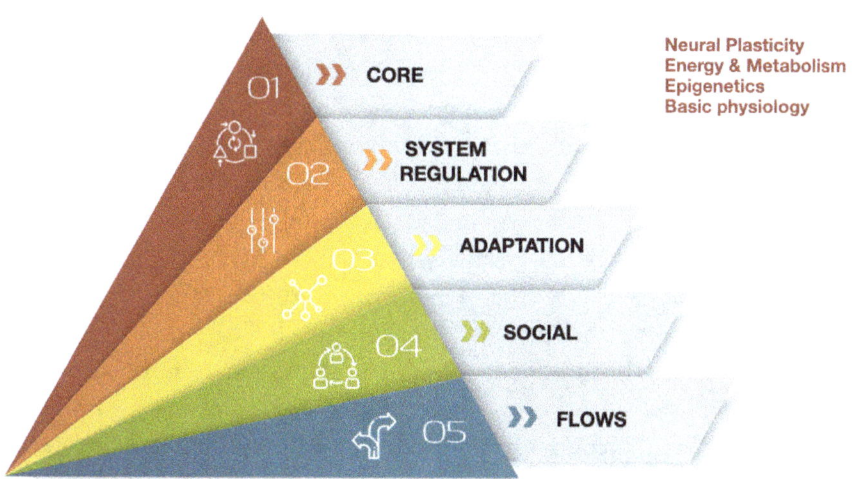

PLASTICITY, ENERGY AND MIND METABOLISM, EPIGENETICS, CIRCADIAN RHYTHMS

One of the worst frustrations when I was little came from the 'bicycle mechanic' (as they called Mr. Bruno, who sold and repaired bicycles in the village where I grew up). At the time I dreamed of being an engineer, designing beautiful and very fast motorcycles. I lived in a very small town and everyone knew it. One day I went to Bruno, the bicycle mechanic, with a broken bicycle chain. He looked at me, then after a long moment of silence, he said to me in a very important tone: "My *dear engineer, remember that even if you design a rocket, you will still have to remember to grease the chains and cogs*". I was dumbfounded, within moments a key concept of not only how bikes work, but how everything works became evident: the basic structures must be kept in top condition. In fact, it is no coincidence that the term 'maintenance' is used for cars and household appliances, but should also be used for human beings.

In this chapter we focus our attention – metaphorically – on the grease and on the chains and cogs of human beings. The health and proper functioning of every cell in the human body are fundamental both for bodily structures and movement, and for every mental and emotional process. We will enter the cell to understand what favours the possibility of having physical and mental energies, understanding that these are mechanisms which can be promoted and literally 'nourished' by taking care of nutrition, physical activity and through a series of daily habits. We will also see that those changing behaviours, emotional and thought patterns, as well as the underlying mechanisms of physical and mental health, are based on neural plasticity and epigenetic markings, which are absolutely dependent on the experiences we live, on the type of oxygenation, on the rhythms and intensity of physical activity. In other words, we will see that change is based on physical foundations and – once the right conditions are created – any process of care, change, learning or development can be more effective, and it will not encounter resistance and will have more relevant and lasting results.

Anyone picking the book up and starting here, without reading the other chapters, might be tempted to see this as a biological or reductionist approach. On the contrary, it is a global and multi-disciplinary approach, which allows you to include many elements in your professional work and to maximize its effectiveness, creating the most favourable conditions. Just take a look at the introductions of all the next chapters to get an idea of how many different aspects will be included.

The basic physical themes that we will see in this first chapter and in the next are usually not part of health and change operator professional training. Often they are only seen as macro-concepts (for example "neural plasticity is useful for learning" or "what we eat influences both physical and emotional pain") but the processes and how, even within one's own professional sphere, it is possible to stimulate these processes or recreate a physiological state, are not well understood.

A final note for those facing these issues for the first time: this first chapter, and in part the second, might appear less interesting to those who are not used to taking these aspects into consideration. This is mostly down to prejudice. In this chapter we talk about fundamental processes for them that can help them understand even better what they usually deal with. Thanks to this knowledge and these tools an even broader understanding of the topics that are already known is achievable with the inclusion of new perspectives to expand the range of action.

ASSESSMENT: WHAT TO OBSERVE AND WHAT TO WORK ON

Before entering into the description of the typical mechanisms of this first area and of how it is possible to intervene on them within one's own profession (or in synergy with other professionals), it is interesting to look at things from the perspective that everything we are going to talk about can be observed in every person we meet. A key aspect consists in starting to look at some data with new interpretations that we previously read only in one way, or that we did not fully take into consideration because, traditionally, we were not taught that observing those data was part of our profession. For example, in a person who seeks counselling for a bereavement, low energy and motivation are classically read as a consequence of the emotional distress they are experiencing. By contrast for a traditionally trained doctor or physiotherapist, when the patient recounts a bad fall, it is normal to stop searching for the causes of shoulder pain. And yet, both case 1 and case 2 can find causes, contributing causes, factors of non-recovery or resistance to therapy in this first switch area.

For example, let's consider the case in which a person, following bereavement, shows a lack of energy. It often happens that this lack of energy is only noticed by family members in the context of the organizational consequences resulting from the loss of a spouse but, in reality, by asking a few more questions, it turns out that their energy had been low for years. They hadn't been noticed because they met with their relative less often and for shorter periods of time or because the ex-spouse himself compensated for this lack of energy, but now he's gone. Mourning certainly plays an important role too – its natural process leads to a reduction of energy, especially outwardly – but previous physical conditions make the situation biologically and mentally unbearable at the same time. The biological cause can be metabolic, linked to the type of diet or to the malfunction of the mitochondria (both in terms of energy production and use of oxygen). Understanding these mechanisms and acting on them, first of all – but not only – offers a direct and immediate sense of well-being and relief. To do this, a few explanations and some clear advice are often enough. If it were then necessary, if our skills or role do not allow us to go further, we can send the patient for a targeted consultation with a nutritionist, doctor, personal trainer or other professional, based on the specific needs that we have identified in this area of the switches. However, it is essential that we take the first steps with the patient. In fact, at that moment we are the professional of reference and we can give information and indications that are already very useful and effective. Furthermore, this creates an allegiance, the person feels understood and accepted in their entirety. In fact, it is precisely the attention to many small details that makes the difference. Even if the lifestyle changes, the psycho-physical integrative exercises or other initiatives proposed are not many and not perfect, they still work better than a single-sector intervention.

Let's start to consider, at least at an initial glance, what our process with the person could be. Let us look at patients and the problems they bring us with different eyes. Among other things, it is also about starting to consider something that might seem 'normal' for that person as potentially relevant clues. For example, let us consider the case of Anthony, a 60-year-old professional who is feeling rather low, who we will get to know as the book progresses along with other cases. It is normal to think that a person of that age and with some emotional baggage might not be full of energy. Thinking about it, however, this idea is based on a negative stereotype and/or on the fact that it is normal in modern society to have an unhealthy diet, a sedentary lifestyle and few positive prospects at that age, but this is not necessarily the case. Certainly, a 60-year-old person will have less explosive energies than a 20 or 30-year-old, but it doesn't mean that they have to be very low. Also, mental energies, clarity and motivation can be very strong and well-structured and can sometimes be more solid and consistent than those of some younger people.

Similarly, we also need to look critically at stereotypes with respect to other age groups. In this switch area we talk about the possibility for change, which we take for granted in a young person, yet the factors that allow neural plasticity and to write new epigenetic markings are often altered even in young people. For example, sleep-wake rhythms are typically out of physiology in that stage of life. In the same way, the times in which we eat are unregulated and sports activities are often at extremes (either absent or too intense), leading to dysfunctions on various physical and mental levels.

These are just a few simple examples for initial reflection. These are ideas, relevant factors but, as we will see throughout the book, there may be different interpretations for each of them. Similarly, there can often be multiple factors that combine to form a particular condition. We will learn about them and to identify them as we proceed.

With this in mind, some typical things and clues to look out for in this area are:

- Low energy (not accumulated or not metabolized)
- States of 'exhaustion' (in the sense of having abused one's energies for too long)
- States of depression (metabolic, that influences the mental one)
- Lack of or little constancy in motivation
- Little or fluctuating vitality
- Altered sleep-wake rhythms
- Physical stiffness, contracted muscle tissues
- Dry skin and hair, wrinkles and excessively damaged skin compared to age and type of life led
- Difficulty changing
- Memory difficulties
- Difficulty with balance and movement
- Physical and mental rigidity
- Slow thought processes (thinking, understanding) or only apparently fast (always repeating the same ideas, without change and without adding value)
- Dysfunctional immune system (tendency to get sick easily)
- Degenerative psychosomatic symptoms (cells no longer function properly)

IMPORTANCE OF THE 'MICRO' LEVEL

To fully understand the processes in this switch area, we have to look at the microscopic level. In fact, in recent years various scientific disciplines, such as molecular microbiology, epigenetics and many areas of neuroscience, have developed new methodologies and ever more powerful tools to fully understand the mechanisms they deal with, offering new perspectives and applications to the study of human behaviour and emotional life. It has thus been possible, for example, to understand how:

- cells use energy to support mental and emotional activities, to create the structural basis of neural plasticity present in all forms of learning and change;
- epigenetic processes, which underlie every form of evolutionary process and development are written and modified;
- how the food we eat and our levels of physical activity play a fundamental role in determining the energy levels available to us for self-regulation processes, motivation and emotional responses;
- how the development of new cells or, conversely, their death, is a physiological mechanism linked to the prospects for development that we have on a mental level, as well as to the daily positive challenges we subject ourselves to (from learning a musical instrument to signalling of hot-cold stimulation obtained with a sauna);
- how the brain and the immune system (and not only) are closely connected in both directions (for example through the T cells that give the signal to the brain of *when it's time to feel sick* or not, to give a clear example).

Understanding these processes and *translating them into practice* allows us to identify and develop a series of concrete directions that are applicable in the daily work of change and health professionals.

Let's take Anthony who we introduced a few pages earlier as our first example. He is a 60-year-old doctor, in the middle of a crisis because work is no longer what it used to be due to the number of low-cost clinics opening in the area and due to a marriage that hasn't been satisfying for years. He wants to carry out projects, but he does not have the energy, so he thinks about them all the time, but in the end he never acts. He forgets to do things, even nice things (like playing golf, having lunch with his son, etc.).

He is diagnosed by a doctor friend of his as depressed. In reality, talking to him and observing him carefully, we understand that – rather than depressed – he is above all a man without energy. In fact, his head is active, his vision of the world and of what is happening is realistic, his thoughts are not always engaged in dwelling on what is negative. Rather we see a man with soft body tissues, even if there are glimpses of a body that until a few years ago must have been muscular and toned. A body that doesn't move is a body that doesn't need to renew tissue and produce energy. Renewal is a mechanism activated by evolutionary urges, while stasis has a sense of recovery and regeneration. In fact, to heal a broken leg, our adaptation system takes away energy and motivation to redirect them towards tissue repair and, at the same time, prevent too much enthusiasm causing us damage. In Anthony's case, as unfortunately often happens, the body is stiff or under-used due to simple habits or social conditions, as a result of trauma (both physical and mental) or of emotional suffering which, however has not been addressed and overcome. Prolonged stasis inhibits developmental and motivational processes, creating a vicious circle in which the problem gets progressively worse.

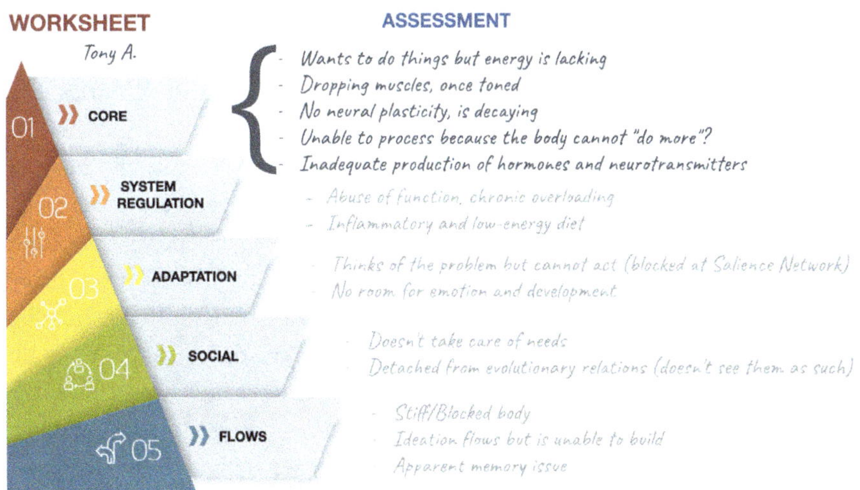

Fig. – Anthony's initial assessment sheet

When Anthony talks to us about his memory problems, we realise that he doesn't really pay attention to what he does because he doesn't have the strength and he certainly doesn't experience intense emotions. This means it's normal that he can't memorize. This is very different from having memory problems because "you are old" or because there is a pathology. Until now Anthony did not know this and, consequently, he felt old and ill. Neural plasticity, but also the correct production of neurotransmitters and specifically stress neurotransmitters (adrenaline, noradrenaline and cortisol), which also have a central role in writing memories from different perspectives – as we will see in the area of switches 2 and 3 – are involved in memorization processes (as we will shortly see in this switch area).

One last element to take into consideration for now is that, as he himself tells us, he eats "as one should eat at his age". After asking him for concrete examples of what he meant, I told him that he "eats like he eats in hospital... and that's not good!". As has been known for years and scientific research has demonstrated, eating mashed potatoes and cooked ham (just to cite the stereotype of this type of diet) not only brings no nutritional advantage, but today is considered a *pro-inflammatory* and, therefore, *pro-disease* diet, as we will see clearly in area 2 switches. It is a diet that is in itself demoralizing and which leads to making our identity coincide with that of the patient.

Anthony certainly needs help to put his thoughts and emotions in order, but it will be essential to help him regain energy with food changes and with the right physical activity to reactivate his body and his nervous system at the same time. We will look at different physical activities and exercises that we have created specifically to fight inflammation (which always connects with mood disorders), but also to favour mitochondria in the cells (which means more real and subjectively perceived energy), greater neural plasticity (also beneficial for many other aspects of mental and physical health), a more flexible and efficient ability to change epigenetic markings (i.e. to change at the deepest level where the parameters with which we function – including resting heart rate – are recorded with respect to risk, ability to trust, and so on). Since we are still at the beginning of this analysis, remember that all these levels can be found in many subjects, but not in all. On the other hand, all the factors of the other switches must also be taken into consideration and, in fact, we will take up Anthony's case in other areas over the next chapters as well.

Together we will develop the ability to look at all these aspects in a systemic way, later discovering how synergistic and mutually supportive these mechanisms are in clinical practice. We will also see that some types of interventions and strategies can impact multiple factors at the same time. In short, it is not always necessary to do a lot, but it is essential to frame everything in the best possible way and to act in a targeted manner and in the correct sequence.

3 LEVELS OF NEURAL PLASTICITY FOR CHANGE, LEARNING AND FLEXIBILITY

Every change and learning process corresponds to a neural network and epigenetic marking change from a neurobiological point of view.

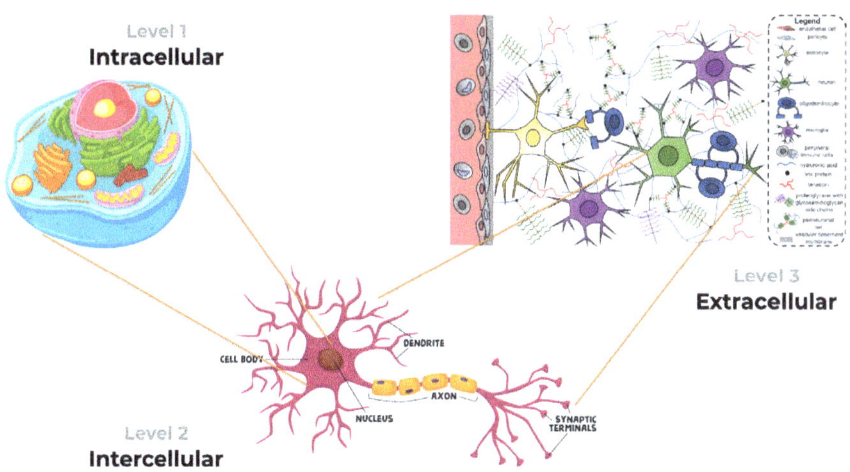

Fig. - The three levels of neural plasticity on which it is possible to act in a targeted way to favour processes of care, change and development.

As for the change in neural networks, the paths previously traced by neurons are modified or even abandoned, creating new, more effective ones that support the most recent behaviour or learning. These modifications take shape for any update or novelty, when we learn a new language, a sport, during psychotherapy or rehabilitation. There are numerous sources that demonstrate the different neural pathways, for example, of a person in front of their phobia (it could be a spider, as well as a place where a traumatic event has occurred) and of the same person after they followed a successful therapy. The two paths are significantly different, as are the emotional response and the self-regulation capacity that the person is now able to bring into play.

The other level at which the change is 'written' is the epigenetic one, i.e. the modification of the markers that make it possible to change the way in which the gene is expressed. This level is also a type of plasticity, so we will take it up and develop it shortly. We often talk about "strengthening and supporting neural plasticity" or "creating new connections" or, again, "developing integration (hemispheric and beyond)". In the same way, there is increasing focus on the central role of epigenetics and the importance of modulating it in a way that is favourable to physiology and well-being.

Our task, once again, is to ask ourselves what this means in practical terms and how it can be achieved. As we will see, it is possible to intervene at these levels through daily life changes and through targeted exercises. We will see, for example: how certain types of physical exercise (alone or in synergy with specific mindsets and emotional states) can literally transform the brain; that they increase the size of the hippocampus, favouring memorization processes (and counteracting the effect of stress which 'shrinks' it); the connections between the prefrontal cortex and the motivational areas increase, allowing us to make more advantageous and less impulsive choices. They also make the self-regulating areas, such as the insula, thalamus, amygdala, etc., less inflamed (i.e. less 'swollen' and 'hyper-sensitive' just like a finger that hurts).

To start off on this path with our best foot forward it is important, first of all, to understand that there are different levels of plasticity, all equally important and very useful for accessing more possibilities for change and greater plasticity in the adaptation processes:

1. Intracellular (more mitochondria, epigenetics and more)
2. Intercellular (between neurons, on multiple levels)
3. Extracellular (Glia + MEC)

THE INTRACELLULAR LEVEL: A POWERHOUSE AT OUR DISPOSAL

The *intracellular level* concerns the number of mitochondria in each cell. Mitochondria represent the powerhouse of the cell and have a key role in managing the development of new neural networks and in eliminating connections that are no longer in use. The bioenergetic metabolism of the mitochondria also influences epigenetic marking processes which, in turn, enable lasting changes in the regulation of a number of *emotional*, *mental* and *psycho-somatic* physiological processes[1].

There is no fixed number of mitochondria but the more there are, the better for the cell and its processes[2]. New mitochondria can be developed while malfunctioning ones can be disposed of via a process called mitophagy. It is an intracellular level of plasticity, therefore, that does not develop new neurons or new connections, but that makes new ones more effective and more powerful ones available. The richer a neuron is in mitochondria, the more signalling duties it will have and the more energy for cognitive-emotional duties it will make available.

This is one of the reasons Anthony couldn't concentrate and focus attention on important things, as we mentioned earlier.

Mitochondria are especially important to neurons as they enable and favour the transmission of signals in emotional, cognitive and social processes. They are also at the heart of processes that support neural plasticity, this provides us with networks that are able to develop all the behavioural capabilities and skills that are part of adult life.

Following the Switches of Change scheme, what happens inside the cell influences what happens outside. This is true in other levels of this first area of Switch, as we will see shortly, and continues to be effective in increasing degrees of complexity in the following Switch areas too.

Metaphorically we could say that intracellular plasticity is not like changing the car we drive or the route we take, but to boosting its engine. This is an absolutely relevant improvement that can radically change our quality of life. In light of increasingly widespread research, the field research activity we carry out with the Association of Integrative Sciences and my personal clinical experience, I can confidently state that this is a fundamental plan on which to definitely intervene. If you are not used to considering this type of level, it may initially seem distant from your usual professional practice, yet there are simple ways and small steps to help your patients or clients act on these levels. We will look at them as we proceed in the analysis of the various factors involved.

EPIGENETICS: THE ROOTS OF CHANGE

Man is born with a well-defined and non-modifiable genetic heritage. Yet there is a very significant margin of action with respect to how these genes are expressed, i.e. what type of information they give to the body and what type of protein or enzyme they produce. These processes are known as epigenetics (from the Greek epi = 'above' or 'after'), so they take place above/after the genetics and shape it.

Without getting too technical, we can think of the genetic code as a library and genes as books. So-called epigenetic markers are like the meta-tags that allow us to quickly find which texts are most important to us. When a situation lasts for a long time, for example a state of stress, a type of movement or posture that we repeat several times at work, the tag is moved to another book (from a biochemical point of view it is basically a methylation and acetylation processes, but not only), in order to express that part of the code that is considered most useful. The problem arises when the 'way deemed most useful' is not functional, as happens in conditions of chronic stress, when you live in conditions of constant uncertainty, when your body is constantly under strain and so on. Fortunately, marking can also move in the opposite direction, which is advantageous for us and modifiable over time.

In other words, epigenetics corresponds to the phenotypic expression of our genes. It can be inherited but is also strongly conditioned by the external or internal environment of the body and by the experiences we live. Sufficiently prolonged and constant stimuli over time can modify epigenetics. This knowledge has revolutionized previous beliefs regarding learning, evolution and transmission of certain features or skills from generation to generation, bringing back into the fore (with the necessary modifications and updates) Lamark's intuitions that had been set aside in favour of Darwinian theories.

It has in fact been proven that relationship styles (attachment or avoidance), as well as greed, are transmissible epigenetically for 3 generations. For example, various broad research studies have found a correlation between grandparents that went hungry during the war and their grandchildren – who had not met them – who had inherited a specific epigenetic marking that activates them more than usual in relation to a lack of food.

HOW TO INTERVENE ON THESE PROCESSES IN A PRACTICAL WAY

In practice, this means that to help the person change at the deepest level, within the scope of their objectives, every professional must find a way to intervene at the epigenetic level.

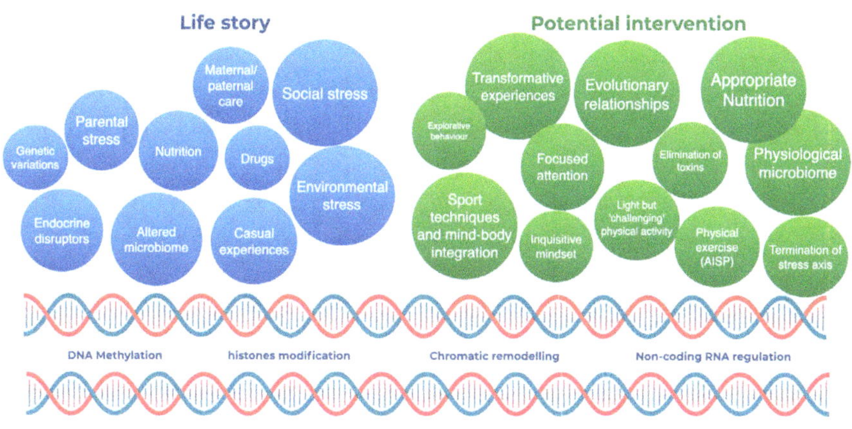

Luckily you don't have to be a geneticist to do this, there are simple ways to stimulate neural plasticity and epigenetic change that are easily applicable. Among them are nutritional style, physical exercise with the rapid alternation of activation-recovery, mental activities, but also games or sports that are "challenging" in a sustainable way.

Diet strongly influences gene expression and, based on what we eat, we can create favourable or disadvantageous conditions on all the switch levels we are analysing. We often talk about the importance of methyl donors, such as folate or vitamin B12, but other micronutrients or bioactive food components are also implicated in epigenetic mechanisms (e.g. through carbon 1 metabolism or by directly influencing enzymes involved in the regulation of epigenetic phenomena). Even ketones, produced during fasting or in some nutritional styles, and the metabolites produced by the intestinal microbiota can contribute to epigenetic modulation (we will further explore these aspects in switch 2, because they are complementary themes with all inflammatory aspects at both the cerebral and immune system levels).

In this area, it is interesting to look at the case of Angelica, a very anxious 26-year-old girl who has recently started having panic attacks. Angelica also has frequent dermatitis and candida, which have not improved with traditional medical treatments. She comes to me because her doctor, describes her as 'a psychosomatic case'.

In addition to other interventions that we will see in other switch areas, Angelica gradually introduced *fasting* in order to give respite to her cells that are constantly bombarded with carbohydrates and, therefore, with insulin peaks (the brain loves insulin levels that are low and constant, while it reacts with anxiety symptoms in case of frequent insulin peaks).

It is good to know that fasting is culturally (at least in Western countries) seen as something dangerous and tiring. In reality, with the right metabolic and mental preparation (which are synergistic) it is easy to introduce intermittent fasting, for example by initially skipping breakfast on some days, then breakfast and lunch and so on. If there are no particular degenerative pathologies, most people can see huge benefits just by skipping some breakfast sometimes. The effect is interesting on several levels: for example, it facilitates the recovery of the intestinal microbiota, at the same time favouring epigenetic change and drastically reducing inflammation (switch 2). Furthermore, this practice allowed Angelica to concretely interrupt her way of filling the void in the face of uncertainty (because well-executed fasting immediately leads you to the experience of not feeling hungry, because you change your metabolism first and then you become aware of the emotional dysfunction and behavioural compulsion, now perceived as meaningless, as we will see in switch area No. 3, in particular around the theme of emptiness and uncertainty). Finally, with an aware and programmatic approach to fasting, Angelica was able to tolerate detachment and frustration, distancing herself from the emotional elements of a vital need (switch 4).

Physical activity also plays a key role in helping move the epigenetic "bookmark". Two interesting trends which we have tested several times and are particularly effective, emerge from the research.

The first trend relates to *light physical activity*, such as slow walking or running, that is only just above the threshold of a minimum effort. In other words, if the heart rate doesn't increase compared to a relaxing walk, if the body temperature doesn't rise even one degree, then we won't get any results. If, on the other hand, these modifications take place and in the end we feel a little tired, but above all activated in our muscles, then, day after day, the possibility of changing epigenetic signature increases more easily. This activity, if repeated at least 3-4 times a week, brings a series of direct benefits, including: neural plasticity, oxygenation (as we will see later in this same chapter), disinflammation (which, as we will see in the next chapter of the switch 2, is a crucial factor for any positive change in mental and physical health), regulation of sensory processes and self-regulation and emotion networks (switch 4), a more elastic body and – conversely – a lower likelihood of developing physical stiffening and contractures with related mental states (switch 5) and more. The exciting aspect is that the benefit also cascades indirectly on other types of epigenetic signatures, so it is also advantageous when compared to the markers that express genes to adapt to stressful situations or to modulate pain.

The other physical activity trend that favours epigenetic signatures but also the correct modulation of stress hormones, relates to activities that centre around the rapid alternation of physical strain with moments of rest. It is interesting to know that these modes are studied in neuroscience laboratories to understand how to improve adaptation or stress responses and, on the other hand, they are also studied to optimize sports training. The results are literally very relevant. People find it easy to do this type of exercise and, apart from the most serious cases that require longer efforts, everyone experiences states of well-being and motivational impulses right from the first session. We have introduced these exercises in this part of the book for the specific effect of favouring new epigenetic markings and, therefore, the deep foundations of any process of care and change. Exercises of this type, however, also have other advantages: better oxygenation (with repercussions on health and mental lucidity); they favour the correct process of transformation from cortisone to cortisol, with significant impacts on the immune system, as well as that of stress; they promote the dopaminergic system, supporting motivational processes; they change the quality of the myofascial system, reducing aches and pains, as well as the related interferences with body image, self-esteem and assessment of dangers.

They are simple exercises and within everyone's reach. To understand what they are, you can browse the internet looking for 'HIIT workouts' or 'Tabata workouts'. The first acronym stands for High Intensity Interval Training, while Tabata is the surname of a professional who has developed workouts that are similar to HIIT ones, but with some differences. There are many free videos for patients to follow. Below we see one of our applicative proposals – the HISP Exercises – which uses these mechanisms.

HISP EXERCISES: HIGH INTENSITY FOR SHORT PERIODS

In line with the principles and training methods that are useful for promoting epigenetic mechanisms, as well as obtaining good results on physical and mental well-being, let's look at a type of training that I have applied myself in the past with great success and that I still propose to many people with good results.

These are exercises that can be done freely at home and the total time required is so little (12 to 20 minutes on average) that you can't find excuses to avoid them.

Basically, it's about doing a series of exercises, alternating every single activity with a break of the same duration.

The time is short, usually between 30 to 60 seconds (starting small and gradually increasing over time).

The typical sequence is to carry out one exercise (for example, push-ups) for 30 seconds, pause for the same amount of time, do another exercise for the same amount of time (this time, for example, sit-ups), pause again, and carry out another three such repetitions by switching exercises. The remaining three exercises can be squats for the legs and glutes, pull-ups for the lats, bench pull-ups for back muscles. This way you work on all the muscle chains with overall benefits and possible synergies with the postural and motor flows of area 5.

At the end of these 5 blocks of exercises, each followed by its break, there is usually a slightly longer break, of about 2 minutes. At this point, the whole block of exercises is repeated.

If you haven't engaged in any sports for a long time, it's advisable to do just a couple of blocks of exercises in the first few days. After a while, you go up to 3 and then 4 blocks. Once you have reached this level, you can begin to increase the time, for example reaching 40 seconds for each exercise, or up to one minute.

For further developments it is advisable to undertake a specific training path and/or contact qualified personal trainer. However, for our purposes of recovering physiology and well-being to reactivate the mechanisms seen in this first switch area, and beyond, this process, carried out for 3-4 months and practised approximately every 3 days, may be sufficient.

Let's see how this kind of knowledge can be applied to the two patients we have met so far. For Anthony, who is very tired and presents little energy, we began by recommending light-intensity activity, without even anticipating that high intensity would then arrive. For him it would have been a discouraging prospect. The concept of always staying on the edge of the challenge, of adding even just one minute each time, of accelerating even a little when he felt that it was becoming a simple walk, was immediately clear to him. With these tricks he found himself significantly more energetic within 3 weeks. We waited another week and then introduced activity at intense and alternating rhythms, starting with short times and few repetitions twice a week, while he kept the light-intensity activity.

Angelica, on the other hand, as she was already very active, immediately started with the activity at an intermediate regimen. This, in addition to being more engaging for her, allowed her to physically release all the mental and emotional tensions that she usually poured into her body.

Epigenetics influences physical and mental health and – vice versa – body and mind care can change gene expression positively. A very relevant example comes from studies on epigenetic markings associated with diseases that are usually considered to only be hereditary or metabolic, as in the case of type 2 diabetes (DT2). The epigenetic markings of these pathologies can be inherited from parents or acquired through foetal and early events, as well as through environments or lifestyles, which can increase the risk of manifesting the pathology in adulthood[3]. However, epigenetic changes are reversible and can be altered through appropriate intervention, thus mitigating risk factors[4]. In fact, the synergistic and mind-body integration interventions induce changes at the epigenetic level of psychological processes (such as the alleviation of depression, anxiety and stress), but also physiological changes (such as parasympathetic activation, reduced secretion of cortisol, the reduction of inflammation and the slowing down of the ageing processes) which are all risk factors for various pathologies and dysfunctions.

An epigenetic change can alter both the primary adaptive response and the memory of events, as well as the sense of mastery and resources we have available to face the challenge of the moment[5]. The term 'challenge' is useful to highlight the fact that the same event can have a negative or positive value, of effort but also of evolution. In fact, epigenetics changes through experiences with an evolutionary purpose. This means that the way in which a stressful event but also an interpersonal conflict is handled can make the difference in developing physiological evolutionary methods which can affect physical and mental balance. This perspective places great emphasis on the importance of planning and carrying out new transformative experiences to implement a significant and lasting change with respect to emotional responses.

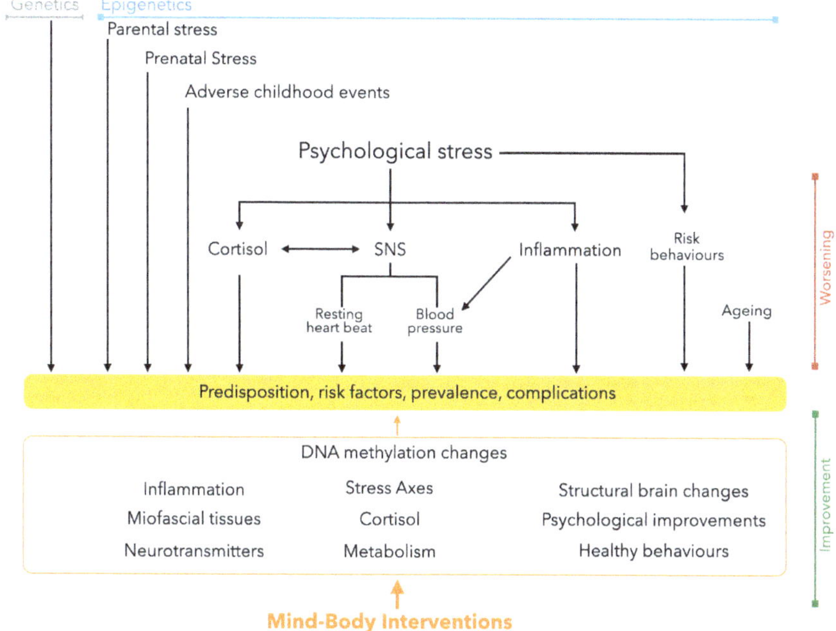

Fig. - Representation of some of the ways through which mind-body interventions are effective in contrasting various pathologies and dysfunctions (even those usually considered exclusively hereditary or metabolic) at epigenetic level.

INTER-CELLULAR LEVEL: LEARNING AND FLEXIBILITY

The level of *intercellular neural plasticity* is the best known and most widespread. In reality, even this level is more complex than usually thought. In fact, it concerns the creation of new synapses and – cascading – of new neural networks, but not only. In fact, changes also occur in dendritic density, number of vesicles, synaptic strength, *gap-junctions*, and more.

In this case too, we are dealing with mechanisms that have historically been tackled in isolation, perceived as purely cerebral aspects. Instead it is essential to have a broad and global vision of the whole living being and its organism in line with the integrated and integrative approach that we hold. For example, it is now known that serotonin receptors play a central role in promoting neural plasticity[6]. Specifically, if these receptors are working well, they become promoters of neural plasticity, while any dysfunction of theirs is connected with psychological and psychiatric problems. This type of information allows us to see the important connections, for example between nutrition and the state of the intestine (serotonin is largely produced in the intestine), neural plasticity and mental health. The perspective widens even more if we consider that these receptors are also involved in the processes of pain perception, regulation of circadian rhythms, thermoregulation, emotional regulation and learning (even independently of neural plasticity).

At a global level, which remains the most relevant for us, these are the structures at the base of the brain networks (which we will see in the switches of groups 2 and 3), and which respond significantly to sensory stimuli, motor outputs and environmental stimuli. Translated into professional practice, this means that plasticity can be fostered through dietary cues, *stimuli and multisensory activity*, introducing and integrating therapy and learning processes with *highly experiential activity* and just the right amount of *adaptation challenge*[7].

Complex activities involving coordination, balance and joint action relating to different domains in synergy (visual, motor, strength and precision, etc.) stimulate neurogenesis. This occurs, for example, in the hippocampus – which is essential for memory, reasoning and stress management – and in the striatum, essential for motivation[8], but also in many other brain regions connected to different networks (see the third group of switches).

Ecker[9], like many other illustrious colleagues, demonstrated that the effectiveness of psychotherapy is based precisely on the ability to carry out interventions aimed at making the most of neuroplasticity on scientific grounds. This can be achieved with strategies and techniques that integrate the mind and body, which address emotional and sensory experiences, by working on multiple experiential, ideational, motor and postural narratives (see Flows, in the fifth group of switches) or with specific integrative techniques (NB: most of the techniques and strategies that we will present throughout the book will have an integrative approach; in particular those relating to Reconsolidation – please refer to the box below – fully exploit the processes of neural plasticity that can be actively stimulated through specific sequences of actions).

FAVOURING LEARNING

To a degree, every feature of our life is something we have learnt. For example, the body learns to maintain an activated stress response at a certain level (usually higher than necessary) after a traumatic event, chronic stress or other salient events.

People "learn" that their personal value is defined in a specific way that is obvious to them; in fact they memorise it mainly without being aware of it, integrating the feedback they receive from the outside, contextual clues, their own way of processing events and various other sources.

Similar processes can be noted at metabolic, postural and physical level but also in relation to self-image and role, in relation to the most effective behaviour selection for different situations, in relation to food and to all other features of daily life.

All this information is recorded in different types of memories; these can be semantic, procedural, emotional, physical maps and so on. Memories that are created and recovered this way are below our level of awareness and direct control. In any case, these are memories that have very interesting similarities in the way they are 'recorded'.

The ways in which different types of memories (events, activation states, subjective feelings, physical maps, etc.) are recorded at neural level are today commonly known as *consolidation* and *reconsolidation* processes.

From a structural perspective, what changes when we create this new memory can be represented as a stable change at synaptic level. In reality, this concept only relates to simple and familiar representations of this process, which is actually a much more ample and complex mechanism.

For synaptic level change to take place it is necessary to achieve intercellular change at internal cascade signalling level and, more relevant still for us, for a modulation of genetic expression to take place.

The two critical moments of learning and change

There are two critical moments that create the ideal conditions to change memories: the first is immediately after the primary learning has taken place (the so-called *consolidation* phase), the other is just after the reactivation of the previous learning (so-called *reconsolidation* phase), which happens when the memory is evoked and the entire connected activation process is also reactivated.

The second process (reconsolidation) represents a new way of thinking: memories are not fixed, but they can be altered each time they are activated.

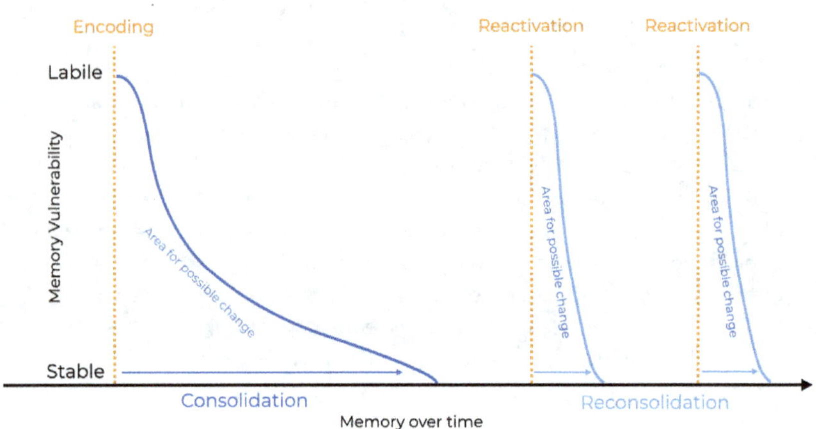

Most of the issues consist in intervening on old dysfunctional learnings (whether relating to a phobia, limiting beliefs, a distorted self-image, excessive emotional reactions in relation to the stimulus and many other cases). By calling up the old response process and stimulating correct mechanisms we create optimal conditions to create a new functional learning.

It is important to remember that we can start from any type of memory or learning: actual memories, procedures, concepts, representations, theoretical models, movements, stress responses, body maps or something else. Understanding the processes at the heart of consolidation and reconsolidation can help optimise therapeutic processes for change in psychology and in education, as well as in care and rehabilitation settings. Let's look at some examples below.

Example 1 - Using emotion and physical activation

Every emotion, stress response or significant physical activation can alter hormone levels in the body. What is interesting is that these are the same hormones that take centre stage in memory processes.

Adrenalin, noradrenaline and cortisol – known as stress hormones – significantly influence consolidation and reconsolidation processes. By contrast, antagonists and their receptors can inhibit their effect (in fact some drugs list memory loss as a side effect).

Research has shown that the use of glucocorticoids can work in synergy with psychotherapy. It is for example possible to increase the effectiveness of traditional exposition techniques for defence mechanisms such as phobias or PTSD, or "appetitive" processes such as pathological wishes, addiction and cravings.

What is interesting here is that similar results can be achieved without drugs but via the application of targeted stress (for example physical activity, emotionally evocative images, light physical shocks such as a pinch, or the application of intense heat or cold).

These stimuli can be provided before or after a therapy session depending on the objectives. Specifically, a pre-session stress helps weaken a dysfunctional memory, while a post-session stress favours the reinforcement of new learning.

Let's take a practical example. We need to apply an imagination technique that weakens the memory such as viewing the painful event like a film, progressively distancing the video camera and letting colours grow less vivid and so on. In this instance the objective is to weaken the memory, so providing a slight stress before the technique such as 2 minutes of lunges or push-ups is a useful strategy.

Example 2 - It's a recent memory...how to intervene?
Understanding the interactions between hormones and memories helps us reconsider emergency intervention strategies: whether a catastrophic event or an accident has taken place, or when we are trying to help a patient that recently went through trauma or an emotional shock (such as a death or "simply" a betrayal of trust, the unexpected end of a relationship), it is now possible to re-evaluate ideal strategies.

It has for example been proven that debriefings straight after an event- which used to be part of the guidelines for traumatic events and emergencies- can actually be counterproductive and end up reinforcing the negative memory. It is therefore necessary to precede the activities with strategies that enable hormone levels to return to physiological state before the debrief even just for a few minutes.

A practical example that is easily applied to daily life can also be educational: a child argues with his friend, hurts himself and is furious.

In this instance it is useful to:

* get him to move about so as to avoid any feelings of impediment and immobility that increase the feeling of impotence and delay termination processes;
* get him to breathe correctly so as to return the stress axis towards a physiological state;
* get him to concentrate on basic presence and awareness elements (self-awareness, not of the event), orientation in space and identification of external environmental and social safety clues;

• only after 5-10 minutes will it be useful to tackle what happened and favour a constructive consolidation of the event.

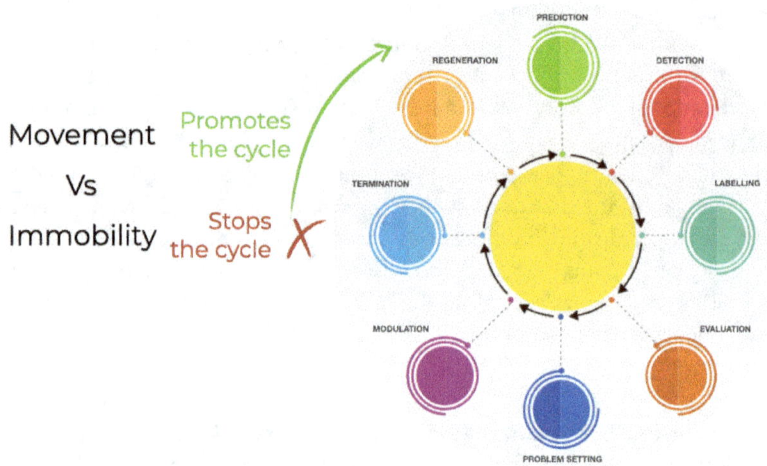

Example 3 - Post-learning rest (and more)

Contrary to certain old beliefs, more rooted in advertising than anything else, it is not possible to learn anything new by listening to it while you sleep. In spite of this, sleep and other similar states can be used in very interesting ways.

Sleep represents a condition of deactivation of adaptation and defensive processes during which various synaptic, immune system, cell recovery and other repair and regeneration processes take place. As far as consolidation is concerned, between slow wave sleep and REM sleep there is a selective refinement of mnestic representations via interaction between the hippocampus and the neocortex.

Three initial practical suggestions that can be applied to any educational or therapeutic environment consist in:

1. Introducing 10 minutes of silent relaxation post-therapeutic session, thus creating the conditions for consolidation of the work carried out. This is valid for both physical activities (physiotherapy and osteopathy), and mental ones (such as the end of a psychotherapy session).

2. In general, it is useful to reduce emotional interference after treatment, so it is not ideal to dive back into a stressful job, or to phone a person that we

might argue with, to read social media or watch the news for about 20/30 minutes later.

3. During a change and recovery process it is critical to return sleep cycles to physiological state. In relation to our specific objectives this enables a large scale synaptic reordering that favours all change processes. In general, improving sleep-wakefulness cycles and quality of sleep enables us to establish energy metabolism, immune systems processes and to adequately regulate hormones and neurotransmitters, creating the ideal core conditions for a better mood, more energy and better concentration.

EXTRA-CELLULAR LEVEL: A POWERFUL ALLY

When we talk about neural plasticity, in reality, we are not only talking about neurons. As now demonstrated by plenty of research, the neuron can perform its tasks effectively only with the support of the glia (astrocytes, oligodendrocytes, microglia, and other structures) and blood vessels, which – themselves – are subject to plasticity[10]. We must, therefore, look at the body in its completeness.

Let us look at this from another interesting angle too: often when we talk about neural, *hemispheric* or *"different brains"* integration (e.g. in MacLean's three brains, see the introduction of the book for a critical review of this and other concepts that have made history, but are no longer scientifically adequate), we are not only talking about connections between neurons, but also between the structures that connect, nourish and support them.

In the past it was believed that glia only had a support function for neurons, now it has been discovered that it has far more important and fundamental roles for our physical and mental health. We must remember that microglia is the immune system dedicated to the brain and that it presents alterations (both a cause and an effect) in emotional and mental health problem. Astrocytes, on the other hand, have various functions, including providing immediately usable nourishment to the neuron, regulating its metabolism, synchronizing the action of axons and neurotransmitters, cleaning up when a neuron dies and so on.

The ECM (Extra-Cellular Matrix) is a macromolecular network composed of proteins and polysaccharides that occupies the space between neurons and glia. Structurally, the ECM serves as a physical barrier to reduce the diffusion of soluble and membrane-associated molecules and cell migration. It functionally regulates a number of key neural stages during brain development and plays a role in physiological and pathological conditions in the adult brain. For us, it is interesting to know that it changes according to the stimuli it receives, for example allowing the cytoskeleton of *neurons* and that of *astrocytes* (glia) to unite in order to exchange organelles and other substances[11].

From a practical point of view the ECM is stimulated by direct contact[12] (such as *massage and manual techniques*) and by indirect movement (such as *stretching, sport-induced movement, physical and psycho-physical techniques*). A *massage* reduces inflammation and enables faster repair of micro-tears that can form in the muscles as a result of exercise, as well as chronic alterations from stress or prolonged negative emotions. This way, sub-threshold painful stimuli are reduced, i.e. which we may not be aware of, but which are in any case capable of altering the state of alertness, emotional reactivity and, in general, the interoceptive processes underlying the self-regulation mechanisms (we will analyse this aspect further in the chapter on third group switches).

In addition to this, *contact with others (and even self-massage*, although at a lesser degree) favours the release of oxytocin, known as the "love hormone". In reality, it would be more correct to call it the *hormone of trust and balance*, since its main functions include facilitating interpersonal bonds and because it has antagonistic action with respect to cortisol (we will return to these aspects in the area of switch 4 which focuses on relationships).

Finally, it is important to know that with the indirect movement techniques of myofascial tissues and viscera (as in stretching, yoga, taiji and our *Psychosomatic Stretching Release, Isometric Emotions techniques*) you develop the ability to calm down more quickly and to centre, thanks to the work on the ECM combined with specific breathing and physiology recovery methods. From a neurobiological point of view, the reduction of pro-inflammatory cytokines and, vice versa, the increase of anti-inflammatory ones can be achieved[13], leading to a condition of well-being which reduces the possibility of developing various diseases ranging from the likelihood of having a heart attack to depression and many others.

Elizabeth is a beautiful 35-year-old girl. She is so beautiful that, looking at her, you would never imagine all the suffering she carries within her. As soon as she starts to speak, however, something immediately emerges, a river of words that struggles to keep up with the torrent of thoughts that come to her. These are all negative and centred on problems, worries and injustices that she experiences. Similarly, when you observe her in motion, you notice a rigidity that does not appear when she is still. She moves in rapid jerks, with stiff joints and almost no flexing. We will then see in switch area 5 how to act on the flows of thought and the importance of fluid movements (that have been lost), while in area 3 we will examine the related bidirectional cause-effect implications with our alert and safety systems. For now, let's focus on the elements that concern this part of the book. Among the various interventions, we immediately proposed that Elizabeth give herself a massage once a week. She was free to choose the type of massage (anti-stress, draining, Ayurvedic, or other) as long as it was effective in lowering the state of activation, restoring plasticity to the tissues and allowing her a moment of passive abandonment to give relief to both the body and to the mind. While she was receiving her massages, I suggested that she pay attention to the physical sensations and areas of contact between these bodily sensations, the emotions she was feeling and any memories and thoughts that might arise. This way we were also starting to integrate and bring back into physiology the relationship between different functions (cognitive, affective, sensory, postural, etc.) and to reactivate the interoceptive processes that are fundamental for self-regulation (see switch 3).

Elizabeth also has a 2-year-old daughter with whom she struggles to connect. This is why I suggest that she give her daughter short 5-minute massages every day. This way Elizabeth can pay attention to the needs of the child, learn to observe her and – indirectly – rethink from a different perspective and with fewer constructs about her Ancestral Needs (switch 4), her own body, observe a breathing style that is natural and that she had totally inhibited, etc. Another important aspect concerns the possibility, through both of these activities, of releasing oxytocin. In fact, oxytocin is released both by receiving a massage and by giving one. In both cases the effect is positive because this hormone counteracts cortisol (for further information on cortisol see the introductory chapter on the stress axes), which is high in Elizabeth considering the level of excess stress she has accumulated through the adverse experiences she has been dragging on since childhood. A further important aspect concerns the fact that oxytocin also has a social function, it promotes emotional ties. This way Elizabeth and her daughter not only spend quality time together and cultivate the attachment-care relationship, but also consolidate its neurobiological level.

BODY AND MIND ENERGY, EFFICIENCY AND PHYSIOLOGY

At the cellular level there are other important switches that modulate the energy and physiology of well-being and change.

As has been highlighted in much research and also shared on a large scale by the *American Psychiatric Association Task Force on DSM-IV* (The Diagnostic Statistical Manual of Mental Disorders) as early as 2000, there is a clear link between human fear and other homeostatic systems. Specifically, they report as a clinical example how all mood disorders are united by an alteration in energy metabolism.

These are processes that are well clarified to date and on which it is possible to act in a targeted way. Let's start with a practical fact. Some **typical symptoms of anxiety** are *disorientation, feeling faint, poor motor control, loss of long-term goals,* etc. Once again, let us ask ourselves what sustains these processes at a basic neurobiological level (we will then look at other interesting processes in the following levels). We analyse the main ones in the following paragraphs.

THE METABOLISM VIEWPOINT

There has recently been a fully-fledged conceptual revolution concerning neuron metabolism. Contrary to popular belief, only 10% of the work of the mitochondria is based on glycogen (derived from sugars)[14], while it uses quality fats which it transforms in ketones far more effectively. The latter represent the most efficient source of energy for our nervous system cells[15], providing them with constant energy to carry out their tasks in support of their functions of being alert, control and resolution of external threats.

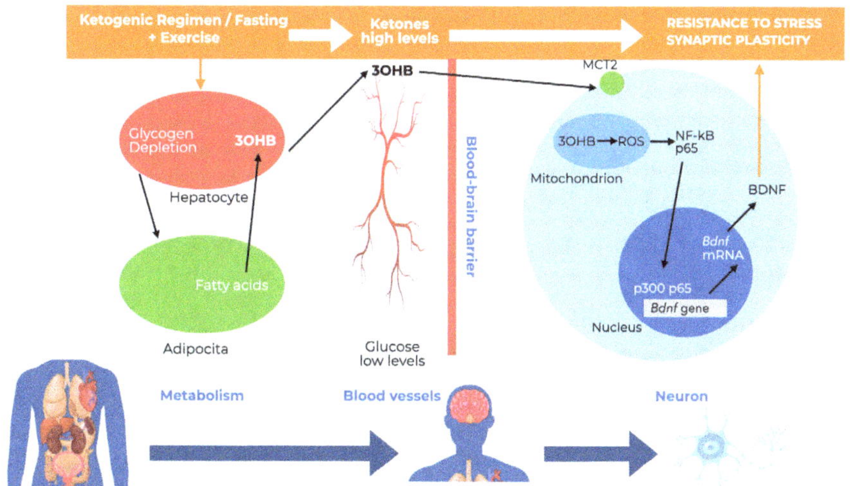

Fig. - Representation of the cellular stages through which nutrition and physical activity change the metabolism of neurons, promoting resistance to stress and neural plasticity.

We have already revealed that from an operational point of view mitochondria modulate the process of neurodevelopment. Let us now focus on the connection between energy metabolism and the development of neural networks. BHB (β-hydroxybutyrate) is one of the main ketones derived from fats and is a molecule that favours the production of energy. It also plays a signalling role by stimulating the production of BDNF (brain-derived neurotrophic factor) that in turn is critical to learning, memory and other adaptive responses in neurons[16].

It is a core growth element that enables neural plasticity and other forms of development with all the subsequent impact and advantages these bring at a therapeutic and change level. For example, it has been shown that – all other conditions being neutral – this type of metabolic circuit enables the development of new synapses in patients suffering from depression. This creates a beneficial substratum for focused attention, motivation and openness to change activated by psychotherapy.

Through a ketogenic nutritional regimen, during fasting (even just skipping a meal) and in combination with exercise, brain cells switch from using glucose to ketone 3-hydroxybutyrate (3OHB). Several studies have revealed that 3OHB has protective functions for neurons against excitotoxicity and oxidative stress. Neurons, using 3OHB, increase oxygen consumption and ATP production (more energy) as well as have a higher NAD+/NADH ratio (better transmission of brain signals)[17]. Furthermore, 3OHB metabolism increases mitochondrial respiration, promoting changes in BDNF expression, which plays a central role in synaptic plasticity and neuronal resistance to stress[18].

Nutrition, and metabolism in general, also has other very important implications on health at an overall level, as we will see in the Switch 2 area, the common factor in all diseases and dysfunctions, both physical and mental, is a chronic inflammatory state and, on the other hand, what we eat and our engagement in physical activity play a central role in favouring or blocking these inflammatory states. Similarly, through nutrition we introduce (or don't introduce) essential substances to give the correct or wrong signals to many processes (just think that type 3 diabetes, linked to nutritional style, is considered the basis for any neurodegenerative disease such as Parkinson's, Alzheimer's, etc.). We will explore these aspects in the next chapter and, in the light of the explanations, we will provide some practical indications on what to eat in view of specific objectives (reducing pain, not amplifying negative emotional states, preventing somatization processes, etc.).

Ageing and other chronic dysfunctional processes are the main risk factors for the development of tumours, neurodegenerative diseases and cardiovascular diseases. Altering nutritional style (such as introducing a calorie restriction and, in particular, a ketogenic diet), reduces the risk of developing these pathologies through the increase in circulating β-HB (Beta-hydroxybutyrate). The increase in β-HB improves the metabolic complications caused by insulin resistance (a process involved in all inflammatory processes, see switch 2), reduces cellular ageing phenotypes (including senescence and inflammation) and regenerates sciatic nerves[19].

It is important to remember that, even more than food, water is essential for our health. A state of dehydration is a critical factor connected to various cellular dysfunctions which, in turn, are at the basis of numerous problems. It is a very widespread condition: at a sub-clinical level we could say that it is a condition present in the majority of the population. If we think about it, our culture leads us to drink little water. This is true on several levels. First of all we are driven to lose our sense of thirst because it is seen as an interference: this starts with preventing children from drinking at school and consequently from going to the bathroom.

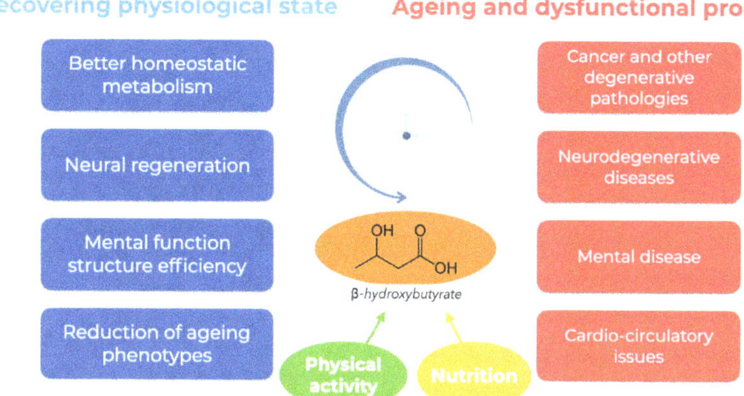

Fig. - The effects of physical activity and nutrition regulation (through β-hydroxybutyrate metabolism) on different aspects of physical and mental health.

They then grow into adults that are totally focused on work, so much so that they no longer feel their somatic needs, or they become people who are ashamed to go to the bathroom frequently because they are judged by colleagues (and their 'frequently' is 2-3 times a day, which would be perfectly normal, but in a dysfunctional culture it is they who seem 'the strange ones' or those who don't know how to manage their bodies). Then there are people who no longer feel vital stimuli such as thirst because they are always wrapped up in engaging cognitive activities, which can be the playful fantasies of a child, the romantic ones of a teenager, but also the concentration of a professional in solving a problem. If on the one hand these people are very focused on their mental flows, on the other hand they are totally detached from the body. There may be several reasons: they have never nurtured a good relationship with their body: because they grew up without the normal physical activity of intense playing when they were children, they have never played sports in a constant way, they have suffered trauma or physical limitations during development, they had adverse experiences as children (so-called ACEs, *Adverse Childhood Experiences*, which include emotional trauma, lack of affection, detachment or relational absence, emotional neglect, etc.). Whatever the reason, it is essential that the body is rightly hydrated: dehydrated cells do not allow a correct exchange of neurotransmitters in the synapses, they damage the metabolism of the muscles and of each organ, they send an alarm signal to the central nervous system, which overrides any other function. This last statement might seem strong, but if we look at the evolutionary significance of this process, it becomes immediately evident: with dehydration begins the process by which the body evaluates that it could die from dehydration, therefore from its point of view it puts everything – thought, logic, affections, medium and long-term motivation, etc. – in the background until the situation is resolved.

In addition to the nutritional element, the other factor capable of improving mitochondrial metabolism, the production of BDNF and also the optimal use of oxygen (which enables better cognitive performance and lucidity under stress, as we will see in the following paragraph) is *controlled exercise*. Good examples of this are *aerobic activity* or *muscle strengthening*, as long as they are exercised within their window of improvement (i.e. they are metabolically challenging but not excessive). There are different mechanisms to take care of, but fortunately in many cases the initiatives to be taken are similar. For example, the types of physical training that we have seen to be favourable to the activation of new epigenetic marking are also ideal for this type of purpose.

Even *passive activities*, which require the adaptation of different regulation systems, can be effective. These may be a few minutes in the *sauna* which is capable of activating the body without wearing it down. This type of activity also increases the functioning of sirtuins (a class of proteins that perform a regulatory enzymatic activity), which play a role not only in the development of neural networks, but also in epigenetic signature processes, enabling deep and lasting change over time.

The basic concept to remember is that we need to give our body, and therefore our cells, *stimuli that push just above the status quo*. This way, they are pushed to adapt flexibly to become more functional or – in cases where there is no room for improvement – to destroy themselves by apoptosis and make room for new cells. This way we guarantee that chronic degeneration, which can manifest itself in symptoms in which the cells degrade, from dermatitis to tumours, but also in many mental disorders, from obsessive thoughts to schizophrenia, can be avoided.

THE ROLE OF OXYGEN

Feeling *disoriented*, a *fuzzy head*, *shaking limbs* (hands shaking and legs that give way) are all symptoms that relate to a lack of oxygen to the brain and muscles[20] which need to function at their best to activate the fight or flight responses necessary to face danger. Another key factor of this first group of switches concerns oxygen and its use.

It is not by chance that *controlled breathing techniques* play a key role in helping people recover from early-stage anxiety and panic attacks. However, once oxygen arrives to a cell, it still needs to be put to use. Mitochondria (they are the users of oxygen) must therefore be in a physiological state and, if they are numerous, they will be able to elaborate a bigger amount of oxygen more rapidly (see earlier paragraph). It is thus possible to gain greater control and speed in basic self-regulation processes with their connected history of mastery and personal efficiency in stressful circumstances.

Breathing should flow attuned to every human activity, adapting to the requirements of the activity and favouring physiological state as much as possible. Occasionally, however, something goes wrong and the lack of suitable breathing rhythm can pose a problem to cognitive and emotional processes. There are various situations in which breathing can become dysfunctional: 1- a fright or intense pain can stop it; 2- there are also forced immobility situations, such as when you remain frozen during an accident or under physical attack or when being abused in some way, that lead to an incongruence between breathing and thorax and diaphragm mobility; 3- less dramatic instances, such as that of prolonged bad posture or non-physiological work conditions, can alter normal breathing flows too.

The problem isn't just with oxygen not flowing properly. As often happens, the opposites are also connected: the dysfunction also affects carbon dioxide. Even the amygdala, which plays a central role in the survival, adaptation and emotion networks (see specific insights in switch area 3) is defined as a chemosensor, i.e. it is able to detect the degree of carbon dioxide - and not only - based on the assessment made. It can give shape to fear reactions[21]. So, we must not only pay attention to how much oxygen enters the body, but also *how saturated with CO2 the air in a room or*  *in the vicinity of a person is.*

All these phenomena, if prolonged or repeated over time, can set off a series of dysfunctions and significant alterations at structural and functional level. This can have a significant impact on memory processes, dissociative episodes, on physiology and muscular memory, on hyper-activation of certain brain areas such as the amygdala and of entire brain networks as well as on the balance between ortho- and parasympathetic systems, and so on[22].

With regards to this latter aspect (ortho-parasympathetic balance) it is important to remember that the view that pits *sympathetic* and *parasympathetic* systems against each other as mutually exclusive antagonists is limiting and dated. It is useful to talk about predominance of one system over the other in different contexts such as at the opposite poles of fight-flight and rest.

Nevertheless, both systems interact and cooperate towards a common outcome of maximum flexibility and adaptation at any one time. Problems arise when this dialogue and balance are not attuned with real requirements. This can happen in ambiguous or murky situations (it will be possible to intervene on these elements with the ideas and techniques relating to n.3 Switches and specifically the uncertainty network)[23], or because dysfunctional systems for evaluating external and internal conditions have taken hold (particularly the Salience Network and expectations, also in area 3).

On the other hand, there are also small constant physiological variations to this balance that are influenced by the regular alternation of inhaling and exhaling. As a result, *controlled breathing techniques* can be very effective especially when associated or put into conflict with *coherent muscular activation states or other processes of active or recovered adaptation*.

Let's see below one of the most effective and transversal techniques that we have developed to act on these aspects at multiple levels.

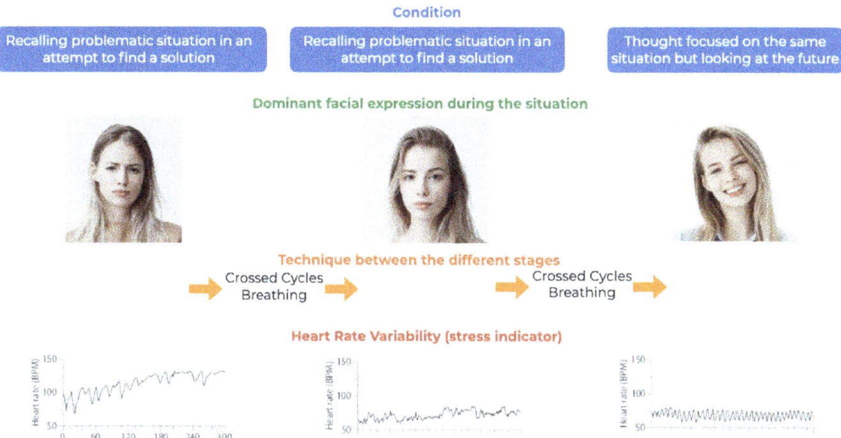

Fig. - Crossed-Cycles Breathing can be used to recreate physiology on different levels (of breathing, of the frontal and posterior muscle chains for different types of stress and fears, position and functioning of the diaphragm, etc.) with effects at a systemic level (instant better cardiac variance, regulation of neurotransmitters and hormones through repeated practice, etc.). In this research the subjects faced three situations: 1- the spontaneous recall of a problem from the past (a quarrel, a disappointment, etc.); 2- a situation similar to the previous one, but after having done a Crossed Cycles Breathing session; 3- thinking aimed at the same theme of the previous situations, but without reliving the past and focusing on constructive future solutions. As you can see, Heart Rate Variability significantly improves during the three phases, in line with the experience reported by the subjects, who felt increasingly in control, serene and optimistic with respect to the situation they were evaluating. During the test, photographs were taken every 10 seconds, those with the most frequently recurring expressions were chosen and, among them, the subject could choose the one that best represented him/her.

A FIRST INTEGRATIVE TECHNIQUE: CROSSED CYCLES BREATHING

We first introduce Crossed Cycles Breathing by focusing on its main objective: that of providing the muscles and nervous system with suitable oxygenation. The technique, however, provides benefits that reach far beyond and intervenes on multiple levels.

While still in the realm of the first switches area it is useful to know that controlled, slow and deep breathing can alter the cascade of calcium in cells.

Calcium in cells is connected to energy and metabolic processes, but also to inflammatory signalling cascades which are a key feature of psychosomatic symptomatology (as we will see in the second group of switches).

Breathing is regulated by different groups of neurons, amongst which are the Nucleus of the Solitary Tract and the parabrachial nuclei that are essential in sensory and perceptive processes. The insula (see the brain networks in the third group of switches) also plays an important role and is in constant dialogue with the breathing system: mediating sensory and perceptive aspects with the processes of danger recognition, context evaluation, marshalling of inner resources and the transition to movement and to different adaptive behaviours.

Working in a targeted way with the breathing system, movement, the alternation of opposite cycles - all key factors in this technique - allows us to stimulate and interact with stress responses and, in particular, with the dialogue and the balance between sympathetic and parasympathetic nervous systems.

Very strong pain or unexpected emotion such as astonishment can stop breathing in its tracks. If the stall is prolonged and combined with muscular stiffening or immobilisation, a series of complications may occur at the level of the writing of our memories.

At the central level, the memories or the event are filed separately so that the narration can be connected to images, sounds or sensations (see fifth area switch flows and related techniques where breathing is controlled and managed in yet another way).

THE BASIC TECHNIQUE

The basic concept of this technique is that there are two main alternating cycles:

- The first concerns the stages of inhalation and exhalation
- The second refers to head movements

NB: the main steps of this technique follow. To understand it fully, however, a video is worth more than a thousand words!

➔ a free video course illustrating all further phases and 5 other variants is available. You can access it free of charge on our website:

www.insciences.co/breathing

Start seated. The back is well against the chair, legs at 90 degrees and hands resting comfortably on the legs.

The head is centered comfortably on the shoulders, in a relaxed, natural position.

The first step is to inhale while slowly tilting the head back. This movement is quite slow, as if in slow motion and happens while inhaling.
In this first instance, most people end the movement before they finish inhaling. For now, that is fine. Remember: we can improve the technique as we go along.
Ask the person to hold the position and finish inhaling by filling their lungs, a movement which pushes down the diaphragm. It should be a deep breath, but one that stays within physiology. We do not want to "fill the lungs as much as we can" but to breathe "in the best way possible".
When the inhalation terminates, we ask the person to hold that position, count two seconds and then proceed with the following step.

Now the head returns to the center and we exhale.
As per the previous iteration we complete the exhalation holding the head in a vertical position.
The principle stays the same: "let's empty the lungs well" but "not entirely". The idea is to go a bit further than we would do naturally, but to stop before it becomes too difficult, distressing, or forced.
We will work within a re-consolidation window, which is essential in generating change and new learning.

Initially, when the head is in the vertical position, it is important to remember that it must be straight, but also relaxed. This is in order to avoid recruiting unnecessary muscles that could lead to a stiffening of the neck.

Once the exhalation is completed, we count two seconds and proceed with the third step.

Now the head tips forward. Here slowness is essential, because the movement is short and the back muscles that we are stretching could be quite contracted. We are aiming to stretch them a little, but always remaining in physiology. Please note that the stretching of the muscles and greater freedom of movement can and must only be an indirect consequence of this exercise. We are not actively seeking that out during its execution.
Once the inhalation is completed we pause for two seconds, then while exhaling we return the head to centre.

Now, at this point there is a crucial step: we take the following breath but hold the head still. Because we finished the previous movement by exhaling, we remain still while inhaling.
Now I start again with the movement of the head that will reverse the previous breathing cycle.

We then start again moving the head in reversal of the previous breathing step. This time, we slowly tilt the head backwards while exhaling (whereas in the previous cycle we were inhaling).
Then we release, pause and slowly take the head back to a central position while inhaling.
Now we tip the head forward while exhaling and we end by returning to a central position while inhaling.
We now keep our head in a central position, exhaling.

We have now completed two cycles, the first starting by inhaling, the second by exhaling. We can now start over again.

➜ Video-instructions available on:
www.insciences.co/breathing

Crossed Cycles Breathing is an easy-to apply, practical transversal tool that often sparks the interest of the people we introduce it to. In addition to giving immediate relief, performed at least once or twice daily it brings significant results both subjectively perceived and objectively measurable. In Angelica's case, for example, I proposed this technique pretty early on, mid-session, linking it to the explanations I was giving her to understand why she always had extreme feelings: she was always either hyperactive or hypoactive, never in between. The technique helped her to experience what we were talking about on her own skin and to have immediate feedback on how it is possible to regain a sense of well-being and control.

Generally, I suggest this type of technique right during the first session, perhaps just as a practical closure and to give something concrete to the patient, especially in cases where there is a significant activation component (anxiety, stress, phobias, PTSD, but also hyper-performing managers, etc.). Among other things, it is a technique that delicately introduces working on interoceptive awareness, on control, on actively shifting the attentional focus, on the interference with nearby people's state of 'agitation' and other aspects on which one can work later, with specific variants of this same technique or with other techniques that we will see later.

Another interesting technique that uses breath is connected to physiological activation, posture, movement and how all this can create or unlock traumatic memories. This technique is called *Inverse Physiological Replay*, which we will see in switch 5.

Finally, it is important to highlight that there is also a direct link between cellular metabolism – seen previously – and respiration. A state of maximum metabolic physiology, in fact, lowers the basic heart rate and increases respiratory arrhythmia, which together allow for better emotional and adaptation responses. From a structural point of view, this phenomenon occurs because the synapses in the dorsal nucleus of the vagus increase and can be favoured in different ways. The simplest modality is *aerobic activity* which, on the other hand, combined with *specific mindsets* (for objectives, scarcity, body maps, etc.) can generate a strong motivational boost, increasing the production of dopamine, essential precisely to move and to maintain motivation, both in terms of constancy and in terms of ideational and creative relaunch.

IT'S A MATTER OF (CIRCADIAN) RHYTHM

FRAME THE PROBLEM

Just a few years ago it was commonly thought that misaligned circadian rhythms (i.e. erratic sleep-wakefulness and nutrition patterns) were the consequence of bad habits or symptoms of anxiety, stress or PTSD. Lately, however, it has been revealed that although these elements can represent a starting point for misalignment, there is also an interesting inverse influence.

In other words, erratic circadian rhythms can create and fuel even quite serious mentally dysfunctional conditions and physical pathologies. Re-ordering these patterns and bringing them back to physiological state used to be seen as an outcome derived from treating anxiety or PTSD, while it is now seen as a primary strategy that should be put in place immediately to enable a faster and more effective intervention.

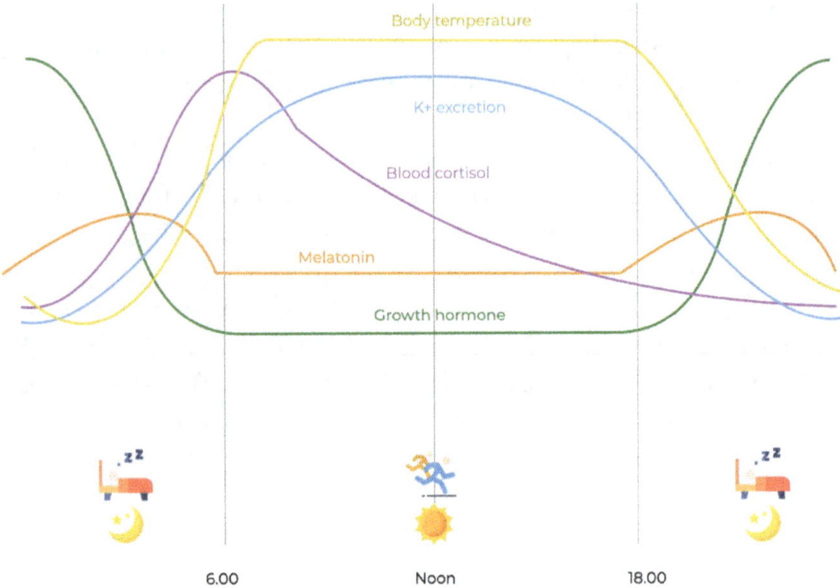

Fig. - Some of the biological variations that occur daily in the human organism with important repercussions on mental, emotional and available energy states. Bringing these processes back into physiology is essential for recovering global health and well-being. On the other hand, it is important to take them into consideration when organizing your daily activities, in order to keep them regular and make the most of the neurobiological conditions in which you find yourself.

This happens because every day, cyclically, certain physiological parameters vary: hormone peaks (including cortisol, melatonin, sexual hormones and more) alterations in appetite, ability to concentrate, body temperature and other parameters. If these cycles are synchronised and adapt to the environment the basic conditions for a return to physiological state of metabolic, genetic, epigenetic and self-regulation processes are fulfilled (including cognition, emotional regulation etc.).

In simple terms there is one central time that sets all the other internal clocks and it is the Suprachiasmatic Nucleus (SCN). The SCN is strongly affected by sunlight even through closed eyelids. To recover the first level of a physiological state in a practical way it is – for example – useful *to not sleep in total darkness* or, if specific conditions (such as winter in Northern Europe and Northern Canada, or if there is artificial lighting just outside the bedroom window etc.) call for it, to use tools such as a *wake-up light alarm clocks* so long as the light spectrum is modelled on that of real sunlight.

The SCN directly connects and influences various brain areas including the Pulvinar Nucleus. The Pulvinar is within the hypothalamus and plays a key role in regulating emotions and in providing synergy between logical thought, motivation and emotional responses[24]. The Pulvinar is the starting point for the *Hypothalamus-Hypophysis-Adrenal Gland* axis so its disfunction influences any response to stress and related hormones (especially cortisone) derived from this axis.

The Pulvinar is also directly connected to the brain stem and thus influences motor and postural states, the perception of pain and all basic instinctive responses.

Regulating circadian rhythms, therefore, enables the recovery of basic physiology starting from the earliest processes that govern it. It becomes a favourable prerequisite to any therapy focusing on basic regulation, from modulation of arousal states to the effectiveness of increasingly complex physical techniques. To intervene at this level, it is critical to *set regular sleep-wakefulness patterns* (initially not necessarily sleeping but resting or exposing oneself to light) with periods of physical and mental activity and rest that follow natural daily rhythms, regular meals and times for socialisation[25].

SEVERAL PRACTICAL SOLUTIONS

To promote recovery of the correct sleep-wake cycles we can implement some useful tricks and use specific tools. The first trick consists in inviting people to *go to bed a little earlier every day*, even just half an hour before what they're used to. They may not even fall asleep, but they begin to let the body rest a bit and gradually get used to new times and modalities. Each week it will be possible to anticipate bed time more and more, approaching an optimal time (between 9 pm and 11 pm) compatible with one's work and family commitments. On the other hand, it is essential *to avoid demanding sporting activities after 6 pm.* If possible, *work and cognitively demanding activity after dinner should also be limited*, even if unfortunately, this is often a common need of modern times.

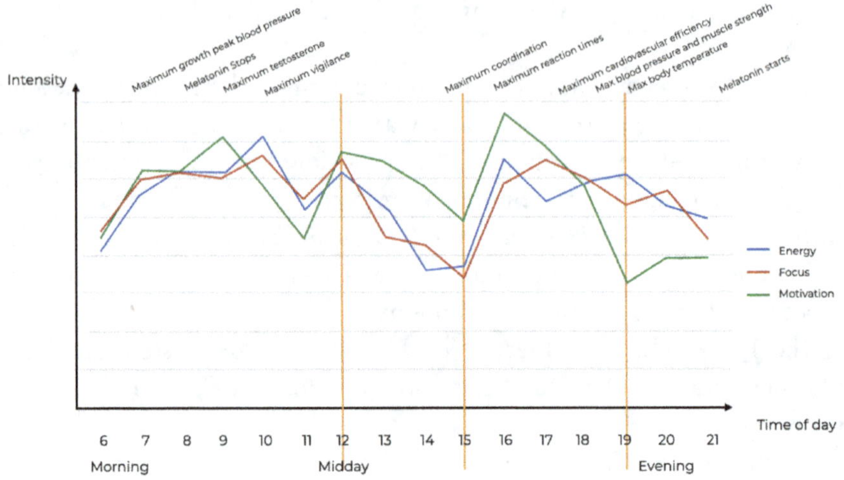

Fig. - This table can be used to illustrate ideal peak activity. The times are indicative; there may be physiological variations of a few minutes up to a maximum of about an hour. Excessive deviations from these times may indicate the need to bring circadian rhythms back into physiology. A simple first exercise is to indicate your current peaks on a white card and note the differences. Then, progressively, one can try to reorganize one's work and personal activities (sports, games, socializing, meal times, etc.) to start moving in this direction. Indeed, these times are partly organized by central cues, but they can also be maintained and influenced through biofeedback of one's daily activities.

An important aspect, that also to be properly clarified, is that often we feel tired even after sleeping due to a metabolism malfunction. Working on nutrition by *reducing the intake of unnecessary carbohydrates* (as we will see in switch 2) will not only help reduce inflammation, but will create less insulin swings, allowing our brain to be lucid after meals and, conversely, to better fall asleep at night.

Technology can be both friend and foe when it comes to these issues. As mentioned above, the use of the *twilight alarm clock* can play a fundamental role in bringing sleep-wake rhythms back to correct levels. There are several studies that demonstrate its effectiveness even with respect to specific problems, from depression to attention deficits. In our research and in clinical practice we have seen that it is very useful for any mood and motivational problem.

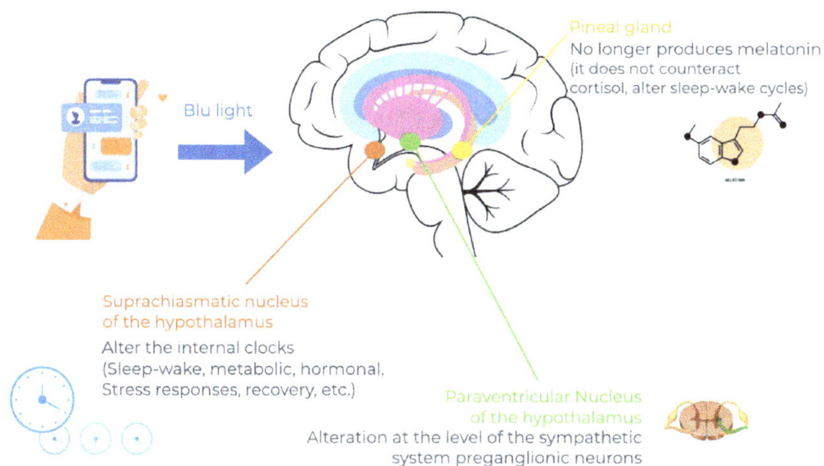

Fig. - The effects of prolonged blue light, especially at night from electronic devices on the brain and, in cascade, on many aspects: rest, attention, hormones, stress responses, vigilance, hyper-reactivity, etc.

For example, the introduction of this tool has resulted in a great and rapid improvement in Anthony's case. For different reasons, it also benefited Hilary, a management secretary who was in danger of losing her job because lately she was always tired, late, distracted and made a series of mistakes she hadn't made before. This was not Hilary's only problem, in fact we will find her again later in the text, but it certainly made a difference for her and made her quickly recover a large part of her standard ways of living and working.

Another important aspect concerns electronic devices (mobile phone, tablet, computer, television), which emit a light that is strongly biased towards blue. It's easy to notice in the evening: with all the lights off you can notice a blue reflection lighting in the room where the television or computer is on, regardless of the type of projected image. A specific frequency of these blue lights emitted by technological devices directly activates the suprachiasmatic nucleus and, through a series of steps, can alter the production of melatonin, with the related negative effects on our sleep. Furthermore, this blue light is also problematic for the eyesight itself, so much so that manufacturers have been forced to introduce the so-called *"night mode"* or *"night shift"* functions. By activating these modes, the screen reduces blue lights and increases orange tones. The result is absolutely pleasant and problematic only if specific computer colours are needed to work. On the other hand, negative mechanisms for our eyes and our hormones are interrupted (particularly melatonin, but cortisol is also involved in these dysfunctions).

These types of tricks are essential for all those who spend a lot of time in front of a computer, especially in the evening. It will be useful to propose it to students during the exam period, as well as to various professionals. In this regard it is important to always have a 360 view, perhaps someone could tell us that they never use the computer after 5 pm, so we could be induced to discard these issues. Yet it often happens that during the hours in which they are at work they're in a basement with only artificial light, a situation that alters circadian rhythms and makes the blue lights of monitors unfavourable even during the day. The other aspect to keep an eye on often concerns the artificial distinction that some people tend to make between 'work' and 'pleasure', thinking that blue lights only hurt if you work. In reality, they should be avoided even if it comes to watching a movie or spending time on social networks.

REFERENCES

[1] Mattson, M. P., Moehl, K., Ghena, N., Schmaedick, M., & Cheng, A. (2018). Intermittent metabolic switching, neuroplasticity and brain health. Nature Reviews. Neuroscience, 19(2), 63–80.

[2] Detmer SA, Chan DC. Functions and dysfunctions of mitochondrial dynamics. Nat Rev Mol Cell Biol. 2007; 8(11):870–879.

[3] Zhou, Z.; Sun, B.; Li, X.; Zhu, C. DNA methylation landscapes in the pathogenesis of type 2 diabetes mellitus. Nutr. Metab. 2018, 15, 47.

[4] Morgan, N.; Irwin, M.R.; Chung, M.; Wang, C. The effects of mind-body therapies on the immune system: Meta-analysis. PLoS ONE 2014, 9, e100903.

[5] McEwen, B. S., & Wingfield, J. C. (2010). What is in a name? Integrating homeostasis, allostasis and stress. Hormones and behavior, 57(2), 105–111

[6] Crispino M, Volpicelli F, Perrone-Capano C. Role of the Serotonin Receptor 7 in Brain Plasticity: From Development to Disease. International Journal of Molecular Sciences. 2020; 21(2):505.

[7] - Yuste R, Bonhoeffer T. Morphological changes in dendritic spines associated with long-term synaptic plasticity. Annu Rev Neurosci. 2001; 24:1071–10789.

- Stranahan AM, et al. Voluntary exercise and caloric restriction enhance hippocampal dendritic spine density and BDNF levels in diabetic mice. Hippocampus. 2009; 19(10):951–961.

[8] Bergmann O, Spalding KL, Frisén J. Adult Neurogenesis in Humans, Cold Spring Harb Perspect Biol. 2015;7(7):a018994.

[9] Ecker B, Ticic R, Hulley L. A primer on memory reconsolidation and its psychotherapeutic use as a core process of profound change. The Neuropsychotherapist. 2013;1:82-99.

[10] Lövdén M, Wenger E, Mårtensson J, et al. Structural brain plasticity in adult learning and development. Neurosci Biobehav Rev. 2013;37(9 Pt B):2296-310.

[11] Damasio, A., Carvalho, G.B. (2013). The nature of feelings: evolutionary and neurobiological origins. Nat Rev Neurosci, 14, 2, 143-152.

[12] McGlone, Francis, Johan Wessberg, and Håkan Olausson. 2014. "Discriminative and Affective Touch: Sensing and Feeling." Neuron 82 (4): 737–755.

[13] Ford, Earl S. 2002. "Does Exercise Reduce Inflammation? Physical Activity and C-Reactive Protein Among US Adults." Epidemiology 13 (5): 561–568.

[14] Fontán-Lozano, A., López-Lluch, G., Delgado-García, J. M., Navas, P., & Carrión, A. M. (2008). Molecular bases of caloric restriction regulation of neuronal synaptic plasticity. Molecular neurobiology, 38(2), 167–177.

[15] - Maalouf M, Rho JM, Mattson MP. The neuroprotective properties of calorie restriction, the ketogenic diet, and ketone bodies. Brain Res Rev. 2009; 59(2):293–315.

- Marosi K, et al. 3-Hydroxybutyrate Regulates Energy Metabolism and Induces BDNF Expression in Cerebral Cortical Neurons. J Neurochem. 2016 published online Oct 14.

[16] Marosi K, Mattson MP. BDNF mediates adaptive brain and body responses to energetic challenges. Trends Endocrinol Metab. 2014; 25(2):89–98.

[17] Longo V. D. and Mattson M. P. (2014) Fasting: molecular mechanisms and clinical applications. Cell Metab. 19, 181–192.

[18] Wrann C. D., White J. P., Salogiannnis J., Laznik-Bogoslavski D., Wu J., Ma D., Lin J. D., Greenberg M. E. and Spiegelman B. M. (2013) Exercise induces hippocampal BDNF through a PGC-1α/FNDC5 pathway. Cell Metab. 18, 649–659.

[19] Han, Y. M., Ramprasath, T., & Zou, M. H. (2020). β-hydroxybutyrate and its metabolic effects on age-associated pathology. Experimental & molecular medicine, 52(4), 548–555.

[20] Radak Z, et al. Oxygen consumption and usage during physical exercise: the balance between oxidative stress and ROS-dependent adaptive signaling. Antioxid Redox Signal. 2013; 18(10):1208– 1246.

[21] Ziemann AE, Allen JE, Dahdaleh NS, Drebot II, Coryell MW, Wunsch AM, Lynch CM, Faraci FM, Howard MA 3rd, Welsh MJ, Wemmie JA. The amygdala is a chemosensor that detects carbon dioxide and acidosis to elicit fear behavior. Cell. 2009 Nov 25;139(5):1012-21.

[22] Van der Kolk BA. The body keeps the score: Brain, mind, and body in the healing of trauma. New York: Viking; 2014.

[23] El-Sheikh M, Kouros CD, Erath S, et al. Marital Conflict and Children's Externalizing Behavior: Pathways Involving Interactions between Parasympathetic and Sympathetic Nervous System Activity. Monogr Soc Res Child Dev. 2009;4(1):1-79.

[24] Pessoa L. (2015). Précis on The Cognitive-Emotional Brain. The Behavioral and brain sciences, 38, e71.

[25] Sinibaldi F. (2018a), Mind Switches: everything that needs to change to favour change. How to work on the 4 key elements at the heart of change: Neuroplasticity and Metabolism; System Balance; Brain Networks & Hubs; Natural Flows. The Neuropsychotherapist, Oct 2018.

SWITCH GROUP N. 2 SYSTEM REGULATION – THE ART OF DARING AND REBALANCING

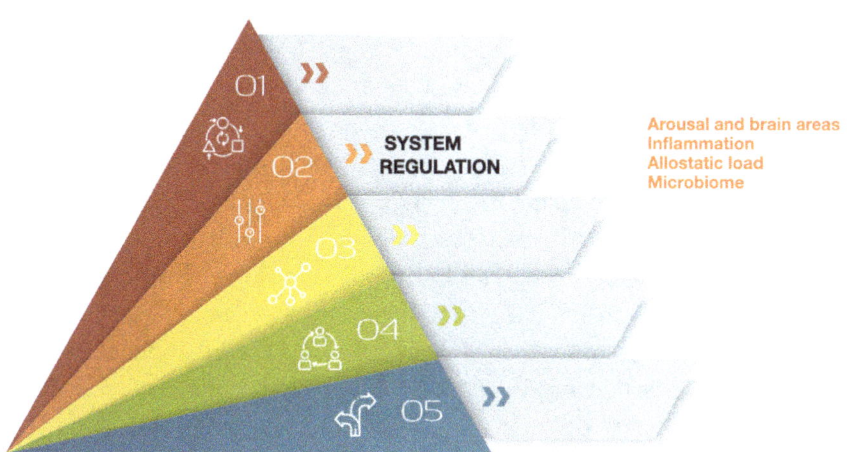

HOMEOSTASIS, ALLOSTASIS, ABUSE OF FUNCTION, INFLAMMATION (BODY, MIND, BRAIN)

I love eating and drinking well, and cooking too. These are activities that are halfway between an art and a science and, for this reason, I find them even more fascinating.

One aspect that has always intrigued me deeply is that in the kitchen there are areas where you can move freely and explore, where you can be daring. Sometimes even what was once considered impossible (such as a type of cooking or a combination of very distant flavours) turns out to be very enjoyable. I still remember when I ate a raspberry-stuffed tomato for dessert. I expect that I had made the puzzled face you're making just now, when I initially read the menu. If I hadn't trusted the chef, I would never have ordered it and, actually, it was an amazing surprise! As much as the kitchen is full of freedom and creativity, there are just as many insurmountable constraints: once a food is overcooked, it becomes hard and will never recover its softness; food that is boiled the wrong way can deposit all the flavour in the broth and remain flavourless. On the other hand, it is possible to transform a food that is not very tasty with a sauce, to make a bitter note disappear not with sweetness (as one would guess, despite the recipe) but with the oil fats. In short, the kitchen is a playground of flexibility for overcoming limits, but certain limits must be acknowledged, there should be no exaggeration and this should – at least – not be protracted for too long.

This second switch area deals precisely with these typically human behaviours: our need to adapt, to the point of hyper-adapting and paying a psychosomatic price for it; our strong desire to be in balance and, at the same time, the inability to remain balanced due to boredom or the desire to follow other stimuli.

A concept dear to me, which well encompasses everything contained in this switch area is that of *function abuse*: that is, the human tendency to take any functionality of their mind and/or body and develop it until it reaches an excess. The first part, the one in which a skill is developed and refined, represents a great talent, such as the talents that have allowed us to create masterpieces of art, develop technology, have materials that make our daily life more comfortable, from the softness of a sweater to the preservation of various products by vacuum. Yet often, too often, there is no limit to this process: I have seen athletes tear muscles in order to lift just one extra kilo or run one marathon too many; scholars that fall ill to add the last minuscule detail to their research, which no one but them probably would have noticed; parents who, in order not to disappoint their children in one aspect, neglect others that are far more important. The list could go on indefinitely, but I think the concept is clear by now: from a positive impulse, from a healthy adaptation, from the desire to surpass oneself, we often end up exaggerating. This drive to *push further* is balanced for a while by our body, while we get used to the effort and evolve, but then degeneration begins. In this switch area we look at some concepts that help us understand what happens in these cases.

Like the previous chapter (switch area 1) this chapter focuses on various biological aspects, but all have relevant mental and emotional implications. In this case too, processes are clearly illustrated and combined with practical cases and examples, identifying pragmatic solutions and methods for intervention that can be easily integrated into daily professional activity.

The main themes around which we will focus our insights, are those of *inflammation* and *allostatic load*.

The concept of allostatic load is used to measure the biological price of over-adaptive mental stress. It is a very useful concept, which can be used in various contexts and which provides clear explanations for us and for the patient on how to proceed to avoid reaching these excessive levels and, above all, how to reverse course before reaching a point of no return. Homeostatic and allostatic systems, as well as inflammation, are two crucial points of the body-mind relationship that point in different directions. This chapter represents a central point for developing a scientific and modern idea of psychosomatic mechanisms. The whole book, the model and the overall method that we present, revolve around the inseparable relationship between mind and body, so much so that they should no longer be separated. However, we come from both medical and philosophical traditions that have separated these concepts for a long time. In order to reason with them and bring them closer together it is now necessary to proceed as follows. In general, the processes through which different domains of our body and of our life influence each other are many and complex. For example, the vagus nerve, the main parasympathetic regulatory pathway (central to emotional and stress responses), also has a central role in anti-inflammatory processes, through the *vagal cholinergic[1] anti-inflammatory* reflex circuit (see the chapter on emotions and the next chapter for further insights into the vagus nerve in clinical practice). As we will see, at the basis of these adaptation and regulation processes there are numerous systems and different networks in dynamic interaction.

The other theme, closely related to the first but with a different perspective, is *inflammation.* The term 'inflammation' makes us immediately think about the immune system, the various pathologies that end in "-itis", such as dermatitis, rhinitis, arthritis and so on. In fact, as we will see more in detail, inflammation is a response that is always active and at our service: just a small *cut* on a finger, unhealthy *food*, but also a *stressful event*, a strong *emotional suffering*, are enough stimulus for the immune system to react. Inflammation is also the neurobiological correlation of so-called states of hyper-arousal, hyper-activation, neural hyper-excitation (sometimes colloquially called "*hypertrophic or hyper-active amygdala/limbic system*", etc.) typically found in those suffering from post-traumatic stress disorder, chronic stress, or those that have a history of abuse or deprivation.

The problem is that often, when you 'abuse a function', the immune system continues reacting, and it never stops. We will see that inflammation can be activated in many ways; therefore our task will be to identify how the patient can take action to avoid activating it continuously. It is often enough to change some specific behaviours to see interesting results. On the other hand, we will see that when there's an ongoing, now chronic, inflammation, it is necessary to put several targeted strategies in place, including physical activity, ad hoc psychophysical exercises, nutrition and more.

ASSESSMENT: WHAT TO OBSERVE AND EVALUATE

For those who have started reading from this chapter, I recommend going back to the preliminary assessment of the chapter dedicated to the first group of Switches in order to have a clear perspective on how to understand and use these indications.

Among the interesting aspects to observe and evaluate from an integrated perspective, and on which to act in this second area of switches, there is:

- Chronic fatigue (in this case energies are present – unlike for switch 1 – but they are consumed to survive and no longer available for motivation, relationships, mental concentration and other higher functions);
- Chronic pains and discomfort (especially related to the intestines, digestion, mouth, the neck cervix, etc.);
- Maintenance of hyper or hypo-activation that are not adequate for the current context and situation;

- Hyper-irritability towards objects, people, unexpected events, etc.;
- Intense emotions that are prolonged and often not commensurate with the situation;
- Moods that does not change over time or, vice versa, that change too quickly and without apparent reasons;
- Weakness (tendency to get sick easily) or hyper-reactivity (intense reactions to minimal stimuli) of the immune system;
- Typical psychosomatic symptoms (skin, gastro-intestinal, etc.);
- Tight, swollen intestine, flatulence, constipation, etc.;
- Extremely contracted or lax muscles;
- Degenerative diseases.

THE STRESS LIMIT: WHERE FLEXIBILITY ENDS AND YOU BEGIN TO PAY THE PRICE

All organisms must regulate their own physiology, their behaviour and also the body structure as they go through their life cycle. These changes occur daily and, in some respects, seasonally. There are challenges and adaptations that are predictably repetitive (eating, working, arguing with a partner, sports, not finding a parking space, etc.) and others related to unforeseeable events (infections, illnesses, risks or accidents, conflicts at work, having to pay a fine and other forms of occasional stress). The classic concept of homeostasis is key to these adjustments, but not sufficient.

RETHINKING HOMEOSTASIS AND ALLOSTASIS

Homeostasis concerns the continuous maintenance of vital physiological variables (such as blood pressure, blood glucose levels, body temperature, etc.) in the event of a deviation from benchmark parameters. It has been defined for years as the main element behind physiological regulation and, although its understanding and definitions have changed over time, the fundamental concept of homeostasis, as captured by Cannon's phrase "Wisdom of the Body"[2], remains central.

As previously mentioned, there are situations in which the concept of homeostasis is not sufficiently flexible. For example, when a woman is pregnant, she experiences changes in her physiology, behaviour and even body structure. Further changes occur when she starts breastfeeding. All these changes do not stem from the need to maintain homeostasis, but reference parameters have changed[3].

The concept of *allostasis* is integrated with the concept of homeostasis, presenting a framework through which it is possible to take an overview of the main foreseeable events of the life cycle alongside the unforeseeable ones. A good, inclusive definition of allostasis is:

the process of maintaining homeostasis through the adaptive change of the internal environment of one's own organism to meet perceived and expected needs.

McEwen defines allostasis even more clearly and synthetically as *the achievement of stability through change*. From this perspective, allostasis can be defined as the active process of maintaining/restoring homeostasis, when with homeostasis we mean the preservation of aspects of physiology that support life (pH, oxygen tension, body temperature, etc.). In this scenario, allostasis refers to the body's ability to produce hormones (such as cortisol, adrenaline) and other mediators (such as cytokines, parasympathetic activity, etc.) that help to adapt to a new situation or challenge of any kind, whether predictable and unpredictable.

The concepts of *allostasis* and *allostatic load* preserve the concept of homeostasis (that is, homeostasis is maintained within a phase of the lifecycle), but also include the anticipatory aspects of the life cycle (perfectly in line with the forecasting mechanisms we will discuss in area 3). Increased allostatic load also heightens susceptibility to disturbances, meaning homeostatic mechanisms can be overcome triggering a stress response. The key point of the concept of allostasis is that it incorporates homeostasis and provides a framework for a model of how individual subjective conditions (body conditions, infection, injuries, age, etc.), status, daily and seasonal rhythms of food availability, predators, weather, etc. as well as habitat differences and so on interact to contribute to the overall allostatic load and thus the energy needed to power it. In the next section, we will examine this fundamental theme in order to regulate the processes underlying the paths of care and change.

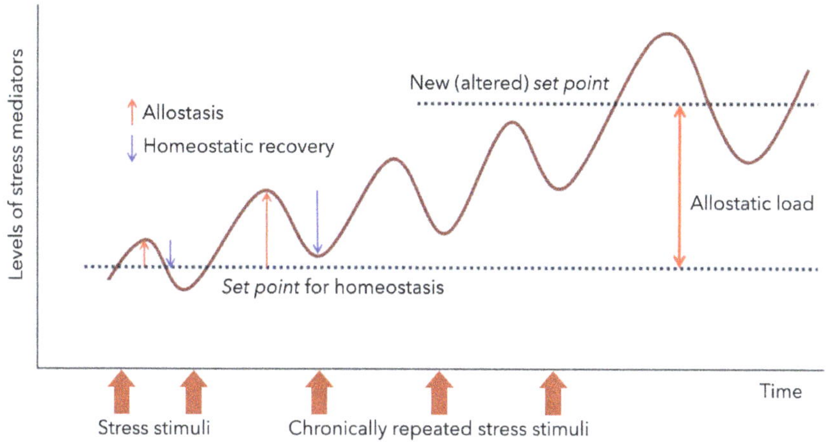

Fig. - The flexibility offered by allostatic mechanisms has a downside: the prolonged adaptation to dysfunctional situations leads the body to create new benchmarks, or consider rapid heartbeat, hyper-vigilance, muscle contraction, etc. to be 'normal', without it being useful, but rather leading to a progressive degeneration.

THE PRINCIPLE OF MINIMUM FREE ENERGY

The concept of energy plays a central role in allostasis: our body must manage physiological, structural, behavioural and motivational variations according to the ratio of total energy (available or recoverable) and the current or planned needs to carry out basic daily activities and to deal with potentially stressful unpredictable events.

In light of these mechanisms, the inflammatory processes we saw earlier that are linked to both nutrition and stress, as well as the idea of how well neural plasticity works, energy metabolism, and epigenetic markers, become even clearer. At this point it is interesting to take another step forward and further broaden our perspectives to include physical aspects, this time more from the sensory and muscular point of view, in our overview on the physiological regulation and management of energy.

To this end it is useful to start from the *principle of minimum free energy*, a simple postulate in itself, but with complex implications on different levels. In a nutshell, this postulate says that any adaptive change in the brain will minimize free energy, i.e. energy not used in some process and, therefore, 'free' for other emerging needs. This minimization could take place in evolutionary time (months and years) as well as in a few milliseconds (for example during the perception of a possible danger).

The principle applies to any biological system that resists a tendency to disorder, from unicellular organisms to social networks. The principle of *minimum free energy* was created to explain the structure and function of the brain. It is the fruit of the interaction of complex disciplines: neuroscience, neural networks, statistics, artificial intelligence, game theory and many others.

The operational synthesis that we have developed over our years of study and research within the Integrative Sciences can be formulated as follows:

 *If we don't use our energy for something useful, we will waste it on something else.*

Conversely, if we use all our energies for:
- postures (*due to stress, physical or emotional trauma, habits*) that are no longer useful;
- thoughts (*narrations, memories, images, etc.*) that are not functional to the present;
- physiological adaptation processes (*inflammation, digestion, cell degeneration, etc.*) that are no longer required.

We must, first of all, free these energies. Only after doing so does it become possible to redirect energy towards healthier and more constructive modes.

In other words, the principle of minimum free energy helps us to understand that in order to begin any healing or change process, we must first identify where energies are wasted and hindered, free them and then proceed with healing processes like the development of new habits, mindsets, body maps, correct postures, cognitive or physical development or whatever our therapeutic goal may be.

PSYCHOSOMATIC RELEASE TECHNIQUES

The psychosomatic release techniques, as the name implies, are aimed at obtaining a release, i.e., a loss of tension, but also a physical, mental and emotional "lightening".

In line with the principle of minimum free energy, we have developed these techniques with the aim of releasing those tensions that consume energies in a pointless way:
* contracted shoulders as a result of a stress response that has lasted too long;
* contracted diaphragm caused by shortness of breath due to prolonged anxiety and/or incorrect posture at work;
* thoughts that continue to remain focused on the problem and not on possible solutions;
* a constant state of anger and resentment that tightens neck and mouth muscles and that, in turn, sends a negative biofeedback that supports a sense of impotence;
* blocked sacrum/tailbone (due to a fall or excessive psycho-corporeal tension in a sedentary job), which tightens movements, supporting a sense of insecurity and vulnerability;
* chronic pain states in specific areas of the body that can be due to several reasons, and which can often be reduced at least in part by releasing mental and motivational energies;
* and so on.

As you can see from the points above, this is a rather varied case list. That's why we developed several psychosomatic release techniques.

One of the most transversal techniques, applicable with almost every patient, is the so-called **Psychosomatic Point Release** technique. It focuses on those pain points that everyone has in their body after a certain age (usually from adolescence onwards). If you ask an anxious person to touch the opposite shoulder with two fingers of one hand, for example on the trapezoid muscles, or near the neck and upper spine, surely you will find one or more points that hurt, even if pressed with only medium intensity. Such points can be found all over the body, usually in the middle of the triceps (behind the arm), on the forearm (near the elbow and about halfway), on the sides of the thighs, on the mid-calf and at several points of the hands and feet.

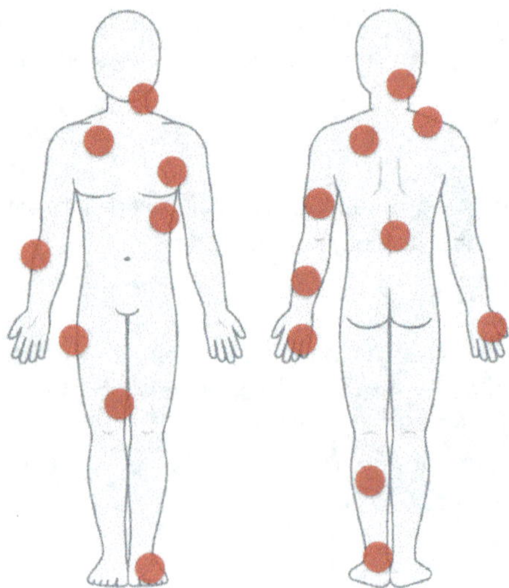

Fig. - The image represents some of the psychosomatic points where patients can easily spot pain or discomfort and apply one of the psychosomatic release techniques. All the marked points can be present both on the right and left side of the body (for graphic clarity only one point per side has been marked on the drawing).

These are some recurring examples. Everyone can find different points of this kind. Inviting people to explore their body, find these points, see if they are painful all the time or if the pain changes (maybe they only hurt in the evening and not in the morning), represents an excellent physical exercise of awareness, self-knowledge and an initial recovery of mastery over one's health.

Once you find these points and begin a process of self-discovery and self-monitoring, you can start the actual technique. Place two fingers on the painful spot. You need to find a position where you can touch it and then relax the whole body as much as possible. For example, if I touch a point on my shoulder with my fingers, then I'll try to straighten and relax head and neck. I will also try to lower my elbow, so that I don't have to work harder than necessary to hold my hand in the chosen position. Then I'll check that the whole chest, pelvis and legs are comfortable and relaxed. All this is fundamental, we cannot unlock a point while there are unnecessary contractions in other parts of the body. The technique is performed by massaging the point in a circular way with the two fingers while exhaling slowly. Once the exhalation is over, the massage stops, while keeping the fingers still in position, without pressing. Meanwhile, inhale slowly and deeply. After inhaling, start massaging again while exhaling. Continue for two to three minutes. Doing this too quickly will mean that the technique will barely be effective, vice versa, overstimulating the area. If this technique - as often happens - offers quick results and people get enthusiastic, it's best to invite them to do it for three minutes twice a day but not for prolonged periods.

Warning: for all muscles on the back of the body the sequence is exactly the same as above. If, instead, we work a muscle on the front of the body (e.g. the forearm, pectoralis, etc.) the technique is the same, but the breathing phases are reversed: massage while breathing in and stop while breathing out. The only exception concerns the piriformis muscle (part of the buttock) that despite being behind, grafts in the front, and must therefore be treated in this way.
We have illustrated an execution that is totally physical, but, as you will easily experience, the relief is physical, mental and emotional too. It can also happen that during the performance you'll notice thoughts, emotions and memories emerging. In this case you simply have to invite them to flow and release them, the same way tension is being released from your body: to feel that they "lighten", move away, fade and so on.

Another psychosomatic release technique that is quite transversal and applicable to different body areas is the **Contraction in Reduction**. In this case you choose a sore point that can be 'pinched' between the thumb and index finger (using the middle finger can help). It typically works well with trapezoids due to their shape and position, but it can be performed on any muscle you can access.
Again, after placing your hand, you relax your body and find the most comfortable and easy position to hold the point with minimal effort. At this point there is an important step: you must somehow 'ease' the situation and reduce the nuisance. So, I find the point that, if pressed between the two fingers, hurts. I relax the body. I squeeze hard enough to feel the pain and try to make movements that change that feeling. For example, if I pinch the trapezoids I can tilt my head in different directions, if I pinch the forearm I can move my hand. The aim is to find a position (always comfortable) where the pain is at least slightly reduced. At this point you stop and tighten your grip on the point for 90 seconds, during which you breathe slowly and try not to contract any muscle at all. Usually about halfway through you begin to feel a softening of the tissues, which then increases as time passes. Also in

this case, the person is invited to release thoughts, imagination, memories and emotions in a similar way to what is happening to the body. You can also favour the process by looking for evocative images and sensations, such as imagining that between the fingers there is a piece of butter or ice that melts with the heat of your hand, a chain whose links widen, a string that frays or anything that helps the process and is a pleasant image.

Other psychosomatic release **techniques** focus on specific areas: the sacrum bone, the shoulder blades, the masseters, the temples, etc. These are mechanisms and details difficult to render in writing, so I invite you to visit the website and watch some demo videos: www.insciences.co.

ALLOSTATIC OVERLOAD

As we have seen, an organism facing stress reacts with a phenomenon called allostatic accommodation, i.e., it rearranges its physiological values on new levels that are suitable to react to those stimuli. If the change is occasional and short lived, the organism will return to physiology easily. If the required adaptation lasts a long time and is repeated often, the body will find it advantageous not to return to the previous physiological parameters, and it will take actions in a complex and systemic way to achieve a new balance that allows it to respond well to the new environment. This makes us understand how our functioning takes into account evolutionary aspects: if a change happens often, our system acknowledges that the environment has changed and we adapt. If we are often anxious, our body assumes that we have ended up in a hostile environment and does not consider that a dysfunctional change may have occurred, that we now predict that all the environments we go to are hostile, without making an accurate assessment each time (a mechanism behind different types of anxiety). That is why it will be important to act on personal awareness, on one's own resources, but also on environmental perception and - where it makes sense - on the environment itself.

The term allostatic load was coined to define the cost of this adaptation[4].

The term allostatic load was coined to define the cost of this adaptation. Adaptation may not be effective in several situations: under conditions of chronic stress, traumatic events, consecutive acute situations, false alarms due to misjudgement, etc. These are different situations that lead to non-flexible and non-reversible physiological changes, with short-term advantages but consequences for the whole organism in the medium and long term.

It is important to remember that allostatic load does not measure the objective weight of certain life conditions, but the consequences of those conditions. Elizabeth, for example, lived in economic, working and social conditions that would be considered extremely comfortable, if not dream-like, by many people. Yet, all her life she had lived in constant worry, thinking that anyone she met, even a waiter at a restaurant, judged her negatively or tried to cheat her.

Following and developing the language created by McEwen and Stellar we can say that to each *allostatic load* should, at least in principle, correspond some *allostatic discharges*, or a series of initiatives and tools aimed at giving flexibility to our system, allowing it to return to earlier physiology as soon as the modification is no longer necessary, while only keeping the really adaptive changes in the long run. If you cannot find a balance, the load becomes excessive and turns into *overload*.

The concept of *allostatic overload* is now widely accepted and developed within the scientific community and represents the flip side of adaptation, i.e., when the allostatic load becomes excessive and the damage becomes consistent on different mind-body levels.

When, in the allostatic attempt to achieve a new adaptation, the disadvantages outweigh the advantages and the situation is prolonged excessively, a structural (organ damage, neurotoxin overload, resistance to neurotransmitters, etc.) or functional (inability to tolerate further stress, motivational decline, unjustified maintenance of reparative or escape positions, etc.) price is paid[5].

In Mark's life the balance between advantages and disadvantages has always been negative. Mark is the typical good guy who is a little shy and who has not managed to have a significant (and probably not even insignificant) emotional relationship until the age of 52. At this age, through friends, he met Meredith, and he married her after 4 months of engagement. He wanted to take his time, but "she cared so much". He wanted to have a ceremony with a few friends, but "she really wanted to" have lots of guests. He would like to have sex, but "she's not interested". He can't listen to the music he likes, because "she doesn't like it". And so on. He wants to leave her and regain his freedom, but she has threatened suicide. Beyond the couple's interpersonal mechanisms and Mark's individual difficulties and dysfunctions, here, I am interested in emphasizing that he was in allostatic overload for years due to the social frustrations and limitations he experiences. This had brought on a series of symptoms united to a general process of premature aging involving damaged skin and hair, sarcopenia, prostate problems, etc. for which doctors could not provide an explanation other than a generic attribution to stress.

In recent months, despite his attempt to fulfil his dreams and redeem his life, the disadvantages have become even more relevant than the advantages acquired and - as a result – his mood and physical symptoms have drastically worsened, and tumour masses have appeared. For Mark it was fundamental to understand the mechanisms at the core of his physical and mental health to find the incentive to take back his life and take his own defences. We worked a lot with different release techniques to act on the points where he had accumulated tensions due to anger towards his wife and towards himself. From a neurobiological point of view, it was fundamental to activate all the interventions seen in switch 1 area in a practical way, while from a personal point of view, we worked a lot on his Ancestral Needs (area 4) and emotional postures (area 5).

This is one of the typical cases where a doctor with a traditional approach could only give relief to some physical symptoms but without having an overall perspective and integrating the concept of allostatic overload, could not identify and solve the common cause of all these symptoms. Conversely, even the best (individual or couple's) psychotherapist with a 'classic' approach could have achieved a series of advances, but without parallel work on physical aspects, the remission of the symptoms would have required a very long time and would always have only been partial (reverse metabolism and somatic memories altered by allostatic overload only through words and thought has strong limitations dictated by the very nature of these mechanisms).

Our tendency to get used to, and to bear discomfort, fatigue and suffering, especially if prolonged in time, is associated with alterations on all metabolic, neurobiological and immune processes seen so far and beyond. In the long run, allostatic overload leads to a reduction in the volume of grey matter and changes in cortical thickness[6], modifications of networks that process pain and interoceptive circuits that are fundamental for self-treatment regulation, the processing of emotions, the development of identity and social cognition[7].

Actively monitoring and managing the switch between raising the threshold (for adaptive advantages) and the establishment of rest and recovery mechanisms (to return to physiology), is a key mechanism to maintain development without paying a price.

TECHNIQUE: THE EMOTIONAL BUFFER

The term buffer indicates something that stands between two systems acting as a barrier to reduce extremely violent impacts, absorb shocks or filter. The buffer function is carried out, for example, by a shield that distributes the impact of an arrow on a harder surface than our skin, so we feel the impact, but it cannot hurt us. The buffer function can also be carried out, in a different way, by a syphon installed by the plumber, which on the one hand, prevents water from entering the boiler at too high a pressure and - on the other hand - acts as a reserve in the case of a shortage or a drop in pressure.

The Emotional Buffer technique, in its basic form, focuses on the possibility of giving a strong signal of Termination with respect to the stress processes and, consequently, allows short but effective moments of Regeneration (see the chapter on Integrative Functional Schemes to delve into this terminology). It can also be re-read as a mechanism that counteracts the phenomenon of allostatic load or remaining in states of alert, uncertainty or execution (see switch of the third group).

There are two particularly effective activities that give a strong signal to our system, so that it can 'realise' that it is no longer necessary to maintain a state of adaptation to stress and, on the other hand, promote the return to a state of body-mind physiology.

The first activity involves deep relaxation, that could be defined as *ancestral relaxation* characterized by a total muscle abandonment. It is what children and tired animals instinctively do, lie down and "let go" of every muscle. It is not a controlled relaxation, but an absence of control over each muscle.
The emotional buffer, therefore, cannot be introduced while sitting on a chair without a back or holding the phone to read the news. In these cases, some muscle is always contracted, while we need to relax all of them completely.
We can recreate the ideal conditions for the emotional buffer by lying on a fairly rigid mattress or on a carpet, on our stomach, with our arms outstretched, palms facing up.
This position must be maintained for at least 3/4 minutes, so that the biofeedback effects can be significant. During this time, it is important to breathe slowly and naturally and try not to think about problems or negative aspects. Since it can be difficult not to think, the advice is to focus on pleasant but not too exciting aspects, as the goal is to deactivate body and emotions (it is better to imagine being by the sea than cycling down a hill, as pleasant as it can be). Another strategy is to think about something neutral, for example by imagining a white screen and repeating the word "white" slowly.
Another way to introduce an emotional buffer, if there is no physical space to isolate and lie down, is through other stimulations aimed at restoring physiology to our organism. The basic idea is to apply the following to a stressful event, in moments of pause, then interrupting for a moment or trying not to think about the problem.

Based on what we have seen regarding our nervous functions and the close relationship between physiology and nature, it is easy to understand how all the stimuli that put the body and the perceptive system in motion are effective. Starting from these reflections and testing different hypotheses we have identified the most effective factors:
• Sensory stimulation: expose yourself to natural light; restore visual field depth, so, for the emotional buffer technique, it is not useful to relax while watching a computer or mobile phone, better to look around in open spaces; pay attention to and try to distinguish scents, sounds, etc.
• Regular asymmetric body movement. Not exercises like classic push-ups, it's better to walk or swim.
• Thinking of pleasure or play, even constructively like what we would like to eat that evening and how to cook it.

• Physical contact, from cuddling to massages, has a strong power to help us detach the mind from the problem and regenerate our ability to use the emotional buffer technique. If in the situation there is not a person with the necessary intimacy to ask for this type of support, self-contact is also effective and that can be socially explained through the relaxation of a contracted muscle. Obviously there are also other implications of physical contact on an emotional and relational level, but here we focus on this regenerative function.

The Emotional Buffer technique is very transversal, it immediately offers tangible results and can be easily applied to different situations. In fact, we carried out this kind of exercise with Anthony, Elizabeth and all the other cases we've seen so far. It is an easily and quickly understandable technique that does not require a lot of explanation, in terms of both its execution and the advantages for which it is recommended.

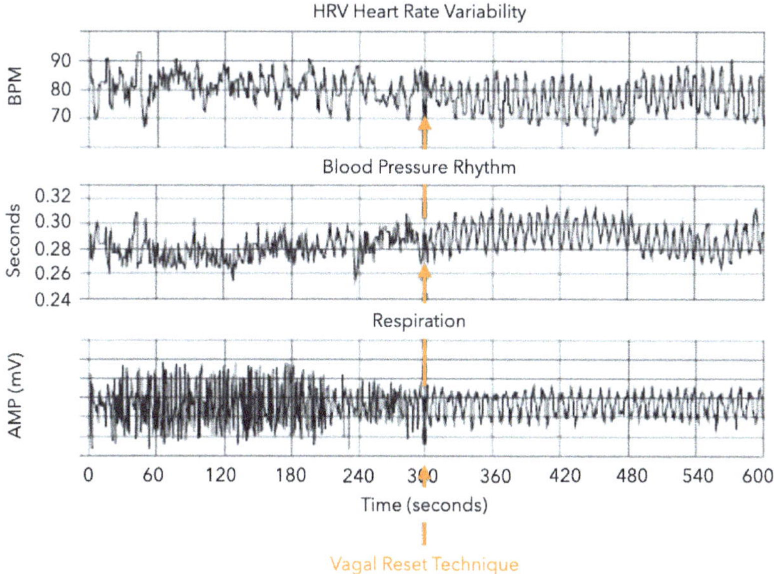

Fig. – In the case of someone who has been practising the Vagal Reset technique regularly for at least 3-4 weeks it is possible to notice significant changes in cardiac coherence, blood pressure and respiratory rhythm, right at the start. In the image a subject is being monitored first under standard conditions for 300 seconds, then while applying the Vagal Reset technique.

The Vagal Reset technique (see box below) represents a further level of depth and effectiveness compared to the Emotional Buffer one. It requires greater awareness and self-control, so it is usually best to propose it later on, when the person can successfully implement it.

After some practice, it becomes a very effective exercise, and can bring significant results in a short time both in terms of energy recovery and return to physiology.

TECHNIQUE: VAGAL RESET

The Vagal Reset technique, as the name suggests, is designed to reset the balance of stress and adaptation responses in physiology, counteracting allostatic-homeostatic imbalances and releasing energies blocked at the postural and/or emotional level, by overloading the principle of minimum free energy. From a technical point of view, this exercise acts on ortho-parasympathetic balance, with particular focus on the vagus nerve and all its implications in the emotional-body adaptation mechanisms, resetting any dysfunctional synergies or activation schemes that are no longer needed.

The ideal position to perform the technique is lying on your back, possibly on a mat or carpet, so as to be comfortable while maintaining a solid base that allows you to control the movements well.
The legs can be bent, with the knees tied together by a bandage or a scarf, so as to stay in that position without using the muscles. The feet (and knees) are not together, but hip-width apart. Alternatively, the legs can be crossed and opened, free to fall outwards. These measures are used to smooth the lumbar curve.

Two important details:
• There should be no contracted muscles. You need total abandonment to the ground, with the mouth slightly open and every muscle of the face relaxed;
• Once in position, the person is asked not to move anymore, not even for some adjustment or to scratch their nose, unless really necessary. One of the criteria of effectiveness of the technique is precisely the resetting of some signals (muscles that we try not to use, sensory receptors that are

deactivated after a constant signal, etc.), which becomes possible only without moving for a long time.

Breathing is initially divided into two phases:
• Inhaling is the only time you use the diaphragm and try to use only that muscle (it's not easy, but just trying causes interesting effects). Any other movements must be passive: the thorax widens due to the diaphragm movement, the viscera move downwards with the lengthening of the lungs, but all muscles other than the diaphragm are relaxed;
• Exhaling is passive. When the lungs are full of air you stop using the diaphragm that, like an elastic, will return to position; the air comes out passively and making a gentle sound; you do not blow and do not push the air out, otherwise you would activate neck and mouth muscles, as well as vocal cords.

This type of breathing, in its minimalist simplicity, can be difficult and initially give you tachycardia. It is normal, but we are no longer used to doing it (although we are recreating the most natural breath there is, clearly visible in all small children when they sleep). With time it will become the standard mode of breathing again, at least in quiet conditions.
After some practice it is possible to add a third respiratory phase. After the first two phases, the exhaling one is prolonged, in order to fully empty the lungs. To do this, you need to contract your core (the muscles typically known as "the abdominals", the so-called six-pack, visible in lean and trained people). This muscle normally serves to bend the body forward, to assume the foetal position for example. As we have positioned the body in this exercise, if the rectum of the abdomen is contracted isometrically, it 'flattens' and moves the sternum slightly downwards (both towards the floor and towards our pelvis). It thus helps us to completely empty the lungs and, moreover, acts as an antagonist to the movement of the diaphragm, allowing its return to physiology.

This breathing exercise should be carried out for 5-10 minutes a day, preferably several times a day.
After some practice it leads to a deep relaxation in a shorter time and, at the same time, to the recovery of energy (freed from psycho-bodily tension that was previously maintained without reason).
There are several variations and focuses to address specific body and emotional areas, also using eye movements or targeted tools to turn on/off

certain areas or topics of interest, work on body maps and other variants that need a guided practice and attention to fine details that would not be transmitted effectively in writing.

POSTURE, MUSCLES AND ALLOSTATIC LOAD

At the basis of any excessive muscle contraction there is always, even if at different degrees, a great emotional and mental component. There are at least 3 classic cases that stem from daily situations through to more extreme conditions.

1. In daily life, for instance, maintaining the same position for prolonged periods of time for work in front of a computer – or in other non-natural stances – causes a series of compensatory contractions and imbalances that are meant to reduce the strain, aches and pains that arise in these conditions. (i.e. the adaptation mechanisms that become allostatic load). Although stress levels may be relatively low, if a person usually experiences boredom, frustration, exhaustion and so forth, posture and muscle contractions are connected to these experiences and so is the mindset that accompanies them and the neurobiological changes connected to them. In these processes we also have to consider the connection with identity, self-image and interlinked body maps. These three elements are in turn connected in a two-way relationship with vitality, energy, motivation, feelings of agency or -by contrast- of impotence. We have just described the simplest and most basic level at which muscles, posture, mind and emotions influence each other (see the following chapters for further details at different levels).

2. At the extreme opposite, allostatic overload and inflammation have a stronger and more intense origin, although sometimes it is hidden in the past: we are talking about emotional and physical trauma. This covers an ample range of situations that range from car accidents, to physical violence and to abuse. However, we also must include less evident, but equally devastating situations such as psychological violence, emotional blackmail, emotional deprivation and stress. In all these instances the body becomes contracted, rigid and takes on

defensive postures that create an illusion of protection but are not actually effective. Instead, they create dysfunctional vicious circles in which mind, body and emotions constrict and impede each other.

3. In between daily dysfunctions and extreme trauma at the other end of the spectrum, we find a series of other situations that should not be taken for granted. These are for example the psychosomatic alterations caused by interpersonal dynamics such as antagonistic and challenging behaviour in social and work settings. The muscle groups involved, the postural alterations that take place and the neurological alterations are different from those that occur in instances relating to fear, stress or feeling of impotence as previously analysed.

WHERE TO START: WHAT TO PAY ATTENTION TO – 2 PRACTICAL MODES

As we mentioned earlier, each person corresponds to one of the above instances to a degree. However, very few people are aware of the impact of the mind-body relationship on these events.

This lack of awareness is in part due to cultural factors that do not lead us to nurture sensory and physical perception as a key element of our well-being, rather focusing on sacrificing the body in favour of cognitive efficiency and hyper-adaptation to external demands (social inhibition or professional performance, to name a couple of the most common ones).

A key process relates to habituation and threshold whereby our body begins to see a prolonged state as a starting point. We may lift a shoulder or use the computer mouse to reduce pain, or as a fear reaction. In both instances, when we lower the shoulder and lift it up again an hour later, we can still feel that that position is not natural. If we keep it lifted for hours each day, however, it will eventually get stuck there and we will start to consider it a normal position, even though it is not.

The conscious mind no longer considers it and focuses on its duty to remain productive on new and urgent issues, while the body remains conscious of the dysfunction and keeps a biofeedback relation to this unnatural pose open along with the adaptation processes that go with it (fear, strain, passiveness, depending on the personal experience relating to the initial condition). It therefore becomes critical to regain physiological order and solve this dysfunctional vicious circle.

It is particularly useful to start from a sensory and perception level to regain awareness of these processes. The feeling needs to have immediate impact and then lead to a more complex reworking higher up at mind level.

There are two routes to achieve this: *the first* starts with daily movements; asking the patient to bend down, to walk in longer strides or stretch a limb correctly. While this is carried out they should note whether the movements are fluid (depending on the area of the body), whether they feel pain or constrictions comparing the left and right side of the body carrying out the movement symmetrically, whether movements are isolated or rigid, and so forth.

The *second* option is an extension of the first. The first is in fact localised at perception level which critically needs to be reactivated. This option stems from the visual perception of these same processes, showing the people that we work with, via a video or a mirror, how they move, maybe comparing them with videos of other people in a physiological state because they are more sporty or less traumatised and so on. This way it is not a frustrating comparison but simply a perceptive starting point outside the self.

PSYCHOSOMATIC STRETCHING TECHNIQUE

This variation of Isometrics Emotions (see Switch nr. 5) is focused on the ability to relax and extend our contracted muscles after chronic stress, hyper-adaptation processes, traumatic events or other mind-body processes that have become dysfunctional.

These exercises are called Psychosomatic Stretching, but the name can be deceiving. Muscle extension represents only the starting point. The results are overarching on emotional memories, thought flows, body maps and identity. These processes return to physiological state even just by following the core version of the exercises in their original form, bearing in mind processes of reciprocal influencing among all the factors involved. We have also developed a series of variations and extensions to further increase these effects.

We will initially focus on the most common muscle groups and adaptation schemes, taking into account: 1- biomechanical adaptation processes; 2- the typical physical behaviour activated in all evolved mammals and therefore also in human beings as an innate response, activated below the level of consciousness in just a few milliseconds to form survival responses and - in rapid succession - development and recovery responses.

Finally, complex emotional-cognitive processes correct and amend the physical response via acquired patterns, compensations, desires, etc. In the same way, we will progressively move from grassroots following the natural sequence of adaptation across three phases.

The basic technique

The main principle of psychosomatic stretching is that traditional stretching techniques only have a temporary and localised effect. If, instead, we introduce some isometric pushes, followed by muscle stretches, we obtain a longer-lasting effect at muscle but also at postural memory, emotional experience and mental flow, level.

After these exercises it is in fact normal to feel freer, lighter, more powerful and in control depending on the specific muscle group worked on. Repeating the exercise over and over you can achieve long-lasting alterations and significant biofeedback in relation to safety circuits.

The process is similar to that of the traditional Isometric Emotions:
• push for 7-8 seconds exhaling,
• then release inhaling 8-10 seconds.
The significant variation is that in the release and inspiration phases I am also extending the muscle group I'm working on.

Let's go over a specific example among the many possible ones, focusing on arm thrusts upwards (the position of Superman when flying, but standing straight).

This type of movement can easily be carried out against the upper part of a doorway or any other solid element taller than us.

This is the basic movement:
  • a forward thrust (i.e., seen from the profile, hand forward from shoulder)
  • One in the middle (i.e., profile, hand in line with shoulder)
  • One in extension (i.e., profile, with the hand behind the shoulder)

From a muscular point of view, we are working on the front muscle chain of the shoulder, but we are also activating pectoral and abdominal muscles.

To be carried out correctly, this movement also requires appropriate activation of legs and hips.

Therefore, although this is an isolated and very precise movement, it still provides ample stimuli.

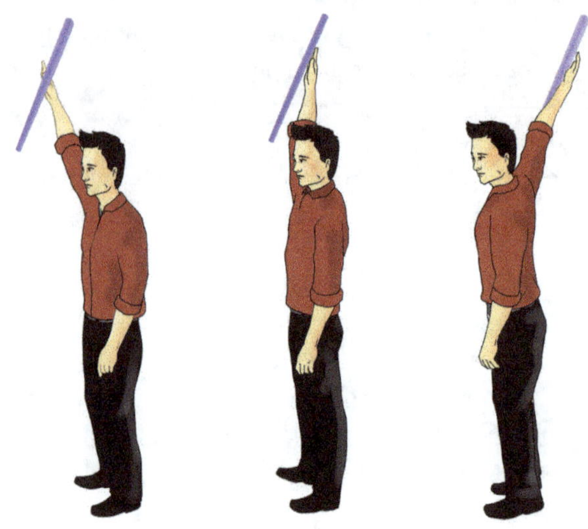

Fig. The three basic sequence's positions: forward, centre, extension.

When it comes to *biofeedback* specifically, this movement can help us activate the inversion of various schemas:

• Of the contraction in *posture* typically caused by a high stress load;

• Of the forward-movement by the dominant arm in circumstances of interpersonal *aggression* (where forward rotation and sliding of the shoulder can be noted);

• Of the physical *submission* response (that is identifiable by the sliding of the shoulder lower down and closure of the chest, ribs and stomach);

• Of direct or symbolic *grabbing* gestures where the contraction of the shoulder shapes a closed fist that grabs and rotates in order to maintain control or release otherwise explosive outbursts of anger.

From an *emotional point of view*, in addition to the biofeedback we have just analysed, this exercise also provides a strong opening up stimulus to the chest that provides a feeling of power, self-confidence and presence in the current situation.

It also favours a "facing" posture (see Switch nr. 4), or in other words the ability to face up to challenging or dangerous situations and people.

DIFFERENT DEGREES AND LEVELS OF PHYSICAL AND MENTAL SUFFERING

Pain, in the wider sense of physical, emotional or mental suffering, is an element that can help us better understand homeostatic and allostatic processes through its many facets and multi-system interrelations. Painful phenomena, although they represent different experiences, partially share the neural circuits and neurotransmitter cascades involved[8], and bring focus back onto the physical components of emotional pain both as cause (for example increased emotional vulnerability sustained by dysfunctional body maps and lack of physical mastery) and as consequence (such as in somatisation processes).

In conditions of extreme anxiety, the perceptive threshold lowers, causing us to feel very painful feelings even in relation to normally simply irritating or neutral stimuli. In these conditions a high-volume sound, touching a rough surface or perceiving a gesture of social exclusion that in normal circumstances would have been interpreted as appropriate to the context (due to being in a hurry, for example) can cause significant suffering.

PTSD sufferers typically display one of two exactly opposing features: hypersensitivity (any stimulus is unbearable be it physical, emotional or relational) or, at the other end of the spectrum, a numbing of sensory perception that leads to apathy and loss of sensitivity.

It is critical to recall that perception (internal or external) is the starting point for all processes at the heart of self-regulation, elaboration of emotions and social dynamics (We'll go into this in detail in the switch 3 section). A case in point is the way the behaviour of someone suffering from bad toothache alters: their priorities change, there is no room for long term planning, there is a loss of empathy and an increase in aggression. This type of change can alter any type of structure and function over time. Those suffering from chronic pain almost always show a de-regulation of the HPA axis[9].

The issue with stress and the liable border – between adaptation and motivation on one hand, and allostatic overload on the other – is therefore down to a system of switches whose regulation processes need to be monitored and actively managed in order to master them and not lose control.

MIND AND BODY JOINED IN INFLAMMATION

One of the most important clinical observations of recent decades, which clearly highlights the large areas of overlap between psychology and medicine, is that each patient diagnosed with different forms of *anxiety, stress, depression* or *PTSD* has an inflammatory immune profile which can easily be spotted through blood tests that is similar to that of patients who have recently been treated for common bacterial and viral infections, or for physical trauma[10].

Another interesting observation, which allows us to go a step further, is that this inflammatory state also coincides with the mechanisms noticed as a result of traumatic events and chronic stress, such as hyperactivation of certain areas of the brain (e.g. the amygdala, which thus amplifies fear responses and anxiety symptoms) and the dysfunction or reduction of other areas (such as the hippocampus, which in these conditions promotes typical symptoms such as loss of orientation, of memory, etc.).

Widening our perspective, it should be noted that in recent years pathologies and inflammatory profiles have also changed among the public. There are increasingly fewer acute inflammatory processes - due to physical trauma, injuries, infections of various kinds - thanks to the increasing levels of prevention and safety. On the other hand, states of chronic inflammation and so-called *non-resolving inflammation* are extremely widespread[11]. These are mainly to factors related to style and quality of life: no recovery time, chronic stress, poor personal and work satisfaction, sensory hyperstimulation, social isolation, emotional deprivation, incorrect nutrition, etc. Anthony, Hilary, Angelica and Elizabeth's cases, seen in the previous chapters, all displayed this though in different ways.

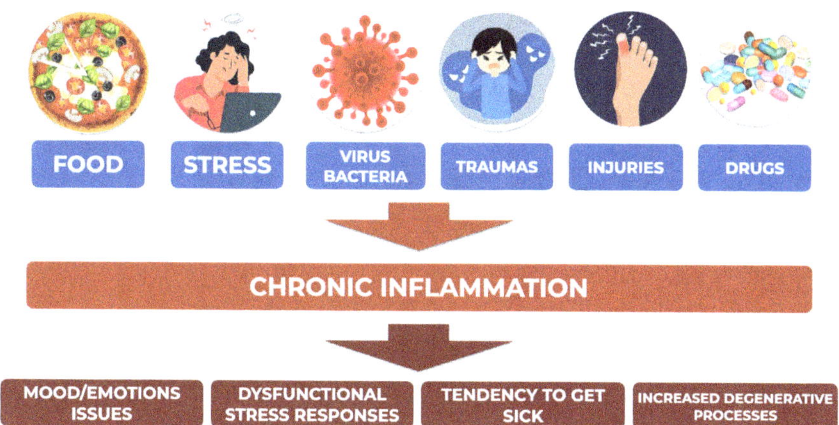

Fig. - Different aspects of daily life lead to chronic inflammation which, in turn, can cause or amplify different problems and pathologies.

Let's look at this from a different perspective. From a clinical point of view, an important discovery has been made in this area. The association of a basic anti-inflammatory product, such as common aspirin, with an antidepressant or with cognitive-behavioral psychotherapy, increases the remission of depression in patients previously not responsive to drug or psychotherapeutic treatment[12]. In other words, inflammation is one of the possible causes of resistance to change. This discovery distorts the approach to a vision of resistance to purely psychological (*secondary advantages, lack of will, etc.*) or biological change (*genetic limitations, familiarity, etc.*).

From a practical point of view, it is important to highlight that drugs are not the only anti-inflammatory tools, but there are also *dietary styles, aerobic physical activity, relaxation techniques, meditative practices, and other structured activities* **and** particularly effective *techniques*.

Joshua came to me after a few failed attempts at psychotherapy. His case was serious: two close-calls with death and an already present health problem that had further worsened during that period. In addition to a concern for his health, the symptoms were very disabling socially and at work: he had bouts of diarrhea several times a day, for weeks. His mood was very low without cause. He had already tried both individual and group psychotherapy. In this case it was useful to work in synergy with a doctor to implement a rapid anti-inflammatory treatment plan with targeted drugs and supplements. At the same time, we used several of the techniques and tricks illustrated in this book, and thanks to them the medical support lasted only three months and allowed us to start working at our best and, once that part ended, Joshua's body and mind were able to continue independently.

Anthony, whom we met in the previous chapter, had a long history of switching constantly between psychotropic medication (that he stopped taking after a while as they did not have the desired magical effect) and psychotherapy. When he came to me, consistently with this order, he was not taking any drugs and I thought it appropriate not to propose consulting a psychiatrist to consider reinstating them, because I evaluated that he could safely develop other lifestyle-based anti-inflammatory techniques, ways of thinking that allowed him to block stress responses, psycho-physical techniques for releasing tension and allostatic load and consuming anti-inflammatory foods.

WHAT IS INFLAMMATION?

Inflammation is - first and foremost, but not only - the physiological reaction of the immune system that is activated to heal injuries or to remove the presence of pathogenic microbes. As mentioned in the introduction, inflammation is an evolutionarily response to these issues, but today it is activated by and involved in many other mechanisms.

When we encounter an asthmatic patient, with symptoms such as dermatitis, vaginitis, chronic pain, headache, anxiety and many other widespread ailments, there is always an underlying state of chronic inflammation. It is, like all other aspects we are dealing with in this text, a two-way mechanism: inflammation can arise - for example - to combat a virus, or due to drug abuse, disrupted sleep-wake rhythms, an excess of sport-related activities, and in turn lead to states of anxiety, moods, etc. On the other hand, physical and emotional trauma, prolonged stress, overwhelming emotional experiences can activate the immune system. The immune and nervous-psychological system are linked on several levels. To understand them we need to start from the biological level and gradually integrate all the other aspects.

As anticipated, from an evolutionary perspective everything stems from the body's physiological response to heal wounds, injuries and to fight viruses and bacteria. To do so, inflammation aims to eliminate the initial cause of cell injury and repair (or eliminate) damaged cells and tissues.

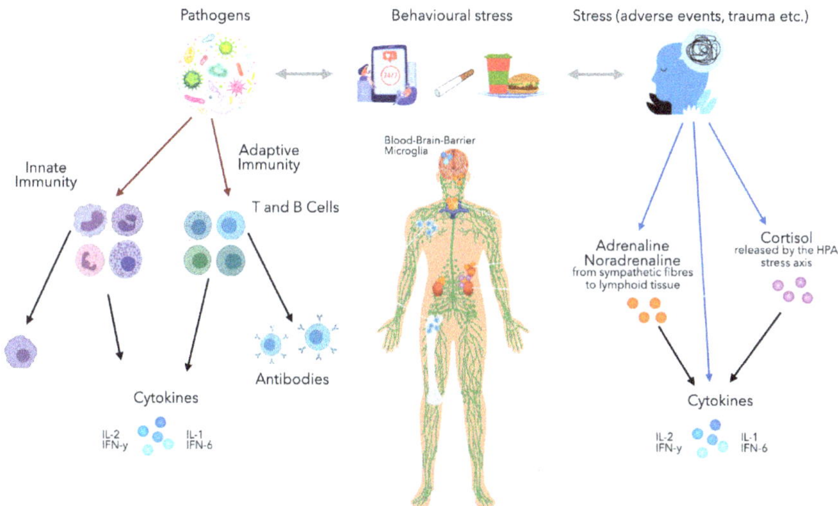

Fig. - Schematic representation of how pathogens (viruses, bacteria, etc.) and stressful mental-emotional events (adverse events, trauma, chronic stress, etc.) both activate immune responses that, in large part, overlap and influence each other. Some compensatory behaviors (smoking, eating junk food, cell phone abuse, *binge-watching*, etc.), used to deal with daily stress, actually activate mechanisms similar to pathogenic ones (and are in fact often 'toxic' elements from a biological point of view) and mental ones (because they are behaviors that temporarily solve a problem and then create another).

This process begins when the body releases cytokines (protein molecules that act as communication signals between the immune system cells and different organs and tissues) that act as emergency signals, bringing nutrients, hormones and immune cells to the site of injury. To facilitate this process, the arteries dilate and the capillaries become more permeable to allow the cells assigned to "repair" to access the injured area. From there, the cells of the immune system do their job until the problem is solved. This mechanism saves our lives, but at the same time it involves a temporary increase in consumption of resources. This becomes even more relevant when the inflammation becomes chronic, that is when the inflammatory process never reaches a final phase, i.e. it does not go into *Termination*, following the cycle of the Integrative Functional Schemes (see the relative chapter).

Elizabeth's tendency to see one problem after another and consider every person she encountered as a possible obstacle to be fought, never allowed her to let her guard down, relax and think about herself and her true well-being.

Hilary, however, was driven by duty and by the desire to be loved by her colleagues, and never rested her body or her mind (i.e., she never went into Termination), thus reaching the point of never being able to regenerate energy and be as efficient as she wanted.

This is a typical issue for professionals, but it is also found in hyper-caring parents: they all go to the extreme, to give their all they put themselves in a position where they are unable to make it anymore due to exhaustion or because they come to pay too high a price (heart attack, cancer, degenerative diseases, etc.) which forces them to stop. To add insult to injury, when these people stop they finally have time to realize that they have done everything for others and/ or for an ideal goal but it has been all useless: colleagues or loved ones are not grateful (at least not as much as they would have liked) and now – after a lesson learned at a high price - they no longer have the conditions to care for themselves and enjoy life.

WHAT ACTIVATES OR AMPLIFIES INFLAMMATION

Most inflammatory diseases begin in the intestine, with a reaction of the immune system that triggers the inflammatory response. The intestine consists of an extremely large and intricate semi-permeable lining. Its degree of permeability (see below) varies in response to a variety of chemically mediated conditions. For example, when cortisol is elevated due to prolonged negative emotions (such as a heated argument or conflict), intense stress or trauma, or when excessive amounts of inflammatory food, such as sugars or trans fats, are introduced, the intestinal lining immediately becomes more permeable.

Even an incorrect posture, often supported by haste and tension, as well as a thoughts that are continuously focused on negative issues, favor the development of inflammatory states in the long run (we will delve into these aspects in the area 5 switches).

Other common causes of inflammation are: drugs (corticosteroids, antibiotics, antacids, and many others); hormonal dysregulation (thyroid hormones, progesterone, estradiol, testosterone, etc.); infections (viral or parasitic infection, yeast or bacterial proliferation); trauma and physical injury; endocrine disrupters (contained, inter alia, in detergents, soaps and other common products commonly, but also in industrial foods); smoking and alcohol excess.

Hilary's case is one of these: her rigid posture stems from the rigid education she received, both in an old-fashioned nuns' school, and growing up in a family that was very focused on formality and appearances. This posture has played a crucial role, both as a cause and as an effect, creating rigid negative thoughts and high-level inflammatory states. In addition to this, her life had been dotted with additional factors that constantly amplified this inflammation: she was a smoker; to save money she used low-quality cleaning products; she washed dishes without gloves; she took daily medications to relieve headaches. Thoroughly explaining the central role of these mechanisms was the first fundamental step to give her a direction and some new certainties to make new choices and set new habits. These aspects, together with the work on posture with the Psychosomatic Stretching technique and some of the area 3 techniques, were the central points to start her path of change.

Let's proceed on our journey by further exploring some important aspects. We will start from the inside, from the crucial role of our intestine, so important as to be called the 'second brain' and to justify expressions such as 'having butterflies in the stomach' to refer to strong emotions or 'follow your gut' (gut=intestine). The centrality of the intestine will lead us towards some nutritional indications to then continue our analysis also on emotional, mental and physical aspects (this time in a more musculoskeletal sense).

THE SECOND BRAIN: THE GUT AND THE IMMUNE SYSTEM

The intestine is widely referred to as the "second brain". This is because its number of innervations is second only to the brain's and it has a significant functional autonomy compared to the brain itself. It also communicates directly (without mediation of the nervous system) with the immune and endocrine systems. The nerve and lymphatic networks lie over each other in the tissue of the small intestine (in the submucosal tunica to be precise).

Therefore, our digestive system represents a system that receives input both from the outside (food), and from the inside (nervous system, especially related to emotions, stress and other adaptation mechanisms) and which processes output on all mind-body levels.

Today, it is well known and demonstrated that the brain and intestines are in direct contact in various ways. In this connection a key role is played by the vagus nerve, which allows a two-way communication between the brain and the intestine. This connection clarifies how phenomena such as stress and negative emotions can significantly damage the production of enzymes that are useful for digestion or cause intestinal disorders that directly affect stress responses.

The intestine, also called the second brain for exactly this reason, has a real autonomous nervous network with a higher number of neurons than the spinal cord. More generally, the whole gastro-intestinal system plays a fundamental role in the health of our body and brain. Let us consider the case of serotonin, the so-called happiness hormone: 95% of serotonin is produced in the intestine and is used to initiate the peristaltic reflex and to regulate movements and digestive activity. Intestinal inflammation activates the enzyme that breaks down this hormone. Consequently, a damaged intestine will produce less serotonin. There are many other substances (peptides) that are produced both by the first and second brain with different functions (for example acetylcholine, ghrelin, opioids, etc.) and it is therefore evident that the communication between the two systems is very close, much more than we have been used to thinking.

Numerous research papers have now shown that a damaged intestine can directly affect mood, stress, depression, lack of motivation, phobias, obsessions, bulimia, memory and concentration disorders, sleep disorders, nervousness, panic, tendency to addictions, but also lead to autoimmune diseases, chronic inflammation and various pathologies, even serious ones. The incorrect digestion of food, the intake of refined or fatty foods, the abuse of medicines, states of prolonged stress, lack of physical activity, are all factors that can cause inflammation in the intestine and drastically compromise bacterial flora and, consequently, the proper functioning of the intestine and the immune system.

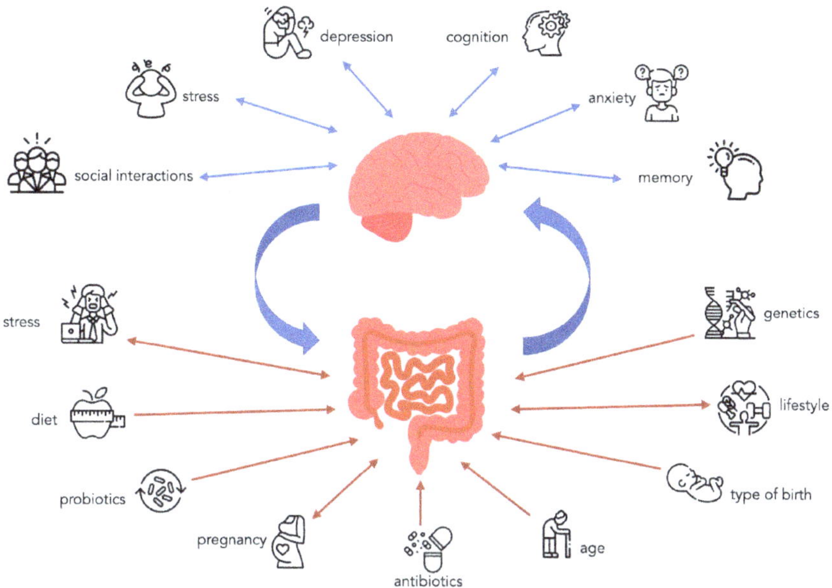

Fig. - Different causes can lead to intestinal health alterations (leaky gut, inflammation, microbiome, etc.) which in turn, through the intestine-brain axis, significantly influence various mental, emotional, behavioral and relational aspects. Acting on the health of the intestine and on the quality of the intestinal microbiome represents an excellent complementary activity to enhance the effectiveness of psychotherapeutic, educational or rehabilitative interventions.

The immune system includes several barriers. One of the *first* barriers is the intestinal microbiome, also known as bacterial flora, i.e. the set of bacteria and microorganisms that live in the mucous membranes of the whole body and in particular in the digestive tract and in the intestine. The microbiome plays a crucial role in immune defense by producing a series of fundamental substances (such as short-chain fatty acids) that regulate homeostasis and defense against pathogens.

The intestinal mucosa acts as a *second* barrier, a single layer of epithelial cells that separates the intestinal lumen harboring bacterial flora from the intestinal epithelium. The mucus prevents large particles from contacting the epithelial cell layer while allowing small molecules to pass through.

A *third* barrier is the intestinal epithelium, a layer of epithelial cells lining the intestine which, in addition to providing a protective function, controls nutrients and substance absorption.

Below all these layers we find the real immune system, composed of a series of cells responsible for the defence of the body. When the layers preceding the immune system are damaged, any substance – pathogenic or non-pathogenic – can cross the barrier, activating the immune system and triggering the inflammatory response.

In these conditions (known as dysbiosis or leaky gut), in fact, not only viruses and bacteria have the opportunity to pass through the intestine, but also many other substances normally considered harmless such as gluten, lactose, or substances produced by body in response to stress or trauma (such as the catecholamines, adrenaline, noradrenaline, dopamine), triggering an inflammatory response. In other words, today we know that a chronic inflammatory processes can also be induced by psychological trauma, the environment, stress, or nutrition.

When the intestine is damaged, the body responds with an inflammatory process which, if not resolved, can become chronic and, over time, can lead to a series of symptoms that can range from allergic reactions to more serious diseases such as cancer.

Michael and Juliette are two siblings. He is 10 years old, thin, very active and reactive, and has been diagnosed with ADHD. She is 12 years old, a little overweight and always a little more emotional than required by the situation. Apparently they are two very different cases, but they have antibiotics and medication abuse as children in common and share a wide range of intolerances and allergies. In this case it was essential to explain the link between the state of the intestine and the different symptoms (to both children and parents). We advised them to repair the intestinal mucosa with aloe arborescens, vitamin D3 and, subsequently, to repopulate the microbiome. This improved the overall immune system, reduced the extent of intolerances and allergies, and improved mood and emotional stability for both children. In respect to this example, we must once again remind ourselves that the approach we present is integrated and integrative, magically changing a dysfunctional family or solving individual symptoms with multi-factorial origins is not enough to fix the intestine. On the other hand, it should be remembered that this step promotes a physiological state that creates the optimal preconditions for other targeted work. With *targeted preconditions*, in this specific case, we mean removing or reducing the state of chronic pain and discomfort related to intestinal problems (tension, constipation, diarrhea, etc.); counteracting immune inflammation, consequently reducing imbalances that lead to disabling symptoms such as asthma, allergies, etc.; reducing neural hyper-excitation and removing energy from inflammatory and allostatic processes, allowing the brain be 'calm' and have energy for cognitive processes, i.e. eliminating the factors that kept the symptoms of attention deficit active. We will come back to this family again later, to explain the work carried out on other aspects, which are just as important.

FOOD AND INFLAMMATION: WHAT TO EAT AND WHAT TO AVOID

Nutrition plays a central role in chronic inflammatory processes. The abundance of cheap and low-quality food that we find in supermarkets favors many negative metabolic processes for the human body.

It is good to remember that we are not talking only about quality but also about quantity. In fact, overeating both in terms of quantity and frequency of meals is not conducive to health, regardless of the quality of the meal.

Among the foods that can *lead to dysbiosis, leaky-gut and trigger inflammatory processes* we find:

- *Sweets and sugary drinks*, i.e. foods such as candies, fizzy drinks, sweets, juices, snacks, etc. that contain high amounts of fructose. Fructose digestion produces byproducts that are toxic to the body, such as uric acid which leads to inflammation, endothelium damage, hypertension, gout, and so on.
- *Vegetable oils*, including cooking oils such as soybean, corn, sunflower, palm, etc., which are rich in omega-6s. An excessive amount of Omega 6 can trigger the inflammatory response with the production of prostaglandins, leukotrienes, thromboxane.
- *Trans fats and fried foods*, i.e. chips, fish sticks and onion rings that we typically find in fast food restaurants and are often cooked in vegetable oils and are high in trans fats.
- *Refined carbohydrates*, such as bread, pasta, pizza, focaccia, crackers, breadsticks and all flours, if in excess, can favor an inflammatory process. Additionally, research has recently shown that wheat contains specific proteins called amylase-trypsin inhibitors (ATIs) that may

trigger inflammation related to chronic diseases such as multiple sclerosis, asthma and rheumatoid arthritis.
- *Foods rich in MSG and aspartame.* In fact, an excessive consumption of MSG and aspartame favors chronic inflammation and all the pathologies related to it. MSG is also capable of overexciting cells, causing various level of brain damage and triggering or worsening learning difficulties, attention deficits, sleep disorders, etc.
- *Industrial and highly processed foods.*

In cases like the Juliette and Michael's, we often meet professionals who remove gluten and dairy products, because they are the direct object of intolerance or, in any case, considered trigger factors for a specific allergy or reaction (for example dermatitis or abdominal swelling). This consideration is correct, but broadening the perspective - in line with what we are evaluating in this chapter - we can say that certain foods are factors that trigger inflammatory responses. In fact, this is why removing them offers relief. By analogy it is like saying that by not constantly touching a wound, it does not hurt, but this does not necessarily change the situation in which the wound was originally developed. It may therefore be useful to remove the food that triggers the problem, but we need to work on inflammation and all its causes globally, so that in the future, in the vast majority of cases, it will be possible to eat that food again, without triggering the immune response.

On the other hand it will be useful to:
• Increase the intake of *Omega 3-rich foods* such as blue fish, *grass-fed beef* or *free-range* eggs.
• Increase the intake of *quality fats,* such as butter, eggs, fatty fish such as salmon, fatty and aged cheeses, cream, dark chocolate, dried fruit, etc.
• Increase the intake of *fiber-rich vegetables* that contribute to the intestinal microbiome's wellbeing.
• And, after adequate preparation, introduce periods of *intermittent fasting* which are very useful for reducing inflammatory processes and promoting the recovery of physiology.

THE POWER OF THE MICROBIOME ON MOOD, BEHAVIOUR AND HEALTH

The bacteria inside the body form the microbiome. We cannot live without it: animals that have been deprived of microbiomes in the laboratory, and are therefore called 'germ-free', die almost immediately. This happens because we are not dealing with parasites or visitors, but organisms that have evolved with us over the centuries and to which we have delegated certain metabolic functions. Without them we are unable to carry out certain digestive or immune system functions.

If we are healthy, the microbiome, and specifically the intestinal microbiome is rich and varied, mostly populated by 'good' bacteria (in a state of eubiosis) and carries out its functions maintaining systems in balance. If we are in conditions of dysbiosis (too few and mostly dysfunctional bacteria), metabolic and immune processes cannot take place correctly and end up cascade-influencing a series of other phenomena according to the Functional Hierarchies principles.

Interesting confirmation for this effect has been provided by the results of transplants in animals and humans; swapping the microbiome of an obese person with that of a normal eater, for example, immediately changes their relationship with food and they are no longer as voracious as they were.

Experiments have also been made relating to attachment style. The microbiomes of two mice, mothers with litters, where one was very nurturing, and the other neglecting, were swapped. Their nurture style changed as a result: the mother that had neglected her offspring started to nurture them and, vice versa, the one that had nurtured them started to neglect them.

Microbiome transplant, however, does not represent a solution as its effect is short lasting and genetic expression and re-colonisation of bacteria occasion a return to initial conditions within just a few days. Nevertheless, this research highlights the power of the gut microbiome not just over our health, but on behaviour such as appetite and attachment that had previously been regarded exclusively as the result of genetics, education, implicit learning and neurobiology.

In order to return the microbiome to physiological state and reactivate this switch to our benefit it is critical to understand what improves and what damages its conditions. A wide spectrum antibiotic taken for five days damages the microbiome to such an extent that, if no proactive intervention to re-integrate it is made, it takes two years to recover completely. Avoiding antibiotic abuse is therefore a critical point. By contrast it is possible to favour a state of eubiosis with a varied diet, reducing sugar intake (which typically feed 'bad' bacteria and influence the hyperactivation of safety circuits in the brain) and increasing intake of fibre.

It is not just nutrition that favours eubiosis, but also physical activity, relaxation of the intestinal area (through yoga or even osteopathy), any activity that regularises or stabilises the functioning of the vagus nerve (that connects the cranial brain and the enteric brain, or in other words the gut), meditation, relaxation, stress-free concentration (ranging from playing chess to friction climbing).

THE EMOTIONS-TRAUMA-INFLAMMATION CONNECTION

We have seen that the intestine and, consequently, nutrition play a central role. There are also other ways in which an inflammatory state can be created and sustained.

Several studies[13] have been carried out to fully understand these phenomena and all agree on the fact that two mechanisms occur: one that i easily predictable, the other less intuitive. The *first* concerns the activation of the well-known fight-flight reaction characterized by an increased heart rate, blood pressure, cortisol and catecholamines, as well as a series of other processes that we do not need to go into further now (we will go back to them later in the book). The *second* mechanism activates relevant inflammatory pathways in peripheral blood cells, including activation of nuclear transcription factor (NF-kB) and leads to marked increases in circulating pro-inflammatory cytokines, including interleukin-6 (IL-6).

But that is not all. There are also significant correlations between this inflammatory response and other factors. For example, subjects exposed to early childhood trauma (in the broad sense of ACEs, or Adverse Childhood Experiences) display a higher inflammatory response in tests monitoring performance under stress.

For example, Elizabeth had apparently lived in a perfect family: the father was a successful entrepreneur but also a loving man, the mother devoted to her children trying to teach them humility, despite their status. The problem is that, despite the affection, her father was not at home for long periods of time (even months) during Elizabeth's childhood. The mother, who later emerged to have had her own trauma, alternated firmness with coldness (Elizabeth does not remember a caress from her mother, not even when she was hurt, but rather lessons on morality and virtue that turned into prohibitions during adolescence). This example emphasizes the fact that adverse childhood experiences are not necessarily blatant, such as having lived in an orphanage or having been abused, but can be hidden in many people's lives, leading to inflammatory states that are otherwise unexplained. In fact, many of these cases of hidden ACEs live in comfort, have satisfactions, eat well and play sports, yet their inflammatory levels are very high.

Looking at things in prospective terms, instead, it has been observed that people who show a higher inflammatory response to psychosocial stress have a significantly higher risk of developing depression in the following months[14], as in the case of Anthony and Joshua.

Furthermore, inflammation favours emotional hyper-reactivity in general and alters cognitive processes as well as motivational ones,[15] as in the case of Hilary.

We have given examples of negatively influencing each other but, fortunately, there is also a mutually supportive relationship between emotional and immune responses. For example, T cells may play a protective role against stress and depression, favouring the proper functioning of cytokines, a change in microglia, neurogenesis in the hippocampus. Similarly the cytokines underlying immune responses may have a relevant impact on the monoamines serotonin, norepinephrine and dopamine underlying mood regulation[16]. These are just a few examples of how these paths can create virtuous circles which, to date, cannot be excluded from any therapeutic, educational or developmental approach.

All these processes also act at an epigenetic level. Inflammation can carry epigenetic markings capable of amplifying depressive or anxious responses in the face of psychosocial stress. Evidence of this bidirectional correlation between stress and the immune system at epigenetic level is the important discovery that childhood trauma is associated with increased inflammation through stress-induced epigenetic change in FKBP5, a gene implicated in the development of depression and anxiety, as well as in glucocorticoid sensitivity[17].

DEPRESSION OR SICKNESS BEHAVIOUR?

One thoroughly analysed example of the connection between mood and inflammation relates to the overlap between the diagnosis for depression and so-called Sickness Behaviour. This term is in fact used to describe the patient's typical behaviour: low energy levels, weakened muscular tone, lack of investment in the future, negative outlook etc. In people with depression, even those without diagnosed pathologies, biomarkers for inflammation are significatively higher compared to non-depressed people. It is even more interesting to look at the cause-effect relationship at a clinical level. When Interferon alpha is used (a standard treatment for chronic hepatitis and some types of cancer) the drug typically tends to induce states of depression in 20–25% of patients that showed no sign of depression prior to taking this medication[18].

In psoriasis patients taking TNF-α antagonist medication, a significant improvement in mood was noted independently to the evolution of the disease[19]. In other words, mood improved in spite of symptoms not improving and, therefore, could not be explained as a strictly cognitive process.

These bottom-up inflammation processes literally extend local inflammation to central level, sustaining states that are typically described in literature regarding trauma or chronic stress of the hyperactive amygdala, hyper-responsive empathetic resonance circuits, reduced hippocampus etc. (see brain-networks in the following section). These *bottom-up* inflammation processes literally extend local inflammation to central level, sustaining states that are typically described in literature regarding trauma or chronic stress of the hyperactive amygdala, hyper-responsive empathetic resonance circuits, reduced hippocampus etc. (see brain-networks in the following section).

Louis's story is a typical example of these processes. He is a tall 52-year-old man who arrives in a very smart suit, even though he seems uncomfortable in it. I will find out shortly that he wears it because he works in a financial company, where that is the standard attire. However, paradoxically, there are traces of this formality even in areas where he could act freely: in his ways of doing things, in the type of gym bag he carries around (and which, I check, he doesn't take to work, where anyone would see it). These first indications point in the direction of over-adaptation. As he later recounts, his life has been devoted to doing what others expected of him (father, ex-wife, colleagues, etc.) "until I wore myself out", he says with great awareness. All this points to a high allostatic load, so high as to become overloaded and give shape to different somatizations through all the mechanisms previously seen. Now focusing on inflammatory aspects, his symptoms immediately catch the eye: he has severe dermatitis on his head and deforming arthritis in the knuckles of his fingers. Perfectly in line with the research and mechanisms we have just seen, he tells us that he is amazed at how his dermatitis had not improved with drug therapy, but his mood did!

In this case we immediately focused on reducing the inflammatory state, both considering the disabling symptoms and because these intense symptoms reveal very high levels of inflammation. In fact, the body puts all its energies and gives the highest priority to managing this inflammatory state, leaving no free resources for changes on a mental, identity or emotional level. Furthermore, high levels of inflammation coincide with hyper-reactivity of the entire perceptual and sensory system. Just think of when we have a wound: we feel a lot of pain just touching it. Just imagining (or, better, predicting) pain is enough. Just thinking that someone is touching us, the pain pathways are activated. The fascinating thing, albeit to our disadvantage, is that from the point of view of the nerve pathways, the circuits of physical and mental pain are almost superimposed with each other and with the interoceptive circuits. As we know, pain wins over other stimuli, activating defensive mechanisms to the detriment of developmental ones, both from a physical and mental point of view. Similarly, interoceptive pathways (see Switch 3) are essential for self-regulation and emotional responses, but they must be able to work freely, without interference. This basically means that to help Louis, and all those in similar conditions, it is essential to reduce inflammation in order to create the mental and emotional space in which to act and change things. In this case we immediately introduced the Emotional Buffer technique to be repeated 2-3 times a day to interrupt the continuous state of activation to which Louis is subjected. We introduced a highly anti-inflammatory nutritional regimen, light physical activity (because intense would be further inflammatory for him at this stage), regulated circadian rhythms (switch 1), used the psychosomatic points release technique to release tension in the body and emotional memories, and took simple but basic precautions, such as avoiding superfluous triggers (switch 3).

In light of all this information, the relevance of implementing a switch from an excessively inflammatory profile towards immune system physiology is evident. The treatment of anxiety, stress, depression and PTSD through mental techniques, from meditation to psychotherapy, reduces the state of inflammatory activation through a top-down approach. In line with what was seen in the group of previous switches, reducing inflammation from the beginning and starting directly from the body (therefore bottom-up) increases the effectiveness of psychotherapeutic interventions and even helps to overcome resistance to treatment. The two routes, from above and below, are not mutually exclusive, but must be synergistic and used according to a clear plan.

Among other things, it is important to underline that inflammatory processes, if normalized correctly, yield advantages on several levels: they reduce the phenomena of pain amplification (both physical and mental) and sensitization; they facilitate the reduction of hyper-arousal phenomena and the engagement of alert networks (see next chapter); bring the calcium cascades and NMDA receptors back into physiology in memorization and learning processes; and other processes as well.

We looked at various ways to reduce inflammation. Some clarifications and other methods could be: physical movement and nutrition measures as already seen in this and in the previous chapter; the use of *natural anti-inflammatories* (such as turmeric, ginger, etc.); reducing inflammation in the intestine (Aloe Arborescens in particular is very effective, provided that it is in the formulation in which all leaves are used - not only pulp and juice - but also bone broth and other natural products); bringing *bacterial flora back into physiology* (see box-out on the microbiome) through prebiotics and probiotics; with *well-targeted supplements* (e.g. vitamin D3, Omega 3, Micellar Turmeric, etc.); *avoiding overload* and increasing recovery times and the efficiency of adaptation systems, favouring *termination signals* with the correct *modulation* of emotional and behavioural responses (see subsequent switch areas and the Integrative Functional Schemas in the relative chapter).

REFERENCES

[1] Matteoli, G., Gomez-Pinilla, P. J., Nemethova, A., Di Giovangiulio, M., Cailotto, C., van Bree, S. H., Michel, K., Tracey, K. J., Schemann, M., Boesmans, W., Vanden Berghe, P., & Boeckxstaens, G. E. (2014). A distinct vagal anti-inflammatory pathway modulates intestinal muscularis resident macrophages independent of the spleen. Gut, 63(6), 938–948.

[2] Cannon, W. B. (1932). The wisdom of the body. W W Norton & Co.

[3] McEwen, B. S., & Wingfield, J. C. (2010). What is in a name? Integrating homeostasis, allostasis and stress. Hormones and behavior, 57(2), 105–111

[4] McEwen, B. S., & Stellar, E. (1993). Stress and the individual. Mechanisms leading to disease. Archives of internal medicine, 153(18), 2093–2101.

[5] Juster, R.P., McEwen, B.S., Lupien, S.J. (2010). Allostatic load biomarkers of chronic stress and impact on health and cognition. Neuroscience & Biobehavioral Reviews, 35(1):2–16.

[6] Baliki, M. N., Schnitzer, T. J., Bauer, W. R., & Apkarian, A. V. (2011). Brain morphological signatures for chronic pain. PloS one, 6(10), e26010.

[7] Maleki N, Gollub RL (2016) What Have We Learned From Brain Functional Connectivity Studies in Migraine Headache? Headache 56(3):453-61. doi: 10.1111/head.12756

[8] Meyer, M. L., Williams, K. D., & Eisenberger, N. I. (2015). Why Social Pain Can Live on: Different Neural Mechanisms Are Associated with Reliving Social and Physical Pain. PLoS ONE, 10(6), e0128294.

[9] McEwen, B. S., & Kalia, M. (2010). The role of corticosteroids and stress in chronic pain conditions. Metabolism: clinical and experimental, 59 Suppl 1, S9–S15.

[10] Michopoulos, V., Powers, A., Gillespie, C. F., Ressler, K. J., & Jovanovic, T. (2017). Inflammation in Fear- and Anxiety-Based Disorders: PTSD, GAD, and Beyond. Neuropsychopharmacology, 42(1), 254–270.

[11] Kowalski EJA, Li L. Toll-Interacting Protein in Resolving and Non-Resolving Inflammation. Front in Immunol. 2017;8:511.

[12] Mendlewicz, J., Kriwin, P., Oswald, P., Souery, D., Alboni, S., & Brunello, N. (2006). Shortened onset of action of antidepressants in major depression using acetylsalicylic acid augmentation: a pilot open-label study. International clinical psychopharmacology, 21(4), 227–231.

[13] Pace, T. W. et al. Increased stress-induced inflammatory responses in male patients with major depression and increased early life stress. Am. J. Psychiatry 163, 1630–1633 (2006).

[14] Aschbacher, K. et al. Maintenance of a positive outlook during acute stress protects against pro-inflammatory reactivity and future depressive symptoms. Brain Behav. Immun. 26, 346–352 (2012).

[15] Beauchaine, T. (2001). Vagal tone, development, and Gray's motivational theory: toward an integrated model of autonomic nervous system functioning in psychopathology. Dev. Psychopathol. 13, 183–214.

[16] - D'Mello, C., Le, T. & Swain, M. G. Cerebral microglia recruit monocytes into the brain in response to tumor necrosis factor-α signaling during peripheral organ inflammation. J. Neurosci. 29, 2089–2102 (2009).
- Maes, M., Leonard, B. E., Myint, A. M., Kubera, M. & Verkerk, R. The new '5-HT' hypothesis of depression: cell-mediated immune activation induces indoleamine 2,3-dioxygenase, which leads to lower plasma tryptophan and an increased synthesis of detrimental tryptophan catabolites (TRYCATs), both of which contribute to the onset of depression. Prog. Neuropsychopharmacol. Biol. Psychiatry 35, 702–721 (2011).
[17] Klengel, T. et al. Allele-specific FKBP5 DNA demethylation mediates gene-childhood trauma interactions. Nat. Neurosci. 16, 33–41 (2013).
[18] Musselman, D. L., Lawson, D. H., Gumnick, J. F., Manatunga, A. K., Penna, S., Goodkin, R. S., Greiner, K., Nemeroff, C. B., & Miller, A. H. (2001). Paroxetine for the prevention of depression induced by high-dose interferon alfa. The New England journal of medicine, 344(13), 961–966.
[19] Tyring, S., Gottlieb, A., Papp, K., Gordon, K., Leonardi, C., Wang, A., Lalla, D., Woolley, M., Jahreis, A., Zitnik, R., Cella, D., & Krishnan, R. (2006). Etanercept and clinical outcomes, fatigue, and depression in psoriasis: double-blind placebo-controlled randomised phase III trial. Lancet (London, England), 367(9504), 29–35.

SWITCH GROUP N. 3 ADAPTATION – RADAR AND COMPUTER TO MANAGE COMPLEXITY

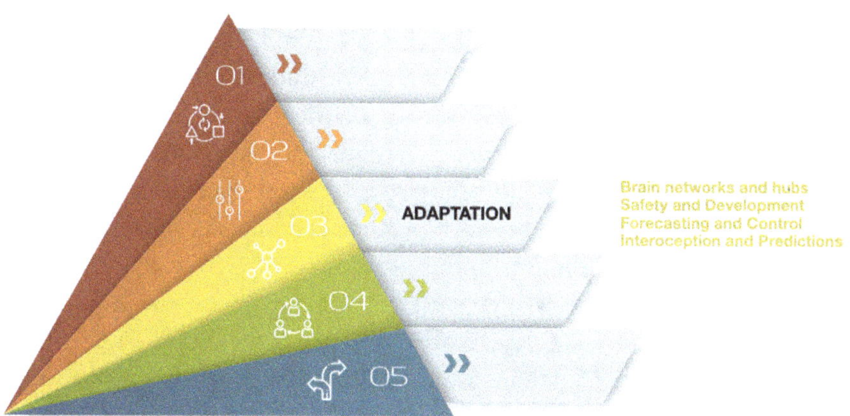

NETWORKS & HUBS: CONTROL CENTRES FOR EMOTIONS AND BEHAVIOUR

Like many of us, I too have always been very attracted by the man-machine analogy, by the similarities between the brain and the computer. I think it is no coincidence that at the age of 18, attracted by so many and vastly differing subjects, I had signed up for numerous university entrance tests (5 if I remember correctly, even though I had reluctantly excluded something!). Among these, there was also engineering. The result had been brilliant, I had positioned myself among the first candidates, even though I hadn't prepared. Yet in the end, I chose something more 'warm' and 'human'.

I have always found there are important analogies between the study of complexity, the laws of physics, mathematics and the complete study of human behaviour and health. It is also no coincidence that among the people with the most interesting minds that I have met in my life there have been many musicians, professionals or amateurs it doesn't matter. The study, and especially the practice of music, changes brain functioning and emotional regulation. All of this (psychology, complexity, mathematics, biology, music, etc.) is absolutely connected, as is now clearly demonstrated by research and various areas of study. Music is an art that is based on: physics (sounds are waves); mathematics (the relationships between notes that give shape to wonderful harmonies can all be calculated numerically); multi-sensory perception; non-innate physical movement which becomes, between practice and automatisms, something extremely fluid (we will return to this aspect in switch 5); creation of links between what I see (the written notes), what I foresee (my expectations based on experience) and the real experience which is always a little different (the sound of our instrument will change just by putting new curtains up in the house); active and passive time management (which clearly reminds us of frustration tolerance, mastery and other fundamental self-regulation themes); the other person, with their and our expectations (playing will make him/her happy or bored, they can compete on performance, etc.). These processes underlie our lives, affecting everything from basic survival mechanisms to the most sophisticated arts.

In this third switch area we will see just how necessary it is to have both an engineering overview, to get away from cause-effect reductionisms with respect to our functions, and an orchestra conductor's vision for flexible modules, i.e. systems that alternate or collaborate with our human experience, which is always at the same time an attempt to harmonize the metabolic, nervous, immune, mental and emotional elements. For example, today it is no longer possible to say that "the amygdala is the centre for fear", but we will see how there are brain networks that regulate adaptation and survival systems, which work by forecasting and correcting these same forecasts on the basis of real data, while being influenced by metabolic and immune processes that are already at play and by those that will be activated with this specific response.

We will also see that the dimensions of the past, present and future are always at play simultaneously in our minds and in our experience and learning. We will see that bodily resources of all kinds (available energy, loose or blocked muscles, levels of hydration, excessive immune responses in progress and other factors) are essential for shaping correct perceptive and cognitive assessments of what is happening around to us, as well as to shape well-organized emotional responses and behavioural patterns for development and growth.

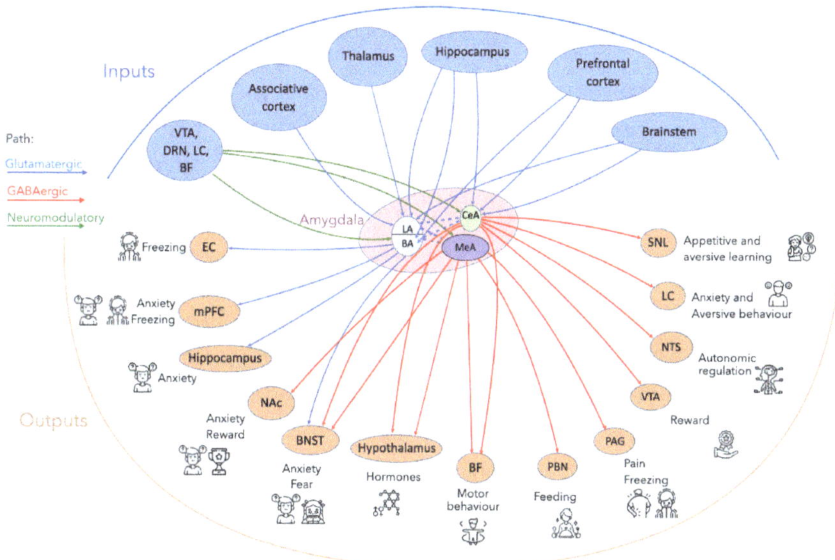

Fig. - The different inputs and outputs of some of the major nuclei of the amygdala. As you can see, the amygdala cannot be defined as a 'fear center', but it is a very important hub in many networks that concern any human function (behaviour, movement, hormones, nutrition, pain, rewards, memory, decisions, etc.).

ASSESSMENT: WHAT TO CONSIDER AND EVALUATE

In this third switch area we will look at some topics that we know well from a different perspective with a systemic vision, through which we will be able to optimize our work, by combining it with further tools and synergistic methods of intervention.

In particular, we can look in this perspective at:
- States of chronic alert;
- Hyper-vigilance;
- Difficulties with trust (situations, new ideas – while for interpersonal trust see switch area 4);
- Difficulty letting go;
- Re-reading of diagnoses such as OCD, PTSD, Generalized Anxiety, based on safety networks and predictions;
- Alterations of the perceptive system;
- Relational or communication difficulties that are actually perceptive-emotional (e.g. a person who often does not understand what others say, misunderstandings that result in: *"if only you could hear yourself!"*, *"are you kidding me? I didn't say that/I didn't have that tone!"*);
- Altered responses in sensory processes, such as hyper-sensitivity, awareness, balance, discriminative ability in various sensory channels, etc.;
- Dysfunctional forecasting methods, such as confused or distorted anticipations, predictions and expectations (e.g. mistaken for intuition, willpower, distrust, etc.);
- Not being able to terminate (with respect to conflicts, work, worrying thoughts, etc.).

THE CRUCIAL ROLE OF CEREBRAL NETWORKS

To fully understand complex phenomena such as behaviour, emotions, cognitive abilities, relationships or affections, we look for explanations and models that can best represent the mechanisms at work in each of us. When dealing with dysfunctions, problems or pathologies, the situation becomes even more complex: in fact, it is necessary to understand which are the normal (or rather physiological) processes and what is not working as it should.

In recent years, the technical capabilities of scientific investigation have increased exponentially. From the first attempts to integrate body and mind, we now study neural networks and the connectome, or rather the study of the structure and functioning of the nervous system, and beyond, at the same time.

Thanks to modern studies, today it no longer makes sense to speak of "language area" or "pain area", of "fear centre" or of other function-specific locations. On the contrary, we reason in terms of hubs and networks. For example, when an anxious mode is identified in a person, when dangers tend to be seen everywhere, the study of brain networks offers us an interesting contribution: the function of labelling a stimulus, a context or a person as 'dangerous' is carried out by a set of brain structures called the Salience Network. To help this network work at its best, it is necessary to act in a targeted way, knowing the specific mechanisms and processes of its components and how they interact with each other. As we will see later, the Salience Network involves sensory processes, integration of body maps with respect to the resources available to deal with the presumed danger, predictions with respect to any physical damage, evaluations and hypotheses with respect to what will happen based on one's own behaviour, and so on. Each of these connections can be favoured or penalized by certain conditions that the therapist, educator or change professional will be able to favour in different ways, for example by acting at a contextual level, creating ad hoc experiences, with intervention strategies or through specifically developed techniques.

In the past, emotional and behavioural neuroscience focused on two opposite extremes: the study of single brain areas (as we have seen for the amygdala identified as the *'centre of fear'*) or very large multi-function systems (for example the 'limbic system' as *'regulator of emotions and sociability'*). Over time, research has fine-tunes and a configuration has emerged, in terms of networks and hubs[1], or groupings of areas, which – in dynamic interaction – perform various functions of emotional regulation, cognition, problem solving, social rule management, as well as empathy circuits and other configurations differentiated by task or domain[2]. For example, perception and cognition are strongly and directly affected by information that has affective and motivational content. The effectiveness of a specific reward, for example, is barely evaluated from a rational point of view, while it is directly proportional to its emotional salience. According to classic interpretations, motivation is an independent activation factor, which requires significant voluntary control. Conversely, it is now clear that synergistic interactions (and not conflict) between motivation and thinking are present in numerous perceptual and cognitive tasks. Motivation shapes behaviour in many ways, for example by reducing challenges and competition, or through selective effects on *working memory*. Reading emotional responses has also changed in recent years. As we have seen in the chapter dedicated to emotions, the work of Joseph LeDoux has clearly clarified that the emotion we experience does not coincide with the adaptation response, but is rather its result, the fruit of the interaction in the *working memory* with a series of other functions dependent on different *networks*[3].

Emotional events cannot be deconstructed and reduced to the activation of specific neurons, brain areas or to a generic system capable of producing emotional responses. Rather, emotions are an emergent phenomenon, taking shape from different interacting systems. To be even more precise, we are able to understand the functioning of any specific network only in the context in which it emerges and in its dynamic co-activation with other networks and hubs. For example, there are some specific networks that interact dynamically just to predict the intensity of different variations of sadness, fear, or anger over time.

In general, there are numerous specialized networks for different functions. Thinking in this way allows us to understand that the problem, the dysfunctional node, is not always necessarily at the most obvious level. For example, chronic pain does not go away if areas of the brain responsible for touch and physical sensations are blocked. On the other hand, it is possible to significantly reduce and modulate chronic by acting on one of the most powerful integrative hubs of our nervous system: the insula. The insula is a structure involved in numerous networks, from the aforementioned Salience Network to all those that regulate attention, control, self-awareness, adaptation to the environment and more. The insula, as we will explore further on, plays a central role in interoceptive processes and can be helped to perform its activities at best in various ways. In this regard, we will look at a series of sensory and psycho-physical exercises that can be easily integrated into one's professional practice.

Understanding the basis of networks and hierarchies of influence also allows to refine the sequence of action. In some cases, this also means creating the conditions to overcome resistance to change in general or with respect to specific therapeutic techniques. We know, for example, that there are mental techniques capable of altering the perception of pain. These take shape mainly via the dialogue between the prefrontal cortex and the insula. If the insula is in optimal working order, mental pain-reducing techniques will take effect. Otherwise, there will be no particular benefits (and this also applies to emotional suffering and relationship difficulties, not just to physical pain). In other words: the prefrontal cortex, even if perfectly functional, cannot give its contribution if the insula is not in a position to receive it. Hence the importance of giving priority to interventions capable of regulating the insula and, only later, to try to introduce more cognitive techniques. This way intervention times are optimized and the client is prevented from experiencing the frustration derived from an ineffective technique.

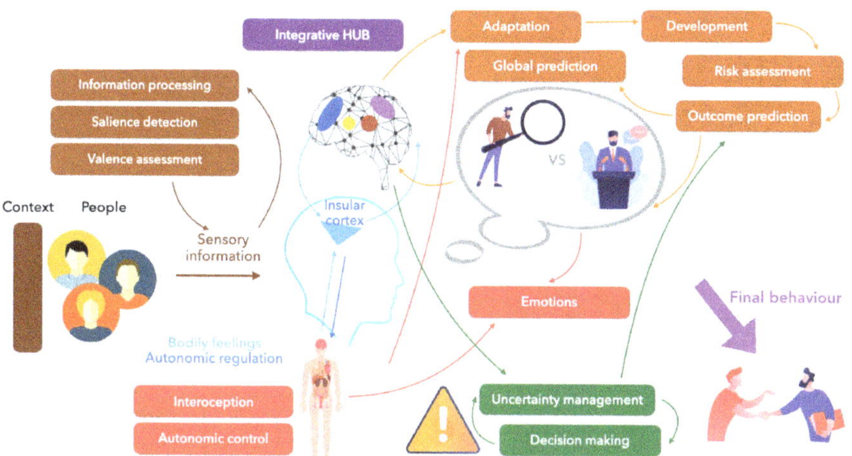

Fig. - An example of different networks giving shape to a social interaction in synergy: some of the networks involved are marked in the coloured boxes which, as can be seen, concern different bodily, emotional and cognitive aspects. The role of the insula is graphically highlighted not for its autonomy or functional superiority, but to emphasize the physical aspects in all adaptation processes (even those in which the body is apparently not involved), as we will see later on in this chapter.

Below, we will see a series of interesting concepts and mechanisms and we will look more closely at two of the main systems underlying self-regulation that can constitute interesting switches on which to focus attention in order to effectively act on *adaptation, development or recovery* mechanisms, among other things, alternating them so that they can support and strengthen each other.

The complexity of these systems and their interactions can be experienced in different everyday situations. The point of arrival for a professional is to get to know these switches and favour their operation in a way that is advantageous and evolutionary in both the short and long term, with a logical design sequence that is in line with what we have seen in the chapter dedicated to the working method.

Before analysing specific networks, their implications and practical applications, it is necessary to delve into some fundamental issues connected to them, especially with regards to the data and information on which we base our adaptive and development processes. We will therefore examine the central role of perceptual processes - i.e. gathering information about the external world, including interpersonal relationships - and internal processes (so-called interoception).

IT ALL STARTS WITH PERCEPTION... WHICH IS OFTEN WRONG

To help us in these considerations, let's go back to the Integrative Functional Diagram, explored in one of the introductory chapters. As we have seen, this model follows the temporal events that occur within us, whenever we have to adapt to an environmental stimulus or an internal need.

Let's start from the beginning, or at least from the one that most clearly represents the beginning (we will see later that everything actually begins even earlier).

We start from the idea that every behaviour we engage in, from scratching our nose to graduating from Harvard, has a starting point. We can visually identify it with a point where we realize that "there is something". In the first example (scratching our nose) the trigger may be when we feel an itch and, consequently, the scratching behaviour begins. In the second case, everything could start from the perception of a need to fulfil one's potential or, in general, the "feeling" of type of need (even a non-functional one, such as having to prove something to someone). In any case, the identification – more or less conscious – of a trigger factor takes place.

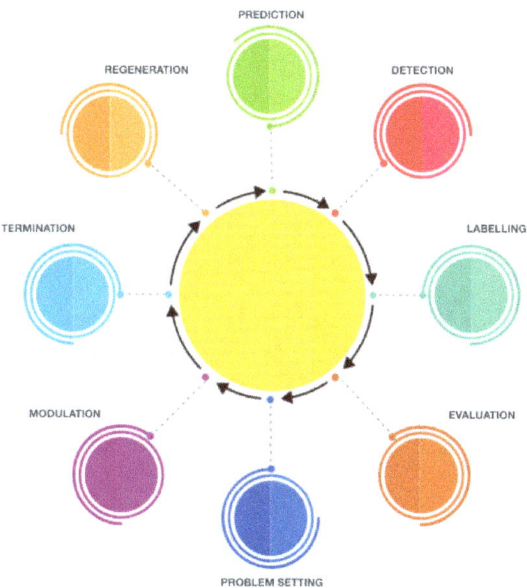

Fig. - The Integrative Functional Patterns.

This is why we call this the Detection phase. The metaphorical, and much more than metaphorical, idea is that *something enters our radar.*

A first central point concerns the fact that this radar (which, as we will see later on, coincides with the *Salience Network*) is continuously in operation, but we are not always aware of it. In our metaphor we can say that the radar is there and works, but we are not always looking at it or, even if we are looking at it, the dot on the screen could be too small or dim.

Looking at the same phenomenon, but from an opposite perspective, the signal might usually be quite bright, but if we've just returned from a walk on a very sunny day, our eyes won't be able to notice it. On the other hand, if our eyes are irritated by too much work in front of the computer monitor, it will immediately appear strong, even annoying, perhaps forcing us to turn away or close our eyes.

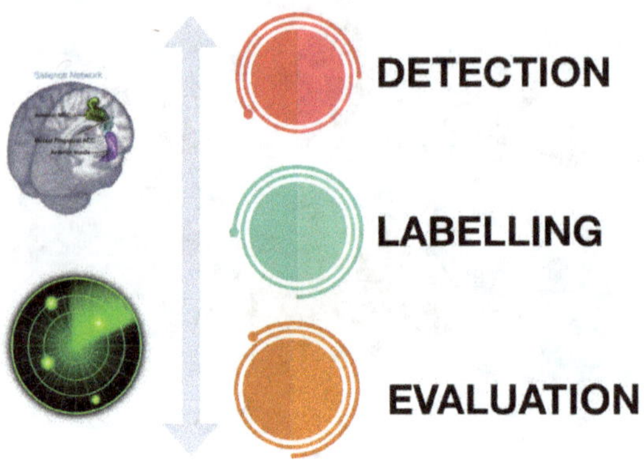

Fig. - The initial phases of the Integrative Functional Schemes are necessary to make sense of reality and, at the same time, to better adapt to environmental demands and internal drives.

Out of metaphor, what are we saying? That a dangerous signal, a threat, a defiant look can be detected, even if not consciously. Furthermore, this detection (conscious or not) can be more or less intense depending on some factors, such as environmental aspects or the psycho-physical state in which a person is in at that specific moment, for example after a run or at a time of day when testosterone levels are particularly high. This is what happens for example in those with post-traumatic stress disorder or for autistic children: sensory detection is hyper-intensified right from the start.

As we have seen, this doesn't only occur in extreme pathological or dysfunctional conditions; it only takes some environmental stimuli or internal dysregulation to distort our sensory capacity. When this altered perception is the starting point of an emotional reaction, a decision or a behaviour, everything that follows will be influenced in some way as a result.

Furthermore, our radar, like any tool, can be calibrated more or less effectively. To function at its best, like any kitchen scale or bicycle brakes, occasional adjustments are necessary. The springs can loosen over time, and cables can wear out. Similarly, our sensory system (both internal and external) is subject to numerous factors that can change its threshold and responsiveness. Trauma, chronic stress, emotional deprivation, as well as medication misuse, improper diet, and lack of physical activity, are all factors that alter the neural networks and neurobiology that govern our perceptual and evaluative abilities. Depending on whether it's a momentary effect (such as temperature changes, daily hormone peaks, etc.) or long-term alterations (trauma, ACEs, chronic stress, etc.), we will need to take targeted action.

To further delve into the topic on the basis of integrative scientific literature and findings from research and clinical practice, the evaluation phase of what enters our radar is so intricate and complex that it needs to be divided into two stages and, to some extent, it needs to begin at the interception phase.

Today, modern research is so sophisticated that allows us to analyse all the mental, cerebral, and physical processes we undergo, providing a clear understanding of these stages. The first evaluative phase is the *Labelling* one. In a matter of milliseconds, to be precise, a few milliseconds, we assign certain generic tags to what is observed during the *Interception* phase. It's similar to what happens in an emergency room where there is no time for a comprehensive diagnosis; instead, triage is performed and preliminary tags are assigned to each case, based on the severity and risk of the situation, ensuring that lives are saved and severe cases are covered.

The second phase is the actual *Evaluation*. This is a more complex process than the previous one and thus takes a bit more time. However, we are not yet in the realm of pure complex cognition and awareness. We are still within the realm of fractions of a second, where access to traumatic memories, hierarchies in relation to other needs, and a series of additional factors that we will explore further is made, largely without consciousness and voluntary control. The more cognitive and logical aspects will primarily come into play in the subsequent *Problem Setting* phase.

THE COMPLEXITY OF FEELING AND PERCEIVING CORRECTLY

Sensory perception is key to life. In fact, every adaptation process starts from an evaluation of the surrounding environment. Usually we are only aware of, or we "notice", just a small part of all the sensations we perceive at any given moment. The reason is simple: if we were to notice all the feelings we perceive at any moment, we'd be completely overwhelmed and we'd become unable to do anything other than feel these sensations. This tendency to exclude sensations initially takes place as an evolutionary advantage: I exclude sensations to focus on other more important things. The problem, however, is when we start to exclude even very important information coming from our environment, other people or ourselves and as a result make mistakes, misinterpret situations and make choices that we end up regretting. Unfortunately, human beings are really skilled at this. Not only do they not pay attention to relevant data and information, but they often do so in the name of unimportant activities.

In frantic modern living, we tend to take this feature to extremes, ending up feeling almost nothing. We seek out extreme sensations in flavour and in daily life, such as sensual touch or extreme sports. This way we forget that sensory perception, as enjoyable as we may find it, did not develop as an end in itself from an evolutionary point of view, but should always be the starting point for something else.

We can observe dysfunctional behaviours every day. For example, Angelica was always busy, jumping from one sport to another, going on adventurous holidays, and in a way, every choice she made involved intense feelings. In her own way, she was somewhat aware of these mechanisms, but she often derived pleasure from intense feelings, losing sight of potential risks or other important factors (commitments, relationships, responsibilities, etc.). I vividly remember when she described in detail the feeling of the ball impacting her arms while playing volleyball, how much she enjoyed feeling the impact on her skin and deep into her bones, her ability to tolerate pain and how eagerly she anticipated the immediately burning sensation that followed. This attitude, present across various aspects of Angelica's life, led her to neglect other more relevant aspects. For example, her teammates often told her that she had "her head in the clouds" and that she didn't notice the signals they were sending during matches or if someone was struggling.

At the extreme opposite we find Mark who, fatigued and disillusioned with life, had almost lost all sensation. Once, while he was bidding me farewell, he stopped under a tree with leaves touching his head. As he spoke to me, he moved his head, and the leaves visibly brushed against his skin and hair, but he seemed to pay absolutely no attention to it. Many people would have immediately brushed them away, and those more sensitive would have found it quite bothersome. However, when I pointed it out to Mark, he was surprised and told me that for a moment, he actually had a doubt that there might be something there: "perhaps a fly had landed for a second", he thought. In reality, he had remained in that condition for about 5 minutes.

Another different attitude is displayed by Joshua. He is the typical person who, immediately adds a generous amount of salt and pepper as soon as a dish is served (whether he's at the workplace canteen, family gatherings, or restaurants), to "give it some flavor". He does this with every food that is not sweet. Moreover, if it's a pasta dish, he also adds a large amount of cheese. The interesting point is that Joshua, like anyone who exhibits such behaviour, cannot truly know if a food will be flavourful enough for him until he tastes it. If he makes an evaluation beforehand, he is simply making a guess, a hypothesis.

An important issue to consider with food – as with other features in life –therefore relates to incorrect anticipations or predictions. As we shall see, these predictions can cause us problems. The underlying neurobiological processes are interoceptive and are at the root of our self-regulation and emotional processes.

Another relevant element that these examples highlight is that although these people are talking about flavour and taste, they are really seeking out something else, unawares. Often people that exaggerate with cheese such as pecorino or supermarket parmesan are trying to give their salt receptors a strong stimulus like the one derived from traditional table salt (sodium chloride) and monosodium glutamate (MSG). Those that seek them out in abundance tend to have salt receptors that have been hyper-saturated by constant exposure to these products, due to eating habits that are heavily reliant on packaged and processed foods. Hyper stimulating these receptors brings hedonistic sensations (mental excitement or activation) and a series of metabolic signals - in the short and long term - that are often damaging to overall health.

The topic of food in relation to the senses, pleasures, and self-regulation is very important. It affects everyone to varying degrees and intensities. Additionally, the daily relationship with food represents a fundamental area where needs, gratification, and the possibility of relieving emotional tensions and stress comes into play. The compensatory mechanisms through which we seek gratification in one area while lacking it in another, or the vicarious adoption of behaviours and motivations, can easily manifest through the relationship with food, but in reality, they can apply to any behaviour.

AVOID UNNECESSARY TRIGGERS

With many techniques and strategies, our goal will be to stay in a situation, to face it, and not avoid it. However, in some cases, it can be beneficial not to trigger negative emotions, especially if they have damaging effects or are distracting. This is particularly valid in the initial stages of therapy, where we need to help the person re-evaluate the situation they are in and the aspects they are focusing on. Avoiding unnecessary triggers, if done consciously as part of a therapeutic approach, can also be a useful tool in later stages, allowing us to focus only on specific situations in a targeted manner.

We can start by identifying unnecessary triggers, which are situations or conditions that activate a stress response, a painful memory, or an overwhelming emotion that serves no purpose and, because it is not managed or processed, only causes suffering. As studies on memory consolidation and reconsolidation show, continually reliving traumatic events (or events with negative value) risks reinforcing their memory and making it more difficult to modify in the future.

A typical way to avoid unnecessary triggers is to avoid situations that lead to revisiting a negative event, such as passing by the house where you lived with a previous partner or being in the location where an accident occurred, keeping a prominently displayed photo of a person whose absence is difficult to bear after their death, and so on. I want to reiterate once again for safety that this is not a definitive or inherently useful strategy, but rather a possibility to be evaluated on a case-by-case basis depending on the individual and their needs at that moment.

For example, Hilary had lost her parents in a car accident several years before. Due to the way her life was organized, she often passed by the location of the accident. She would also find herself standing still in front of their photographs at home, frozen, holding her breath to prevent herself from crying. In this case, we agreed that for a month she would change her route to avoid that place and put all of her parents' photographs in a drawer. This way, after a brief period of disorientation, a sense of lightness and emptiness emerged, revealing the real reasons why she couldn't accept the loss of her parents. After working on those issues, all connected to her lack of perception of her own resources and ability to be autonomous, it became possible to reintroduce the photographs and let her freely choose which routes to take in the car. An interesting note: after some time, she noticed on her own that she now passed by the location of the accident without any issues, but it happened less frequently. As she herself said, "I used to make sure to pass by there before, even if it wasn't always the shortest route, but I only realize it now."

Sometimes these triggers are not obvious and can be hidden behind false solutions of technological efficiency. For example, receiving constant real-time notifications for every new email that arrives on the computer or through the phone are all distractions and potential sources of stress. The stress lies in the partial information provided by these notifications: seeing a name or the beginning of a sentence immediately triggers a thought in us that wants to attribute a complete meaning to it. The problem is that we don't have enough data to do it correctly, so our fears will move more easily than positive options. Later on, when we'll address the themes of uncertainty and unpredictability, we will delve into the underlying mechanisms and factors of this process. In the meantime, let's use an example to better understand: if I receive a notification of an email from my accountant, I will easily think that there is some tax to pay or a missing document, in any case something burdensome and unpleasant. This evokes a negative emotion until I read the email. Maybe then I discover that he just wanted to verify a simple piece of information that I know by heart, so I can respond to him in a few seconds, but by now the negative emotion has already started, my physiology is altered, and it will take some time for my body and mind to return to normal mode.

The paradox is that all of this can also happen with positive news as well: think about what happens to a teenage girl when she sees the name of a boy she likes as the sender of a message on WhatsApp, an SMS, a message on Facebook, or an email. Maybe the optimistic thought immediately arises, such as "he's thinking of me!" or "he's interested in me!", but during the time that passes between that notification and reading the message, doubts arise in her mind that the content may not be what she desires. Even if for a few seconds, the girl experiences strong mental, physical, and emotional effects.

If the girl is not very self-assured, these reactions are amplified, and these reactions reinforce her insecurities in a vicious cycle. The same can happen to an adult, just replace the boy's message with an email related to an important work matter, the outcome of a medical exam, etc.

The solution is simple: deactivating these notifications, at least for most of the time, especially when people are working, studying, or even enjoying an evening with the person they're with, so there is no looming shadow of a third person or entity (work, taxes, etc.) on the horizon. The pleasant surprise will be that, in addition to reducing the moments when negative emotions are experienced without a valid reason, they will be much more focused on their work or on the people around them. Electronic devices now have advanced functions to disable notifications during certain hours or for a specified period of time set by the user. It becomes a good habit and gradually allows for an important transformative experience: to emotionally remember that impulsively fulfilling others' demands is rarely beneficial for either party. If there are true emergencies, they can be easily identified, but in almost all other cases, they tend to be dysfunctional emotional urgencies. Not catering to them creates the conditions to become aware and, conversely, provides concrete proof that nothing serious happens if we're not connected all the time. In the worst-case scenario, dysfunctions will surface, allowing them to be intercepted and resolved; in the best-case scenarios, one immediately realizes that they have saved time, energy, and regained power (in a positive sense) over themselves and their relationship with the person who sent the message.

A final type of unnecessary triggers is more indirect, and we could say environmental. Some examples include noisy places that make it difficult to concentrate, background conversations that enter our mental radar even if they're irrelevant, artificial lights that irritate the same perceptual system we need for more productive tasks. Avoiding or reducing these aspects allows us to waste fewer resources and exert less effort in any activity, whether it's work-related or a journey of personal change where individuals seek to modify their mental patterns, emotional responses, relational behaviour, or other aspects. Sometimes, small adjustments are enough, such as turning a desk around or changing the position of the computer monitor to avoid seeing something in the background, or using headphones that have active noise cancellation when listening to music. Additionally, or alternatively, it's important to take breaks from these constant interferences (also to avoid transitioning from allostatic load to overload, as we discussed in the previous chapter). To do this, one can use the Emotional Buffer technique or simply try to have a lunch break in the nearby park, listen to relaxing music with their eyes closed for 5 minutes before approaching a task in a different way.

Louis, for example, wanted to change the type of interactions with his son and create a more direct and affectionate relationship. He had realized that as soon as he entered the house, tired from work and commuting (taking both the subway and the car during rush hour), he would always fall back into the same patterns of superficial exchanges with his son within moments. After explaining the concept of unnecessary triggers to him, being reflective and analytical, he made a list of all the factors he encountered throughout the day, seeking a solution to most of them: he stopped listening to the news radio in the car, which led him to think (without usefulness, only with frustration) about negative aspects such as corruption, the economic crisis, etc.; at work, he turned off the phone ringing and personally checked for important messages or calls every hour; before entering the house, he parked the car in the garage and sat there quietly for 5 minutes, breathing calmly and focusing only on his son and what he wanted to say and do with him.

FROM ALLOSTASIS TO PREDICTIONS

In the chapter dedicated to Group 2 switches we've encountered the concept of allostasis. In that context, we focused primarily on system overload due to hyper-adaptation, related to the theme of inflammation and the psychosomatic price we can pay whenever we do not return to physiology for a long time.

In the Group 3 switch area, we can revisit the concept of allostasis and extend it further. As previously seen, allostasis is our way of increasing chances of survival and development by optimizing the efficiency of the system. The most natural way to do this is by anticipating the potential problem and its corresponding solution. If we think about it, this happens in every aspect of life, and it should not surprise us that our nervous system is organized in this way. If we usually come home from work at 6 PM, in winter we know that to find the house warm, we need to start the heating at least at 4 PM. Therefore, we anticipate the potential problem (finding the house cold) and its corresponding solution (turning on the heating when we are not home yet, because experience has taught us that our specific boiler takes about 2 hours to warm up). From this example, we understand that predictions are based on past experience, they are refined over time, but they originate from and can be improved thanks to the perception of the external environment.

With this analogy, we can also understand that if we maintain a fixed prediction without integrating new data, the advantage turns into a problem. Keeping the heating on based on what we did in previous years, even if that year spring arrives particularly early and not considering that the house is already naturally warm (thanks to the sun), creates several negative consequences, including unnecessary expenses that could have been avoided, family arguments about that unnecessary expense and different priorities we could have invested in, feeling too hot, sleeping poorly due to excessive heat, and so on.

The example we just gave may shift the focus too much on predictions made through logical thinking (which can be better clarified using the term *forecast*, such as weather forecasts or economic budget forecasts, clearly made through deliberate study and reflection). In reality, the predictions we are talking about are quick and subconscious. Our neurons communicate rapidly and develop numerous predictions about every little aspect. We even need to reconsider how we understand perception. In the previous paragraphs, we saw that perception is the start of any adaptation process. To avoid confusion, I find it clearer to use the broader term of *Detection* (see the Functional Integrative Schemes in the relevant chapter), which includes perceptual processes and more. In reality, our perceptual system does not directly absorb complete information from the external world as if they were exact photographs of reality; rather, it deconstructs various components and reconstructs them in our brain. In reconstructing them, always to optimize processes, speed up our responses, and gain advantages, our nervous system creates predictions about what we are seeing, hearing, touching, and perceiving. This happens in every instant. Think about it now, what is the biggest... Your mind, in those three suspension points you just read, in that brief pause, tried to guess what the next word or general topic would be. Maybe you noticed it. In reality, most of the time, we don't notice it, but our mind does it constantly: it tries to anticipate.

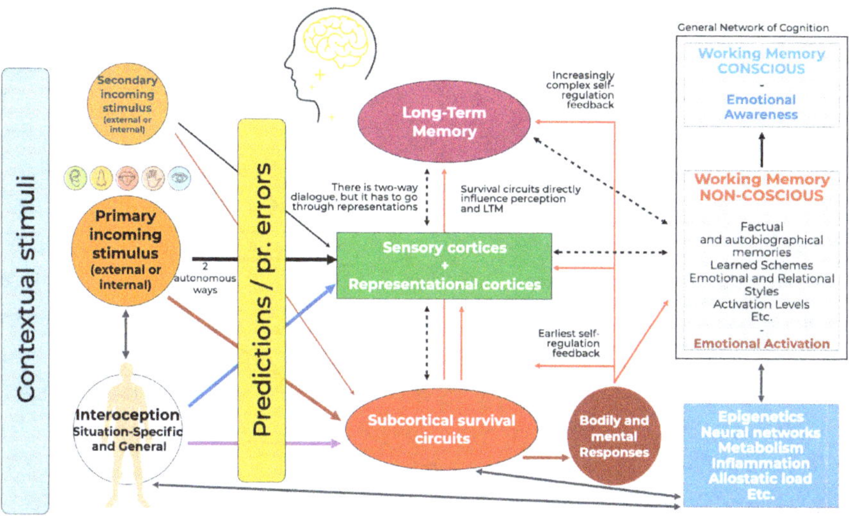

Fig. - We have already seen this image in the introductory chapter, and we are including it here to focus on the relationship between incoming perception, predictions, and error verification cycles of predictions.

Another way to understand this is to think about when you are listening to someone speaking in your native language, or a language that you are less fluent in. In the first case, you can get distracted and still understand, as you are able to correctly identify each word even if mispronounced or spoken at a very low volume. However, if you are not a native speaker, you have to pay attention, and the possibility of not understanding is quite high, even if you know the individual words the other person is using. Your mind hasn't had enough experience to predict them, so it has to pay attention. In this case, your brain is engaging in the opposite process of prediction, which is categorization. It is trying to create a broader register, for example, of the word "dog", including how it can be pronounced and the meaning it has in that context. It is a process that is not under our direct control but is still active and demanding.

Prediction, on the other hand, is quick and easy, but like all automatisms, it can be incorrect. That's why there is a mechanism to verify the error of the prediction by comparing it with real experience, allowing us to reach a more accurate perception of what we are witnessing.

So far, we have focused only on perception, but this entire system of predictions also applies to determining the most appropriate behaviours to enact. These are sophisticated mechanisms connected to many other systems (e.g., memories of past experiences in switch 1, as well as the fluidity or rigidity of thinking in cognitive flows of switch 5). Furthermore, we have indirectly introduced some important aspects, such as the possibility that a prediction may no longer be contextualized or never be error-tested. We have also hinted at the effort required for an active approach compared to the ease of automatism, which often leads us to expend much more energy in the long run (in the sense that there is slight to moderate and prolonged fatigue or suffering for months or even years, for example, by not changing, not evolving, constantly being in conflict with others because contextual or interpersonal clues are not grasped, etc.). In the continuation of this chapter, we will delve into specific mechanisms and, based on this knowledge, explore how we can make our change and healing strategies more effective.

PREDICTION–ADJUSTMENT LOOPS

We have introduced an important theme that now needs to be further explored due to its significant practical implications. Predictions occur not only for what we perceive but also in relation to our possible reactions. In all of this, there are also predictions concerning our internal state (see the concept of interoception mentioned previously). Various types of predictions take place, and they have relevant interactions with each other. For example, there are specific brain networks that dynamically interact with the sole purpose of predicting the intensity of different variations in sadness, fear, or anger as time passes. These networks exchange information and influence other systems that evaluate external and internal data, the effectiveness of our potential responses in that specific context, our self-image, our image of others, and many other factors. There are even networks in the microglia that, in turn, influence neuron networks processes.

All these predictions are not separate and consecutive; it couldn't be so. They must occur simultaneously and on multiple fronts. In fact, many daily activities leave us less than a second to react. It would be impossible to shape any form of art or engage in any sport, let alone sustain a fast-paced dialogue if it were a serial and linear process.

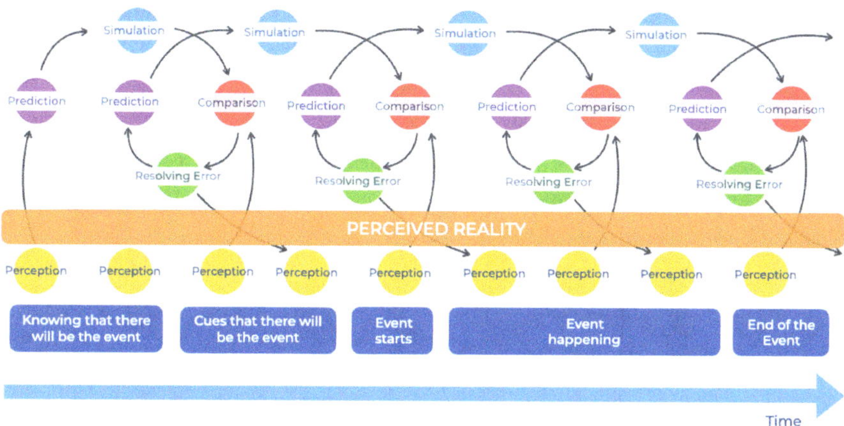

Fig. - The reality we perceive is the result of the ongoing dialogue between cycles of prediction and error correction with incoming stimuli. For the sake of graphical simplicity, only a linear flow of predictions is represented, but it would be accurate to have multiple levels that influence each other.

Basic predictions can be seen as feeling and action simulations generated by our brain. These simulations are compared to the actual sensory input we receive from the external world or from within ourselves. At this point, if everything goes well, we come to a crossroad: if the prediction and sensory input match, meaning the predictions are correct, the simulation becomes the lived experience; if they don't match, the brain must resolve the errors.

I mentioned "if everything goes well" because this is a path fraught with possible difficulties. One structural difficulty is that the cortices that transmit predictions are granular, while those carrying sensations are a-granular. In terms of signal speed and transmission quality, it's like saying predictions travel in a Ferrari while sensations travel in a Fiat 500. The former will arrive faster and stronger, while the latter will arrive a bit later and with less force to assert themselves.

The other risk, connected to this structural aspect but not only, is that we are always in a hurry and not accustomed to paying attention to our feelings. Sometimes we don't even give the perceptual system enough time to adapt and receive accurate information. For example, if we go from darkness to light, it takes a few seconds to see someone's face clearly and accurately deduce their intentions. When we drink or eat something, the receptors in our mouth need at least 6-7 seconds to fully activate, but we typically judge the quality of the food (and consequently influence our mood, choices of where to buy, etc.) based on inaccurate data, influenced by erroneous predictions (based on a product tasted in the past) and external factors (the kindness of waiters or the luxury of the decor). Our predictions are even influenced by internal self-regulation mechanisms: for example, the levels of certain hormones (which vary daily or from day to day) make the predictions less accurate in reading the emotions experienced by another person.

In light of this information, it becomes crucial, first and foremost, to make patients aware of these mechanisms that shape our way of being and experiencing daily events. Immediately afterwards, it will be necessary to implement a series of measures and strategies that allow us to restore the proper functioning of the prediction-verification cycle in everyday life, particularly during crucial moments of change (techniques that we perform in the clinic or that the patient will need to practice on their own).

INTEROCEPTION

Interoception is an interesting theoretical concept with important practical implications. It is crucial for better understanding the mind-body unity in its so-called top-down and bottom-up dimensions. The concept was introduced by Sherrington in 1906 and began to take hold in the scientific community in the 1940s, but its greatest expansion came thanks to Bud Craig's contribution.

We can define interoception as an internal sense, analogous to the classic five senses, but focused on what happens inside our bodies. Craig defined it as the "sense of the physiological state of all bodily tissues". Today, we can say that interoception collects data about the body's state (heart rate, respiration, blood pressure, glucose levels, temperature, hormones, metabolism, acidity, sensations of pain or discomfort in different body areas, etc.) and conveys them to the central nervous system to regulate allostatic and homeostatic processes.

Already a century ago, Sherrington sensed the motivational aspect of interoception: interoceptive afferent pathways (from the periphery of the body to the central nervous system) allow fine-tuning of the body, primarily for optimal survival but also for movement, interaction with others, pleasure, achieving goals, and more.

Just as the brain tries to understand the external world through data received from the five senses, it similarly tries to interpret signals that come from within our bodies. Interoception is precisely the process of collecting and analysing this data. The information considered includes some elements accessible to our consciousness, such as stomach-aches or knee ligament pain, but also all the subtle signals of which we are not usually aware. Some of this information can be brought to awareness, such as the tension in the intestines that we can detect by touch, while others are inherently inaccessible, such as the level of acidity detected in various parts of the body (while we can only consciously perceive acidity and alkalinity in the mouth and the very early stages of the digestive system). The detection of internal perceptions, like external ones, is subject to the prediction mechanisms we discussed earlier, always with the purpose of anticipating functional adaptation.

Both in the prediction-correction processes and in the various stages of processing, there are continuous interactions with different types of learning and memories, expectations, contextual and interpersonal data, movement, posture, balance, and other factors. In other words, interoception originates physically from the body but influences—and is influenced by—mental and emotional states.

For every movement of our body, there are modifications that are detected by interoceptive processes. The act of anticipating any movement - from picking up a pen on the table to imagining discussing a problem with a colleague at work - begins to generate a multitude of interoceptive predictions that prepare the body to carry out those future movements.

While interoceptive predictions are complex and sophisticated mechanisms, from an evolutionary standpoint, they are still tied to life in natural environments, where prediction and action are closely linked to the moment or to seasonality. The body prepares itself to leap to catch prey or to escape from a perceived danger, just as it prepares for hibernation by sensing the signals of winter's arrival.

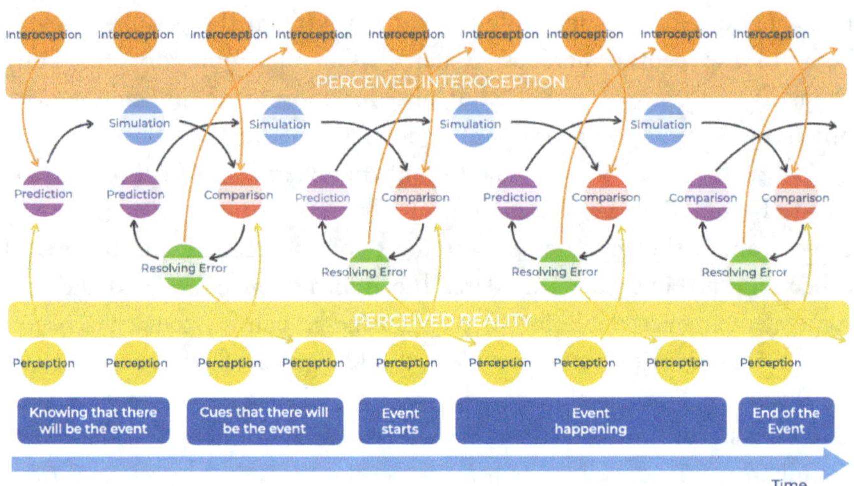

Fig. - This image is more accurate and comprehensive than the previous one because it considers both external sensory perception and interoceptive perception. However, even in this case, multiple levels of parallel cycles that influence each other should be added, but the graphical representation would be chaotic and unclear.

In human life, we encounter many false signals: we often see photographs of food or potential sexual partners that don't exist in reality but still activate a series of hormones that won't be utilized by the body in the short term; we receive letters and electronic messages reminding us of a problem to be addressed in a month's time; we watch TV shows and video games so well made that they completely alter our physiology. In all of these cases, and many others, interoception activates predictions that have no corresponding reality or have been distorted. For example, the mistaken prediction of needing to defend ourselves can drive us to contract muscles already contracted due to the weight of the work bag we are holding, further confirming the erroneous prediction. Or, while looking at an anxiety-inducing photo, we may suddenly perceive that our diaphragm is contracted when it was already in that state due to poor posture or chronic anxiety. This creates a great confusion and mutual disruption between external and internal perception and their respective predictions and errors.

INTEROCEPTIVE TESTS 2

An interesting test to make people experience these connections is the following. The person is asked to stand with their feet together and arms by their sides. They are asked to remain still and balanced. They are encouraged to pay attention to bodily sensations and have a smooth (i.e., 'soft' or 'non-rigid') control of their balance.

After a while, they are asked to close their eyes and notice differences. Usually, people start to sway more (it is normal to sway in this position, although many are not aware of it). With closed eyes, the external reference parameters for balance are missing, so the adaptation processes have to get used to having one less input.

At this point, we can start experimenting with perception, interoception, and their predictions. The person is asked to briefly open their eyes, find a distant point to focus on, memorize it, and then close their eyes again, trying to remember this image and adjust their balance as if they were seeing it. They are given a moment, and then asked how it's going. Most people respond that there is more stability and a greater sense of bodily self-control.

Then we tell them to let go of this image and make the person spin around two or three times, leaving them in a slightly different position than they started in. This way, any external cues that may be perceived through closed eyes, such as passing lights and shadows are also lost. These implications are explained to the person, so that even at a cognitive level, the predictive references are lost.

At this point, the person will feel their balance, awareness, and muscular control worsen. They are told that balance usually improves, purely due to the laws of physics, by extending their arms. They are asked not to physically do it, but to imagine doing it. To be precise, they are asked to 'imagine being about to do it and intending to do it,' just to ensure that the predictive cycles we are interested in are set in motion.

The person is given the opportunity to listen to themselves, both on a physical and emotional level, and they are asked to share what they feel.

Then, they are asked to slowly initiate that movement, but they are stopped after a few centimetres, so that the feedback is different from what was expected. One can gently hold back one arm and allow the other to rise, always with the purpose of forcing error and prediction mechanisms. Then, they are allowed to reach the correct position with arms extended and are encouraged to listen to bodily, emotional, and mental sensations. They are then asked to perceive their own body map from within and also to imagine themselves from the outside. To evaluate what they think of themselves with that body and what they would think of someone else who in that body. The final step is to return to reality data and simply integrate present sensations with a correct perception of oneself.

Other variations of this interoceptive test can be developed by moving the eyes upwards or placing the tongue against the teeth or palate to make one feel how much the balance of the whole body can change with only minimal variations and how this connects to significant emotional and mental changes related to these specific organs or their dysfunctional synergies.

Furthermore, incoming perceptions can be deliberately altered, for example, by tapping the feet on the ground to reset the receptors or by using bandages or dry ice (like the spray used for sports injuries) to numb a part of the body (numbing the sensory signal but not the prediction, creating an interesting mismatch).

The interoceptive networks are now well-studied in all their complexity, and it is extremely clear that interoception plays a fundamental role and is an integral part of every self-regulation, adaptation, and development process. As it takes shape, interoception primarily uses two brain networks (but not only): the Default Mode Network and the Salience Network, which we will explore furth in this chapter. For now, we can begin by saying that interoception develops gradually, passing through various "stations", becoming increasingly complex, and integrating with other afferences and different processes of adaptation and development. For instance, in the reticular substance, an initial pre-cortical homeostatic processing occurs (without our consciousness), which is then repeated, updated, and further integrated at the level of the posterior, middle, and anterior insulae. We can envision these progressions as a series of cycles that become increasingly refined, similar to mixing different colours of paint, gradually achieving harmonious and uniform shades.

This knowledge has significant practical relevance: it helps us understand that the neurophysiological basis of how we perceive external sensations and integrate them into new body maps and motor patterns, giving us a sense of security and mastery, requires continuous changes and updates. For example, all *grounding* exercises, whether referred to as the "knight" or by other names depending on the discipline, work much better if the position is not static and prolonged over time (this is effective when developing muscle endurance). Instead, maximum effect is achieved by maintaining postures with continuous slight variations, even microscopic ones, and with a diffuse focus on both muscular and visceral aspects, along with their corresponding emotional and mental correlates.

According to Damasio, the neural substrate of the Self is found in the interoceptive stations. This representation begins to form in the brain (the Proto-Self) and further takes shape in the anterior insula (particularly the right side), where it interacts with the prefrontal cortex, creating the perception of a Sentient Self.

Interoceptive data usually travel beneath our consciousness. This is beneficial because it allows us to do other things in life besides simply paying attention to our sensations. However, it can be problematic when we raise the bar too high (like those individuals who are "too much in their heads", have excessive commitments, chase constant deadlines, live in overstimulating environments, etc.). In this latter case, we experience continuous interference with all our processes, but we are not aware of it, leading to self-blame (feelings of inadequacy, etc.), blaming others ("they are mean", "they don't understand", etc.), or blaming the real or supernatural world ("it's bad luck", "destiny is cruel", etc.). This ruins our performance, life, and, in the long run, creates psychosomatic damage because we disrupt the system for too long, without returning to a physiological state.

FEELING THE BOUNDARIES OF PERCEPTION

Let's look at an example of this working process that you can use in synergy with many of the techniques found in this book. It is an application that can also be used with other tools you already use in your professional practice.

When we massage or apply pressure to a point on our body (such as in our psychosomatic release techniques discussed in switch 2, for example), we can bring conscious attention to different levels of subtlety. We can focus solely on the fingertips, pretending that the area of the body we are touching, such as the leg, doesn't provide direct, interior-derived sensations, as if we were touching a piece of wood. In the fingertips, we can feel sensations right on the surface of the skin and then descend millimetre by millimetre, perceiving how these factors change and new ones emerge (e.g., the internal pressure of the bone pressing against muscles and skin from within; the circulation of blood altering over time due to prolonged pressure; different types of warmth), and if desired, ascend – even in a not precisely anatomical but still interesting way – to the hand, arm, shoulder, and so on. This allows us to greatly refine perception, discover new sensations and new awareness. Moreover, it enables us to activate the comparison between real sensations and predictions, as well as expectations, imagination, body maps, and many other factors, as seen in the preceding paragraphs.

So far, starting from the hand, we have focused only on one half of our experience. Now we can perform the complementary process, trying to isolate the sensations in the body part being touched, pretending that the hand gripping or massaging us belongs to someone else.

We can shift our attention to the skin of the massaged area, which feels the fingers and possibly the fabric of clothing in-between. We can perceive pure tactile sensations (the type of fabric, the shape of the fingers) and their qualitative evaluations, such as the pleasantness of silk, the texture of the fabric, the pain of nails sinking in, the discomfort of hair being pulled, and so on. The more we feel, the more we differentiate, the better it is for recovering correct perceptual and interoceptive processes, which are highly useful for self-knowledge and self-regulation starting from primary processes. In this case, we can take further steps by descending into the body, feeling the different layers of skin, fascia, muscles, and potentially bones, perceiving their individual sensations or how they influence each other. All these evaluations can be accompanied by refined vocabulary, as well as other strategies (using other languages, metaphors, deliberately using only images without words, looking or not looking, wearing gloves, using moisturizing creams, etc.) precisely to develop interoceptive finesse and avoid distorted predictions, negative expectations, and other assessment errors.

THE PRACTICAL BENEFITS OF THINKING IN TERMS OF NETWORKS

As we have seen, when we want to have a deep understanding of complex phenomena such as behavior, emotions, cognitive abilities, relationships, or affections, we look for explanations and models that can best represent the mechanisms at work within each of us. Understanding these mechanisms allows us to immediately know which processes and modalities are active and which are dysfunctional. We can then understand at which level it is most appropriate to intervene, what is needed to support them and to restore effective functioning.

For example, when an anxious mode is identified in a person, for which they tend to see dangers everywhere, the study of brain networks offers an interesting contribution to develop a new perspective. The task of labelling a stimulus, a context, or a person is carried out by a set of brain structures called the Salience Network. To assist this network in functioning properly, targeted actions are required, based on an understanding of its components' and their interaction's mechanisms and specific processes. As we will see in the following paragraphs, the Salience Network is involved in sensory processes, integration of body maps with available resources to deal with presumed danger, predictions regarding potential physical harm, assessments and hypotheses about what will happen based on one's own behaviour, and so on. Each of these hubs can be facilitated or hindered by certain conditions that the therapist, trainer, or change professional can promote in different ways, for example, by acting at a contextual level, creating tailored experiences, using intervention strategies or specifically developed techniques.

Reasoning in terms of networks and hubs also allows us to understand that the problem, the dysfunctional node, is not always necessarily at the most obvious level. For example, migraine, back pain, fibromyalgia, IBS (irritable bowel disease) don't go away if we block the brain areas responsible for physical sensations. On the other hand, it is possible to significantly reduce and modulate it by acting on one of the most powerful integrative hubs in our nervous system: the insula. It is a structure involved in numerous networks, from the previously mentioned Salience Network to all those that regulate attention, control, self-awareness, adaptation to the environment, and more. The insula can be assisted in various ways to better perform its role, including regulating pain.

It becomes therefore evident that thinking in terms of functional networks and hubs has a significant impact on professionals in the fields of healthcare and personal development, with interesting applications in various domains, from psychotherapy to education, counselling and business coaching.

Thanks to brain networks, it becomes possible to gain a thorough understanding of behaviours, self-regulation processes, as well as their dysfunctions, and potential pathologies. This perspective provides an integrative framework to accurately assess the situation and establish targeted and effective interventions.

Brain networks serve as an additional lens that can enrich and complement other approaches and methodologies. They provide knowledge and information based on scientific evidence, capable of fulfilling their role as a network of integration and synergy, even at a theoretical level. For example, understanding brain networks allows for a refined understanding of the mechanisms through which they are effective that can be integrated and optimized in various forms of therapy: from classical cognitive-behavioural therapy to more modern somatic therapies, disciplines such as meditation or mindfulness, various forms of counselling and coaching, as well as expressive activities such as theatre and writing, sports and martial arts, even as complementary elements to the therapeutic journey.

There are two additional advantages derived from the knowledge of brain networks. The first is the ability to access a system of techniques specifically created to support, develop, and integrate all these networks and their hubs. In this section, we will explore some of these techniques, but the book also presents many others that work on these mechanisms. Another advantage of the functional network approach is that once the mechanisms are understood, professionals become more flexible, effective, and creative in their practice. By analogy, it's like transitioning from being a sous chef who memorizes the set recipe given by the head chef, to becoming the actual head chef who skilfully balances all factors at play and can make infinite variations because they master all the elements and their characteristics. To give a concrete example, when trying to enhance the salty flavour, the most obvious solution is to add more salt, but this can have implications on overall flavour and on health. A chef must consider all the balances and have foresight. For instance, they know that the perception of saltiness changes based on the temperature of a food or that if they offer a small taste of something bitter beforehand, the perceptual threshold decreases, making the subsequent dish taste even more flavourful. Similarly, understanding the processes of control, attention, socialisation, affection, strategy, action, and others puts us in a position to use various tactics, to leverage activities that the client may already engage in out of passion (such as drawing or writing) with minor adjustments to enhance their transformative power. Likewise, we will have the tools to make targeted alterations to familiar techniques, making them even more effective towards the achievement of our goals, or even to create new ones.

THE RADAR–SWITCH THAT ANALYSES DANGERS AND RESOURCES

When it comes to the self-regulation, adaptation, and development mechanisms – and the emotional and cognitive processes associated with them – a significant step forward has been taken with the identification of three important brain circuits. In fact, they allow us to highlight what happens in our brain when we shift from a condition of quiet and introspective thought (the Default Mode Network) to one of alarm and evaluation of danger (the Salience Network, connected therefore to conditions of anxiety, fear, stress etc.), right through to putting into action resolution or adaptation (the Executive Network, that activates processes of fight, flight and self-regulation). We are about to see how this enables us to provide an operational reading that is steeped with practical suggestions compared with traditional diagnoses for anxiety, stress, PTSD, obsessions, addiction etc. Let us first analyse some of these processes.

As the name suggests, the **Default Mode Network (DMN),** was initially regarded as the condition of 'non-activation' in which our body is functioning, but not focused on any specific task. The DMN is in fact connected to these states but also to internal thought processes such as the building of mental simulation and the formulation of forecasts by drawing on previous personal experience. This type of circuit has a direct connection with balance, sense of direction, motivation, empathy, nervous system activation, self-regulation, attachment and perception.

As we shall see, stabilising the DMN and its correct alternation with the Salience Network and the Executive Network, represents a critical factor for intervention in order to achieve integration and bring various adaptation and development systems back to physiological state[4].

The *Salience* Network (SN) is a veritable switch in that it allows the activation between one system and the other between the *Default Mode* Network and the *Executive* Network[5].

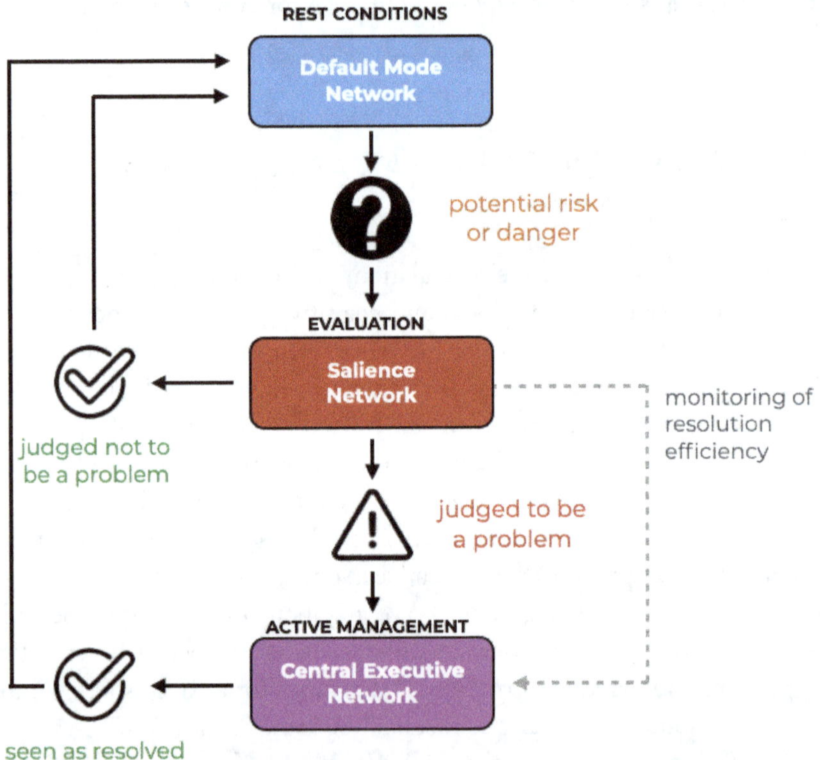

Fig. - An illustration of the relationship between the three networks. The *Salience* Network acts as a switch opposite a problem: if it identifies it as a real risk it activates the Central *Executive* Network to actively manage the problem, otherwise it reactivates the *Default Mode* Network to allow a return of rest conditions.

As the name suggests, the SN evaluates what is salient, or relevant. A sound, a shape, a change in temperature, a texture, are all signals that the SN evaluates to understand if there is a need to adapt at a physiological or behavioural level. It is easy to see that it represents the starting point of all emotional and defence processes and of adaptation to an environment.

In this light, a condition of continuous alert, such as the anxiety caused by PTSD, can therefore be seen as the prolonged and dysfunctional maintaining (no longer suited to the context) of SN activity. We can therefore ask ourselves what keeps it in this state, which of its functions is not finding a response that enables it to deactivate, to recognise Termination signals (See Integrative Functional Patterns in their respective introductory chapter) or to engage another functional network.

Many psychological methods (from clinical to managerial) focus on assessing a danger by considering external factors (such as the type of danger, risk, context, etc.) and internal "mental-emotional" ones (coping skills, self-esteem, emotional resources, etc.). The study of the SN, instead, highlights how these considerations also largely depend on the insula that gives much importance to information such as body maps, readiness and muscular power, freedom of movement and, in synergy with the Periaqueductal Grey (PAG), the potential physical damage that can be caused or suffered. Techniques and psycho-physical exercises that integrate these data will make the therapy process more targeted and effective in recovering the basic functions of self-regulation.

All these considerations also take place in relation to risks that are not very physical at all, such as an argument with a colleague or a financial problem, because DMN, SN and EN have ancient evolutionary roots as they developed and formed when risks were mainly connected to physical survival.

Centuries have passed, but the neurobiological survival patterns remain predominant and activate in response to any risk, even if it pertains to emotional and identity-related survival rather than purely material survival. The body still constitutes a central element to protect and utilize as a resource. In the modern world, although risks are rarely life-threatening in material terms, the struggle for emotional survival, earning a social role, and safeguarding something important to us may be even more ruthless and frequent than in the past (for further insights on these aspects, you can refer to the discussions on stress and emotions in the introductory chapter).

Let's explore a first simple self-analysis exercise that can be done after explaining these three networks and their functions. We can ask the person we are working with how much time they spend each day actively engaging in each of these three networks. They can look at their schedule or reflect on their typical day. It is helpful to advise them not to focus on specific activities (such as attending a meeting, working on a computer, etc.), but rather on how they experience different moments within those activities. For example, if during the first half of a meeting they find themselves lost in their thoughts, the Default Mode Network is active, while if they feel anxious about interacting with others and trying to understand the problem, the Salience Network is active. Similarly, while attempting to read a book, if they keep thinking about why their ex-partner left them and can't understand the reason, the Salience Network is active, or if they constantly take notes to become a better writer, the Executive Network is active. Once the daily (or weekly) activation of the three networks has been analysed, it is useful to question whether it is functional, beneficial, or simply a waste of energy. Additionally, one should inquire whether the individual feels in control and satisfied with this allocation or if they would like to change something, even if only in specific moments or areas.

Although in different ways and for different reasons, Elizabeth and Hilary were always on high alert. Their radar – their Salience Network – was constantly active and hypersensitive. Elizabeth would notice every slight change in tone of voice or shift in the gaze of friends and family. The problem was that she noticed these differences with great skill and based on actual data, but she didn't interpret them correctly. She would relate every signal to her own problems and perceive them as negative judgments or malicious intentions from others. In reality, those variations were often present, but unrelated to her and stemmed from completely different factors, such as feeling hot or having personal concerns. Sometimes they were indirectly connected to her, like when people physically suffered from sitting in the same position for too long or grew bored listening to her worries, but there was no real issue, and they weren't plotting behind her back; they were simply fatigued. It was crucial for

Elizabeth to work on these aspects and objectively evaluate relational and contextual cues.

On the other hand, Hilary, due to the experiences she had gone through and the level of hyper-activation and inflammation she had reached, became hypersensitive to any stimulus. A loud sound or a label on a piece of clothing was enough to trigger intense and disproportionate states of alertness compared to the initial stimulus. She often "saw" judgmental gazes that weren't actually there (her predictions imposed themselves on reality, as seen in the previous mechanisms). After normalizing all the factors in area 2, we worked extensively with Hilary on perceiving her genuine sensations and developing an accurate assessment of her resources to cope with potential risks and challenges in the external world, using various strategies and techniques presented in this chapter.

The **Executive Network** comes into action when the risk evaluated by the SN is high enough to make it useful to activate a measure of adaptation or safety. The EN, therefore, helps transition to action. This is an action that can also be static, in the sense that there is no physical movement involved, but rather focused attention is directed towards making choices in regards of actions to be activated in the future. Hyperactivity, when not justified by need or context, can therefore be seen as a way of maintaining EN even if unnecessary[6]. At the same time, repetitive pointless behaviour ranging from *obsessive rituals* to simple *insistence* such as repeating the same concepts over and over again, or *being unable to reduce control* over one's children or co-workers, can be seen as a dysfunctional phenomenon of the Executive Network that is not finding alternative value-add processes or is unable to identify valid internal or external signals indicating either its inefficiency or that it has reached maximum efficiency already.

This is what happens to Enrique, a successful manager and entrepreneur who is always active – perhaps even too much. He wakes up at 5 in the morning, organizes his schedule, and goes for a run. He returns home for breakfast with his family (that he forces to wake up at 6, even though they could and would like to sleep longer) and then enthusiastically goes to work. He carefully monitors all the activities of his 14- and 16-year-old children, even though they are very responsible and do not cause any trouble. In fact, the only issue is that they complain about their father's excesses, treating them "as if they were still in primary school". Similarly, he leaves no space for his employees, constantly checking and controlling everything and everyone. When he goes on vacation, he gets bored quickly. He tells me that he has chosen dream vacations in wonderful places several times, organizing various excursions and activities. However, after a few days, he feels empty, as if he's not doing anything productive. Sometimes, he even left his family on vacation to return to work earlier than planned (even if not necessary) or just to take care of household chores.

The *Default Mode Network* is not to be considered the opposite of the *Executive Network*. The fact that the DMN is also a state of calm directed towards self-reflexive thoughts does not mean it is a good idea for it to remain active all the time.

If self-reflexive thoughts are mainly devoted to negative repetitions (For example, the dream role one wants to have among friends or at work, a negative behaviour that isn't accepted, the obsession with a particular body detail that one wishes to change, or continually obsessing over a traumatic event.), DMN activity is not synonymous with being in a state of calm, but means we are maintaining a dysfunctional state active.

In addition to this, considering the executive switch dynamic, remaining in DMN means remaining inactive. As we have seen constant activity for no reason is a problem, but so is never becoming active. The alternation between networks is another perspective providing a new reading on emotions, alertness, anxiety, but also anhedonia and motivation.

From a neurobiological perspective, the balance between networks is also established through the action of cortisol and other glucocorticoids. Factors such as childhood adversity, sensory stimulation, specific types of physical training, the development of complex skills (such as playing a musical instrument, learning a new language, etc.), daily habits, and every significant life experiences influence the release of glucocorticoids and the subsequent rebalancing of networks following stress. All of these factors (which can be both risk and protective factors) can tilt activity towards the Salience Network, leading to a continuous evaluation of danger (accompanied by experiences of anxiety and fear) without transitioning into action, ultimately resulting in an inability to cope with environmental demands.

RESOURCE BALANCE TECHNIQUES + RECONSOLIDATION

The Resource Balance techniques are very flexible techniques that can be declined in different ways.

1- They can be used on their own to develop interoception and favour the perception of resources in the initial phases of Detection, Labelling and Evaluation.

2- They can help to interrupt incorrect motor or thought flows (see switch area nr. 5) and restart with a new focus.

3- They can also be used as very powerful forms of awareness and dynamic meditation. This is because they fully exploit neurological features that connect movement to safety, self-regulation, introspection, mediation, emotion and cognition circuits.

These are complex physical exercises in terms of balance and coordination specifically because these elements activate the circuits described above.

A **basic exercise** involves isolating movement in a single leg (by placing the other foot against a chair behind us) and moving very slowly focusing specifically on the different phases of movement and the specific emotions felt. For example, we analyse the specific differences in the generic description provided by 'it hurts': tension, heat, burning, itching etc. At the same time, we carefully define the topographic borders of sensations both in extension (i.e. 2, 5, 10cm from the knee) and in depth (on the skin, under the skin, near the bone etc).

In the second stage we introduce variations and different modes to actively transform these sensations and manage their relationship with emotional experiences, feelings of control and power and other relevant experiences.

A central element of the technique is to regain control in a flexible manner and on multiple levels, understanding what is truly needed. For example, the exercise improves rapidly if the head is aligned with the shoulders, and the shoulders are not too far forward in relation to the pelvis. This spatial perception can be initially facilitated with a mirror but then needs to be internalized and verified exclusively through proprioceptive (body parts in space) and interoceptive mechanisms (muscle tensions, varying degrees of visceral compression, freedom of movement of the diaphragm despite the search for balance, etc.).

Similarly, any energy waste, such as contracted muscles in the hand or face due to fatigue, which do not contribute to improving the exercise but rather create an additional dysfunction and amplify negative experiences unnecessarily can be identified.

Possible *variations* can be introduced using external tools, such as boards with a semi sphere underneath or soft cushions, to facilitate finding balance or make it more challenging or playful.

Other exercises and modes can also be utilized, such as bodyweight exercises (e.g., the butterfly used in artistic gymnastics or certain martial arts), alternating lunges with or without jumps, using a trampoline, and other variations that engage the patient's motivation and emotional involvement.

Another very relevant application of these techniques for the development of new learning and at a pre-cognitive level is their association with **reconsolidation processes**. Reconsolidation techniques, in fact, represent the highest expression of balance and return to physiological state in adaptation processes. They enable the targeted and strategic alternation between old and new processes, thus providing new forms of reaction.

Among the various possible modes, let's explore a variant that is closely related to the Resource Balance techniques. In this case, sequences are used in which the following alternations occur:

- A masked stimulus (thus not consciously recognizable) of the triggering factor of the problem - this represents the modern and laboratory-based version of mechanisms known as "subliminal stimuli."

  ➡ You can find a tool to do this and further instructions at www.insciences.co/repro;

- Approximately 5-8 minutes are allocated to explore the elicited dysfunctional responses.

- A session of Resource Balance with a neutral mental focus of about 3-5 minutes;

- Another masked stimulus.;

In this case, a swift transition is made to physiological modes through a simplified repetition of the previous Resource Balance technique and active management of mental focus (5-8 minutes).

These procedures are structured and can be varied in many possible ways to maximize their effectiveness. The previous example should be considered as a concise illustrative demonstration of a wide range of possible variations

➡ For further information and instructions, please visit www.insciences.co/repro.

For Enrique – the manager with the constantly active Executive Network  we already met – applying the Resource Balance techniques was very helpful. They helped him feel first-hand how rigid and out of control he actually was, contrary to what he had previously thought. With the basic exercise of managing his legs separately, he noticed asymmetries in his body and how little balance he had. Additionally, he realized that he quickly experienced pain and a series of dysfunctional synergies (such as holding his breath, making facial expressions, curling his toes) that wasted energy instead of using it - referring to the principle of minimum free energy, switch 2. After a period of initial frustration, he transformed his anger into motivation, practicing the exercise multiple times a day, aiming to regain a sense of control and mastery while understanding that he needed to do so with flexibility, graduality, and proper environmental management. Moreover, for Enrique, these exercises represented, as he himself explained, "the best way to not think about anything else, emptying the mind of problems to solve and goals to achieve, but at the same time, recharging and starting again, focusing the right energy where it is truly needed".

For Hilary, on the other hand, the basic exercise would have been too  physically intense. Therefore, we chose to do variations on balance boards. This allowed her to find a fun activity that brought her attention back to her body, which she had previously neglected. After gaining some confidence and achieving a reasonable balance, the balance board became a test for her. When she had doubts about her worth or how she should interact with others, she would step onto the balance board and think: if her balance worsened, she would try to see things from a different perspective; if her balance improved, she would have confirmation that she had found an interesting perspective to explore. Hilary, although very emotional and impulsive, was also very clear-headed, so she knew that her test was not perfectly reliable as a final decision criterion. However, she understood that there were short circuits between thoughts, body, and effectiveness that she could work on and reflect on constructively.

TASTE AS A WAY TO HEAL AND GROW

Developing attention to flavours and perceptions is an excellent way to act on various levels, all of which are primary and fundamental. Tasting, choosing, and preparing food to the best of our ability allows us to engage with the mechanisms we are analysing in this switch area and beyond. In fact, we can stimulate and integrate awareness, interoception, sensory perceptions, emotions, needs, and their respective connections with primary survival and adaptive reflexes. From a theoretical standpoint, it is also possible to integrate a fundamental aspect of life, namely eating, with all the sciences revolving around emotions, thoughts, socialisation, neurobiology, and more.

In each of us there is an innate drive to enjoy food and want to get the best out of it. By contrast, culture and mass distribution work against this tendency. Our objective is to bring the situation back into balance so that it works to our advantage. Eating is connected to survival not just in terms of "putting something under your teeth" to stay alive; our bodies are far more elaborate. We innately know how to find and identify what can bring us more nutrients. The problem is that we do not train this ability and therefore we forget how to use it.

Let's now explore some relevant aspects to better understand these mechanisms.

In our search and selection of food, evolution has equipped us to avoid what is toxic. In this instance too we have deactivated a lot of potential. We've also created conditions that cause confusion and overlap between the roles of the different processes. For example: at a certain point in life, we overcome our disgust for bitter flavours and start to feel revulsion - with the same distancing reflexes such as vomiting - for people and behaviour that we regard as "toxic". We are the only animal to do this and there are positive as well as negative implications.

The world of flavour has a lot of overlap with adaptation and development circuits. For example, identifying smells helps manage danger and advantages of non-nutritional nature. This happens in interpersonal evaluations that go from sexual compatibility to identifying reliable people (in the wider sense of the term: identifying people that are not stressed, aggressive and that are able to be autonomous, healthy and so on).
Many choices that we call "instinctive" or that we attribute to our "sixth sense", are actually based on the non-conscious evaluation of biological factor variations (hormone changes, body temperature, toxins in sweat etc) that we pick up with our sense of smell and other senses. All this is critical to help sharpen our evaluation skills.

Considering the role of metabolism from an energy perspective can also be very rewarding. How do we know how much energy we have available? It's a refined interoceptive process that doesn't evaluate the quantity of energy we have introduced (otherwise we'd feel full of energy after stuffing ourselves and we know that's not the case!). It's a perception of energy resources, but also of our ability to use them effectively. It applies both in the short term, to save our lives if necessary, and, more often, to help us perform over time, not just at work (which is a nonsensical myth rather than something useful! But this is a whole other subject…), and most importantly in relation to energy to use with our children, partners, for our hobbies and other important activities.

At an individual evolutionary level, cooking means developing mastery and self-sufficiency. For example, cutting rapidly and precisely, even when simply chopping vegetables is an aggressive act that destroys but at the same time transforms things into something beautiful and good. From this stand-point you can start to guess what the various connections with different levels of interpretation of destructive or, by contrast, pleasure behaviours (innate drives, needs, survival processes, primitive social regulation, Eros and Thanatos, entropy and so on). Cooking is a great way to try out, experiment and learn how to manage all these processes.
Another example is the preparation and consumption of meat ranging from the enjoyment of eating it raw to eating it ravenously. In all these instances we are reactivating ancestral predatory processes in addition to a series of other mechanisms such as the need for iron, enjoying the succulence of

animal fat and so on.

From a social point of view, preparing food and enjoying it means taking care of others. Often here in Italy, but I've seen something similar in many other countries, we see an almost excessive drive in this direction that can end up confusing attachment with social interaction and survival. One sentence we hear far too often goes: "if you don't finish everything, grandma will be upset, with all the time she devoted to preparing this!" A sentence like that, even when it is said with all the love in the world is emotional blackmail. It also drives a child to not listen to their feeling of fullness in favour of affection. Respecting others, their effort, the quality of the food, our personal tastes and feeling of fullness are all important but separate. It is important not to overlap them and confuse them, or they will only cause disadvantages in place of the benefits we hoped for initially.

Understanding these mechanisms, paying proper attention, removing automatism and bringing back awareness, making thoughtful choices - all of these aspects allow us to restore these processes to their physiological state and derive direct benefits (in terms of pleasure and metabolism) as well as indirect benefits (in relation to all the sensory, emotional, and survival processes associated with them). Additionally, it is possible to engage in targeted exercises, leveraging the common neurobiological processes of adaptation, emotions, taste, and smell. This approach is not to be confused with the well-known practices of *Mindful Eating*, which have different scientific foundations and objectives. Our approach is called "Brain-informed Tasting & Cooking" and integrates all disciplines of Integrative Sciences with the tasting techniques used by chefs and sommeliers. Given its highly experiential nature, it is challenging to convey in a text like this. We invite those interested to visit our website to learn more.

UNCERTAINTY: LIFE IS UNPREDICTABLE. PROBLEMS AND SOLUTIONS

The theme of *uncertainty* or, from a slightly different perspective, *unpredictability*, has gained increasing prominence in recent years. It is discussed more and more in the media, considering the political, health, and economic developments of the past decades. Everything is less secure and less certain than we once thought: financial markets can collapse overnight, a pandemic can emerge and overturn every notion of modern medicine that we believed in, political balances—whether of a single country or the entire world, that had been carefully constructed over years, can be shattered in an instant due to the sudden decision of a single person with great power. In reality, beyond recent events, there have always been very few absolute certainties to rely on.

Louis was on vacation with his family. In the middle of the night, the hotel room door suddenly opened, and a drunk man entered. As Louis would only discover much later, this man's friend worked at the hotel and had given him the key in the afternoon, mistakenly believing that the room was vacant misunderstanding the reservations. At the moment of the intruder's entry, Louis could have predicted many things, but not this. There were no clues just moments before (no drunken commotion outside the hotel, or noise in the hallway given that the hotel was a luxury establishment, etc.).

Furthermore, we must remember that the central point is not the prediction of the event itself, as if it were merely an exercise of imagination or a game of probabilities. As we have seen, the purpose of prediction is to optimize our response to that event. For example, in Louis's case, the entry of the drunk man was unexpected, yet he quickly found a good behavioural response to manage the situation and safely escort the intruder out. The crucial factor that Louis had not anticipated and was unprepared to handle was his daughter's loud and prolonged scream. Moreover, in an attempt to make sense of, and manage this secondary event (secondary in terms of sequence but primary in terms of emotional importance), Louis was concerned about his daughter's well-being, while his daughter was screaming because she was afraid for her father's safety. As a result, the attempts to rescue his daughter only made her scream louder, creating a dysfunctional and traumatic cycle for everyone involved.

Let's analyse the mechanisms we are discussing, starting from something that happens every day and concerns practically everyone. Meteorologists have understood how to make fairly reliable weather predictions, but in reality, there are still many cases where they can be partially or completely wrong. This detail, in its simplicity, creates several problems: for farmers who need to organize their work, as well as for an individual who has to decide how to dress and whether or not to take an umbrella to work. What we often do to have a greater sense of control over this limited predictability is to make seemingly rational choices and delude ourselves that they are certain and secure: we check three different weather websites (without considering that they might all be drawing from the same source of information), or we determine which one is the best and decide to trust it exclusively. Studies on User Experience tell us that 80% of trust in a website is determined by graphic clarity (readability of fonts, colour contrast, easily readable graphics) and the speed at which the pages load. Looking at the data the other way around: we choose to trust an information source using only 20% of the data that could be reliable (scientific method, long-term efficacy verification, authoritativeness of the authors, etc.) while making a highly irrational choice (based on aesthetics and convenience).

Throughout history, humans have often tried, in various ways, to delude that they have control: superstitious rituals, popular beliefs, magical thinking, seeking secure employment at the expense of personal satisfaction, and so on. Even in our field, there has often been a success in reductionist theories to interpret behaviour, illness, or even personality traits. As we are witnessing in our journey, patterns and models are meant to navigate complexity, not to be rigidly applied.

Our relationship with predictability and unpredictability is further complicated by the fact that we have ambivalence towards it: predictability offers us security and tranquillity, but it can also bore us and make us lose interest in something. Conversely, unpredictability can evoke fear and induce stress, but it can also be enticing because there is something new to discover. It can be stimulating and facilitate change.

These mechanisms take shape at multiple levels, from mental and motivational aspects to biological responses. In fact, many of them are innate processes upon which more complex processes have evolved. For example, our eyes attentively follow random movements and curved lines (even less predictable in their future direction) while they quickly lose interest in linear and repetitive movements. The reason for this, even in evolutionary terms, is easily understandable: repetitive movement can be natural, like leaves in the wind, while an unpredictable movement is more likely to be that of prey or a predator and requires greater attention. These mechanisms are now utilized in reading (rapid eye movements allow us to go to the next line without losing the thread of the discourse), video games (changes in movement maintain attention and activate emotional engagement), as well as in a magic shows (the magician's distracting movements are always curvilinear and unpredictable). I have used the example of eye movements for explanatory purposes, but similar mechanisms exist in various domains. For instance, repetitive sounds have a calming effect (from lullabies to popular music), while complex and unpredictable musical patterns attract and stimulate passionate individuals who seek more intense and intricate sensations, which require a state of activation rather than relaxation.

A GENERATIONAL READING: PREDICTABILITY, AGE, AND MASTERY

When a stressing situation takes place, the processes described above (and various others we shall see in the upcoming sections) activate.

Let us look at a condition of extreme unpredictability and how it can change the way it is approached based on experiences, preconceptions, and physical resources available. A dog, when it finds itself on a surface with no grip (such as an icy surface) slips and is unable to predict its movements and the direction to take. To tackle this situation the dog activates a series of uncoordinated movements and then feels powerless.

Humankind, thanks to greater structures and potential compared with this beloved domestic animal, has a wider variety of available responses. It is interesting to note how different life-circumstances occasion different reactions.

- *A very small child* (2-3 years) reacts like the dog.
- *An older child or an adolescent* transform unpredictability into something positive activating the playful aspect, a sense of fun and of challenge, as well as the quest for an effective strategy. If other people are present, amplification takes place and social dynamics are leveraged (nurture, affection, cooperation, antagonism etc but we will analyse these better in later sections of this book).
- *An adult*, who potentially has access to all the dynamics used by youth, typically does not activate them. There are various reasons for this: lack of headroom for playfulness due to cultural or contingent reasons (such as being late for work); lack of control over the body and little confidence in their own motor skills; muscle stiffness or contraction – which may or may not be connected to the earlier point on motor skills

– due to lack of exercise, or allostatic load which in turn leads to a lack of perception of physical resources and to a keener fear of falling; embarrassment at the thought of appearing clumsy or pathetic either in absolute terms or in relation to other people etc.

On the other hand, an adult that has some similar experience or skill, such as for example someone that can ski or skate, can maintain control even though forecasting is not perfect thus increasing self-confidence. This can in turn be used constructively (helping others to manage control with some initial rules such as lowering the centre of gravity and bending the knees – in this instance the rule is correct and based on physics) or it can be used negatively, fuelling other dysfunctions such as arrogantly feeling superior to others (and confirming superiority is limited to that instance specifically).

THE SWITCH–MANAGER ANALYSES THE ENVIRONMENT, RESOURCES, GOALS, AND ACTION PLANS

Uncertainty or, in other words, the idea of *unpredictability*, carries with it feelings of *hostility* in the environment and of a *lack of safety*. These characteristics, combined with the ones seen earlier, make talking about anxiety, stress, or insecure individuals a matter of utmost importance.

Uncertainty is a multi-faceted concept that impacts various different aspects of daily life: parental behaviour, that of your partner, work security, lack of social support, features of the outside environment, unstable sentimental relationships, work that is based on volatility (such as trading, negotiating etc.) and other similar situations that are – unsurprisingly – connected to high heart attack rates, neurodegenerative diseases, acute somatisations and premature mortality.

In this perspective we can also identify three types of reactions to stress:

- At the *first* level stress is simply positive; the environment is simple to forecast, and risks are low. Stress thus becomes a source of activation and motivation; mastery and self-esteem remain active and grow stronger.

- The *second* type concerns stress that cannot be tackled but that is tolerable, medium intensity risk is perceived and there are some forecasting difficulties. Uncertainty is reduced, managed and compensated in different ways: through natural regulation actions such as habituation, through structured processes like relaxation techniques, meditation, through reframing (from classical reframing to Possible Scenarios, which we will see shortly), through Emotional Buffer techniques (as seen in switch 2 and applicable in this context as well), and others, as well as problem-solving tools and strategic thinking combined with consistent thinking techniques and modalities such as Ideographic Thinking.
- The *third* type is toxic stress. In this instance adaptation processes have failed and we feel trapped in a hostile environment with no mastery, self-esteem or other resources available[7]. In this case, it will be important to undertake a more comprehensive and multi-faceted approach to regain a sense of control and trust in one's resources and effectiveness, with various tools and methods across all switch areas.

To better understand how these mechanisms work, let's take a schematic look at how the brain network that helps us manage uncertainty and low predictability is organized.

While looking for balance between adaptation and development, the brain receives sensory data from the inside (interoception) and from the outside world. Integrating these data it selects a switch based on the evaluation of whether it is more useful to: 1) carry on trying to reach *its objectives*; 2) *act on the outside world* altering it; 3) *act on its own body*, changing its physiology (so called 'stress responses' and more).

This brain network evaluates the pros and cons of a situation, but not necessarily those factors that we typically consider when trying to make a rational choice. For example, when deciding to purchase a new car, we consider factors such as cost, associated expenses, tangible features (fuel efficiency, garage space), as well as emotional factors (status, the potential for self-gratification, which needs it fulfils, etc.). This brain network evaluates external resources (e.g., available funds) as well as internal resources (from freedom of movement to any bodily pain that may indicate heightened risk and limitations). It also considers the ability to tolerate physical impact (even though the direct and immediate connection may not exist in the context of purchasing a car, it could relate to feeling physically secure in that vehicle, financial security in relation to the loan payment, and protection from potential verbal provocations indirectly linked to the new car).

This network also takes into account potential risks. For example, if we were to choose an expensive car, it could activate additional states of uncertainty, which we may not be able to tolerate because our immune system is already strained (leading us to choose a fixed-rate financing option, even if it is less advantageous than a variable rate). Among other factors, the sense of security inspired by the seller is also considered, and this often taps into our emotional vulnerabilities (switch 4), even though it may not be based on logic (as everything is now controlled by the parent company, while the seller's role is solely to sell, although we often pretend not to remember that).

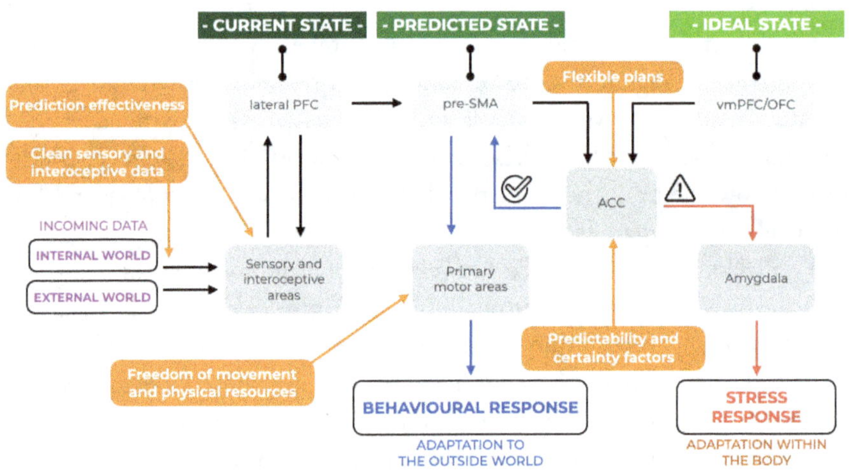

Fig. - A schematic representation role of the Anterior Cingulate Cortex (ACC) as a switch: in conditions of certainty, it activates a strategy, while in situations of unpredictability, it triggers a stress response. The orange boxes represent the criteria for effectiveness to best mediate between the current situation and the ideal one, ultimately developing a predicted state that is realistic and achievable in a concrete manner.

At the mental-cerebral level, this switch involves two main mechanisms and is based on the evaluation of three different factors, which affect specific networks and hubs[8]:

- The information regarding the *current state* of one's body and the external world, which is managed by the lateral prefrontal cortex, that looks for maximum objectivity. Our task will be to support this process from the beginning, both for internal and external sensory perceptions, as well as in the attribution of meaning.
- The information related to the *predicted state*, in the sense that we consider this state as the realistically achievable outcome. Interestingly, this process involves the pre-motor areas, precisely because it simulates the actual realization of the predicted state to evaluate its feasibility. Here, it is important to assist the individual on multiple levels, from the mental flexibility of representing different possible scenarios to concrete problem-solving.
- The third aspect taken into consideration relates to information on one's *ideal goals*, which involves the prefrontal and orbitofrontal cortices. This localization helps us understand that the term "ideal goals" should be understood broadly to include motivation, desires, self-image, compensation mechanisms, and one's deepest needs (further explored in switch 4). In this aspect, it is possible to work in various ways, but the central point always involves gaining clarity on how genuine and balanced these goals are with other objectives and how in harmony and balance they are with different aspects of life.

Beyond individual interventions and in-depth analysis of each of the three factors, the great added value of this network lies in its global functioning. The anterior cingulate cortex (ACC) interacts with all this information and representations, the neural hubs that process them, comparing the achievable state with the goals. Based on this evaluation, it selects the best strategy for future well-being.

This mechanism allows us to act on two affected areas. The first relates to the perception of predictability. If there are conditions of certainty, the pre-SMA (pre-Supplementary Motor Area) and PMC (Primary Motor Cortex) initiate their respective behavioural responses. However, if the conditions are characterized by unpredictability (e.g., low environmental predictability or great uncertainty in choosing the optimal strategy), the amygdala activates the stress response.

As we have seen with the previous switch, this evaluation is largely influenced by incoming sensory perception. Therefore, techniques that we have already discussed, as well as those we have referred to as "Reboot Techniques" (see detailed box below), will be helpful. Other strategies involve managing emotions and impulsivity, using concepts and techniques that we will explore in switch area 4. From a behavioural and organizational standpoint, it can be beneficial to alternate between physical and mental environments with varying degrees of hostility throughout the day, thus avoiding the possibility of overload beforehand.

REBOOT TECHNIQUES

With the term "Reboot Techniques," we metaphorically refer to the process of restarting a computer when an application is stuck or not functioning correctly (e.g. pressing *Control+Alt+Delete* to restart the computer).

Indeed, we have gathered a series of precautions and strategies to promote the proper sensory perception and physiological functioning of the initial stages of evaluating a situation to which we need to adapt, which will then shape stress reactions, learning, behaviour, and decisions under this name.

The underlying idea is to leverage the neurobiological processes and mechanisms that underlie these evaluations and how they can be in synergy or antagonism with anticipated predictions in order to facilitate them.

Starting from the beginning of the perception mechanism that initiates every process of adaptation (stress, emotions, relational and power dynamics, etc.) and development (learning, evolving relationships, etc.), it is useful to understand how different sensory organs function, how their processes integrate with our systems, and how to use them to our advantage.

For example, our skin has numerous sensory receptors specialized in detecting various sensations such as heat-cold, pressure, stretching, mechanical bending (like with a pinch), burning, affectionate touch, itching, and so on.

There are even receptors and entire somatosensory systems that are completely different for discriminative-exploratory touch and affective touch. Without going into the details of the neural and integrative pathways that interact with all the described systems concerning the phases of Interception, Labelling, and Evaluation, it is important to know that:

The *discriminative-exploratory* pathway begins in naturally hairless skin (primarily the palms of the hands, at least for our purposes) and represents the sensory foundation for somatomotor activity.

The *affective* pathway starts from the hair-covered skin (including the non-visible micro-hair present over almost all the body) and, in contrast to the previous pathway, represents the sensory foundation for autonomic activity and has high emotional, homeostatic, and motivational significance.

These characteristics allow us to provide salient signals, or signals that have the strength to be noticed and, consequently, reactivate the perception process that may have been distorted or bypassed by states of hyperactivation or by the imposition of beliefs or predictions.

One way to provide this signal is by offering unnatural and inconsistent stimuli that our system doesn't recognize so that it is, therefore, obliged to carefully verify all subsequent signals. This can be done in various ways, such as touching close stimuli at different temperatures or made of significantly different materials (cold and hot, smooth and rough, dry and wet) using the same hand. It can also involve creating incorrect expectations (placing a hot beverage in a can that has apparently just been taken out of the refrigerator) or calmly breathing through a straw (the reduced oxygen supply triggers alertness, but in reality - if the supply is constant - one can remain relaxed).

Another method is through sensory spectrum amplification or limitation. For example, attempting to face a challenging situation blindfolded or with reduced external audio, or wearing a bandage that restricts movement. As a practical example, this technique could be used in a simulation to prepare for public speaking by delivering a presentation while blindfolded or, conversely, facing very bright lights.

The second key factor of this network concerns the *flexibility of plans*. In fact, to adapt well to this world, you don't need a perfect plan; on the contrary, this would be limiting and problematic due to its very nature. This network functions well when it recognizes that we need flexible plans to achieve our goals. Flexibility is determined by various factors, including the ability to quickly change even a single step of our plan, replacing it with one that better suits an unexpected change in the external environment or in our priorities. This also means being able to tolerate a moment of standstill or inaction, as long as it makes sense in our vision, even if it hasn't been well incorporated into the strategy we had initially set out. It also means being able to observe things from a different perspective and having good mental flexibility.

To support this type of flexibility in action plans, it is crucial to develop projects that are organized into flexible modules, which allow for an easy transition from the overall vision to the specific details that need to be explored. These modules can be easily modified, reordered, and updated, intervening only where necessary. This type of project becomes a more flexible way of thinking that is applicable in any field. That's why we have developed *Modular Thinking* as a sub-mode of Ideographic Thinking (see the following box for this application, while Switch 5 provides an overview of the method in general).

Furthermore, it is possible to cultivate more flexible thinking from various perspectives and with specific approaches: one can train the ability to consider multiple scenarios in parallel (see the Possible Scenarios technique and the Pre-Solutions technique), to have more mental energy available (nurtured by the strategies mentioned in previous switches, which provide quick access to mental resources, clarity, and motivation), and to have the freedom to accept that a plan may not go as expected, which is a mental, emotional, and physical resource (in line with the principle of free energy in Switch 2, as well as the flows of Switch 5).

In the case of a stress response related to the malfunctioning of this network, significant modifications are activated which, in the *short* term, can literally save our lives and bring other benefits. However, in the *long* run, they tend to degenerate into allostatic overload (see Switch 2) and, therefore, the malfunctioning of the adaptive mechanisms themselves (*resulting in chronic anxiety, panic attacks, or depression*) and systemic degeneration of the organs involved (*heart attacks, chronic fatigue, gastritis, irritable bowel syndrome, neuropathies, postural and motor dysfunctions, etc.*). Therefore, recreating a well-coordinated switch mechanism between the achievement of one's goals and stress responses is key.

MODULAR THINKING TECHNIQUE

Modular Thinking, even though it only takes shape in our minds, has a visual and synthetic nature, allowing us to move quickly and flexibly across multiple dimensions, with agility and without always starting from scratch. Serial thinking, on the other hand, corresponds to sentences as we write them: it is rigid and static, following only one line of thought at a time. Changing it requires great effort and time. Modular Thinking is naturally open to change and flexibility, both due to its typical modular function and because it requires less effort to modify it since we don't become as attached to our thoughts as we do to writing, which is typical of serial thinking (resulting in a single, rigid, and unchangeable block). Instead, modular thinking corresponds to the system-project represented visually by blocks that are modifiable in terms of content, form, sequence, and connections. This allows for the development and resistance-free acceptance of new hypotheses, verifying them, maintaining them as possible variations, testing them, and modifying them as we proceed.

Modular Thinking is a way to manage our own thoughts but also to work with another person or in a team. It is an excellent ally for professionals in both clinical and business settings. It provides a working and analytical method with its own features and strategies, but it can be filled with content and techniques specific to one's profession. It enables collaborative work side by side, focusing on constructive aspects, objectively seeing opportunities, opening parentheses without losing the main thread of the discussion, and simultaneously preserving all the valuable ideas that emerged. It provides the opportunity to literally see critical points, identify breaking elements, and explore different hypothetical scenarios without immediately confining the person to a single train of thought.

The use of Modular Thinking in groups of people reduces conflict and promotes collaboration, facilitating integration. Thanks to its active and playful dynamics, it increases participation and engagement. It facilitates, speeds up, and makes meetings and group work more productive, whether this involves brainstorming, problem analysis, project ideation, decision-making, or other activities.

To give shape to Modular Thinking, there are a series of precautions and approaches. Here are some key points in summary:

- Write concisely, focusing only on keywords. Long sentences tend to become restrictive and less easy to modify.

- Use a visual approach to highlight key points, such as flowcharts or comic strip scenes.

- In training courses, I often encourage people to try describing what needs to be done using only images, like the instructions for assembling furniture invented by a famous company but now used by everyone. This process helps identify the salient nodes, the points around which the process is articulated. Furthermore, it helps reflect on what truly needs explaining and what can be assumed as known (in our analogy with furniture instructions, there's no need to represent an instruction just to say "pick up the screwdriver" or "turn it clockwise"). It would be wasteful or even offensive to the recipient.

In many real-life cases, projects cannot be carried out solely with drawings, but attempting to do so develops a more flexible way of thinking that focuses on what truly matters.

To help in this direction, post-it notes or entire worksheets can be used for each key point, allowing room for further insights or changes that can be easily applied.

Discussion, comparison, and integration between different processes are also easier, whether it's colleagues collaborating with each other or a patient wanting to integrate therapeutic proposals into their own habits. Indeed, comparing two serial thoughts is difficult: it's like having to read two articles and constantly scroll through them to find analogies and differences, struggling to find the space where one sentence fits into the other without disrupting the flow of the original narrative. On the other hand, when comparing post-it notes or visually represented diagrams in a series of interconnected circles, similarities and differences immediately stand out, making it easy to integrate them into a single sequence.

Now let's see two techniques that can be used to work on the switch between uncertainty and non-predictability, but which can very well also be considered mental-emotional integration techniques.

THE PRE-SOLUTION TECHNIQUE

This technique constructively provokes for the person who puts it into practice by making them accept that their negative fantasy could come true. Usually, people have a worry that takes shape in a specific situation, such as *"if I give a bad presentation at the meeting, I'll get fired/lose an important career opportunity,"* and they do everything to avoid it.

With this technique, we start from the opposite perspective: assuming that it definitely will happen. The very act of accepting that the event could occur, admitting its possibility, even hypothetically, takes away its seriousness and reduces the emotional charge. However, the value of this technique goes beyond that. In fact, it allows for the initiation of a sort of practical problem-solving process that is rich in cognitive and emotional implications. You work to understand what the breaking points are, the critical moments that can bring about the feared negative consequences. In our example, it could be that the boss, focusing on the poor presentation performance, fails to recognize the real value of the work done to create the content, and doesn't move beyond the manner in which it was presented. Alternatively, in a different hypothesis, the problem could be that they consider the person is too emotional to be promoted to the desired managerial position.

At this point, a *pre-solution* is activated, finding a way to prevent the breaking point from occurring, regardless of how things go. Following the first example, the pre-solution could be to ask the boss to review the slides together and, through comments, highlight the value of the work done a week before the conference. In contrast, in the second hypothesis, the person can identify the individuals who will play a role in evaluating their emotional stability for the managerial position and dedicate time to each of them by engaging in work and social activities that showcase this characteristic, in the days leading up to the presentation.
In addition to the specific advantages of dismantling fears and providing real benefits to the individual, the strength of this technique also lies in offering a broader and more constructive perspective of one's sphere of influence over events and people, despite varying degrees of unpredictability.

The pre-solution technique, as we have just seen, provides a way to work on a specific problem-solving process that, even if it never takes shape, serves to act on the thoughts and emotions involved in that type of issue.
The next technique, on the other hand, starts with a mental-imaginative exercise that opens us up to multiple solutions, with the objective not to identify the right one, but rather to develop greater flexibility, no matter what happens.

POSSIBLE SCENARIOS TECHNIQUE

Restoring multiple alternatives and *being able to choose* are two of the greatest resources and liberties available to humans. There are many ways to devise alternative responses and make them an integral part of our repertoire, from a shift in mental paradigms to overcoming old behavioural "engrams", from creative-generative thinking to visual tools, and so on. Let's now look at a simple and effective application.

When our mind is unprepared to face a particular situation, it seeks behaviour from its repertoire that has been frequently used, even if it is not suitable or may be counterproductive. In other words, having acted many times in the same way makes that behaviour readily accessible. In times of doubt, fatigue, haste, and confusion, that old pattern is easily retrieved at the expense of new behaviours that would be preferable. To counteract this mechanism, it is useful to create multiple different scenarios in which we enact various behaviours, training ourselves to imagine different possibilities, concretely fantasizing about what we would do in each of them. Exploring mental, emotional, and behavioural elements, as well as the relational and contextual consequences, allows us to create new, more easily accessible patterns.

This technique is particularly effective when the number of scenarios is high, ideally ranging from 10 to 15. However, it is important not to have fewer than seven scenarios. This way, we gain several advantages, it is easy to choose the strong alternative over the weak one, and between a strong one and many new ones, the old automatism is less likely to kick in. Furthermore, it is important to create many scenarios, including some that are absurd or paradoxical. Precisely because they represent extreme conditions, these latter scenarios lend strength to the more realistic alternatives. Finally, the high number of scenarios, the mental activity involved in identifying them, and the fantasizing about different reactions and behaviours support the feeling of having more resources and possibilities than previously believed.

A pivotal aspect of this technique's effectiveness lies in collecting a variety of scenarios and then delving deeply into each one, exploring the nuances of different representational, perceptual, and sensory aspects. This involves visualizing the situation as if it were a scene in a movie, capturing all the visual details, examining the context and the people involved with an observant eye, tuning in to the surrounding sounds and voices, and being mindful of the emotional fluctuations, thoughts, tactile sensations, muscular and visceral responses, smells, and more. This immersive exploration enriches the experience, making each scenario a vivid and transformational journey into new potential responses.

REFERENCES

[1] Pessoa L 2013. The cognitive-emotional brain: from interactions to integration. The MIT Press, Cambridge, MA

[2] Barrett, L. F., & Satpute, A. (2013). Large-scale brain networks in affective and social neuroscience: Towards an integrative functional architecture of the brain. Current Opinion in Neurobiology, 23(3), 361–372.

[3] LeDoux JE. Anxious: Using the Brain to Understand and Treat Fear and Anxiety. New York: Penguin Books; 2015.

[4] Sinibaldi F. (2018), Lavorare con l'unità corpo-mente per favorire pensieri, emozioni e sviluppo personale in: La Pnei e le discipline corporee (Barsotti N, Lanaro D, Chiera M, Bottaccioli F), Edra - Elsevier.

[5] Brooks, S. J., & Stein, D. J. (2015). A systematic review of the neural bases of psychotherapy for anxiety and related disorders. Dialogues in Clinical Neuroscience, 17(3), 261–279.

[6] Daniels JK, McFarlane AC, Bluhm RL, et al. Switching Between Executive and Default Mode Networks in Posttraumatic Stress Disorder: Alterations in Functional Connectivity. J Psychiatry Neurosci. 2010;35(4):258-66.

[7] Peters, A., & McEwen, B. S. (2015). Stress habituation, body shape and cardiovascular mortality. Neuroscience and biobehavioral reviews, 56, 139–150.

[8] Peters A, McEwen BS, Friston K (2017) Uncertainty and stress: why it causes diseases and how it is mastered by the brain. Prog Neurobiol 156:164–188.

SWITCHES GROUP 4 SOCIAL - MAN: THE LOST ANIMAL

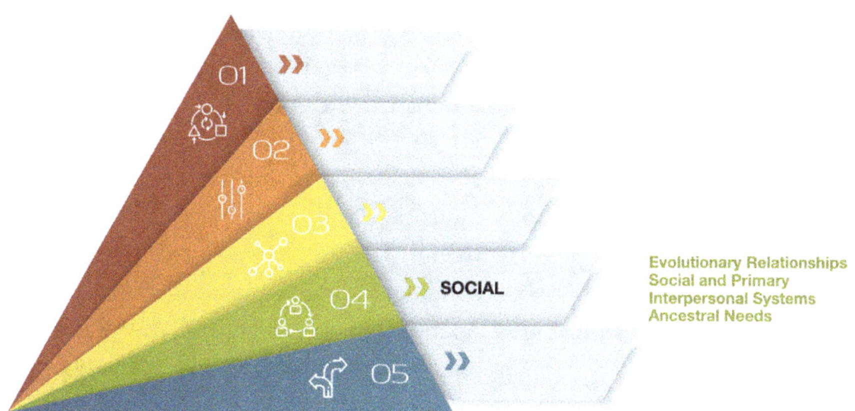

EVOLUTIONARY RELATIONSHIPS, PRIMARY SOCIAL AND INTERPERSONAL SYSTEMS

"Mighty", like the Norse mythology god Thor. This is the name I gave to my dog when I was 17. I chose the name based on the strong interest in Norse mythology that I was nursing at that time. In hindsight, however, it was also a very fitting name for that dog, although I wouldn't have said so at the beginning (I later discovered I had misinterpreted him!). In fact, when we went to see the litter at a nearby farmhouse, that adorable little puppy was on his own and not playing with the other puppies. We chose him thinking that he was shy and in need of affection. After a few months, Mighty's personality began to take shape and it was strong and powerful just like his name, to the point that he wanted to be the one in charge at home. Fortunately, we immediately sought help and (I must say, quite luckily) we found a truly skilled dog expert. The first interesting discovery was the true meaning behind his initial behaviour: little Mighty wasn't playing with his siblings because he had already completed the dominance rank rituals (at least in their initial puppy version), he had established confidence in his resources, and as a result, he had decided that he was the pack leader among his siblings. This was followed by a series of other intriguing discoveries, even more relevant as they were observed in action (quite literally, as we were always in parks or gardens training). Later on, I had the opportunity to verify many of these discoveries – with necessary adjustments for the human species – with friends, in the musical group I played in, and, later, as a parallel perspective to my various studies and experiences in psychology, both in business and clinical settings.

Among the most significant themes I was able to delve into were: the connection between activation/excitement states and social dynamics, the games of trust and power that operate on hormonal and postural levels (often with interpretations far removed from the typical indications of human nonverbal communication), the role of the recognized pack leader who must serve the group not for personal benefit (quite different from the concepts of leadership we're accustomed to in modern society), and many other fascinating topics that we'll explore in this chapter.

In switch area 4, we'll delve into the deepest levels of social interactions and interpersonal relationships, which are ingrained in our mammalian nature and have developed over centuries of evolution. We'll explore, for example, the constructive value of aggression, which is an excellent mode of social regulation and protection of what is important to us. This emotional resource can be well utilized when its neurobiological autonomy from destructive anger is recognized, and when times and spaces in relational dynamics are accurately managed. In this area, we'll also analyse ancestral needs, those deep-seated needs rooted in the brain networks and neurotransmitters of all evolved mammals. These types of needs can be found transversely in several switches, but we've placed them here because, even though they are individual needs, they are infused with relationships, both in the presence and absence of the "other".

Social behaviour and emotional life, in fact, are among the most complex and transversal phenomena of human experience. They are largely rooted in ancestral systems, as they arise from a primary survival need, even though they have become structured and sophisticated over time, evolving through power dynamics, challenges, acceptance, rules, and other complex systems[1].

All the relational and social mechanisms in this switch area interact in a highly articulated way with each other and with other elements of safety, motivation, self-regulation, and development. For instance, the brain networks we saw in area 3 grow and develop through interaction among themselves and through interpersonal dynamics, just as neural plasticity and epigenetics in area 1 can be significantly altered - for better or worse - by the types of affective and social relationships we experience.

ASSESSMENT: WHAT TO OBSERVE AND EVALUATE

In this fourth switch area, it's interesting to observe various aspects from different perspectives and with a multi-systemic view. These include:
- Emotional-relational difficulties;
- Self-regulation and self-esteem problems with an interpersonal dimension;
- Significant changes in personality traits in different contexts (while we all adapt and respond differently to various environments and people, excessive change can lead to identity loss and lack of centeredness);
- Loss of control in relationships (such as raising one's voice excessively in front of someone sexually attractive or seeming aggressive, displaying emotional vulnerabilities in unprotected contexts, etc.);
- Issues related to dimensions involving dependence, autonomy, attachment, possessiveness, etc.;
- Trust issues;
- Struggles with social motivation;
- Limited perception of one's own resources;
- Weak internal focus;
- Impulsiveness;
- Poor timing, both in daily life (saying the wrong thing at the wrong time, not being able to take turns in conversation, etc.) and

pathologically (such as the intrusion into other people's personal space and time which is typical of psychotic behaviours);

- Imbalances in one's needs, demotivation, loss meaning in life.

SOCIAL INTERACTION AND RELATIONSHIPS FROM AN ETHOLOGICAL PERSPECTIVE

Human beings are social animals. Our mind-body system is designed to engage in relationships, and in a virtuous cycle, good relationships keep us in optimal condition.

Even from an evolutionary perspective, we descend from socially organized species. The primate closest to us, the chimpanzee, shares 70% of our DNA and exhibits innate behaviours like attachment, caregiving, cooperation, and play. Humans, like other primates, possess innate social responses, such as tendencies towards forgiveness. This means that in conflict situations (arguments, disagreements, confrontations, etc.), we are naturally inclined to forgive rather than perpetuate the conflict. It would be "less costly" in practical terms to sever ties with someone who wronged us, yet we prefer to reduce the emotional cost of separation and the material cost of forgoing the benefits of cooperation over being alone. In essence, we have several valid reasons that naturally drive us towards social interaction.

The herd, across all species, comes into existence to increase advantages compared to being solitary, although modern humans often experience conflicting tensions in this regard. We seek the benefits of society, like a sense of protection, reduced personal responsibility, ease of obtaining what we need or want, but simultaneously desire private property, no intrusion from neighbours, complete autonomy, to gain more than we yield, managing as many aspects of life independently as possible, and so on.

Generally, we can say that the benefits of the group come at a price, yet humans often exhibit ambivalence towards this. As we've seen, humans need a group, and, in absolute terms, this is an easily attainable condition, there are many other individuals with the same need. However, to stay united and provide more advantages than disadvantages a group requires *structure* and *order*.

By *structure*, we mean a hierarchy with a pack leader providing guidance and directions to other group members (technically referred to as "followers", though this term has taken on a negative connotation) who are willing to follow. In many animal species, the hierarchy can be more complex; for example, in wolves, there's an alpha male and an alpha female. There's a beta who serves as the alpha's right-hand, and so on.

By *order*, we mean that the group's rules must be clear, shared, and consistent. Otherwise, they might not be understood, not everyone might feel involved, and they wouldn't be credible. Animals manage to stay within these guiderails fairly easily and – through clear, transparent, and consistent communication – derive security and balance. However, when it comes to clear, transparent, and consistent communication, humans tend to encounter difficulties. Often, the benefits an individual claims to want or receive from a group are not their real ones. Rarely will a person say to their colleagues, *"I only need you to make money"*, or will a person tell others, *"You're boring, but I hope to find a girlfriend through you"*. I've given two extreme examples to make the point clear, but I'm sure you'll be able to identify many shades of situations in line with these in personal and professional life. As they say, "it's only human" to have such tendencies, the problem lies in internal clarity and then in ethics towards others in how they are regulated and mediated with other factors.

ATTACHMENT AND OTHER INTER-CONNECTED AREAS

The critical issue of *attachment dynamics* towards caregivers in children can be re-read and analysed synergistically with other areas of study, harmoniously with our integrative science outlook.

The dynamics of attachment and caregiving between parents and offspring constitute a natural and spontaneous phenomenon in all mammals. Unfortunately, humans tend to hinder part of this natural process due to the significant interference of fears and concerns, often propagated by certain cultural "degenerations". Let's provide some examples: for some mothers, the fear of bodily changes during pregnancy is terrifying, both for aesthetic reasons and for the feared repercussions on their health. For instance, it's not uncommon today to hear that *"a caesarean delivery is statistically safer for both the mother and the baby, even in the absence of complications"*. This viewpoint is supported by some medical professionals, generating and perpetuating often unfounded fears that disrupt the mother's (and often the father's) relationship with the baby even before birth. This can lead to significant attachment-caregiving repercussions from the very beginning. Following our integrative approach, we must remember that other levels are also in play, the mother will experience the entire pregnancy with her stress axes hyperactivated by this fear, damaging her own physical health and creating an unfavourable environment for the proper development of the unborn child. This, in turn, can lead to complications during gestation or at the time of birth, paradoxically generated by the fear of potential complications that has been instilled.

In any case, a caesarean birth certainly does not allow for the neurological activation of the baby that comes from mechanical stimulation during the birth canal passage. Similarly, contact with the vaginal microbiome doesn't occur.

This example should not be the sole focus; attachment issues are not confined to this scenario. The example serves to highlight how humans themselves often create conditions that exacerbate things. In nature, for instance, no animal experiences concern about economic possibilities to feed or nurture their offspring. No one has agonizing doubts about their true paternity and so forth.

Fig. next page - A schematic representation of the main underlying mechanisms behind alterations in attachment style in a broad sense (not only according to Attachment Theory but considering relational security in general, the tendency to trust others, self-image in relation to other people, degrees of autonomy, etc.). This generates the need to act on all levels in an integrated and integrative manner to restore physiology and well-being in these dimensions.

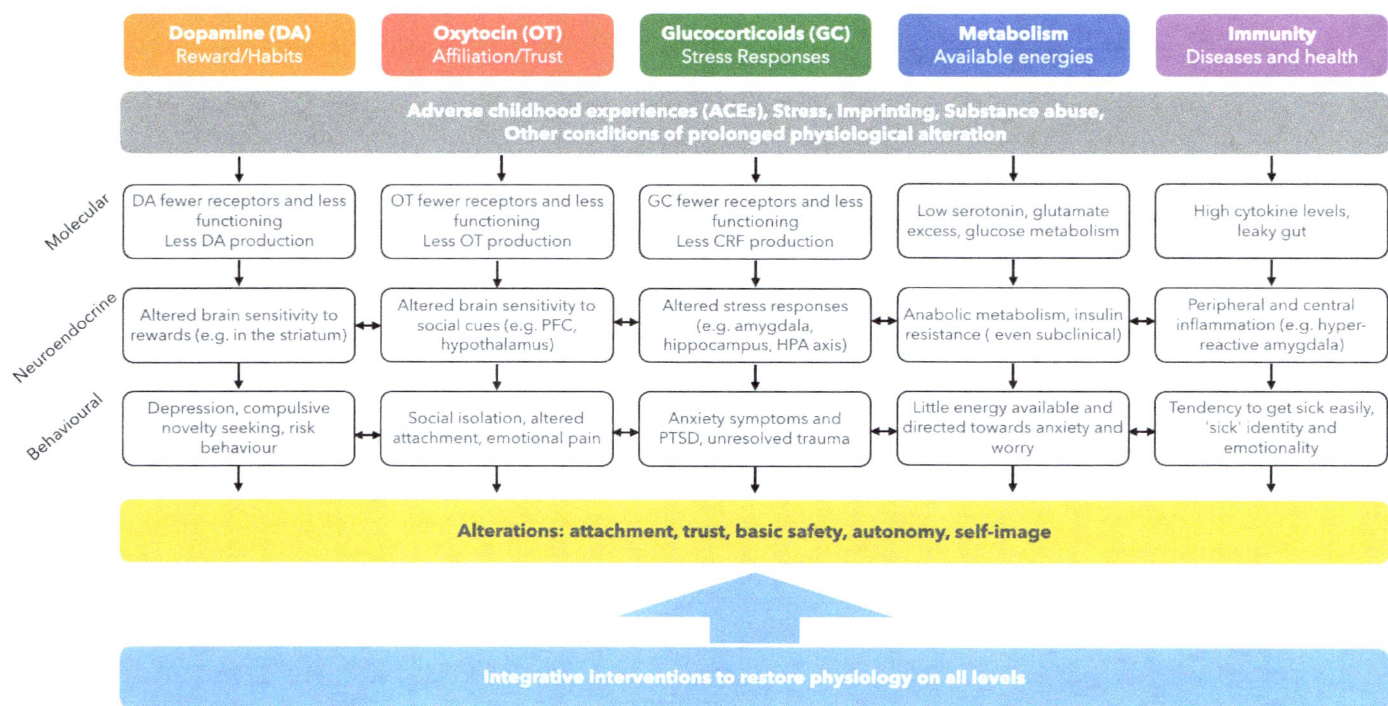
Dopamine (DA)
Reward/Habits
Oxytocin (OT)
Affiliation/Trust
Glucocorticoids (GC)
Stress Responses
Metabolism
Available energies
Immunity
Diseases and health
Adverse childhood experiences (ACEs), Stress, Imprinting, Substance abuse, Other conditions of prolonged physiological alteration
Molecular
DA fewer receptors and less functioning Less DA production
OT fewer receptors and less functioning Less OT production
GC fewer receptors and less functioning Less CRF production
Low serotonin, glutamate excess, glucose metabolism
High cytokine levels, leaky gut
Neuroendocrine
Altered brain sensitivity to rewards (e.g. in the striatum)
Altered brain sensitivity to social cues (e.g. PFC, hypothalamus)
Altered stress responses (e.g. amygdala, hippocampus, HPA axis)
Anabolic metabolism, insulin resistance (even subclinical)
Peripheral and central inflammation (e.g. hyper-reactive amygdala)
Behavioural
Depression, compulsive novelty seeking, risk behaviour
Social isolation, altered attachment, emotional pain
Anxiety symptoms and PTSD, unresolved trauma
Little energy available and directed towards anxiety and worry
Tendency to get sick easily, 'sick' identity and emotionality
Alterations: attachment, trust, basic safety, autonomy, self-image
Integrative interventions to restore physiology on all levels

As we have just seen, a situation of chronic stress during pregnancy can create the conditions to alter the basic regulation of the main physiological management systems of the organism, and in particular, the stress axis. The same can also occur due to trauma or drug abuse during pregnancy.

Studies on imprinting and attachment are very interesting and testify to how these processes have effects at the psychological, neuro-endocrine, immune, metabolic, and epigenetic levels. For this reason, even if the issue doesn't seem to be interpersonal in nature, it will almost always be important to intervene on the mechanisms we are addressing in this area dedicated to relationships.

Taking a genetic and epigenetic standpoint, it is interesting to discover how the genetic expression of a specific serotonin transporter can influence neural plasticity (at the heart of change and learning – see group 1 switches) and the level of serotonin available to the brain, critically impacting emotions and mood. The genetic expression of the alleles involved in these processes is highly sensitive to the type of environment experienced (aversive Vs supportive) and to the level of maternal care received, especially relating to protection[2].

In practical terms, this means that early positive experiences of this type change gene expression, positively influencing mood and the level of social competence exhibited. Although early years are critical in the definition of genetic expression, fortunately, even in adult life there is significant margin for change. For this reason, it is strategic to introduce targeted action on concrete environmental and safety elements as well as on emotional and cognitive aspects. It is thus possible to guarantee change that optimally leverages the synergy between these interconnected systems at every level.

From taking care of the physical environment where one spends most of their time, to developing relational and internal safety factors, much can be done. For example, Louis had many external safety nets and protective factors (a high-income job where being fired was impossible, a beautiful house, etc.), but he lived in a constant state of insecurity. He was like a child abandoned in the body of a fifty-year-old. For him, it was essential to be able to incorporate explicit safety signals into his home. In fact, he furnished it in a minimalist hi-tech style, so his rational mind knew he had high levels of security, but his emotional side lacked tangible, daily sensory experiences that would generate this type of feeling. It was important to accompany his psychotherapeutic journey with a series of concrete initiatives that then merged in synergy with the therapy itself, for him to feel secure in that house, offering deeper insights and bringing to light new themes and key issues. First, I encouraged Louis to try to sensorially identify what might make him feel secure or not in that house, focusing about sensations experienced in friends' homes, his childhood home, but also by exploring the displays of furniture stores. In light of these reflections and experiments, as a first step, he decided to replace the cool-toned, white lights throughout the house with warmer tones similar to natural sunlight. Then, he decided to remove a couple of very modern paintings characterized by strong and saturated (thus unnatural) colours, replacing them with realistic images of the sea and countryside without human figures, which he found very relaxing and *"free from bothersome people"*. Initially, he wanted to try to increase his sense of security in a tangible, even if irrational, way. When he wanted to relax and *"shut out the world"*, he placed a trunk in front of the entrance door to block it. It was an irrational choice; his door was already reinforced, and the house had a state-of-the-art alarm system, but as he put it, *"all this security wasn't visible, whereas the trunk was there in all its solidity"*. Furthermore, the trunk – as he only realized later on – symbolized his grandparents' home, which for him were the only figures capable of providing him with real security. That trunk, using reconsolidation techniques and Parallel Worlds (see box below), was then transformed into a symbol of the *theatre actor's trunk*, carrying around just enough to make him feel secure and comfortable wherever he goes.

From another perspective, as we saw in the second group of switches, the intestinal microbiome can significantly alter many behaviours and relational attitudes, including a mother's caregiving style. Michael and Juliette, the siblings respectively diagnosed with ADHD, weight issues and allergies, had a mother who was quite detached and not inclined towards physical and emotional contact. As we saw in switch area 2, we worked with them to rebalance the intestine, the 'second brain' and for its central role in inflammatory processes. In this context, we can add that, to achieve comprehensive results, we didn't just propose interventions related to the children's diet and nutritional supplements; we included the entire family. This improved everyone's immune system (which was also beneficial for the parents) and, thanks to collective, shared well-being initiatives and related care rituals, this also positively impacted the collective mood and the propensity for more open and constructive attachment-care behaviour.

Meanwhile, we worked with the parents on developing knowledge that could change their perspective on their parental role (providing security, protection, development) and practical activities to promote these aspects concretely (cooperative games, physical contact, discussions to avoid in the presence of children, etc.).

On the other hand, individually tailored paths were implemented for the children in terms of neural integration, involving activities that focused on balance and coordination for Michael (switches 3 and 5), and activities that were more anti-inflammatory and metabolic (switches 1 and 2), as well as emotional regulation in relationships (discussed later in this same switch) for Juliette.

In addition to this, neural pleasure circuits and child care are also connected; just think of the hyperstimulation of pleasure centres such as that caused by drug or alcohol abuse and how it tends to prevail over almost any development and adaptation function[3]. This type of consideration has a huge impact on two levels.

The *first* is a moral point; a mother who does not nurture her offspring is not necessarily devoid of maternal instinct or a 'bad mother'. She may be a mother in whom the nurturing functions have been altered by a series of dysfunctions.

The *second* point is the practical result of the former; there is a need for wide range clinical intervention where different issues can be triggering each other, or where there are reciprocal influences and apparently disconnected elements that affect each other. These can be old traumas, lack of socialisation, poor nutrition and drug abuse (these two elements can radically alter the microbiome and the inflammatory profile even at brain level).

ATTACHMENT... OR CONTACT?

Touch is connected to the level of self-confidence and trust among people. Those who develop a tendency to touch and feel in a refined manner (musicians, architects, tailors, etc.) generally show higher self-confidence and lower stress levels (measurable objectively with parameters like cortisol, HRV, etc.). This phenomenon is understandable by considering: 1- touch as the first form of knowledge, which fortunately is rarely denied; 2- the fact that touch allows us to have an active role and extend our limits; 3- the neurological stimulation associated with these gestures, which richly and complexly activates our nervous processing system.

Physical contact has significant emotional effects: it calms us, activates reward centres in the brain, and generates a sense of security. Through contact, trust is increased, as is cooperation. In elementary schools where teachers have contact with their students, higher levels of cooperation and study are observed. It doesn't necessarily entail hugs and kisses or other visibly affectionate behaviour. In this regard, let's consider a case proven by multiple studies: teachers are asked, while individually correcting a mistake, to take half of the students and provide a simple explanation, while for the other half, they must explain the correct solution while affectionately touching the students' forearms. The results indicate that children who were touched remember the correct solution over time more easily, and if they're asked to do something like go to the blackboard, they collaborate willingly- four times more so than other children.

Even in professional sports among adults, a strong connection between contact and trust is noticeable. The frequency with which players on a basketball team touch each other (high-fives, pats, jumping together with chest bumps, etc.) is directly related to how often they win, their evaluations, and improved compensation.

Contact plays a fundamental role in our evolution and well-being. It's not just one of the first forms of communication, it's a way to activate the senses, provide pleasure, convey trust and acceptance, offer security, compassion, etc.

The skin is our largest sensory organ. Specific neurons in the skin perceive and evaluate touch. The immune system is also connected to these neurons, and it's not surprising that a significant amount of interpersonal contact is directly linked to a longer than average lifespan.

From a neuroscientific perspective, contact activates areas in the frontal cortex responsible for *reinforcement* (in terms of reward-punishment) and *compassion*. It also activates areas involved in *cooperation* and particularly in the sense of *mutual relationships*. Furthermore, it also stimulates the vagus nerve and regulates heart rate.

When parents lovingly caress their children, oxytocin levels rise in both parent and child. A well-functioning oxytocin network counteracts the effects of stress (reducing stress-related hormones, modulating cardiovascular responses, reducing amygdala responses), and significantly promotes family attachment, social bonds, and friendship.

Simple and warm contact even between less intimate individuals has specific social functions that have been extensively verified by neuroscience, it creates a shared sense of reward, reinforces reciprocity, signals security, calms, releases oxytocin, and makes individuals more cooperative.

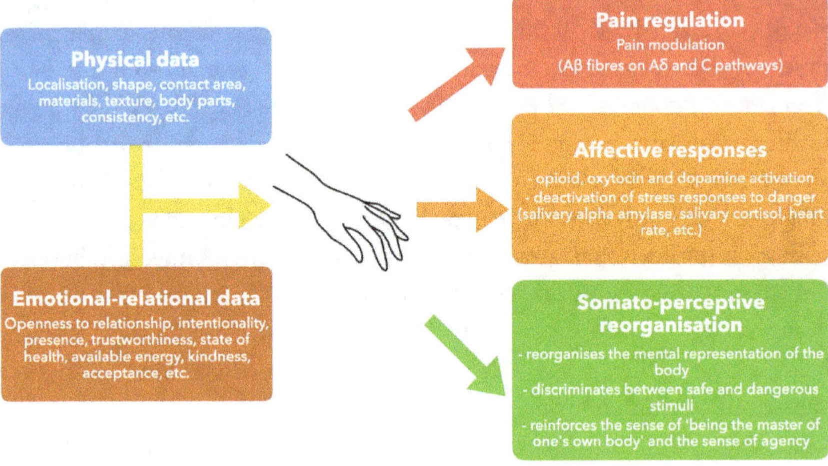

Fig. - Contact processes complex and multi-dimensional responses at the level of pain regulation, emotions, somatosensory processing (self-awareness and understanding of the world through the body) through incoming information.

There are particular areas of application worth mentioning because, given that they are characterized by extreme suffering and limited cognitive presence, we can assess the actual impact of physical contact in isolation, excluding all placebo effects. Physical contact with prematurely born children results in a 47% greater weight gain compared to those who do not receive it. In orphanages where frequent physical contact is provided to children, premature deaths decrease by 75%. In patients with

Alzheimer's, symptom reduction increases by 44%, compared to patients receiving the same care but without physical contact.

In comparison to other mammals with regard to the use of contact, unfortunately, we come out as losers: other species spend an average of 20% of their time touching each other, while we humans – depending on cultures – range from 0.3% to 2%. We humans live in a culture of physical contact deprivation, and given the benefits listed so far, this certainly penalizes us. On the other hand, many people have much more physical contact with their pets than with their relatives. A common domestic scene is one in which a person returns home, quickly greets family members, and then enthusiastically stops to cuddle the dog or cat. This image might make us smile – it's often used by comedians – but it should make us reflect on how innate our need to express affection through physical contact is, while also regulating stress and trust within the group. If we're better at doing this with animals than with people, it's interesting to work on the subjective or relational factors that support this situation.

CHANGING PERSPECTIVE: DETACHMENT

We usually tend to view attachment as a resource, as something positive that needs to be brought back to physiological state, and this is correct. It can, however, also be useful to turn that view point on its head and look at the opposite extreme: *detachment.*

Various Oriental and Western philosophies have seen detachment as a source of mental and emotional strength. Some disciplines, for example, encourage followers to give up or reduce their personal belongings because they are seen as a frequent source of personal stress and conflict. It is true that if we do not own a new car, for example, we cannot worry about it being stolen and nobody can envy us for it. In modern life, however, it is difficult from a practical stand point, and also not very satisfying, to own nothing at all. Giving things up, therefore, also risks causing a cascade of further stress (not getting a new car can lead to worries about sourcing spare parts for an out of date model and related fear for loss of time and money increases, for example).

Detachment can, however, be a mental and emotional exercise. Imagining that we have no bonds can be frightening, but it helps view things for what they really are. There can be no emotional blackmail if there is nothing to lose. Even symbolically detaching ourselves, via our lifestyle and behavioural choices, provides a great sense of freedom and mastery over decision making and self-regulation capabilities.

TECHNIQUE – PARALLEL WORLDS

This is a useful technique in helping individuals think outside their own patterns and move away from well-established thought and behaviour modes that are not always effective. Often, these modes were once helpful but are no longer suitable for current needs or context. In some situations, individuals might not even be invoking their own patterns but are adhering to patterns proposed by others to avoid the effort of choosing or taking on responsibilities. In these cases, real utility and the concrete impact of a choice are not being evaluated.

Let's consider an example where, as often happens, (illusory) rationality is invoked to make irrational choices. In certain cases, taking out insurance isn't rational due to extremely low risk. Sellers, to convince us, talk about "making a rational choice" while leveraging our fear that the minimal risk might occur, perhaps using slightly skewed data to support their argument. Moreover – and here the lack of rationality depends entirely on us – when we choose, we rarely consider that insurance companies will do everything to avoid paying (even though we know this from direct experience or from that of a friend). Therefore, the probability of using that policy becomes even lower, as conditions must be met for the insurance to actually pay out. If we consider a time perspective, not paying for insurance (for example, car theft insurance) often costs less than having to buy a new car with the money saved during years when it wasn't stolen (how many people do you know whose car has been stolen more than once in their life? How many have never had their car stolen? Think about the money spent, how much did it amount to?).

The parallel worlds technique forces us to analyse different scenarios, even extreme ones, to break free from personal biases or the influence of others, who might have a benefit – even in good faith – from influencing our choice (it could be a salesperson, but also an apprehensive parent or an envious friend, or someone afraid of losing us).

Phase 1) The first parallel world leads us to think about how the world would be if everything were purely rational. To clarify: in a purely rational world, there would be no fashion or extremely expensive clothes; only a few car models would exist without too many variations; things that cost more than necessary (phones, cars, houses) would not exist, and so on. In this phase, focus should be on how a world that is solely rational, with respect to the theme of our choice, would look.

Phase 2) The second world focuses on how a perfect world would be from our point of view. Without external influences, what would we choose? What do we truly care about? What brings us real advantages (even though there are negative ones for others, but they are not an issue in this world)? What brings us more "lightweight" advantages (like feeling successful, putting in less effort, etc.), how important are these, or can we do without them?

Phases 3, 4, 5) The technique works well even with just two parallel worlds. However, it's even more effective if more worlds are considered, pushing the mind to be even more flexible and consider extreme or paradoxical scenarios. For instance, one can imagine worlds without parents/children, where your current job does not exist in any form or variation, worlds where you're the last person on Earth, and so on.

Final Phase) Consider what the best mediation could be between World 1 and World 2 (and potentially others) at that point in your life, while also considering what might work well in the medium and long term.

In all phases, the imaginative effort should be as realistic and multi-sensory as possible, thoroughly exploring the world for its environmental characteristics, along with all the bodily, emotional, and affection sensations that might be experienced in those conditions.

THE POWER OF SYNCHRONY AND CONTEXT IN EMOTIONAL–INTERPERSONAL DYNAMICS

Interpersonal regulation and its connection to safety, self-regulation and immune system processes features a series of evolutionary systems that have been refined over time to help contextually manage the present in real-time. These processes are extremely powerful and are, almost always, prioritised in behavioural hierarchies, stress axes, emotions and behaviours. One typical example from daily life is provided each time that we receive a message or an email on our smartphone. If the content sounds aggressive – a personal slight, a lack of respect for our professional self or the imposition of something we do not deem right – our immediate reaction is to reply in the same tone, defending ourselves or returning the aggression. If we give in to this instinct it is common to feel a momentary sense of relief and then to remain suspended as we await a signal of victory or a counter-move to respond to. If, instead, we do not respond, it is likely that we will continue to go over and over what we would like to write, trying to provide the anger and aggression that have been triggered with some release, at least in imagination.

The dysfunctional aspect of this process is that our system for the management of invasions, conflicts and challenges has evolved over centuries to manage a real, physically present adversary whose behaviour we can read in non-verbal behavioural traits, whose changes in attitude we can see and can connect to the overall context. By interacting in synergy with these manifestations we take part in a dual interaction whose objective is to transform reality or the status of the relationship. These are deeply rooted process that humans have in common with all mammals[4].

We can safely say without exaggeration that Elizabeth spent a significant portion of her days waiting for notifications messages on WhatsApp. She awaited signs of love from her boyfriend and confirmation from her parents. Her anxiety grew with every minute that passed without a message, leading her to create the most dreadful fantasies. However, even when the message arrived, the mere notification increased her tension as she tried to guess the meaning of the entire message from the few words visible in the preview. This triggered further negative fantasies and fears; she began to think about how to respond, either by defending herself or attacking the other person. All of this happened in a few endless seconds, which led her to states of psychosomatic activation so intense that to those who saw her from the outside without knowing her, it seemed as if she had just received terrible news, like the sudden death of a family member. Instead, all of this occurred for every message, even positive ones. She was always so agitated and projected into negative anticipations, with all the axes of stress activated, that she never managed to read any message calmly, thus distorting content and tone. This led her to respond quickly and aggressively, trying to prevent her deepest fears from coming true, without thinking about what she was truly doing.

The first step in supporting Elizabeth was to reduce unnecessary triggers (see the technique in switch 3), which involved periodically disabling notifications on her phone and more. Given her constantly active mind, it was crucial to address the brain networks discussed in area 3 in various ways, as well as address altered neurobiology, inflammation, and allostatic load, following the perspectives outlined in the first two switch areas.

Regarding the specific topics we're addressing here, it was crucial to create a new mode of response in which she could read the message calmly and understand it. I encouraged her to contextualize the specific message with recent and past events, to consider the person's circumstances when writing the message (were they in a hurry? Distracted by a chaotic environment? Emotionally altered due to factors unrelated to their relationship, etc.?). Another useful approach was to evaluate their message exchange as though it were written by someone else she knew well or, conversely, someone she didn't know at all. Elizabeth found these and other adjustments very practical in terms of achieving a broader and more objective assessment.

The next step was to implement the *Delayed Action* technique, where she'd write a response immediately after reading a message as a way to vent, but she'd save it as a draft without sending it. At this point, Elizabeth would return to her activities. Only after an hour would she revisit the message she wrote as a draft and question its short-term and long-term effects. She also needed to consider the impression she was giving and whether she was truly safeguarding her relationship with that person. Regardless of the evaluation's outcome (which was rarely positive), she needed to delete the message, think about the constructive goal she wanted to achieve, and then write the message to be sent. These steps might seem long and cumbersome, but they're often the only way to interrupt certain automatisms that have been ingrained for years and are supported by altered neurobiology. These strategies don't need to be maintained over time. Through them, individuals will naturally and spontaneously develop a new mode of behaviour, free from excessive interfering factors.

The ideal endpoint for Elizabeth and many others, especially concerning crucial discussions and relationships, was to respond by scheduling a face-to-face conversation. This way, genuine real-time communication and emotional-affective management were restored. This prevented the loss of contextual and relational clues, enabling them to adapt to the ongoing exchange on all levels in real time (while messaging only provides limited data and drives many assumptions that are amplified by personal fears and insecurities).

This final aspect is particularly significant in critical moments of emotional relationships, as well as in intense workplace conflicts. For instance, with both Enrique and Hilary, despite having different professional roles, we worked extensively on their initial emotional reactions to triggering emails. They departed from their typical response patterns, of which they were both quite proud, but which was actually self-destructive. The turning point was when they started responding by inviting the individuals to discuss matters in person, within protected environments, and with an unexpected attitude. In fact, people that like to provoke are well aware of how to infuriate others and anticipate a particular reaction, deriving pleasure from wielding this power. Once this perverse satisfaction is removed, most individuals lose interest and change their approach.

Fig. next page - Some examples of different levels of human activity synchronization. These spontaneous features can be positively activated only in face-to-face meetings, and only minimally in live online platforms. On the other hand, asynchronous and non-face-to-face interactions (emails, smartphone messages, etc.) don't use these advantages. Conversely, they increase self-referential thinking and the likelihood of misunderstandings.

Bio-Behavioural Synchrony in human relations

	Bio-Behavioural synchrony	Heart rate alignment	Endocrine alignment	Brain-brain synchrony
Parents 	Synchronysed behaviour concerning: gaze, affection, tone of voice and touch mother-specific father-specific	HR (Heart Rate) is synchronised during coordinated interactions	Coordinated OT (oxytocin) response after contact Coordinated CT (cortisol) response to stress	Oscillazioni cerebrali coordinate in onde alfa e gamma
Romantically-involved couple 	Non-verbal synchronised schemas Coordination of empathy self-revelation	Coordinated HR during or after interactions	OT and CT coordination between parents OT and CT coordination between lovers	Parent brain network mentalisation response coordination Coordination of gamma oscillations in lovers' temporal cortex
Friends 	Social reciprocity patterns	Coordianted HR during group activity	OT released during interaction with friends	Alpha response in the social brain connected to behavioural synchrony Coordination between mirror neuron networks
Strangers 	Coordination of cultural-specific rule display (i.e. meeeting gaze)	Occasionally HR coordination in case of extreme closeness (i.e. queuing together)	OT implied in empathetic actions	Coordinated activation in mentalisation areas during interaction

With respect to the topic of synchronisation of emotional responses, another very interesting aspect concerns the existence of primitive protection systems that impose themselves on logic – literally bypassing it. Think about when an insect or a bird hits the windscreen of your car for example: your mind is well aware that the windscreen is much more solid than these little creatures, but your safety system makes you wince and cover your face with your arm[5]. These types of responses are also activated by mechanisms that defend us against potential relational dangers, causing alterations in our bodily responses (we will address this in the next chapter regarding postural and motor flows; here, I wanted to highlight the connection at this level).

The above observations do not make the analysis of higher or more sophisticated logic and forecasting systems, or of projections into the past and future of interpersonal relationships and their value any less interesting. On the other hand, it is once again important to highlight that to manage and help these sophisticated processes it is critical to intervene on the lower level switches that support them and/or enable their activation.

It therefore becomes useful to note the importance of the effect of context, of combinations and of various other primary elements on interpersonal interaction processes. Research has in fact extensively highlighted how context can influence emotional perception, scenes seen, voices heard, presences, people's faces (even when there is no direct interaction with them), cultural setting, the employment of certain words as opposed to others, can all radically change the evaluation that is made of the emotional impact of a face[6].

This perspective debunks various preconceptions such as those relating to the innate ability to read emotion on someone else's face. This is a skill that should not be confused or mixed up with other adaptation processes such as the ability to immediately subconsciously identify higher or lower danger configurations on someone's face. This information is then integrated and processed along with other external clues and information relating to internal resources to come to a decision as to how to behave socially.

Emotional-interpersonal dynamics can be brought back to their physiological state and then improved upon by using certain strategies:

- Exercising the skill of finding and evaluating relevant contextual clues that are often erroneously pushed into the background while focusing on our counterpart;
- Actively managing the time-span of events by methodically looking at correct and real connections between facts and judgement and vice versa, unreal or incorrect ones;
- Introducing beliefs and expectations in this wider representation and seeing them as components that in part contribute to evaluation and forecasting although they are not conclusive in themselves;
- Moving along different time scales, increasing and reducing the time lapse considered and evaluating how this can radically change the evaluations started, the emotional experience triggered (not to be confused with past ones, as correctly highlighted by Khaneman) and subsequent behavioural choices.
- In the switches of area 5, we will explore a series of strategies and measures to change communicative flows (both verbal and bodily) that can act on these processes within us, as well as in the perception of the counterpart.

Right at the start of the twentieth century the Russian film director Lev Kuleshov perceived how an emotional, affectionate and interpersonal tone in a scene could be evoked by contextual clues and by the tone of the scenes immediately preceding. Recent neuroscience studies[7] have proven this idea correct and shown the huge difference between *static images*  (often used in research but also in emotional education), and *dynamic images* (videos) that are far more powerful and effective as they reflect more closely the natural process of interpersonal adjustment in real life. This has critical fallout on methodological choices in clinical and educational practice.

FACING TECHNIQUE: KNOWING HOW TO FACE THINGS

Learning to "face" something is an emotional skill, but also a mental and, above all, a physical one. Facing an emotion allows us to gain awareness of real risks and consequences, rather than those hypothesized by our mind. It also enables us to be more conscious of our resources, activate self-control and self-esteem mechanisms that, as we've seen in various parts of this book, don't largely rely on verbal and cognitive aspects. There are numerous ways to practice facing, or "being in front of" an emotion, ranging from the concrete to the symbolic.

Standing physically still, not just as a stance, in the face of danger or a problem is a powerful act of empowerment. In fact, we tend to respect and admire those who do it. It's the opposite of fleeing. However, this doesn't mean it's an attack. It's more about the mental, emotional, and relational stance of "*I am here, ready to face this, to do what's needed, with serenity and determination.*"

Knowing how to *face* things is not the same as assertiveness. Assertiveness pertains to the issues of aggression or communicative evasion. Behaviours of *fight* or *flight* can be right and constructive. *Facing* is the opposite of *flight*, as it doesn't allow us to run away (a choice that would reinforce this behaviour and the related identity of 'insecure', 'inadequate', 'fearful', 'coward', or more). *Facing* is a foundation and peaceful level of *fighting*.

To frame *facing* correctly, we can focus on avoiding fearful thinking, not fleeing from danger. Young children, for instance, increase their heart rate and avert their gaze when faced with a potentially dangerous stranger, but once they perceive that the person isn't doing anything threatening, they proceed to become more familiar. The essence of *facing* is this: to give ourselves time and use strategies to return to a physiological state, much like animals studying each other from a safe distance before interacting. It's an adaptive sequence that also takes place in other contexts, avoiding, analysing from a safe distance, testing, engaging, or ignoring.

The mere act of facing emotions and those who triggered them has tremendous effects. It allows us to tell ourselves and others: "I'm here and I'm not budging, I won't let myself be manipulated, I won't be influenced." It's a way of rebalancing responsibilities among the different players in an emotional-relational dynamic. It leads each involved person to assume their own responsibility, not the other's. For example, if my anger is triggered by feeling cheated or mistreated, I remain where I am and request a change in product or attitude. If I'm right and I stand firm, the other person will have to do something, consequently reshaping the situation and the relationships.

Facing also concerns not procrastinating or not addressing things directly. It's important to distinguish between situations where it's beneficial to address the issue immediately, and others where waiting is genuinely advantageous, rather than simply a way of avoiding confrontation.

Let's start with the second case, which occurs when we let something simmer down that would be unmanageable or harmful if confronted in the heat of the moment. For example, when unfamiliar people are involved, it's worth observing how they react (perhaps in a business negotiation). It's also important to differentiate whether our action would be constructive *facing* or, conversely, an act to compensate for our guilt, our inability to tolerate an offense (which might not even be real), etc.

In the first case, the situation is crucial; the price to pay if something went wrong would be too high, and if we already anticipate that "it won't end there." In such cases, facing confronts us with dysfunctions or unhealthy emotional habits. Particularly in this case, our physical presence in person or - at the very least - over the phone rather than via email, has effects on various levels. The first effect is that it prevents asynchronous back-and-forth communication (my emotions don't engage with the other person's, but are purely reactions to the meaning I attribute to their written words or their absence; essentially, they're just my own fantasies and projections). In this context, let's remember two important aspects of our neuroscientific premises: social emotions are finely regulated by the amygdala's ability to read the other person's facial expressions, but if there's no face and no tone of voice, what can we base ourselves on? *Emojis* attempt to fill this gap, but they are still detached from the other person's face and represent their communicative choice rather than an automatic ancestral signal (of emotional response but also of trust, openness, acceptance, etc.). Emotions have an immediate adaptive value, so experiencing them asynchronously contradicts their function.

A second significant effect is that when we confront an issue in person, we also put our counterpart in a different position. People can be more aggressive and resentful over email, but their tone changes over the phone or in person. This is due to the emotional-relational synchronicity reasons just discussed, but to another crucial factor: by directly addressing the situation, we position ourselves as an alpha individual (the so-called leader of the pack in ethological terms), that is responsible and authoritative. The message is profound and powerful; indeed, people who are confronted in this manner dramatically change their communication and relational style.

There are two ways to implement the "facing" technique: Static Facing and Active Facing.

Static Facing

Backing away or leaving in response to aggression indicates submission and fleeing. Practicing *static facing* means remaining still and solid, without averting one's gaze, when others try to impose something. Otherwise, whatever is said won't be believed. The classic threat of "you'll regret this" shouted as you walk away holds no weight because it's inconsistent. This type of threat is equivalent to saying "I'll face this tomorrow." Today, you're effectively walking away, leaving the situation unresolved and the impression that the other person has won.

Active Facing

A more advanced stage of static facing involves creating consequences for your counterpart not taking responsibility. This not only preserves what's important, but it's as if you're making it evident that you're paying a price and, through a logical and responsible choice, you're turning that price back onto the person who caused it.

For instance, if you're mistreated in a bar, you can stay at the cash register until your issue is resolved. If this creates a queue behind you, politely explain the reason to those waiting, so that others are aware of the mistake. You can also anticipate and explain these consequences to your counterpart, if they don't realize it themselves. If they have nothing to hide, they'll continue on their way, but if they know they're wrong, they'll have to change something. Worst case scenario, they'll lose their temper and make a scene, losing customers. In any case, you'll have achieved some form of compensation, even if it's just moral. But in reality, there's more, you'll have reinforced your awareness of your strength and your ability to not be passive, while also receiving external feedback on the other person's mistake.

All of this can be seen through the concept of "*stronghold*." I often tell people who come to me to "protect what's important to you." The term *stronghold* captures the idea *of standing firm* with determination and calm steadfastness: just like alpha dogs do when there's a threat in their territory or towards something they care about deeply.

TOLERANCE TOWARDS AMBIGUITY AND SOCIAL ENGAGEMENT SKILLS

Human existence features a constant and omnipresent state of unpredictability (see the switches in the previous section). This means that when faced with a new interpersonal relationship a person needs to evaluate whether contact with the other person will lead to advantages or disadvantages[8]. This process takes place in every environment and on various levels, trusting someone with personal information can lead to receiving help and understanding, but it also shows weakness. It can provide relief, but also fosters reciprocity. Including a person in a work team can help finish a task faster, but also dilutes satisfaction and control as well as impacting all the other members of the team.

Most social decisions (such as that to trust or not to trust someone, to compete or to cooperate by contributing to a certain degree etc.) hold an intrinsic level of uncertainty that requires a constant evaluation of potential risks and advantages, personal and at group level, over more or less distant timescales. Insecurity and unpredictability are elements that can significantly influence the way that people evaluate the options available to them[9]. In most instances, when the decision takes place in a non-social environment, people tend to prefer a small low-risk advantage to a potentially larger advantage, but in highly unpredictable conditions. In a social context, however, the influence process is more complex, first of all, in a pro-social choice we place at least part of our wellbeing in someone else's hands.

If the situation is favourable and reciprocal this can bring great advantages to both parties, but it also carries a high risk and a significant loss of personal control[10]. The evaluation underlying the attribution of trust – or in other words whether we should trust the other person or not – is very complex as the true motivations of the other person (for their generosity, kindness, cooperation, affection etc.) may be unknown (hidden or regarded as unreliable). In this complex scenario most people tend to base their social decisions more on ambiguity (unexpected outcomes) than on risk (expected outcomes). The more tolerant a person is towards ambiguity, the more likely will they be to engage in cooperative and trusting pro-social behaviour even when it is onerous. In other words – in line with the standpoint of this book – to sustain any change or development process in interpersonal dynamics, it is important to intervene on the ability to tolerate ambiguity, which is an important switch underlying the willingness to open up to others in egalitarian relationships of trust and cooperation.

RETHINKING AGGRESSIVENESS

The sight of two puppies playfully wrestling tends to evoke thoughts like, *"How cute, they're playing and testing themselves"*, while two children engaging in the same behaviour might lead many people to think, *"Your child is aggressive, you should fix him!"* or *"What do I do now? This is a problem!"*.

From an ethological standpoint, two kids engaging in a play fight are essentially the same as two young elks sparring or two puppies playfully rolling around while wrestling, aiming to discover themselves, their limits, and their resources, and to compare themselves with others. If we inhibit these activities, we prevent children from discovering all this. Children and teenagers need it. They can do it in a "socially acceptable" manner through sports or by trying to excel in their hobbies, but this isn't always enough. Natural instincts should be accommodated, partially at least. Children, like animals, can regulate themselves; they know how to *play-fight*, which is different from real *fighting*. The young of all mammal species never let their experiments turn into something harmful. So why should human children? In fact, they won't. To be honest, there's an exception, but the mechanism is easy to identify, and in that case, it's right to intervene. Children only allow play-fighting to escalate due to adults; they are in an experimental phase and don't need to exaggerate. If they do, it's because they're using play-fighting dysfunctionally. A child who doesn't feel loved and is encouraged by their father to be stronger and more manly might take it too far, but they only do it to gratify their father. A child who is very angry (accumulating long-standing frustrations and resentment) might use the game to vent all that anger at once, towards someone who doesn't deserve it. A child who thinks the world is harsh and unreliable might want to reclaim their power through fighting.

How can we discern the boundary between play-fighting and real fighting? Once again, animals teach us. A puppy is serene before and after *play-fighting*. It doesn't hold grudges against anyone and, is even less likely to act arrogantly or submissively towards its playmate. A child should do the same. If, however, we observe a child or teenager who is frequently resentful, angry at the world, or emotionally unstable, who can't tolerate frustration or rejection, then we might wonder about the satisfaction of their needs, whether they are having the necessary developmental experiences, and how this might potentially influence play-fighting, distancing it from its original value of experimentation and understanding.

Children who don't properly pass through this important developmental phase often display two opposing behaviors as adults. On one hand, there are the *insecure* individuals who always view others as superior to themselves, struggle to evaluate themselves accurately, appear to forget their own successes, and consistently focus solely on limitations and difficult moments. For these individuals, everything is dangerous, everything is a risk. This mechanism becomes clear when you think about what they haven't done, they haven't had the opportunity to measure themselves and put themselves to the test, haven't discovered their own resources. To face the world and its dangers securely, you need to have and to know the resources at hand.

On the other hand, there are those *who appear confident* but are, in fact, insecure and - to convince themselves that they're not insecure - they constantly put themselves to the test. Sometimes, they "disguise" themselves as successful people, as this constant daring and testing can offer advantages, but in reality, they live poorly and are tormented by insecurity. Think about those individuals who are always in competition, who, when they go running with friends, keep saying, "Let's see who gets there first", and consistently discuss who's faster or more powerful. Consider professionals who love to win and have chosen a job of constant challenge, like being the best salesperson, the lawyer with the most cases won, or the surgeon who wants to become the head not so much for the quality of the work as for the competition with colleagues, and so on. These are professional examples, but sometimes this attitude is highly prevalent in everyday life. For instance, you can take into account certain common behaviours that many of us have to some extent but are exaggerated to the point of obsession. This includes wanting to always have the last word in a discussion, wanting to be the most knowledgeable on a topic, and enjoying teaching something that others don't know (unlike a wise person who enjoys sharing and watching others grow, who considers even exchanges with the humblest person as mutually beneficial).

THE DIFFERENT PATHS OF AGGRESSION

Aggressive behaviour is often culturally identified with a single category of 'dangerous and negative' behaviour. Ethology and neuroscience have, however, clearly shown that there are various types of aggression, some defensive and some even highly valuable from an interpersonal and constructive point of view. Negative aggression is, in fact, just one degeneration of a healthy and useful way of interacting with others. The same degeneration takes place in relation to any behaviour and type of motivation. The application of these adaptation methods becomes problematic when the objectives, methods, duration, or specific context are not consistent and functional.

An interesting starting point for analysing the constructive aspect of aggressive behaviour relates to the anatomical and functional aspect. All mammals in fact have three independent pathways for aggressiveness *towards a predator* (an animal from another species), *towards a conspecific being* (an animal of the same species) and *towards a painful stimulus*[11].

We will see that these three pathways and their sub-variants allow us to understand the processes at the core of different reactions in which anger, rage, aggression and tenacity decline in different ways to shape social regulation, respect of personal and professional *boundaries*, *trust*, understanding of one's own and other people's *resources* (through play fighting – an activity human 'puppies' also engage in – and in any healthy challenge even among adults), *inclusion* and *acceptance* by the pack/group (that is different from affection), and *interpersonal evaluation* tests.

To accurately distinguish between the different pathways, it is necessary to look at the functional subdivisions of each brain area. All these pathways go via the amygdala, hypothalamus and PAG (Periaqueductal Gray) but via different areas with functional connections that only relate to certain brain networks and to central intersections with their relative specific functions.

Typically, when we hear about the functions of the amygdala, speakers refer to it as a unitary brain area. In reality, this area is divided in 12 different subsections, each one with different objectives and ways of working including: activation, vigilance, evaluation of environmental risk, primary decoding of menace and friendliness of a face etc. This latter function also goes through various stages and evolves over time. In fact, initially it is only based on visual aspects (shape and layout of eyes and mouth), then it grows richer thanks to contextual (distance between self and the other, brightness of the environment etc.) and perceptive clues (posture, muscular tone etc.). Only after all these stages is the information gathered and are initial evaluations integrated with memories, associations and other more structured and cognitively complex evaluations.

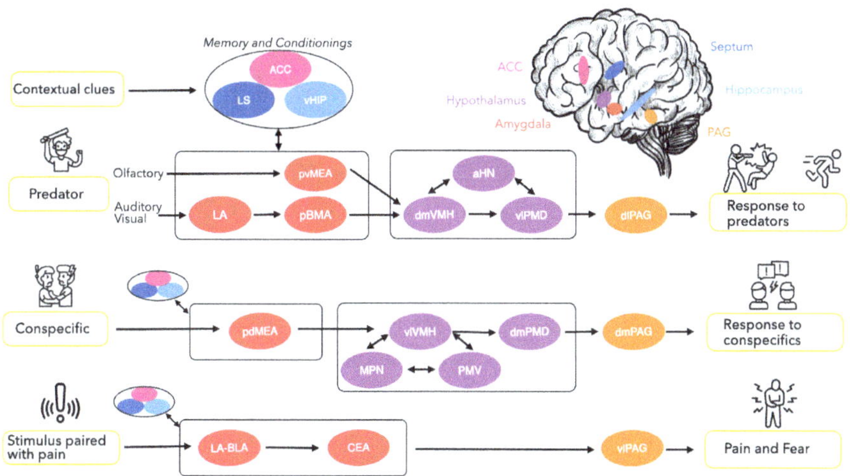

Fig. - The three different neural pathways that shape responses: defensive aggressiveness (real or metaphorical survival, triggered by someone who can 'prey on various types of resources'), constructive aggressiveness (social regulation, e.g., setting boundaries for intrusive people, defending roles, making the social group function, etc.), and protective aggressiveness (associated with pain, even independently of sociality, for example, when we have a toothache).

Some of the processes we just mentioned interact with the PAG, which can provide information in the evaluation process but also shape final

adaptation behaviour. The PAG can also be divided into sub-areas that function differently and are connected among others to:
- The evaluation of the potential physical damage in case of a clash;
- Information relating to currently available physical resources;
- Separate motor and behavioural activation;
- Sophisticated self-regulation via the freeing of endocannabinoids in nurture relationships and in the placebo effect[12];
- and more.

These types of insights, when viewed from the right perspective, have immediate practical implications for those involved in change or care. It becomes possible to act on all factors involved in the evaluation process of a relational danger or risk, for example, by introducing *contextual aspects* and all *environmental* and *interpersonal cues* into the analysis process at the discussion level, as well as in training and recovery of appropriate functionality. To do this, we could use *some of the techniques seen in the previous chapter*, but shifting the focus not only on fear or stress responses (which more easily come to mind compared to the themes of insecurity and uncertainty that we illustrated earlier), but also including the spectrum of aggressive, choleric, or angry reactions. Some of the advice and techniques seen earlier in this chapter also lend themselves well to working with anger (for example, if it is linked to dysfunctional attachment dynamics or the inability to confront one's interlocutor, consequently using *facing*). Below, we will also explore the technique of *Emotion Modulation with Post-it Notes*, which is suitable for any emotion but particularly effective for regulating overly explosive or inhibited impulses, as often happens with anger and aggression.

Following this perspective, it's also possible to develop new interpretations regarding the value and the meaning that can be attributed to a certain symptom. For instance, brain areas involved in managing a potential *predator* are the same areas involved in a *panic attack*[13]. A new path of enquiry therefore opens up relating to the perception of the other person and how to develop an adequate evaluation and functional management strategy. Panic can therefore be seen as part of a wider perspective and not just as an anxiety phenomenon, but also (and not rarely) as a dysfunction of anger processes. When these conditions prevail, it is highly useful to intervene in a targeted way.

If the other being involved *is not a real predator*, it is critical to make this clear so as to deactivate the survival circuit that was erroneously involved. This can take place via logical evaluation, via the elimination of an incorrect or skewed association, with better use of contextual clues, but also by turning around the perception of the self from that of prey to *non-prey* etc.

If, instead, there is a *real predator* it is useful to contextualise and contain this phenomenon. Another human should not by definition be a predator as they are a conspecific creature. On the other hand, the setting may make them a predator depending on their: role, power, affection, sexual intentions and much more. It is possible to investigate whether that which is at risk of predation can be safeguarded or not, whether the risk coincides with a real loss or with a representation, or whether it coincides with its consequences through weakness (lack of resources or inability to nurture them) or replacement (such as when the role of predator is the only element of self-esteem as we shall see later on relating to *Ancestral Needs*).

Enrique had often been accused by his own collaborators of being lacking in empathy. They told him he was authoritarian, didn't listen to them, and would destroy their proposals even before they finished explaining them. After denying it for a while, initially claiming to be an open-minded leader, Enrique eventually admitted that from his point of view, his collaborators were all not very bright and had nothing interesting to say. *"After all, if they are collaborators and I am the boss, there must be a difference in our abilities"*, he once said. Besides the content of the statement, what struck me was his disgusted expression towards the inferiority of the collaborators. I pointed out, provocatively, *"It's as if you belong to two different races"*, intending to highlight his distorted perspective and to later introduce an explanation of the different pathways of aggression. To my surprise, he responded satisfactorily, *"Exactly! That's it!"*. At that point, I explained to him that the view in which he considered himself as if they were two different species was problematic on several fronts, it kept an aggressive and destructive stance active in him, making the disparity clear to the collaborators, even though he tried to use different persuasive and leadership techniques (he was an avid consumer of books to develop persuasive or rather manipulative leadership and communication skills). Thanks to this clarification, supported by the underlying ethological and neurobiological explanation, Enrique understood and convinced himself that he needed to change his approach. To assist him in this process, I suggested that thinking of himself and his collaborators as a pack of a different species, stepping out of the over-stereotyped human framework in his thinking. He chose gorillas. At this point, as in many natural packs, I suggested he evaluate his collaborators in 3-4 categories, considering that each could have a current role and a future role that aligned with their character and was also motivating. Each role had to be useful both in the present and future of the group. Since he considered himself the top-ranking pack leader (alpha), he had the responsibility to evaluate them all and to help them grow. To do this, he could enlist the help of the most suitable individuals (betas). He also had to mentally exercise the thought that in the future a member of the group, sooner or later, should be able to replace him. This depended only half on the collaborator's qualities; the other half was his personal responsibility. We extensively discussed these aspects, the criteria to use for these choices, and most importantly, what to do in practice to activate these changes. As he identified the most suitable people for growth roles, work life became simpler. His staff, involved and empowered, became more proactive. At some point, Enrique noticed that he no longer got angry and that he was no longer reproached for not listening or being empathetic. The change happened on multiple fronts and as a spontaneous consequence of this way of viewing and organizing. Enrique's case is exemplary from this perspective. It's not always enough to go through these steps alone, and often, it's necessary to work directly on self-regulating emotions and behaviours. However, activating these mechanisms makes everything simpler and facilitates other change processes too.

EMOTION MODULATION TECHNIQUE: ANGER AND AGGRESSION

Any aggressive behaviour can be subdivided in a crescendo of different behaviours and states of activation. Aggression is an adaptation ability that has been refined over time. All mammals in fact exhibit 8 to 12 different modes for any emotion.

BEHAVIOURS

| 1 | 2 | 3 | 4 | 5 | 6 | 7 | 8 | 9 | 10 | 11 | 12 |

A first draft of a graphic representation of the entire range of reactions that can develop. Using post-it notes helps the individual become aware of the significant difference between their current behavioural repertoire and the great potential and flexibility they can develop.

The main problem for human beings is the fact that these modes are usually inhibited and there is no practical way to exercise them or to learn to use them correctly. Cultural mores smother ethological and evolutionary dynamics. When two children start to argue adults typically intervene to stem the argument at the start so as to avoid any injury, out of politeness, or to stop them getting upset.

Aggressiveness between equals is a function of social regulation and is managed by different neurobiological circuits compared with aggression activated towards different species. Empirical proof for this is provided by puppies play fighting without hurting each other and never going beyond the objective of the game; they are exercising discovery of the self, of others and of the limitations and resources available, the definition of roles and social rules negotiation. For all these reasons it is critical to provide people with the opportunity to understand, explore and learn to confidently use all the expressive and realisation modes for each emotion.

In order to do this, in the *Emotion Modulation* technique we invite people to define these 8-12 levels trying to find coherence and effectiveness for each one in relation to specific:

- Context
- Objectives
- Risk type
- Risk entity

- Social relations
- Hierarchies (to be respected or re-negotiated)
- Social norms (to be respected or re-negotiated)
- Potential effectiveness of each behaviour exhibited
- Direct audience
- By-standers
- Expectations relating to other people's reactions (remembering they are simply hypotheses)
- Forecasts on short, medium- and long-term consequences (remembering that they are only hypotheses)

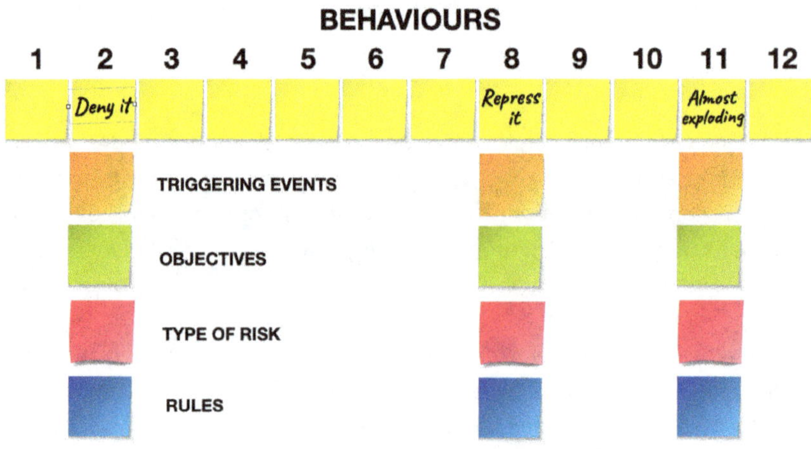

Simplified example of analysis starting from three behaviours currently exhibited by the individual. Subsequently, different levels are examined, and new behaviours are sought to enhance one's repertoire and its effectiveness.

There can, therefore, be no 'right or wrong' ,'positive or negative' emotion, but only 'adequate and functional' emotion.

In this technique the role of the professional is to help the subject reflect on the adequacy and coherence of each 'emotional modulation' identified.

Having defined the different degrees and having perfected them, it is time to look at elements and clues that help identify them correctly in daily life. After that, it is necessary to evaluate the capabilities required to activate them in the best possible way, also potentially planning how to develop them at a later stage. The final stage is that of experimenting and identifying safe environments in which to become more comfortable with these new modes of behaviour.

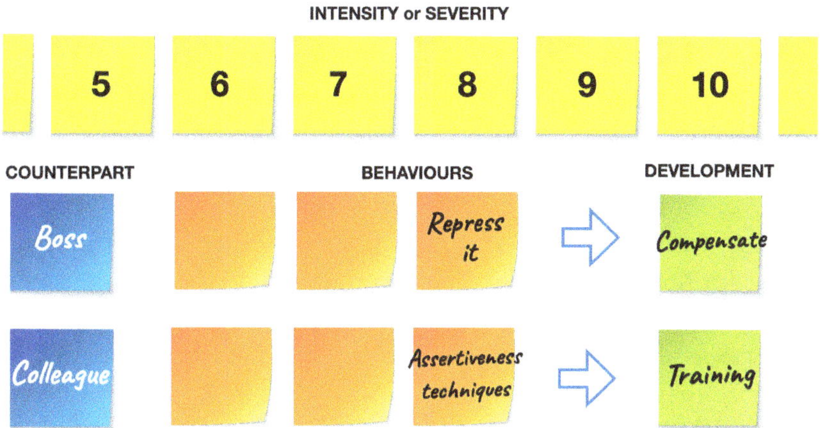

Targeted exploration, tailored to each specific counterpart, of alternative behaviors and the corresponding ways to put them into practice.

INCORPORATING RELEVANT FACTORS

In the previous paragraph we used the connection between panic and aggression as our starting point to later analyse a series of aspects that can be found in other situations too. Even in absence of the exterior symptoms of a panic attack, the relationship between aggression and predation is active in a number of other instances that are less evident, but nevertheless very damaging to quality of life and relationships. It is possible to note levels of dysfunctional aggression (hidden, latent or explicit) in many daily dysfunctions.

Just think of the times when you feel the need to impose yourself or give others instruction that emerges from the excessive use of expressions such as '*do this*', '*you must*' etc., or the need to find a scape-goat as a knee-jerk reaction to any unexpected problem. These are dysfunctional communicative and relational flows (see the next section) connected to the distorted perception of the dynamics of antagonism and cooperation in which aggression provides an illusion of control and personal safety.

In all these processes neural networks and specific organs have a significant role. For example, the resources that we rely on to feel safe in a clash, even when it is not a physical encounter, are mainly found at the body map level (via the insula and its involvement in the Salience Network. See level 3 switches), but also in the feeling of balance and mastery largely managed by the hippocampus and its networks. A hypertrophic and hyperactive amygdala, for example, responds with avoidance and difficulty in thinking to an interpersonal provocation[14]. It is worth remembering that the amygdala can be in these conditions as a result of trauma, chronic stress or inflammatory states of various origin (poor nutrition, pharmaceutical, irregular sleep cycles etc.).

Similarly, there are subgroups of neurons in the hippocampus that are fundamental to emotional activation and related regulation as well as to motor behaviour that specifically respond to the identification of a social danger such as recognising a potential predator[15]. Such circuits are strongly influenced by balance (in the most physical sense), smells, and rhythmic brain waves, thus subject to states of mental flow, as well as stimulations and rhythmic motor or sound activities. To this end, we can utilize many of the activities mentioned throughout the text to effectively act on the neurobiological foundations of these aspects with integrative and multisensory objectives, as well physical, mental and emotional balance.

ANCESTRAL NEEDS

The Ancestral Needs model provides a useful tool to re-read the different Change Switch levels and it is applicable to the different phases of the Functional Integrative Schemas. Ancestral Needs can for example be seen as integration between social switches (4th group) and safety brain networks (3rd group) as applied to relationships. These two levels in turn, can create psychosomatic dysfunctions if Ancestral Needs are not met (2nd group).

Ancestral Needs (AN) are shared with other mammals. We identified them[16] through field observations, compared them with studies in comparative ethology, and through neurobiological research that has mapped the neural areas and processes activated in life situations related to motivations, needs, emotions, and other responses of active and reactive adaptation.

AN's strength lies in their incorporation into adaptive behaviours developed through evolution. Classic ethology had already grasped that these are partly innate systems that then need to be exercised and refined over time and according to one's specific reality. In this process, they also become the foundation for developing increasingly sophisticated and evolved behaviour and abilities.

As with other themes we have already addressed, to properly frame Ancestral Needs, it is useful to refer to the idea of humans as "failed animals" or "denied animals", in other words, as mammals that, in the name of social superstructures and logical thinking, have often placed their instincts and primary needs in the background. In this analysis of needs, we will see that many are often neglected or simply not considered, even though there are clear indications that our instinct knows what we require.

On the other hand, not exercising them, not keeping them in balance, or satisfying them incorrectly can all lead to obstruction, demotivation, and cascading dysfunctions at other levels.

THE 6 ANCESTRAL NEEDS IN SUMMARY

Ancestral Needs are six and can be divided into three more "conservative" and three more "evolved" ones. In brief, they are:
- Control and Safety
- Loving and Being Loved
- Self-affirmation and Recognition
- Freedom
- Creating and Making
- Experiencing Pleasure

Let's see a concise description of the 6 needs below. These are broad and transversal concepts, difficult to summarize in a few pages. However, in the following sections, we will develop them further with examples and insights into how they interact with each other.

The Need for **Control and Safety** leads us to engage in activities that allow us to: experience the world and our ability to influence it; evaluate possible forms of self-control and self-management; analyse and implement the best forms of adaptation; be able to face the majority of everyday life situations. To achieve these goals, the Need for Control and Safety drives us to carry out behaviours through which we can test different tools and resources to address challenges and tasks related to survival, as well as to manage our development and social relationships.

To give an easy example, in the animal world, biting a small stick relieves toothache for puppy dogs, and in doing so, they also discover a pastime and an effective anti-stress tool. Throughout this process, the dog self-regulates and, in a physiological and natural way, develops a sense of Control and Safety (the sense is derived from the satisfaction of the need). Humans, on the other hand, tend to immediately remove something a small child puts in their mouth to alleviate toothache, fearing they might hurt themselves, choke, or get an infection. In this way, we inhibit the child's reflex of self-care and make them feel powerless against the pain of toothache. While the concerns that lead us not to let them do it can be valid, we're not saying it's right to take this risk. We want to highlight the natural development mechanism of certain needs. Once understood, we need to find safe and practically applicable ways to promote these processes. Another example concerns cases where we give children pain-relief medication, creating a passive idea of overcoming pain and difficulties. This example pertains to a single event, which might not have negative consequences and may not leave traces. However, if the same approach is often repeated, even in other areas – for example, helping the child with their early math difficulties by providing them with a support teacher or pushing them to give up playing the piano if they can't do the proposed exercises in the first week – then the mechanism becomes acquired. Please note, we're not saying to endure and impose gratuitous suffering on the child; quite the opposite. Yet, an excessively "analgesic" culture in which the child is never allowed to figure things out on their own can also create problems in the development of self-control and internal safety.

Conversely, repeatedly attempting effective ways to satisfy the Need for Control and Safety will develop the awareness of being able to handle different situations, guaranteeing healthy self-esteem, physiological emotional responses, and freer choices. In a group context, this need can manifest along an axis ranging from functional (focused, conscious, reciprocal) living within a protective group to dysfunctional modalities (like passive dependence on group protection).

Loving and Being Loved is a need that animals express through unconditional love. They don't even question whether or not to express it, whether it might hurt them in the future, or if it's better to attach to one person over another. In nature, we can observe clean attachment and care generated by the need for physical survival rather than emotional fears like "*don't you love mommy?*" or attempts to motivate through guilt, as with requests like "*don't make me worry*". The purest trust can be found in relationships based on love (given and received) unconditionally, typically in couples but also in small groups. In these conditions, we can be ourselves and allow ourselves to deactivate all control mechanisms.

The need for intimacy and a unique bond is also present in many animal species, which manage to maintain this bond because they aret attracted by dysfunctions of other Ancestral Needs (such as losing control for a moment through a one-night adventure, feeling special because seduced by an authoritative or famous person, etc.). To evaluate the quality of how this need is satisfied, it's important to understand how capable we are of being present in relationships, without being distracted by thoughts or compulsions, often as trivial as continuously checking the phone. These behaviours can tell us two things, either what we are experiencing at that moment isn't truly nurturing, or it is but we can't enjoy it because we're distracted by a dysfunction of the Safety need through ineffective obsessive control. It's extremely important to evaluate these two perspectives because it means that we'll have to work on different ancestral needs.

In humans, the need to care for and be cared for evolve and naturally merge into love, but problems arise when they compensate for other unsatisfied Needs (like Control or Affirmation). In social groups, positive manifestations like the sense of acceptance can exist alongside dysfunctional ones like accepting and enduring anything to obtain (illusory) love from other members.

To understand the functioning of the Need for **Self-affirmation and Recognition**, it's useful to analyze its purest animal version. As we've seen, competition and the struggles among animal cubs are the natural way to get to know oneself and others, to understand limits and possibilities, to establish social dominance hierarchies, and to define alpha (leader), beta (right-hand), and subordinate roles. Furthermore, through the modulation of aggressiveness (displaying teeth, growling, barking, biting appropriately for the situation, etc.), the dog gains insight into its impact on the external world and triggers reactions in others that constitute crucial feedback for self-definition and self-worth. Healthy competition entails constructive and evolutionary challenges; it doesn't involve destroying others but rather aims to measure oneself and define roles and limits. Healthy competition can be experienced with serenity because it holds clear meanings and defined boundaries within the group or pack. It's built on trust and fosters further trust in oneself and others. Earned trust and merit are two fundamental criteria in this context. For example, the sense of belonging in a group is expressed differently from what we have seen for the need to be loved (which was unconditional acceptance). In these cases, the emphasis shifts to actively deserving inclusion in associations, groups, organizations, or other forms of community.

Contextual feedback is important, more so than many mind-focused approaches usually propose. While it's true that we need to assess our own value, the context plays a significant role. Too much or too little feedback – both positive and negative – about our value doesn't help us objectively gauge our worth. Experiencing a variety of situations, contexts, and people is beneficial, providing diverse feedback on our perception of value, which can be regarded as subjective and contextualized insights. Integrating this variety of feedback with our autonomous reflection enables us to create a balanced and evolving self-assessment.

Freedom: dogs and cats move freely, following instinct or their own interest, without fearing the loss of anyone or anything, and this, in any case, doesn't limit them. They know well that they wouldn't want to lose someone dear to them or something important, but they don't see it as connected to the act of making free choices. This approach is valid in different domains, whereas human beings struggle with it. Animals choose to sleep when they want, without fearing to offend someone beside them; they take a walk alone without asking anyone's permission; they abruptly interrupt an activity just because they no longer feel like doing it at that moment; and so on. Humans can and must mediate these needs with education and respect for others. "*Mediating*" doesn't mean "*giving up*" or "*sacrificing*".

Human reality presents paradoxical situations that everyone would like to end but no one dares. Consider, for instance, dinners among ill-matched people or boring conferences. Everyone would like to leave, but no one has the courage to do so. Often, the cause is that we've been taught that it's worth giving up our freedom for the sake of politeness or for some advantage (meeting another need), but this view is dysfunctional. If the advantage is having a job (thus Security), let's ask ourselves if there are no other jobs to do with people more aligned with us (besides questioning how real or illusory the cause-effect possibility of having a job while remaining bored is). In this context, our ideals and values play an important role. They should guide us in setting a boundary between what we are willing to tolerate and where to stop, between the direction we want to go and the sense of reality or respect for others' freedom.

Sometimes, unfortunately, they become an excuse to give up our own freedom: *"Friendship is so important to me that I won't tell them in order not to offend them"*.

Spirituality is a more human than animal need. If it's healthy, it's a way of transcending, of going beyond material and earthly things. In this sense, we consider it an extension of the Need for Freedom. Being able to choose and practice our own spirituality (not necessarily religious) is a high form of freedom. It's important to distinguish between Spirituality and adherence to philosophies or religions, which often can – on the contrary – limit freedom.

Creating and Making. All evolved animals love to play, both as infants and adults. Here, we specifically refer to creative play, whereas competitive play was the object of the Need for Self-Assertion and Recognition. Another type of play will be the focus for the Need for Pleasure.

Thanks to our opposable thumb and the prefrontal cortex, we humans derive even more pleasure from creative play than mammals: building objects, drawing, sculpting, etc. After a certain age, this kind of play is penalized in the name of becoming adults, being responsible, etc. This approach makes sense when considering historical periods in which children had to contribute to the family's survival from a young age, but it no longer makes sense today. The paradox is that we all admire creative people; we would like to be creative ourselves, but we perceive it as something impossible. A mammal is creative and generative by nature, putting its all into everything it does. Suppressing creativity means taking vitality away from people. Furthermore, remember that curiosity and focused attention are the foundation of neural plasticity.

Being creative doesn't just concern material objects, but primarily a form of free thinking that creates, transforms, and elaborates. The possibility of perceiving ourselves as creative and productive can remain abstract or take concrete forms; it can be entirely futile, fun, playful, but also help solve problems or contribute to adding value. One mode can coexist with another (for example, problem-solving can be fun). In both cases, humans exhibit a need for persistence and usefulness in their creation. Seeing our creation go to waste or be destroyed (both prevent it from persisting over time) leads to demotivation and sadness. If others or we ourselves don't perceive it as useful (even if it's just a fantasy for playful purposes and our well-being), we question our value as individuals and disinvest in creative thinking.

Sensory **pleasure** and positive emotions are at the foundation of the motivation to live and learn. Only humans, in their vicissitudes, have attempted to deny themselves pleasure: from proper philosophical and ideological movements (stoicism, overworking, etc.) to folk wisdom ("duty before pleasure", "you snooze, you lose", etc.). An animal would never give up a cuddle or a good bite of food; humans do! This can be due to personal choices ("I don't have time", "I don't want to gain weight", etc.) or imposed by others (parents, bosses, etc.). In both cases, it's often a surface choice that hides something else. In fact, it's not the time required for a cuddle that prevents us from delivering work on time, just as it's not the calories in a piece of chocolate that make us gain weight. On the contrary, it's likely the opposite, with gratification, we'll be more productive and effective, just as our metabolism and immune system will function better.

Children learn easily because they do it with interest and enjoyment. It's the same for us, if we read a magazine about travel, sports, or anything else that interests us, we remember many of the things we read, while sometimes other concepts that we need to learn for work just won't stick in our heads. Let's then ask ourselves how interested we are in what we do or what kind of environment we're in when we study.

Two of the most primitive forms of pleasure are controlling our own bodies and self-perception; that's how babies learn to move. Through the pleasure of repetitive play and physical mastery, we learn and refine more complex actions, like learning to play the piano or playing tennis. Research shows that a pianist derives pleasure from the harmonious movement of fingers and hands, even if they can't hear what they're playing. Learning, fluently executing, and mastering a musical or athletic activity, juggling, improving a workflow – these are all ways of expressing the need to experience functional pleasure.

Restoring the physiology of the Need for Pleasure doesn't necessarily mean always partying; it's not necessarily a matter of hedonism. It's more about rediscovering the inherent ways we feel good and have fun in different situations and contexts. Nature gave us pleasure because it helps us regenerate, be creative, and learn. We all need it, and it's absurd that we don't take advantage of the natural mechanism we have at our disposal.

Pleasure isn't necessarily tied to overt enjoyment. Think about a great accomplishment like climbing a mountain or starting a project from scratch. There are sacrifices, tough moments, difficulties. Yet the pleasure of building, creating, seeing our project progress – despite the odds – is absolutely enjoyable and motivating.

THE IMPORTANCE OF NURTURING ANCESTRAL NEEDS

Ancestral Needs must be safeguarded. Neglecting even one of them for an extended period can create significant imbalances. Denying an ancestral need leads to a situation known in ethology as *learned helplessness*. Safeguarding a need means functionally fulfilling it – not neglecting it, not indirectly gratifying it through another need, but also not over gratifying it, unless for short periods and with a clear awareness of what's being done. All ancestral needs safeguard basic functions of Recovery, Security, and Development but through different methods and sub-functions.

The way to satisfy a need can and should vary over time and with respect to context. Flexibility is a key factor. There can and *should* be evolution in needs and ways of satisfying them that's consistent with age and personal maturity.

For instance, Anthony had been working tirelessly for years, seeking gratification solely through his professional success, which he measured exclusively by the number of patients he saw each day and the monthly revenue. This had worn him down; he never allowed time for recovery and regeneration. Even his relationship with his wife, his way of feeling loved, was based on her appreciating him in terms of work success and spending hours listening to his tales of achievements. When he no longer had "big numbers" to share and, conversely, she experienced an increase in work, he suddenly felt unloved and unlovable.

Ancestral Needs should be balanced and virtuously reinforce each other. For example, the transition from feelings of fear to a sense of security (Control and Security Need) during a process of change is possible only when dopaminergic projections come into play, supported by active social motivation (e.g., Self-affirmation AN) or developmental motivation (Creating and Making AN). In other words: *Confrontation and social interaction, together with investment in personal passions or interests (from work to hobbies, as long as they are deeply engaging) create the neurobiological foundation to utilize security networks and overcome mechanisms that sustain fear, insecurity, or anxiety.* The Ancestral Needs Model therefore helps us actively intervene on these two areas from the start, favouring emotional change.

Returning to Anthony he found golf to be beneficial to help him recover from his state of depression and demotivation. He chose a sport that he found enjoyable, that could be practised in a natural and peaceful environment. Moreover, this sport provided him with a sense of open and unrestricted social interaction for the first time, without the need to compete and win to stand out. To facilitate this mechanism, he decided to practice and play alone, not taking part in any competitions or tournaments, so he didn't see any competitive perspective in others, they were simply people with the same passion, discussing techniques and strategies to improve their mastery.

Another similar example of virtuous interaction is that serotonin released through pleasure (Pleasure AN) supports exploratory behaviours (Freedom AN), which in turn support self-esteem and social effectiveness elements (Recognition and Security ANs, respectively).

As we've seen, a central part of Louis's resistance to change was that all his security was based on a fixed salary and a job he was certain not to lose. This wasn't enough, and more importantly, it didn't bring him any joy. It had become a cage that prevented him from enjoying life and finding new passions. Louis, like many others, asked me this question: *"How do you find a passion?"*. This question accurately represents the situation where needs are out of balance with physiology. Starting from small daily pleasures and attention to detail (among other things, he became an expert in coffee blends and making the perfect espresso), Louis began to reactivate exploratory behaviours (e.g., visiting different coffee roasters to try their blends), which then expanded to other active behaviours, stimulating mental curiosity as well.

All ANs impact various personal and interpersonal levels for individuals, couples and groups. In so-called '*alfa*' individuals – known as '*natural leaders*' certain specific features relating to ANs are clearly recognisable:
- The ability to preserve ANs both for the self and for members of the group;

- The ability to act and be motivated to be openly sociable while clearly establishing boundaries and rules for others;
- The ability to remain alone serenely even for long periods of time, always remaining open to helping others in a functional way (not a priori, out of sense of duty or of guilt or other factors that safeguard others but also limit them by stopping them from becoming autonomous and evolving).

The case of Enrique and the activities he undertook to regulate his aggressiveness were further reviewed and explored using the key interpretation of his own and others' ancestral needs within leadership roles.

In relationships ANs allow us to distinguish between the unconditional acceptance that we need (Loving and being loved) and the acknowledgement of our worth (Achievement). It is a fine line that is often blurred; many people would do anything to be loved by their parents just as many others strive for affection and unconditional acceptance at work.

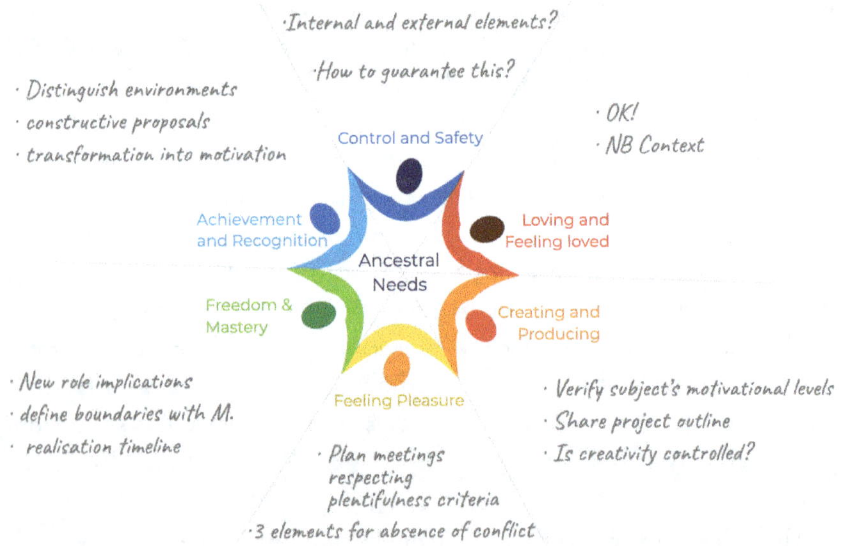

Fig. - An example of an Ancestral Needs worksheet with some suggestions for analysis and possible actions.

From an ethological and neuroscientific standpoint, which helps to distance oneself from the emotional suffering implied and to separate environments, it is possible to clearly see the two phenomena as quite distinct and unconnected, acceptance is part of the AN to be loved, while acknowledgement of our achievements (by definition) cannot be unconditional and relates to the AN for Achievement and Recognition.

This is exactly what was happening to Hilary who was always in search of approval as a human being in need of unconditional love, mistakenly seeking this type of validation from colleagues and especially from her own boss. This had led to several misunderstandings and awkward situations, with male colleagues misinterpreting her and inviting her out romantically. To avoid feeling unlovable, she would accept these invitations and sometimes even end up in bed with them. It was crucial for her to first clarify her own needs and decide beforehand which ones needed to be fulfilled and how it was appropriate to do so. For instance, she eventually admitted that with some colleagues the sexual encounters had also been enjoyable, but she couldn't admit it to herself as it conflicted with her need for control. Hilary used the needs visual map, and week after week she tried to better define her real needs and find the best ways to fulfil them. The visual representation greatly helped her understand how much she risked penalizing one need to make space for another.

Another interesting instance related to the AN for freedom is that it may initially be interpreted as coinciding with the adolescent drive for independence, or with the limitations of working life and life as a couple. In reality, this need spans across all the switch levels analysed in the first part of the book.

First of all, physical and mental movement (such as exploration, curiosity and other constitutive elements of the AN for Freedom) represent a key initial trigger for metabolism and for neural plasticity (see switch 1). This critically happens to improve metabolic efficiency as it enables the optimisation of energy consumption, given that movement increases the potential for survival (you need energy to find other sources of energy).

There is also a strategic evolutionary advantage in the connection between exploration (both literal in terms of territory and in terms of widening of mental boundaries) and plastic-metabolic development, via neural plasticity it is possible to memorise places better and to develop more complex strategies for survival and development.

These aspects in turn activate the immune system because in the hunt for food and exploration it is possible to meet new pathogens or harm by encountering competition or predators. This latter stage also relates to the level of emotional, stress and social unpredictability switches and as a result to all ANs that have an interpersonal aspect.

All these elements can also be found in the Flows of the fifth group of switches. Feeling freedom of movement and thought are two early elements of well-being that are typically absent in emotional inhibition and in PTSD that – in contrast – are found and recovered with sporting activities, manual treatments, etc.

This also applies to communication and creativity flows when there is an obstacle to free thinking and unfettered exploration. These processes are usually seen as creative abilities, but this is just their highest manifestation. Let us remember that exploration is first and foremost an adaptation phenomenon needed to discover the environment, reduce risk and increase opportunity.

Finally, we need to bear in mind that freedom makes room for activity (movement, sport, art, music, unfettered mindsets etc.) that works off excessive neurotoxins accumulated through stress responses without recovery (allostatic overload).

REFERENCES

[1] Krueger, F. et al. Neural correlates of trust. Proc. Natl Acad. Sci. USA 104, 20084–20089 (2007).

Jesus E. Madrid, Tara M. Mandalaywala, Sean P. Coyne, Jamie Ahloy-Dallaire, Joseph P. Garner, Christina S. Barr, Dario Maestripieri, Karen J. Parker. Adaptive developmental plasticity in rhesus macaques: the serotonin transporter gene interacts with maternal care to affect juvenile social behaviour. Proc. R. Soc. B 2018 285 20180541.

Kringelbach, M. L., & Phillips, H. (2014). Emotion: Pleasure and pain in the brain. New York, NY, US: Oxford University Press.

[4] Crofoot, M. C. & Wrangham, R. W. in Mind the Gap: Tracing the Origins of Human Universals (eds Kappeler, P. M. & Silk, J. B.) 171–195 (Springer, 2010).

[5] Sinibaldi F., Achilli S. (2016) Transformative Mindfulness: 45 exercises: An idea-a-day workbook to develop awareness and favour change. Association for Integrative Sciences.

[6] Barrett, Lisa & Mesquita, Batja & Gendron, Maria. (2011). Context in emotion perception. Current Directions in Psychological Science. 20. 286-290.

Calbi, M., Heimann, K., Barratt, D., Siri, F., Umiltà, M. A., & Gallese, V. (2017). How Context Influences Our Perception of Emotional Faces: A Behavioral Study on the Kuleshov Effect. Frontiers in Psychology, 8, 1684.

Vives, M. L., & FeldmanHall, O. (2018). Tolerance to ambiguous uncertainty predicts prosocial behavior. Nature communications, 9(1), 2156.

Behrens, T. E. J., Woolrich, M. W., Walton, M. E. & Rushworth, M. F. S. Learning the value of information in an uncertain world. Nat. Neurosci. 10, 1214–1221 (2007)

Penner, L. A., Dovidio, J. F., Piliavin, J. A. & Schroeder, D. A. Prosocial behavior: multilevel perspectives. Annu. Rev. Psychol. 56, 365–392 (2005).

Gross, Cornelius & Canteras, Newton. (2012). The many paths to fear. Nature reviews. Neuroscience. 13. 651-8. 10.1038/nrn3301.

Benedetti F. Placebo effects: from the neurobiological paradigm to translational implications. Neuron2014;84:623–37

[13] Wilent, W. B., Oh, M. Y., Buetefisch, C. M., Bailes, J. E., Cantella, D., Angle, C., & Whiting, D. M. (2010). Induction of panic attack by stimulation of the ventromedial hypothalamus. Journal of neurosurgery, 112(6), 1295–1298.

Buades-Rotger, Macià & Beyer, Frederike & Krämer, Ulrike. (2017). Avoidant Responses to Interpersonal Provocation Are Associated with Increased Amygdala and Decreased Mentalizing Network Activity. eneuro. 4. ENEURO.0337-16.2017.

[15] Mikulovic S., Restrepo CE., Siwani S., Bauer P., Pupe S., et al. Ventral hippocampal OLM cells control type 2 theta oscillations and response to predator odor. Nature Communications, volume 9, Article number: 3638 (2018)

[16] Sinibaldi F., Achilli S. (2016) 45 Esercizi di Mindfulness Trasformativa. Un quaderno di lavoro – un'idea al giorno – per sviluppare consapevolezza e favorire il cambiamento. Real Way of Life.

SWITCH GROUP NO. 5 – FLOWS – HARMONIES AND RHYTHMS OF LIFE

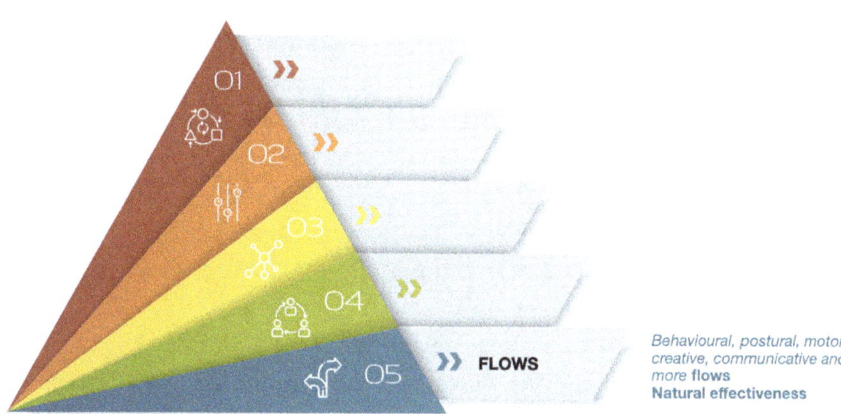

NATURAL FLOWS: AUTONOMOUS, INTERDEPENDENT, AND INTEGRATIVE PATHWAYS FOR IDEAS, THOUGHTS, MOVEMENTS, POSTURE, LANGUAGE, ETC.

Without music and (fiction) writing, I wouldn't be the person I am today. Just like for many others, music has – among other things – also provided an outlet for emotions that are too strong and difficult to convey in words. However, it was starting to play a musical instrument that made the real difference. From that moment, I developed a new awareness, had formative and transformative experiences, and experienced individual and group dynamics that were critical to me. Many of these elements later played a central role in understanding and managing some of the mental, physical, and interpersonal dynamics we will discuss in this chapter better. In a different way, writing has also played an important role, but let's focus on music first.

When you start playing an instrument, the notes are separate, both in your mind and even more so in your hands, which struggle to produce even one note at a time in a controlled manner (so that the sound you want to produce comes out as you intended). Later on, the notes group together in various ways, you sense rhythmic groupings and can immediately distinguish a triplet from a quadruplet; you realize that what you used to call a 'nice passage' becomes a 'descending E7 arpeggio'. This is satisfying; it helps you understand the structure of the world you are exploring. It's not just related to music; it also happens when you learn to taste wine or notice an athlete's harmonious movements. Similarly, it occurs in any form of awareness and mastery of what we do while we talk to a friend or face a challenge at work.

Another important lesson that music taught me is the relationship with time: time marked by the metronome at the beginning is a constraint to abide by, then it becomes a friend to interact with, and eventually it transforms into an element that – while respecting it – can be shaped. There are rhythmic musicians (drummers, percussionists, bassists, etc.) who play some notes with a very slight delay, which makes the rhythm warmer and more enveloping. It's an almost imperceptible delay, yet the listener recognizes it, not so much from a rhythmic perspective but from an emotional one, labelling that musician as 'warm', while the more precise players come across as 'cold'.

In music, time also teaches us to dwell in emptiness, to savour anticipation, to understand if we are filling it too much or too little. Great musicians occasionally shift the rhythm's strong accents or insert an unexpected pause. This creates a brief void and then, as the rhythm resumes, a sense of euphoria. Something similar happens when a swing is at its highest point and, for a fraction of a second, we hang suspended without feeling anything beneath us. We thus experience a brief thrill, and then as the descent begins, euphoria sets in. These mechanisms are crucial in communication and in quality relationships, as well as in the dynamic connection with one's own body in games and sports. Thelonious Monk, a great jazz pianist, taught us to pay attention to the silence between each note, just as we will pay attention to the silence between each word and to what is not spoken through words or expressed by the body. It is just as important as what is shown or explicitly stated.

Musical harmony is created on multiple levels, all the notes heard at the same moment, even produced by different instruments, interact with each other but can be perceived differently depending on the notes played just before. The same happens with the subjects of this chapter, ideas, the spoken word, muscles involved in stress responses and posture, movements, looks, and every other way of existing in the world are connected and influence each other in the moment and as a result of a process. We will analyse each separately to understand and manage each one, but we will always keep in mind their interconnections and the organic view that governs them.

Music has taught me and allowed me to experience firsthand all of this and so much more: the meaning of training, intuition, the word 'performance' in all its positive and negative shades, the power of playing together as a group, the harmony between group members and with the audience, and so on.

Writing has also been rewarding when it comes to experience and transformation. I'm referring to fiction, to the magic of crafting a story that follows your own ideas and, as you write, the roles almost reverse: characters start to shape the story by veering in directions you hadn't planned, and you find yourself putting into words something that is unfolding quite spontaneously.

I have never had problems writing, whether it was a fantasy story or a book like this one; it has always been natural to me, a need to be fulfilled. However, writer's block a is well known phenomenon. From someone aspiring to write a book to a student facing a term paper or a dissertation, sometimes we find ourselves staring at a blank page, not knowing where to start. This can happen for various reasons. Partly, it's about our genuine interest in a topic, which might be something we are dealing with due to a past choice – such as a course of studies or a job that isn't truly aligned to our interest – even if often we are not conscious of it. This can be understood by examining the Ancestral Needs, which we introduced in the previous chapter, and how they can be linked to different mental, physical, and behavioural practices that emerge in this context. As we will see, there are often flows that inhibit each other; for instance, a rigid posture can hinder the smooth flow of ideas and words.

ASSESSMENT: WHAT TO OBSERVE AND EVALUATE

In this fifth and final switch area, it's interesting to observe various aspects, from different perspectives and in a multi-system perspective, including:
• Self-evaluation issues;
• Obstructions (at a physical, mental or emotional level);
• Rigid behaviours (movements, posture, thoughts, emotions);
• Unnaturalness or lack of spontaneity;
• Ways of thinking, moving, speaking that are too fast or too slow, without it being useful or advantageous;
• Individuals who look uncomfortable in their bodies;
• People who seem to want to say something but can't, as if something is holding them back;
• Issues in changing one's mind and believing "emotionally" as well as cognitively;
• Negative thoughts and predictions despite rational evidence to the contrary;
• Postural and physical pain in individuals not engaging in particular muscular efforts;
• Frozen or incongruent flows (motor, ideational, communicative, etc.);
• Clumsiness, poor coordination;
• Significant changes in behavioural style in fairly similar contexts;
• Out-of-place postures, meaning postural and motor patterns that are not consistent with the situation.

(NO LONGER) NATURAL FLOWS

As we mentioned in the introduction, this level regards final stage switches for the processes described so far. It looks at how to act on *behavioural, creative, postural, motor, interpersonal and communication* flows that are activated in order to adapt to an environment, to develop something new (i.e. an ability or potential relationships) or to recover energy and maintain a condition of balance.

One key point that relates to all flows is that of the feeling of naturalness and spontaneity. People often refer to their way of speaking, deciding or acting as 'spontaneous', but at the same time they do not perceive it to be entirely free and feel the urge to improve this. We'll look at some examples that highlight how often this feeling emerges from the awareness (maybe only just hinted at) that complete freedom and flexibility of execution are not present. By contrast, recovering the physiological state of these flows and of the processes that compose them allows us to support more natural ways of being. It gives a feeling of mastery and performs biofeedback which favours the physiological state of the previous level switches.

Various disciplines and teachings ranging from ancient philosophy to traditional CBT, right through to modern third generation, physical and sensorimotor psychotherapies have focused on direct intervention at this level. On the basis of what we have analysed so far, it becomes clear that it is necessary to work across all levels of switches that support flows, whether these are metabolic, regulation or network switches, in order to maximise their physiology and plasticity to release the full potential and natural flexibility of change processes. On the other hand, it is possible to integrate and increase the effectiveness of therapeutic approaches and strategies that are already in use by exploiting some processes that favour all the switches acting on this level's specific features.

Let us now review some types of flows and emerging features on which to focus our attention in order to favour change, care or development processes.

FRAMING THE DIFFERENT FLOWS

From the end of the 1900's to today, many disciplines – starting with Embodiment studies (*Embodied Cognition* and other approaches), *Enactment* (initially Varela) and in parallel the Theory of complex systems, games theory and PNEI (Psycho-Neuro-Endocrine-Immunology) – have clearly indicated and scientifically proven that: cognition, emotion, perceptions, body (in all its aspects: from muscles, to digestion, to the immune system etc), social interactions, needs and motivations are all connected. They all influence each other and can either support or pose an obstacle to each other.

Flows have the great advantage that they can be observed and categorised into types and recurrent patterns that open up clear vistas on how people work, what motivates them and what obstructs them.

Fig. – The Flows symbol visually represents the fluid flow and connection between the different levels that flows are formed in.

Flows pertain to any way in which we adapt or simply 'exist in the world'. Below we'll look at the main macro-categories to begin acquainting ourselves with their nature and the respective implications in practice. As we progress, we will delve into more detailed aspects.

Ideational flows concern the flow of thought. They should not be confused with *communicative flows*, which can be independent. However, listening to how a person presents their ideas can provide interesting insight into how thoughts flow in their mind. For example, there are individuals who express their ideas very slowly, trying to shape them as they are there with us, even for simple concepts on which they should already have their own opinion. If we are reasonably certain that there are no particular emotional or social obstacles at that moment, and if –

conversely – the conversation flows well and quickly as soon as the topic shifts to familiar informational data (such as the names of colleagues they've worked with for years, or steps to perform a well-known repetitive task), then we might be facing an interesting cue concerning the construction and/or sharing of their ideas.

Another typical case involves individuals who constantly get lost in an endless series of details, opening so many parentheses that they lose track of the original point. In this case as well, we may wonder whether the issue lies in the communicative or in the ideational flow. An interesting way to analyse this is to *understand whether the person is really addressing the other or merely thinking out loud.*

Even though formally one is answering a question, and as such speaking to the other person, there are individuals who lose eye contact and interpersonal connection in general. They don't initially consider the underlying need behind the question, don't look and don't verify whether the person is following the conversation and is satisfied with the response. In all these cases, the dominant flow is ideational, while the communicative-relational aspect has taken a back seat or has been completely lost. *Other clues* that help us understand that the focus is on ideation, for instance, are when one observes intellectual enjoyment in certain reasoning. This can result in a complete disconnection between the flows.

When Enrique talked about his own projects, his face would turn red, his chest would swell, and his eyes would sparkle, activating postural, movement, and vocal tone flows that he could very well have used while charming a beautiful woman over dinner (to use these parallels in a structured context, you can employ the *Out-of-Place Postures technique*, as explained later).

Conversely, you may notice that the dominant flow is relational when the content takes a back seat, and all attention is on communication and on the relationship. Quite simply, though often unconsciously, words flow faster and with a richer vocabulary depending on the audience. Sometimes it's very evident, as in shy and studious individuals who speak with great fluency and confidence to their friends but get tongue-tied in front of an attractive girl. The intriguing part is that this occurs, to a lesser but still significant extent, even with certain friends.

Hilary, for example, always spoke at a fairly brisk pace, but she noticed that when talking to one of her close friends, her speed slowed down significantly, and she seemed to "look for the right words" more carefully than with others. We tried to reflect on whether the reason was a specific topic or its emotional connection, but there didn't appear to be major differences compared to what she discussed with her other friends. Shifting the focus to the relationship, however, she realized that she sought the approval of that friend, who was, as Hilary said *"kind of how I would like to be in many ways"*. This dual game of relational and identity dynamics was blocking everything; she didn't feel spontaneous and thus, in her attempt to gain approval from her friend and become more like her, paradoxically, she was losing the very spontaneity she admired in her friend. Moreover, she wasn't being herself, and this undermined the possibility of naturally structuring new behaviour and approaches. Finally, the friend began to sense this filtering of thoughts and words in Hilary's conversations, causing a distance to develop and damaging the relationship.

The most evident *body flows* are *postural* and *motor*. The former are more static, in the sense that they pertain to the postures we adopt at a specific moment, triggered by interactions with other flows (ideas that come to mind, relational dynamics, or specific communicative contents) or those we frequently return to – almost like clothes we "wear", providing a sense of safety. Motor flows, on the other hand, involve the movements we make to pick up an object, to go somewhere, or to carry out any adaptation mechanism that we need in that instance.

If you start paying attention to your conversation partners during lunch, or even just casually observe the tables at a restaurant or in the cafeteria during a lunch break at work, you will be surprised to notice that many people keep their non-fork-holding hand clenched into a fist. This is a postural block; there's no reason to have that fist clenched; it's likely an expression of suppressed anger from earlier. It's important not to become overly interpretive. This example represents just one possibility; the actual reason for each person should be investigated specifically. The key point to emphasize for now is that keeping that clenched fist maintains unnecessary tension and triggers a series of biofeedback loops that keep stress responses and negative emotional experiences active.

The first step is to make people aware of these patterns and encourage them to identify any others that might exist. The subsequent step involves attempting to interrupt this automatic response. For instance, simply relaxing the hand and resuming speaking and eating calmly. Later on, individuals can be encouraged to perform a *Schema Inversion* – temporarily stopping the activation and, for at least a couple of minutes, engaging in the opposite pattern. For instance, if they were clenching their hand, they could extend it, assisting with the other hand, or place their fingers against the table to lift the metacarpal and extend the underside of their fingers and the palm of the hand. After a couple of minutes, during which they are asked to keep the rest of their body relaxed and breathe slowly, they will explore a new natural hand position that lies halfway between these extremes (further details on these techniques, *Inversion of Schemas* and *Interpersonal Accommodation*, are provided later on in this same chapter).

Other interesting body flows, inbetween postural and motor ones, are *suspended actions*. Think of people you shake hands with, who are so engaged in the conversation or the topics being discussed that they inadvertently freeze their hand in place, so that you find yourself struggling to remove your hand, but you can see from their vacant expression that they aren't intentionally holding it; they simply got stuck during that behavioural execution. Conversely, it can also happen that you easily withdraw your hand, and you notice that theirs remains suspended in mid-air, in a position no longer useful but certainly uncomfortable.

When Mark was speaking, he would often scratch his head as if to concentrate and find the right words. Almost every time he found inspiration and began to talk, his hand would stay on his head without scratching anymore, in a noticeably uncomfortable position. Only after a few minutes would he start feeling the weight of his arm, realize the situation, and awkwardly – and quickly – lower it. When I pointed out this pattern to him, he immediately remembered that the same thing used to happen in high school, when he was called to the blackboard, he would start scratching his head or chin, and then continue to do so while writing on the board and talking to the teacher. Unfortunately, this memory was linked to the image of his classmates laughing and teasing him later. In this specific case, we first worked on the anger associated with the helplessness he felt back then, which in various ways was also connected to his current experiences with his wife. To address these issues, we employed the techniques and strategies discussed in the previous chapter (balancing Ancestral Needs, constructively revisiting aggression, etc.) and those from switch area #3 regarding the meaning of and ability to self-regulate and accurately perceive one's bodily resources. When we reached a good point with this work, we moved on to directly managing his body flows. Dealing with them earlier on, in Mark's specific case, could have been perceived as another confirmation of his inadequacy in handling the situation. In cases that don't exhibit this feeling of inadequacy, however, it's useful to begin with this element immediately. Addressing bodily flows breaks automatisms, provides relief, and often opens the door to new insights and awareness.

Let's quickly look at a few more illustrative examples of these recurring flows:

- The breath holding that occurs in some individuals when they're told something they don't want to hear and becomes so intense that they become as stiff as a statue.
- The chest constriction that's constantly visible in some people. This tension often extends to the neck and face, so when observing them for a while, you get the feeling it's a freeze-frame from a film, evoking that typical sense of anguish in the observer at the sight of a seemingly breathless body (those who are highly empathetic can easily experience this sensation).
- The arching of the back that occurs as a result of surprise or irritation, and should only last for a few seconds or minutes before returning to normal physiological state but instead persists even after several minutes.
- Changes in postural patterns that reflect in balance. Take, for example, individuals who stand firmly on their feet but start swaying and crossing their legs as soon as someone emotionally significant – either positively or negatively – approaches them.

These are unnecessary patterns, that often prove disadvantageous. In fact, to avoid looking at something, it would be enough to avert your gaze, while lowering the head shifts the body weight forward, creating unnecessary tensions in the back and a sense of physical instability. This cascade effect also impacts mentally and emotionally.

OBSERVING FLOWS

Flows also serve as an excellent system for understanding what's wrong when it comes to Ancestral Needs (as discussed in the previous chapter). At the same time, they offer a practical way to teach people greater self-awareness and provide daily practical insights for change.

To help identify what happens within the Flows and their corresponding Ancestral Needs processes, we've identified several sub-categories of flows that area easy to observe and created an observation sheet for them. On the next page, you'll find this framework with a series of typical examples. Keep in mind that different modes and dynamics can also be identified beyond those presented in the table.

The *Mindset* flow generally concerns how one views the world, the kind of attitude adopted in daily life situations. It's an overall assessment that should be made after observing all the other flows. *Mindset* is linked with a person's self-image; it's easy to notice a certain pride when you acknowledge whether they're a reactive and responsive person or a curious and innovative one. On the other hand, people often fail to see the flip side of the coin – for instance, that someone who is 'reactive' often reacts when it's unnecessary, lives in a state of hyper-vigilance, and risks doing everything for others. Similarly, the curious and innovative person sometimes spends time thinking about value-added details without having established solid foundations or being certain that the project will move forward. This can lead to strain and frustration.

The *Ideational Narrative* is the flow of a person's most recurring thoughts, what their mind consistently goes back to. It's not about the topic they're discussing at that moment, like bicycles or the Rubik's Cube, but the topic that drives them or instils fear in them. For example, they might always talk about bicycles, but the nature of their thoughts could be focused on being the best among their friends (linked to the need for self-affirmation) or to being the most creative in repairing them (Ancestral Need for creation and production). In a different way, the ideational narrative is also evident in those who constantly need to innovate, have fun, etc; otherwise they become demotivated.

Let's look at a *partially ideational and partially relational mode*; this mode is noticeable for the pattern of denying or belittling others' ideas and shortly thereafter presenting a very similar idea as one's own. Aside from those who cunningly do it on purpose, many people aren't aware of this mechanism. It often stems from the fear that others' ideas might be better than their own, so these ideas are pushed away. However, like a seed that has landed in fertile soil, the idea starts growing within them and attaches itself to the desperate need to be creative while simultaneously self-affirming.

The *Content Narrative* flow pertains to the domains and ways in which a person concentrates to develop a theme and the underlying need. For instance, whether they're discussing cooking or vacations, their focus always centres around organisation. In this case, depending on whether the emphasis is on control, perfecting the project, risk avoidance, or the grandiosity of the undertaking, the underlying ancestral need could be Security and Control or Creation and Production. It might also involve the pleasure of the activity itself(Pleasure), the freedom to do things one's way without constraints (Freedom), or the happiness they provided their partners with as a result of their choice. In the latter case, it could relate to Love and Being Loved or Pleasure extended to the couple dimension.

In light of these initial examples, it's important to clarify that there are no inherently positive or negative modes. The key is to identify various flows, look at the big picture, and understand whether the overall balance is positive and physiological or something should be modified. In the last example given, a person focusing on their partner's pleasure during vacation displays good empathy and interest in the other person. However, it's necessary to determine whether this significantly constricts their personal space (such as their self-affirmation and freedom, for instance) both within the relationship and in other contexts.

The *Form Narrative* flow is transversal and independent of the subject being discussed. It's discerned from recurring linguistic patterns. For instance, individuals who frequently use phrases like *"yes, but…"* often do so due to the need to leave nothing to chance (Control), showcase their observations (Self-Affirmation), seek agreement (Being Loved), or to feel they have left room for action (Freedom).

	Control and Safety	Achievement and Recognition	Loving and Feeling loved	Creating and Producing	Freedom and Mastery	Feeling Pleasure
Mindset (way of thinking and mental models)	Reactive and Adaptive	Engagement and Strategy	Care and Development	Passion and Self-realisation	Curiosity and Experimentation	Learning and Recovery
Creative Narrative (impassioned, obsessed, afraid of)	Risks	Compare & Confront	Relational void, Loneliness	Inactivity	Constraints	Sensorial emptiness; addiction
Content Narrative (macro and emerging themes)	Procedures, complex systems	Ideas, projects & resources (compared to other people's)	Feelings / Moods	Ideas, projects (mainly personal ones)	Ideas, projects, challenges (with a constructive hint of omnipotence)	Feelings and perceptions
Form Narrative (recurrent schemes)	Can't exclude anything (*and... and...*), can't accept imperfections or incompletion (*yes, but...*); Talk a lot and very quickly, are difficult to interrupt	Amplifies him/her-self; criticises others to stand out above them; always talking about his/her epic achievements; doesn't let the others finish their sentences	Amplifies the other people's virtues; never criticise, always praising and confirming	Enthusiasm; constructive criticism (focused on the end product, not on improving the other person)	Exaggeration; out-of-the-box and/or visionary thinking; multi-level hypothetical thinking	Following different ideas driven by enthusiasm
Interpersonal Narrative (trust, delegation, seduction, reciprocity, etc.)	Interrupts others because he/she can't wait; finds it hard to delegate responsibilities to others	Interrupts the other to impose himself or to limit the other person's power, seductive or conflicting, never reciprocal; delegates to let the other grow; reactive to provocations.	Panders to others (on ideas, decision, etc.); passively follows or seeks consent	Brings innovation, is a game changer and leads others in this direction; creates productive and added value connections	Delegates to gain personal freedom; he/she likes to be alone and seeks occasions to be on his/her own	Positive attitude: reciprocity, conviviality, tension release / Negative attitude: greed and solipsism
Social Regulation (power, aggression, rank, roles etc.)	To survive (literally or metaphorically) -mors tua vita mea-	For self-affirmation and to protect what is key	To protect the other (eventually to the extent of sacrificing yourself); developing autonomy and not dependency	Anger towards creative and expressive limits; being able to promote different resources in the others	Anger caused by not daring to experiment; tendency to cut binding relationships	Anger caused by frustration (development Vs resentment); modulation from individual to social dimension
Somatic Narrative (activation, enactment, expression, action etc.)	Defensive, Blocked, Solid, Constructive, Flexible, etc.	Power, Challenge, Submission, Cooperation, etc.	Giver/carer or taker? is there monotony or flexibility (in style, giving, receiving)?	Free and coherent flow; ability to move smoothly from useful schemes to recovery or to physiological state	"Feline exploration" (like a jaguar stalking in its territory); free running; self-feeding energy	Enjoyment; alternation between climax and release; specific focus or multi-sensory engagement

There are people who don't finish their sentences or insist on providing details, even when it's clear the other person perfectly understands the topic. This behaviour can reveal insecurities related to Control or Self-Affirmation. Other people feel the urgency to say something just to avoid silence. This might stem from an inability to tolerate emptiness, fear of judgment, feeling inferior, or from other reasons. Conversely, frequently stopping while speaking, taking long pauses, looking upwards, and using vocalizations like *"uhm"* are elements of form that may reflect the need to look for the exactly perfect word to avoid misinterpretation. If the reason for not wanting to make a mistake is related to risks, then the underlying need is security. If the reason is the fear of not being intelligent enough, we're in the realm of self-affirmation or being loved (as we discussed in the previous chapter, many attempt to satisfy one need with the processes pertaining to another, in this case seeking affection through performance).

The *Relationship/Interpersonal Narrative* flow provides valuable insights into how a person interacts with others and the interpersonal dynamics they, often unconsciously, engage in. A typical case involves individuals who always justify themselves when initiating a conversation, even when it's unnecessary. This mechanism is often rationalized as good manners, but it's actually an over-explanation. Their behaviour and communication would still be considered polite even if they didn't constantly apologize. On the other hand, those who frequently justify themselves lose relational power and others tend to assert themselves instead.

There are people who start answering a question before it has been properly formulated. Their answer is often defensive as they perceive the other person as an accuser/predator (as discussed in the section on aggression in the previous chapter) and can't bear to be exposed to their threats. Individuals with this attitude often encounter genuinely aggressive people, but in at least half of the cases, they also don't fully listen to questions from genuinely interested individuals. As a result, they come across as disengaged, dismissive, and not open to listening. The result is that, while they are trying to protect themselves from certain kinds of relationships, they end up damaging other types.

Another recurring case concerns people who must immediately identify a culprit as soon as anything happens. If they get stuck in traffic on their way to work, they immediately blame the poor municipal organization, without considering that they could have left five minutes earlier; if they drop a glass, they think or say, *"Who put them in the cabinet like this?!"* without thinking that perhaps they grabbed it improperly, and so on. This attitude is an attempt to absolve oneself of responsibility, often driven by the need to redirect anger towards someone else. This anger is almost never solely tied to the specific event but frequently accumulates and magnifies along with the frustration caused by grievances from previous days and months. This is largely an individual mechanism, often only experienced internally, without involving the alleged wrongdoer. This type of behaviour, however, significantly influences one's self-image and the image of others around us, ultimately distorting the foundations of trust and reciprocity in all relationships.

The *Social Aggressiveness* flow is a subtype of relational narrative, but it deals with themes so important that they deserve a dedicated level. Furthermore, as we have seen in switch area 4, aggression and anger constitute a theme rooted in our neurobiology and heavily influenced by our culture, leading to frequent issues. A typical dysfunction is constantly seeking challenge, perhaps even with healthy competition, but without the ability to refrain from it to feel one's own worth, to maintain control of the situation, or even as a perverse form of pleasure or freedom.

On the other hand, there are people who quickly forgive those who have wronged them, even severely, just to avoid losing emotional or financial benefits, sometimes even devaluing themselves in order to salvage the relationship.

In general, by observing the timing and manner in which people engage in a discussion within a couple or a group, it's possible to discern what they are attempting to achieve on a relational level. They may be seeking to gain more power or take it away from others, intentionally provoking conflict just for the satisfaction of it or to break up others' connections and alliances, assigning or avoiding responsibility, hoping that a problem will emerge so that they can address it and avoid the conflict, and so forth.

The *Somatic Narrative* flow is very intriguing and equally susceptible to various interpretations. To approach it accurately, it's important to identify consistent patterns and activations or deactivations linked to specific themes or contexts. While observing a pattern, one should always begin with a correct anatomical reading, then move to a potential ethological meaning (which still respects functional anatomy, biomechanics, and muscular chains), and only in the end attempt a more symbolic and/or cultural assessment. For example, if a young boy frequently walks on his tiptoes, some theories might suggest that he's "escaping from earth, from reality, wanting to live in his fantasy world". If you understand anatomy and functional biomechanical connections, you need to check if the shoulders are kyphotic, if the head is slightly tilted forward and the tongue doesn't move freely (e.g., he speaks with a 'sibilant *s*", can't stick out his tongue much, or has an open bite). In all the mentioned cases, the reason for walking on tiptoes is muscular and motor-related. Working with Psychosomatic Stretching (switch 1), Isometric Emotions (later in this chapter) and various Release techniques (switch 2), the situation can be reversed or at least improved (in some cases, balanced muscle strengthening exercises might also be helpful, along with interventions by a system-oriented osteopath, and sometimes functional orthodontics). On the other hand, it's possible that this "tiptoe walking" is only (or more) visible during moments of stress. Therefore, it will be interesting to work on the connections between this and other flows to develop a synergistic and physiological response during moments of stress.

After providing this initial example to understand the approach clearly, it's still important to consider typical postures associated with fear, anger, or other reactions, while keeping in mind the considerable and subjective variability within these emotions themselves (for more details, refer to the in-depth discussion on emotions and stress in the introductory chapter) as well as in relation to postural and motor patterns. You might observe segmentations in the body, meaning certain areas are highly active – even when speaking emphatically – while others remain completely immobile. Some individuals completely deactivate their muscular chains and seem to "melt" into it when they lean against a chair, while others remain rigid even in the most comfortable armchair.

Some individuals start leaning as soon as they find support, pressing their head against the pillow on the bed or against the headrest in the car, for instance, or gripping a fork while waiting to be served lunch and squeezing it against the table; in fact, many people share the habit of resting an elbow or a leg on the other and then unconsciously pushing when they, or someone they live with settles on the couch to watch a movie. Those who engage in these behaviours do so automatically, without thinking, only realizing what they are doing when someone points it out or when the tension becomes excessive. In all these cases, we need to understand, together with the individual, what tension they are trying to release in this manner, from which part of the body, and which needs – such as seeking a presumed benefit (which, in practice, doesn't exist and instead leads to accumulating even more tension)- are driving this movement.

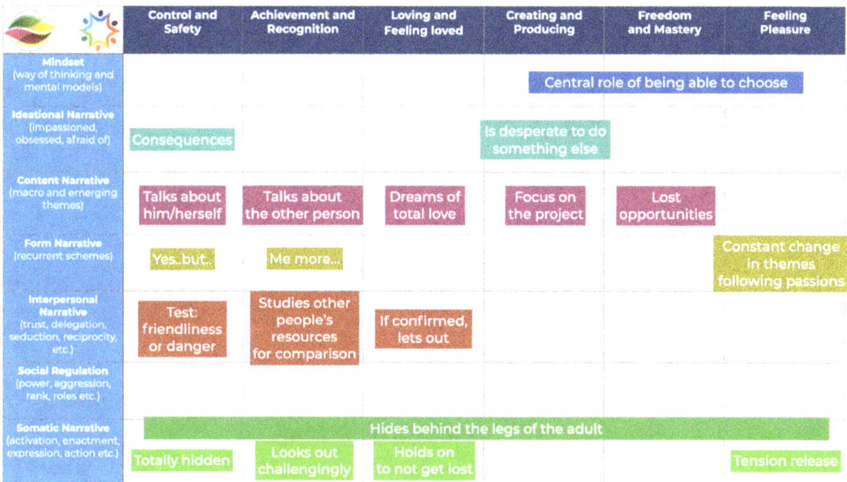

	Control and Safety	Achievement and Recognition	Loving and Feeling loved	Creating and Producing	Freedom and Mastery	Feeling Pleasure
Mindset (way of thinking and mental models)					Central role of being able to choose	
Ideational Narrative (impassioned, obsessed, afraid of)	Consequences			Is desperate to do something else		
Content Narrative (macro and emerging themes)	Talks about him/herself	Talks about the other person	Dreams of total love	Focus on the project	Lost opportunities	
Form Narrative (recurrent schemes)	Yes..but..	Me more...				Constant change in themes following passions
Interpersonal Narrative (trust, delegation, seduction, reciprocity, etc.)	Test: friendliness or danger	Studies other people's resources for comparison	If confirmed, lets out			
Social Regulation (power, aggression, rank, roles etc.)						
Somatic Narrative (activation, enactment, expression, action etc.)	Hides behind the legs of the adult					
	Totally hidden	Looks out challengingly	Holds on to not get lost			Tension release

Fig. – Sample sheet compiled while observing a child

In addition to direct observation, active methods can also be employed to identify each individual's specific flows. Below, we discuss two different approaches.

The first technique, *Dysfunctional Automatisms Mapping*, involves directly engaging the individual, inviting them to observe themselves and gather information about their own modes of operation. This simultaneously becomes a valuable exercise in self-awareness.

TECHNIQUE – MAD MAPPING OF DYSFUNCTIONAL AUTOMATISMS

When emotional pressure becomes particularly intense (at least from a subjective point of view), a series of behaviours and ways of acting emerge. These are particularly interesting to observe, Among them, we are particularly interested in the behaviour that we automatically engage in under stress, such as working faster and harder, overthinking (obsessively ruminating over thoughts), being physically tense, activating ineffective multitasking, socially isolating ourselves, becoming hyper-reactive to stimuli (whether they are lights, sounds, the sensation of a clothing label against the skin, requests for help, or anything else), holding our breath (sometimes literally–there are people who experience hypoxia in these situations), blaming others, getting angry over small things, perceiving everyone as unintelligent and uncooperative, deluding themselves into relying on food or coffee, or feeling the need to relax with cigarettes and alcohol, and so on. These behaviours are useless and almost always counterproductive, both in the short term (making us less effective and more dispersive) and in the long term (damaging our self-image, poisoning our neurological system and affecting its performance, creating favourable conditions for immune system decline, leading to weight gain and somatic symptoms).

Let's see more examples. When they feel uncomfortable, many people tend to tense up, which creates problems for them (physical tension, not knowing where to put their hands or what posture to adopt, increased embarrassment and resulting relationship difficulties) and others, who perceive all of this and as a result, become less spontaneous themselves. Their levels of trust also grow lower.

Sometimes we implement irrational and counterproductive mechanisms when, for example, our computer or the internet are slow and we start talking to our laptop. We try to encourage it, ask it to hurry up (someone even say 'please' or insult their technology), press harder on the keys, as if all this could really help. The computer has no ears and doesn't want to tease us, talking to it makes no sense, and the computer is not ignoring us so there is no point in insisting after the first click that didn't work. Yet we do it, thus deluding ourselves that we have control and are not helpless in the face of the situation. These behaviours represent the working version of making "um", "uhm" sounds when we were asked a questioned we didn't know the answer to in school. Did we really think the professor believed we were working on an answer? No, but we liked to believe it. These behaviours help us release some immediate stress, but in the long run they turn against us. For example, if waiting for a slow computer is just about bearable, we postpone the decision to change the hard disk for a faster one or to call the internet technician or to activate any other real solution to the problem.

Sometimes, when we are tired and stressed, we snap at others, and paradoxically, we treat those we care about worse. The excuse is that 'we can afford to. We know they will put up with it,' while it would be helpful to do the opposite; treating the source of the problem poorly would likely make *them* behave differently. When we release tension with our loved ones, we must remember that accusations and aggression activate the animal centres in our counterpart, quickly and powerfully damaging trust and affection at their core (see Switch 4). At a later moment, when we regret it and apologize, our words will be gentle signals and it will take a long time (if ever) to recover from the damage done. Here are two metaphors that illustrate this well: a crumpled sheet of paper cannot be ironed out anymore, the fold marks remain despite all our motivation and insistence in trying to make them go away; a vase can be broken in an instant, while repairing it takes hours, and the cracks will always be visible.

Another example of dysfunctional behaviour occurs when we fixate on something that needs to be done at a particular moment. Many people tend to see an action as a burden to be removed. Whether it's retrieving a document at the office or doing the cleaning, at some point their thoughts fixate, making them think, 'I have to do it now.' On that 'I have to,' they then build fake rational excuses, but the reasons are always emotional, like getting rid of a burden, doing this to avoid doing something else, etc.

In this technique, we propose that the person maps out the dysfunctional behaviours they engage in. An initial part of the work can be done together, but it will be necessary for the person to self-observe in daily life, looking for behaviours similar to the ones we have presented as recurring patterns. Sometimes you may identify conspicuous behaviours, but often you will also notice small modifications in your behaviour, such as speaking slightly faster than usual. These observations should be encouraged and used as well. In fact, precisely because they are minor changes, it will be easier to be successful in what follows. The next step is attempting to counter these patterns. It should be done without forcing things but by helping yourself regain control and focusing on the awareness that these are not functional behaviours. For example, when you're tired - instead of having a full coffee - you can have only half. Similarly, you can tolerate 2 seconds of silence between one vocalization and another.

The second technique, unlike the previous one, concerns us first-hand operators directly. It is a way to actively generate some changes in flows through questions that engage our counterpart more directly in the communicative-relational exchange we have in progress.

REACTION QUESTIONS

"Those who ask lead" is a slogan that struck me from the beginning of my training. Initially, I thought it was a provocation, then that it referred to manipulation. Finally, I understood what it really was about. Have I piqued your curiosity? Do you understand the true meaning?
Well, we've just given a live example of what I was trying to convey about the slogan "those who ask lead".
To my questions, some of you might have mentally answered "yes," and in this case, the idea that this text might contain something useful has been reinforced. For some of those who responded in this way, the desire to know more about the slogan may have increased, or they may have become interested in how to use questions. In these two scenarios, we could think that there is something related to power: what do you need these questions for? For instance, to become better professionals (power as "mastery") or to manage people with whom communication is challenging (relational power), and so on.
Some may have mentally answered "no". Among them, some might have felt frustrated at not understanding the true meaning, others might have taken it as a challenge ("I'll understand it faster than others!"), and some might have reopened an emotional wound from the past (e.g., "I never understand anything" or "my father always said this, how annoying!").
I've given just a few examples, but the scenarios and nuances can be infinite. What interests me here is to highlight how a seemingly simple and innocent

question can activate various types of thoughts, reactions, memories, identifications, and so on in a very powerful way. Whether a person answered yes or no, everything that happened afterward has little to do with me, except for having created the starting point. If I hadn't asked a question, if I had used different phrase, I wouldn't have triggered all of this.

"*Those who ask lead*" can be understood in the sense that whoever asks inevitably leads the listener into some emotional, cognitive, relational, etc., world. Seeing this world is the greatest gift a person can give us to understand them. It's their way of thinking, of experiencing emotions, and of relating.

That's why I've called them "Reaction Questions". If, on the other hand, we ask direct questions (the classic content-related questions like "*what emotions do you feel?*"), they will probably tell us what they think they're feeling, not necessarily what they truly feel.

It is thus possible to bypass prepackaged responses, avoidance due to fear of judgment, an inability to self-evaluate correctly, and other phenomena that make direct answers to questions less useful. If you try asking someone, "Do you trust me?" how many do you think will respond honestly (with you or themselves)? Furthermore, there are areas where direct answers are not possible because the subject of the question can be the problem itself (for example, someone who cannot engage in mutual relationships might not even know they exist).

To seize the precious opportunity to get to know someone through their worlds, we need to:

• Use targeted questions, asked correctly.

• Be able to observe where the other person is being led.

• Stay in the relationship with them.

Make hypotheses to verify or falsify with other questions or additional tools.

Come up with endless reaction questions based on what we know about the person and the ongoing communication exchange. To give you a starting point and a better sense of their meaning and ways of behaving, let's look at some examples of particularly interesting reaction questions:

What are you NOT thinking about right now?

This is a schema-breaking question (in this case, it's not just a question but a whole technique that I rank among my favourites). People are not expecting this question, and it can lead to interesting reactions: disorientation, anger, towards the questioner ("only an idiot would ask such a question!" or, conversely, "you're a genius!"), or towards oneself ("I don't understand what you're asking"), cognitive overload, engagement, or fleeing from the challenge, etc.

Can I borrow/try/see it?
This needs to be asked referring to something important to the person, like "that watch looks nice, can I see it?" or "nice car, can I try it later?"
I believe this can be the only question about possession and/or generosity that generates a reliable response. Someone may try to inhibit their true response, but a delayed "yes, you can" spoken with muscle tension, swallowing, pulling the object towards themselves, etc., will indicate that it's better if we don't borrow it. This can open up different worlds related to ownership, control, trust, personal resources, etc.

The unexpected question
As the name suggests, this question comes unexpectedly, so it's out of context compared to the ongoing dialogue. For example, suddenly shifting from talking about work to saying, "I think you love brown ale, right?"
It's not an explicit question; in fact, there's no question mark right away, but it includes a rhetorical question at the end ("..., right?"). This question is very useful for assessing the rigidity of mental patterns, flexibility, willingness, or even the desire to switch to a more personal context, to the theme of pleasure, etc.

Saying the forbidden
This technique involves using socially unacceptable phrases, such as "I'm getting bored."
Again, it's not an explicit question, but it usually prompts one or more questions in the listener's mind, triggering a search for answers. For example, after hearing the sentence "I'm getting bored," it's normal to wonder: "Is it my fault?", "Should I take responsibility for your boredom?", "Should I change something?", "Why are you doing this to me?", etc. This opens up a series of fascinating reflections on security systems, assumption of responsibility, role and identity, managing one's own and others' emotions, etc.

Finally, let's look at some other useful questions in various situations:
• You're surely special; can you help me understand how?
• Are you sure you're making that choice?

- How much does freedom scare you?
- How many things that you want to do are you giving up on?
- Let's be honest for 5 minutes, why do you do it?
- How much of your energy do you give to others that you could use for yourself?
- Are you living against your nature?

Teaching these techniques, I've noticed recurring resistance from some professionals who, despite their enthusiasm, struggled to implement more interactive reaction questions. The motivation was often based on the fact that certain professions need to maintain a distance (or at least that's how it's taught in some schools) and cannot afford to ask their patients/clients to try something or ask provocative questions. I want to reassure these professionals that these are pretext questions to generate certain reactions, which can then be explained to the patient. We're not really interested in trying their car or watch. Similarly, we don't need to justify the validity of the hypothesis regarding their beer preference. However, usually, there's no need for an explanation; the richness of the reflections that arise from this stimulus is so interesting and stimulating for the person that they are no longer interested in the initial question.

These are not questions to be asked forcefully or necessarily in the first meeting. These are questions you can add to your repertoire and, with your experience and sensitivity, decide when and how to ask them.

From the next paragraph we will start with a series of insights into the functioning of the different flows and how to work with them in an integrative way.

IDEATIVE FLOWS: SCHEMAS AND RHYTHMS

Ideative flows concern more than just content and structure of thought; there are a series of other sophisticated elements that are in close interaction with each other too.

Let us take a series of daily observations as the starting point to identify their main features. There are deep connections between the way people speak, think and feel. These go beyond feeling connected to a specific thought. Rather, we are referring to the coherence that a single thought may have with a wider thought environment, with the contingent

situation and its potential interaction with other people's thoughts and beliefs. When a child is obliged to say sorry or to say hello to a relative, for example, the speed of their words, the melody and the way the single letters are enunciated are totally different to when these actions are spontaneous. These alterations alert us to the effort and unnatural strain these words and associated thoughts require.

These processes are also clearly visible in adults when there is no external obligation, but some other intervening factor. Typically, this is what happens when we say "Noooo" lengthening the 'o' sound to underline our rage, or to push back further pressure. By contrast we often hear people say "come on" with different intensities and durations depending on how comfortable they feel about motivating the other person. Although these are very short words, the person's embarrassment, anger, worry regarding potential consequences or unwillingness, clearly transpire.

The cinema and theatre also provide interesting food for thought: great leaders are always represented as slow speakers that do not follow traditional punctuation. These elements are intuitively perceived by the spectator as indicators of self-control and independent thinking in real life too.

Another important feature of thought flows relates to the more-or-less flexible employment of specific thought schemas. So-called *overthinkers*, or those that tend to think all the time, for example, go over the same content again and again in the same fashion. They cannot stop doing this as it is the only form of (attempted) control available to them. Anyone that is familiar with studying music will notice an analogy with that process of learning a new instrument; when the amateur tries to play freely they will continue to repeat the same accompaniments and key changes. This happens because these are the only modes of expression with which they are confident. As the repertoire for expression increases, more targeted choices are made and new more personal structures are introduced. Overthinkers do the same thing; they only have a few modalities that they continue to apply repeatedly, but these are rarely suited to solving a specific problem and rarely provide added value.

THOUGHT: IN-BETWEEN LANGUAGE LEARNING AND CULTURE

To truly understand thought processes, it is essential to consider the relationship between thought patterns, language usage, learning mechanisms, and the culture in which one grows up and lives. When one learns a language naturally, it is imbued with cultural factors on various scales; national to regional culture, a rural or urban environment and the type of family and friends one associates with. Each word carries with it emotions, semantic networks, a sense of duty, shame, and many other aspects that influence our way of thinking, how we perceive the world, and how we judge ourselves. I became acutely aware of this firsthand during my years of living and working in London. The tone of conversations, emotional involvement in activities, and the type of thoughts in response to any concern were different from when I thought or spoke in Italian.

In light of these observations, we began to delve deeper and discovered that there is a wealth of research on these aspects, ranging from studies to facilitate language learning to the examination of different neural connections and patterns of reasoning and emotions in individuals who are bilingual from birth, in adolescence, or in adulthood. As we often do in Integrative Sciences, we initiated a process of reverse engineering, which means trying to understand how to use this knowledge to benefit processes of healing and change, as well as to promote well-being.

The central and common point in all these processes lies in the ability to promote the development of new concepts[1], in order to shape different and more functional ways of perceiving reality and oneself, as well as to create different mental and emotional pathways. Words play a central role in shaping these concepts, which are then often retrieved from below our consciousness and are frequently influenced by a predictive mechanism that involves the entire organism. This mechanism can be both advantageous and detrimental (as seen in switch 3) in shaping reasoning, as well as in evaluation, feelings, sense attribution, motivation, and emotional responses. Consequently, the richer and more diversified our vocabulary is, the more easily the networks in our brain can function optimally to orchestrate a general response to adapt to the environment according to the principle of minimum free energy (switch 2). This allows us to focus only on what is necessary and to do it well, while keeping our energies available for real adaptation needs, to develop new skills or to pursue our passions and interests, rather than keeping them tied up in unnecessary activities (rumination, seeking blame, self-pity, as well as stress or trauma postures, etc.) making them available for real adaptation needs or to develop new skills or dedicate ourselves to our passions and interests instead. For this reason, in many of our exercises (such as Isometric Emotions, Interpersonal Accommodation, Psychosomatic Stretching, Release Techniques, Vagal Reset, Emotional Buffer, and many others mentioned in this or other chapters), people are often *encouraged to define what they are feeling in that moment precisely and with more words, using different vocabulary, drawing from images and metaphors as well.* Furthermore, the work becomes even more elaborate when seeking linguistic differences for specific bodily and sensory areas, making distinctions of even a few millimetres and exploring the boundary between different levels of depth (from the surface of the skin, gradually descending to muscle and bone, as in the *Feeling the boundaries of perception* technique) or even trying to distinguish between what can be felt inside the body and what a hand, touching that area, feels.

Returning to the topic of language specifically, when non-native speakers think in a language they have learned later in life (for example, the typical Italian adult who studied English or French in school), they tend to think with fewer errors or emotional interferences. The reason is that the younger a person is when they learn a language, the more of its emotional halo is acquired (both cultural and specific to the environment in which it is learned, both positive and negative). This mechanism can be harnessed positively: training oneself to rethink specific episodes in a foreign language, evaluating oneself, one's worth, fantasizing about how things will go next time, all in the foreign language. Just try it to immediately perceive the difference. For example, thinking "I'm late" while reading this book with a bit of conviction, even if we're just pretending, activates a series of sensations, mental patterns, emotional and bodily alterations. Thinking "Sono in ritardo" in Italian or "Estoy retrasado" in Spanish, if you are not a native speaker, sounds much more neutral and activates little or none of what was perceived before.

If you don't know a foreign language, if thinking in this way becomes too tiring, a good alternative is to use a vocabulary (in the sense of the set of words we use) that is not your usual one. This is not the classic ploy of removing negative words, e.g. use "situation to be resolved" instead of "problem", because even the first expression can be a well-established concept with emotional implications for the subject and – consequently – the rest of the sentence will always have a correlated analogy. Rather, it's about replacing many of the words, including the verbs. Sometimes it is even enough to introduce distortions of certain words (endearments or dialects that are not typical of our childhood) which allude to other emotional and cultural areas.

Thinking *"I'm running slow"* is different from *"it's a bit late"*, both because I remove the personal reference to myself (the "I'm" in the first person) and because I can choose "slow" which reminds me of the expression of an always cheerful shopkeeper where I usually buy vegetables.

Joshua, whom we have met in several previous Switches, was a very witty and refined man, with a great passion for the so-called B-Movies, which is not uncommon among this type of genuinely brilliant people. As a result he used the strategy of thinking with the language and intonation of a character from these movies that seemed most suitable to defuse the situation in which he found himself. He thus achieved the double result of changing his flow of thought, abandoning ruminations and destructive thoughts, but also of changing perceptive patterns with respect to the outside world and towards himself (thus also acting at the level of the networks seen in area 3).

We have talked a lot about language in the strict sense however there are many other ways to develop new concepts and obtain the same mental benefits. The first case is within everyone's reach, it's enough to *read books or watch documentaries* on unusual topics written or narrated in different styles. Another mode is obtained by *developing skills with different structure* from those we usually use, such as learning to program the computer, even in the playful way to develop a video game, or learning to play a musical instrument and its theory. Furthermore, *any form of free and curious experimentation* can be useful, such as trying unusual foods (both in eating and cooking them), doing different activities in your free time, whether it is board games, changing the type of TV series you watch, or the type of travel you do in your free time. As you may have noticed, this approach makes sense with respect to the topic we are talking about in this section on stream of thought, but it is also absolutely in line with what we have seen right from the first switch area regarding neural plasticity and epigenetics, as well as being consistent with many other aspects seen in the previous chapters.

Considering what we have seen, it is critical to expand our repertoire of thought-modes to regain control and produce value-add in the management of complex situations and as ample as possible timeframes and standpoints. This repertoire can be extended to cover modes and schemas that are suited to the objectives, context, audience, dominant culture, social mores etc. To achieve this, some of the schemas and suggestions provided in the *Emotion Modulation* technique can be used (these are covered in the fourth group of switches in relation to the example of aggression, but are applicable to any other context of emotive-cognitive regulation).

There are also more targeted techniques that focus specifically on thought flows such as the *Mind O'Clock technique*, or ones that focus more on the integration of thought flows and movement, such as the *Turn your Mind technique*.

MIND O'CLOCK & TURN YOUR MIND TECHNIQUES

If you drive a sports car at top speed over a bumpy road you are not using it to its full potential. The same goes for thought, although we often have the dysfunctional tendency to think that 'rapid thought' is 'efficient thought'. As soon as we are faced with a problem we try to think as rapidly as possible, but this often doesn't work, rather we generate more anxiety. It's not the number of words thought, but their quality and the structure of thought that makes a difference!

1. The **Mind O'Clock** technique includes a series of exercises that help thought practice a more useful rhythm in a specific situation, whether you need to remain concentrated, face a stressful event or danger. It can be carried out in interaction with an external sound stimulus such as a metronome, or through two-way interaction with other adaptation rhythms such as that of breathing, heartbeats or pacing.

You can start with any thought and repeat it at different speeds, carefully separating words or changing their natural flow, which is often just the result of old automatisms.

Words can be broken down, for example by thinking of a syllable for each stroke of the metronome, giving the mind a breather and us the possibility of perceiving the real meaning of that word. It is also possible to mark the pause between one word and another, thinking "pause" or creating a void in that beat. This stage is very relevant: it offers relief to our mind and helps us catch our breath, even if we are just thinking.

You can even try thinking anxiety generating thoughts at a slow rate and pleasant thoughts rapidly, thus highlighting how often it is just the way of thinking that poses a problem, regardless of the content.

2. The **Turn your Mind** technique also works on thought flows, but mainly focuses on the ability to rapidly change themes within your control. It's a veritable 'switch' technique as it works on simultaneous changes of mode.

The basic version involves the change of thought themes at regular intervals, such as every 30 to 60 seconds. Our suggestion, based on research and experience, is to alternate positive and negative pairs of thoughts on the same theme and then decline them across various levels.

A typical basic sequence is to think about these themes in rotation, for 20 or 30-second cycles:

• Negative things about me;
• Positive things about me;
• Negative things about others (friend, partner, colleague etc.);
• Positive things about others;
• Negative things about a group (of friends, of co-workers, of the family etc.);
• Positive things about the group and so on.

Significant changes to other flows combine with these "mind swerves". You can, for example, change the direction you are walking in, the way you walk, the music you are listening to and so on.

There is a lot of potential in working on these alternations: changing themes and durations, mixing the order of sentences, slotting in other changes.

The mind thus practices focusing willingly and single-mindedly on the desired theme.

On the other hand, this is also a way of teaching the mind important abilities through experience such as:

- Serenely leaving an issue unresolved;
- Awaiting the right moment to tackle it with confidence;
- Analysing the issue from different angles;
- Distancing ourselves from our flow of thought;
- Differentiating between exploratory thought, evaluation and decisions.

Mark found the Turn your Mind technique very useful. He made it coincide with many of his walks, which we introduced to get all the metabolic and anti-inflammatory benefits of switches 1 and 2, but also to avoid unnecessary conflict with his wife. At this point we introduced the Turn your Mind technique with the aim of regaining value. Initially, after some trial and error, he found it effective to have more time to think about his qualities and those of the social group in which his wife was not included, while decreasing the time spent dwelling on negative aspects, which were so well known to him (and indeed, he had to learn to contain).

METHOD – IDEOGRAPHIC THINKING

We have already encountered some variants of Ideographic Thinking, for example in the introductory chapter with the graphics cards we used to analyse a person in their entirety and with the Modular Thinking technique in switch area number 3. Now let's look into this tool in its broadest perspective to support all forms of thinking and learning.

Ideographic Thinking stems from the desire to develop a way of thinking that is more in line with the natural tendencies of our mind and which is able to exploit all the neurobiological elements of our brain. It consists of a very broad and transversal method comprised of a large number of techniques to make thinking more flexible and less subject to cultural constraints and automatisms.

Especially in Western culture, our way of thinking is strongly influenced by the academic approach to reading and solving initial mathematical problems, both of which are fundamentally characterized by a serial process; once one thing is done, one moves on to the next, then the next and so on.

Our mind, on the contrary, is predisposed to a broad and fluid thought that is capable of overseeing recovery, security and development functions very well but then - in its process of greater structuring - at times risks leading to the opposite extreme by causing obstruction or creating very limiting constraints and associations.

With Ideographic Thinking we develop a way of representing one's thoughts in a dynamic way (both in the sense that it is fast and interactive, and in the sense that it favours change over time) and to communicate it easily and by starting constructive dialogue with others.

Ideographic thinking is closer to the natural way of thinking. It is pleasant to realize and has a strong impact since it involves all the senses and brain areas in realizing it. This also happens when we look at the result of our work to rework it or as a simple reminder.

Our perceptual system is naturally attracted to colours and shapes, not to a sequence of black characters like written text. The graphics are attractive, motivating and pleasant. You want to look at them and it's easier to find the information that interests us- as well as process quickly. It is no coincidence that the personal computer has become widely spread with the advent of interfaces with graphic icons. Graphics go directly to the emotions. This also happens in science. There is, in fact, plenty of research which confirms that a website or an article is perceived as "more reliable" if the characters are more legible, the spaces balanced, the colours well matched and there is some chart to underline important concepts, even though the content is identical.

You don't need to be an artist. Just use a few tricks: pens of different colours, felt-tip pens with a square tip or a brush (more or less long and soft), etc. The way we write or draw a line remains the same, but the graphic impact is incredibly increased.

Es. 1 - Just by holding a pen or marker with different tips, the exact same hand gesture can lead to very different graphic results.

Even just paying more attention to the size of the fonts can make a difference. Think of the headlines of a newspaper, the subtitle and the body of the text. Why not use such large elements in our notes too? If we look at the modern websites or the newsletters we receive every day, it is also possible to find interesting ideas on fonts and colours to use even when we write by hand. In fact, writing a title in a strange font is not as difficult as it seems; it can actually be fun.

Someone might think that - while taking notes or having a group meeting - changing pen, choosing colour or trying a new font could be a waste of time. In reality it is quite the opposite: we usually spend more than two or three minutes trying to stay focused, re-reading all the written discursive text because we don't remember something well or inventing ways to keep the attention of the audience alive. In reality, using a slightly more graphical approach saves time right away. Furthermore, even more is saved when one goes back to the notes which will be clearer and more concise and which will have (at least in part) already been fixed in memory thanks to the visual component and the physical motor gesture.

Ideographic Thinking allows rapid, effective communication on many levels and can carry many meanings (hence the reference to the ideogram that inspired its name). Indeed, the symbol is immediate; it conveys numerous concepts and nuances simultaneously that would require many adjectives and explanations. Simple graphic elements such as an arrow or a stylized gear are within everyone's reach, but they make the message far more effective and evocative.

Es. 2 - In this example, Ideographic Thinking (right) is easier and faster than traditional notes (left). Furthermore, the glance at the agenda will be faster and more pleasant.

Es. 3 - Also in this example, Ideographic Thinking proves to be faster than traditional notes and allows for a greater level of privacy (for an outside observer it is not obvious that the building is the bank).

Es. 4 - This example shows us how it is possible to represent a delicate topic in such a way that it cannot be interpreted by anyone other than ourselves.

Ideographic Thinking concretely but also mentally amplifies the space of action and thought with the use of wider supports, offering a potential space without a priori limitations.

Due to its nature it allows you to manage complex thoughts more easily. It breaks down highly articulated systems into modules, which are often not just representations, but the identification of the key elements that structure a specific reality. On this aspect you can refer to the technique Modular Thinking presented in switch 2, which is a sub-mode of Ideographic Thinking.

Ideographic thinking can be declined in various ways to:
• take more effective notes, both in the moment of realization and in the moment in which they are subsequently resumed;
• study the various components and elements of problematic events and situations (through specific methods for various areas of application);
• analyse interpersonal relationships and relationship dynamics;
• map the dynamics of power and influence between people, groups, institutions;
• manage projects (from personal to more complex corporate ones);
• brainstorm and search for innovative solutions;
• conduct meetings (to share, analyse, solve, decide);
• evaluate motivational schemes;
• represent and share a complex case or problem;
• study and develop alternative modes of action;
• analyse and develop processes;

- and for storytelling (with educational objectives, analysis, development, modification, etc.).

In all these cases, Ideographic Thinking innately supports and facilitates the transformative potential to modify or change the central nodes (modules) or part of them (replacing them, changing their path, deleting them without substitutions, increasing the alternatives, etc.).

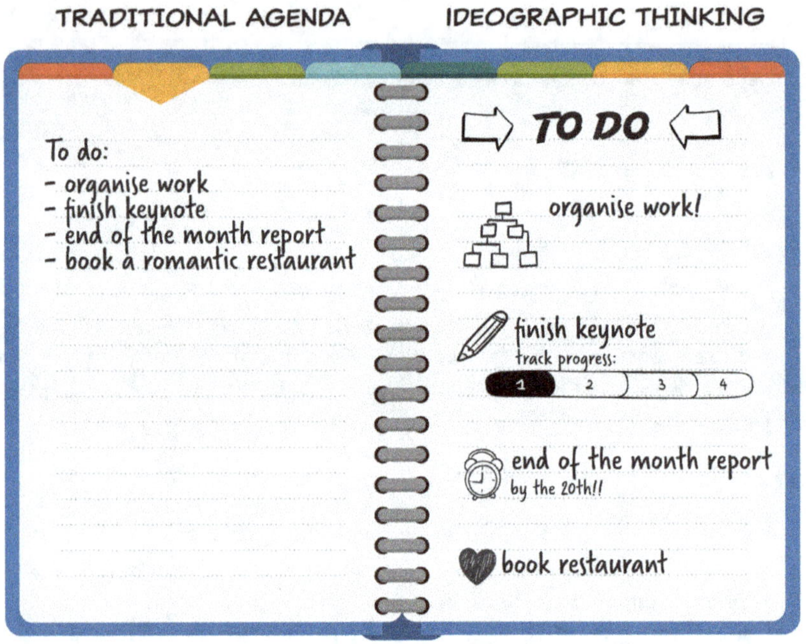

Es. 5 - Traditional agenda and Ideographic Thinking compared: improved first-glance, favours mental organization, is more motivating to update and control, emotionally enhances the positive aspects and constructively depicts more tiring ones.

Given the visual nature of this tool, for further information, please consult www.insciences.co/ideothinking.

ACHIEVING SELF-ASSESSMENT AND IMPROVEMENT

When the ideation flow is directed towards oneself, your own ways of thinking and behaviours, we talk about *metacognitive ability*, or being able to accurately judge our own performance (in the broad sense of 'how it is performed' any communicative, relational, decision-making act, etc.). There are specific networks and systems that, if functioning appropriately, can have a significant impact on metacognition abilities and access to different levels of awareness with impact and interactions on self-confidence and feelings of mastery, elements that are critical to the feeling that something is natural and to any action that balances spontaneity and control.

Various studies have shown the areas that support metacognitive management in the frontal and parietal lobes[2] and have identified the features that make it a capability that can be exercised in a structured way.

It is therefore possible to develop an initial and basic ability to change; the ability to self-observe and appropriately identify the aspects that need to improve to make a switch from poor metacognition (that is not self-responsible) to a flexible and evolutionary mode.

One of the most effective ways relates to the *use of direct, immediate feedback in real-life circumstances*[3]. This is a method that is easily achievable today and highly appreciated by end users. In fact, we have noted in daily life – through workshops, research and clinical practice – that, thanks to modern technological support, the therapist or trainer can assist the patient/client remotely and provide feedback or timely suggestions to try alternative strategies. Behavioural training, the development of new skills, educational processes and therapeutical dynamics therefore can bolster each other in synergy with skills that are context-specific (negotiation, artistic performance, effective communication etc.).

Elizabeth had difficulty being aware of her behaviour with her daughter. Indeed, she thought she was a model mother, but her parents pointed out a number of shortcomings. To get a more objective idea of the situation and not have to side with her or her parents, I suggested that she use the Objective Eye of the camera method (see box below), so I asked her to video herself in some moments of interaction with the child, for example during dinner, in the morning before going to kindergarten and while playing a game together. Watching the videos together, it was possible to point out to her some recurring dynamics of which she was unaware (for example that in the morning she scolded her daughter to hurry up, but in reality the child was ready and she was the late one; or the fact that in a ten minutes game she picked up her cell phone more than 20 times to reply to messages). In light of this new-found awareness we tried a field session; while she was at the playground with her daughter, I watched from a distance. When I noticed some dysfunctional behaviour – for example if she lost herself in thought for a long time despite her daughter's calls, or if she continued to scold her because she was getting dirty (the mistake was the clothing chosen by the mother, not the child's behaviour) – I sent a short message to invite her to find a new, more functional way. Given her problem with the tendency to look at her cell phone often, for the occasion we used the classic text messages, while she kept the application with which she usually interacted with friends and relatives deactivated. This way Elizabeth was able to directly notice some of the behaviour of which she had little awareness and, at the same time, she was able to experience firsthand how easy it was to regain control and enjoy positive feedback from her child.

METHOD - THE CAMERA'S OBJECTIVE EYE

People are not always aware of their way of being and how they are perceived by others. In fact, many anxious people think they are just quiet and many aggressive people think they are authoritative or confident. Surely in your professional career, as well as in life, you will have met many such people.

There is a very interesting way to develop this awareness; seeing oneself from the outside, i.e. in a more objective way, which today is feasible with more than just a simple exercise of mental abstraction. In fact, with the help of a video camera or a cell phone you can really see yourself from another point of view. Also, you can review this at a later time, when you are no longer intensely involved in the situation and relationship dynamics. In this way, time and space (mental and emotional) are created to better observe the coherence of one's own behaviour (verbal and non-verbal) with the situation and the reactions that are generated in others.

From a practical point of view, it is a question of positioning a camera in contexts potentially at risk of non-functional reactions. You can use the small ones, the so-called action-cams, which easily go unnoticed. Many modern cameras have a function that allows you to start recording automatically in certain situations such when there is a loud sound, a human voice or a change in brightness so you don't have to keep them active all the time. In some cases it is also possible to ask reliable relatives and friends to record at that specific moment with their mobile phone. The moments you choose can be the ones where a dysfunctional reaction is most likely to take place, for example when you come home stressed from work, when and where tension usually arises with your partner or children, etc.

KNOWING HOW TO CHANGE YOUR MIND

Dealing with a person that will not change their point of view or, conversely, keeps changing their mind illogically, is a difficult experience to manage both professionally and in our personal life. In this instance an integrated approach that uses different disciplines enables us to take new study perspectives on these phenomena and on their practical implications. Neurobiological and statistical studies on the way that human beliefs change show how people that change their mind easily and continuously or that, by contrast, remain fixed in their beliefs in spite of counter evidence, have specific neural activation schemes[4].

To give some practical examples, we are talking about those who: cannot focus on all the exams that went well because they keep concentrating on the idea that the next one could go badly; those who put all their energy in finding clues about potential risks and unexpected events while taking facts and objective realities for granted; those who do not include new information in their reasoning in spite of understanding and evaluating it as positively worthy of attention. These two opposite extremes (*extreme rigidness* and *ease in changing beliefs*) typically feature either high or low stability schemas in relation to neural activation paths. Excessive rigidness and excessive instability are, in turn, connected to the massive presence of neuro-exciters such as aspartate or glutamate (that leads us back to group 1 switches) or chronic states of inflammation (switch group 2).

Angelica's thought process presented all these problems. In fact, she always had a very fast flow of ideas in her head, which she chased after with difficulty, speaking at a high speed. This didn't solve her problem, on the contrary it made it worse by creating anxiety and difficulty in speaking.

This way of being of hers was perceived, among other things, as anxiety-provoking by her counterparts, negatively affecting her relationships. Also, Angelica was very firm in her beliefs and had a hard time accepting new information or points of view. To support her in this process, we combined her diet (moving it towards an anti-inflammatory direction for the reasons seen above) with a reduction of all foods that could contain glutamate, in order to avoid external inputs. To help 'tame' and channel her mind she practiced the *Mind o' Clock* and *Turn your Mind* techniques.

In these processes the strength of predictions (expectations, prejudice, forecasts etc.) also plays a significant role on the objective incoming data that we need to evaluate to adapt and choose the most suitable behaviour. This is a multifaceted issue that intervenes on many levels.

As we mentioned in switch area 3 though under a different perspective, the *first level* concerns *predictions* as anticipations that are automatically and not consciously activated. From a structural point of view, it is important to remember that organs that send messages to the insula (and the insula itself that has the role of 'integration centre' for a variety of incoming information), are agranular structures. These types of cortices, as they are simple and have fewer interactions towards the outside and less modulation ability than granular ones, ensure that – unless you are aware of physical sensations and sensory input – predictions based on experience and physical maps previously stored prevail more easily. Visceromotor agranular cortices are, on the other hand, central hubs in the communication of central networks putting the interoceptive processes and prediction elements at the heart of any perceptive, cognitive and emotional phenomenon. Any problem in these processes (such as inflammation, neurodegenerative processes, hypo- or hyper-activation) can be at the core of, or be the cause of an amplification of different dysfunctional pathologies[5].

In addition to this, the predictions we make have a central role in the activation of the PAG and its role in the release of endocannabinoids, the most powerful natural painkiller innately available. *Habits* and nurture or *self-care rituals* can play a key role in actively managing automatic predictions to our own advantage rather than passively experiencing them[6]. Considering all these observations, it becomes fundamental to use *movement, self-perception* and *interoceptive sensory* processes in *synergy* to make thought flows more fluid and functional. These objectives can be reached by subverting the prediction process with Reboot techniques (see switch area 3).

In addition to this, it is possible to intervene on this level while working on the perception of our own emotional-physical resources and on self-regulation capabilities at the same time (through *Emotion Modulation* and *Resource Balance,* also in switch area 3), as well as on Detachment skills (see the section on attachment in the fourth group switches).

Up to now we have analysed some of the features of *non-conscious predictions*. From another perspective it is equally important to look at *conscious predictions* in the most logical sense of the term as they represent a second distinct level of *forecasting* (see switch area 3 for more insight).

These are processes that are subject to significant risk of deformation or errors. In this instance it is therefore important to keep track of elements of *uncertainty* (see group 3 switches) that tend to easily impose themselves during the evaluation phase.

In addition to this, when we talk about *conscious predictions* it is particularly useful to identify what the prediction is focused on: prediction about the impact that a specific behaviour or choice will have *on external elements* needs to be kept distinct from the emotional and *intrapsychic consequences*, because they have independent neural pathways and are involved in completely different evaluations and emotional experiences.

At the same time, it is important to increase attention on the present in order to disengage defensive automatisms, implicit schemas and over-evaluation of past learnings. As we will see later on, it is far more effective to intervene with *Reboot Techniques* at sensory and neurobiological level than on attention and cognitive awareness features to achieve these steps. This last level must be addressed anyway, but synergy is essential: for example, working first with more bodily and neurobiologically active techniques, and then with more mental techniques like *Possible Scenarios.*

WHEN WE TELL STORIES ABOUT OURSELVES AND TELL OURSELVES STORIES

Another very interesting creative flow relates to narratives, or in other words, the stories with which we narrate our lives, adventures and misadventures. The way that we tell these stories or tell ourselves these stories, to justify a mistake or a moment of weakness, is a way of rewriting the past or an attempt to define the future.

These processes can be motivated by the need to bring reality closer to ideal standards or to the image we have of ourselves and of our objectives. They can also be driven by other forms of mediation between opposing poles in our internal world or with other people with whom we have some kind of interaction or connection.

These can be *'reconstructions' of reality with positive features*, because they rework and make things acceptable, or shift focus on positive aspects favouring motivation and wellbeing but without bringing disadvantages or loss of touch with reality. They can, on the other hand, be *negative* if they become a way of 'lying to ourselves' and turn into strong self-deceit systems. In these instances, they support or lead to incorrect decisions even in critical issues such as the decision to attribute interpersonal trust to someone or to make significative financial or emotional investments.

An element that they are very responsive to is uncertainty[7] (a key element, in a different way, also to switch groups 3 and 4). Reducing uncertainty and ambiguity helps to develop more linear narratives that are more adherent to reality. To do this and to obtain a relevant result, there are two aspects with their various implications that can be addressed distinctly with specific strategies and these are: *outcome uncertainty* (what will change in reality) and *impact uncertainty* (fallout on people involved).

Another interesting way to act on these aspects is to break the automatisms of these flows. Let's look at two interesting ways below.

The first involves *complaining in a foreign language* that we don't know well. Poor command of the language and limited vocabulary will make the task less easy and we will not be able to use the usual mental automatisms. In this way we realize more easily that, when we think in our own language, we do it automatically and without there being a real purpose of venting or an attempt at a solution. Furthermore, having a limited linguistic register, it is clear that the basic problem is only one and that describing it in many different ways is of no help.

A different way of highlighting this issue is to *count the types of thoughts* (and possibly related behaviours) *dividing them into categories* such as: complaints, accusation, finding a culprit, proving it's not my fault, claiming past injustice etc. It thus becomes immediately clear that the issues in question are always the same, linked more to our frustration than to the single problematic event on which it focuses and too much energy is wasted. This process can be implemented mentally or with the support of Ideographic Thinking which helps to clarify things visually, thanks to minimalist representation (a symbol, an icon, or at most a word placed on a post-it).

A final extremely relevant element relates to the *direction of the narrative.* There are interesting studies[8] that highlight how the same story – when told back to front, from end to beginning – enables a more vivid and accurate reconstruction of details. There is an improvement in the quantity as well as the quality of information thus recovered. The impact is so relevant that this process has become routine in courtrooms and in law enforcement interrogatories. We will exploit this process later in the *Inverse Physiological Replay* technique.

FOCUSING OTHER PEOPLE'S EMOTIONS

Learning to understand where one's emotions end and those of others begin is essential to restoring the right physiology to emotional responses. We must learn to read the emotions of others on them, not on us and vice versa. It is a phenomenon that can be seen very clearly in the dynamics of the couple. Sometimes they are so obvious that even comedians play on these misinterpretations. Take a couple arguing then he or she gets up and goes to another room. The other person will invariably say something like "and you leave me here like this?" or "you leave so you don't have to admit that I'm right!". There are two possible hypotheses, but only two hypotheses. The first hypothesis to be made focuses on the protagonist of the action, not on the person who suffers it: he/she no longer tolerates the discussion and moves away, or has decided to cool down to feel better and speak constructively in a few minutes.

We are led to interpret other people's emotions in a distorted way and often in reference to ourselves because we read them on the basis of our fears and this creates a process of endless distortions.

Objective analysis can be very useful. To facilitate it you can use some expedients such as:

• asking the person to initially forcibly exclude themselves as a possible cause or factor at play;

• write different hypotheses in random order on a sheet, paying no attention to cause-effect connections or sequential logics;

• force them to search for other, even improbable, hypotheses;

• reason absurdly as if they were never to see that person again or, conversely, with the certainty that they will see them again and everything will be fine.

FROM TRAUMA TO FLOW OBSTRUCTION AND RELEASE

When trauma occurs, two phenomena that it is important to know and manage in the subsequent phases also take place.

The *first* phenomenon concerns the different memories in which we record the information of our experience: narrative memory (the story that takes place), visual memory (what we perceive with our eyes, to be kept separate from what we imagine visually), the thoughts we are thinking (to clearly distinguish from a posteriori evaluations which then often overlap), the emotions experienced (to be focused well with respect to those reworked, desired, etc. in this case too), the position of our body in space, and other levels as well. These logs contain related information. When a traumatic event occurs, some of this information is not written down adequately and often lacks correct connections with other memories. For this reason it is so difficult to recover parts of the memory of a traumatic event (e.g. you remember the image but not the emotion, or you feel a strong emotion but do not remember the sequence of events well). For clarity, we specify that the phenomenon we are describing concerns the registration at a neurological level, which occurs before (in temporal and hierarchical terms) any phenomena at a psychological level, such as removal, dissociation or modification of the memory for self-healing purposes.

When we talk about memories it is important to know that there are more kinds of memories in addition to those exclusively recorded as conscious memories and mediated by thought. Even muscles, tendons, viscera and other organs have their own autonomous memory. For this reason, a global involvement of the body is always necessary in order to work effectively on the traumatic memory.

Another important *phenomenon* to be aware of is that when a trauma occurs, our breathing almost always stops for a few moments. Think for a moment about when you hit your knee against a corner or burn yourself with the stove; the first thing you do is retract the limb while you inhale sharply (it lasts less than a second and is usually done with the mouth). This is then followed by a moment of apnoea. This sequence has an immediate analgesic value, but if it lasts too long it leads to altering the memorization processes seen in the previous point. Furthermore, this reaction leads to locking the muscles, in particular the diaphragm and the paravertebral muscles, but also those involved in the specific trauma in a non-physiological stance. Working on all these muscles, on posture, breathing and – in general – on the recovery of the physiology of all the mechanisms described above, will be essential to restore the overall balance of the mind-body unity.

INVERSE PHYSIOLOGICAL REPLAY + OBSTRUCTION RELEASE TECHNIQUES

We have developed several release techniques over the years. These are tools that we have developed and verified over time to bring about real change at a neurobiological level. Indirectly, they can also have a cathartic or suggestive effect, but this is only a secondary aspect with added value compared to our primary objectives. We have seen some of these techniques in the previous chapters, below we see two more.

The **first** is called **Inverse Physiological Replay** and, as the name suggests, it is based on redoing the movements that occurred during the traumatic event but in opposite temporal order and in physiological conditions. For it to work well, some conditions must be met:

• The recall of the movements takes place in the opposite sequence, respecting the criterion (seen in the previous paragraphs) whereby the existing associative links are not strengthened, but new ones are activated (which will be positive given the state of physiology and the other precautions put into practice);

• The place of realization should be the same as where the trauma occurred or, if it is not possible, it must be well imagined in all its details, recalling or reconstructing visual aspects, sounds, any specific smells or scents (wet asphalt, petrol, a nearby pastry shop, etc.) and other sensory re-enactments;
• You must recreate the same posture, movements, and the same gestures that took shape, starting from the end and going back up to a little before the event began (for example if it is a fall, you go back up to 5 minutes before starting to lose balance);
• In the various repetitions some modifications can be made: the gaze, even if this is not what happened in reality, must lock onto the place where the trauma occurred, towards other significant people and must look for contextual elements of reference that give orientation and security;
• While repeating the traumatic gesture, breathing must be as when locked (it is often the inhalation phase, but it is not always the case). If in doubt, do it both ways. In any case it must be increasingly physiological and be accompanied by bodily and emotional states consistent with a controlled and flexible management of the situation that is being relived;
• The sequence of events should be repeated slowly 7-8 times;
• If the event is very long and articulated in several phases, it may be useful to divide it into single pieces (for example working separately on the loss of control of the bike, on the fall, on waking up in hospital).

Possible reactions at the end of the technique, which demonstrate its effects, are: a sensation of lightness, of an empty mind and, sometimes, a sense of tingling or itching in the nape of the neck or in the upper part of the head. These reactions may or may not emerge and should not necessarily be understood as a criterion of efficacy. It is useful to know that they can happen to help those who try them make sense of their experiences.

The **second** technique is **Obstruction-Release** (which is part of the Psychosomatic Release Techniques seen in switch 2 area) and is based on the opposite principle to the previous one. In fact, it does not force physiology, but takes non-physiology to the extreme to give the body a strong signal which makes it clear that the current mode of functioning is not adequate. To make a fairly well-known simile, we can say that it is a mechanism similar to that of muscle relaxation techniques which contract the muscle to the extreme and then bring it back to relax. Once you understand the mechanism it can be implemented in many ways. The basic way that we have tested in different contexts and seen that always brings interesting results is the following: the person is lying on their back thinking about the traumatic event or the source of stress (even quickly and detachedly, for many it is enough to think of the word "trauma") meanwhile they inhale to their maximum capacity and hold their breath. At this point they wrap their arms in a sort of self-hug that is as strong as possible. When they just can't hold their breath anymore, they let go, abandoning their arms and relaxing every muscle, exhaling deeply and concentrating on the sense of pleasure and release.

POINTS OF CONTACT BETWEEN CREATIVE, POSTURAL AND MOTOR FLOWS

The processes described above are aligned and coherent with another two levels of flows: *motor* and *postural* flows. In fact, we have been built and designed to move forwards and have no innate structures or schemas to help us walk backwards. It is not perchance that traditional rehabilitation techniques after an accident or for anyone with motor disorders such as Parkinson's disease, include practice walking backwards. This enables the development of new motor schemas without calling on old habits, associations or dysfunctional learning.

At the same time, it is possible to use this asymmetry to our advantage via the synergy between creative and motor flows. Making new and unnatural movements supports new, free neural activation, in turn favouring creative and flexible mental processes such as those used in the *Reboot* and in the *Resource Balance* techniques (switch 3) as well as through the simple, but always effective *Schema Inversions* technique.

For example, Jack (whom we saw in the introductory chapter) felt obstructed in various aspects of his life, from control over his body through training to poor flexibility in his movements, especially in contexts that were socially stressful for him. Even emotions and thoughts flowed slowly compared to what he felt was his real potential. For this reason, we often worked by unlocking the body, thoughts and emotions in a synergistic way. The *Reboot* and *Schema Inversion* techniques have been particularly useful to him, in particular by applying them before facing challenging situations, in order to give a strong neurobiological signal to his system and return to being in physiology and focused on the present. Furthermore, we worked on the position of the shoulders and the related emotional experiences and his identity with both *Isometric Emotions* and *Interpersonal Accommodation* techniques (both feature later on in this chapter).

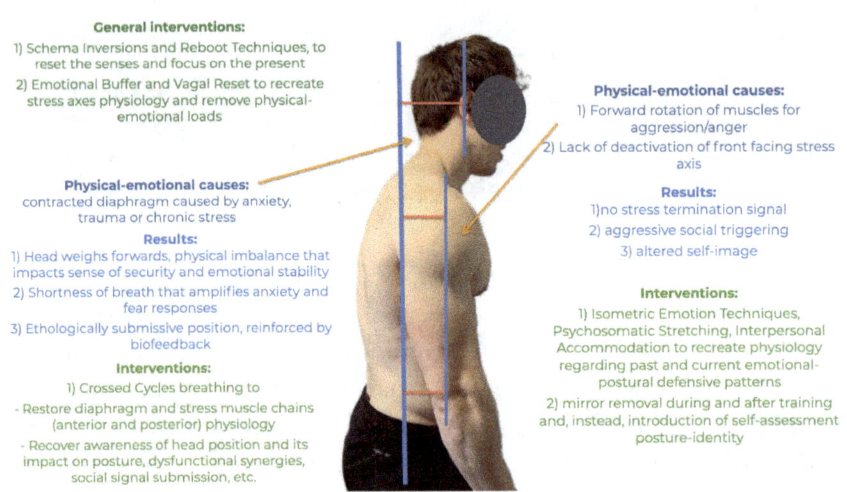

Fig. - Some of the evaluations and related interventions for Jack (find more information and images on this case in the introductory chapter).

SCHEMA INVERSION TECHNIQUE

As we have seen in several previous sections of the text, the mind and nervous system activate the body to adapt to the environment and vice versa. An interesting observation – which early medicine and disciplines such as yoga made centuries ago and which are now reconfirmed by neuroscience – is that a relaxed or tense state of the body, in turn, influences the mind and emotions. Research has well demonstrated that a person who is injected with adrenaline tends to experience anxious states and have more negative thoughts than usual when evaluating the unfavourable or ambiguous circumstances in which they find themselves. On the other hand, a person who (with the help of a drug or through specific techniques) relaxes their muscles will be more serene and benevolent. These effects occur in the short term and, if repeated over time, permanently change our response methods.

These postural tone changes not only bring well-being and positive changes in the perceptions of oneself and of the surrounding environment, they also affect the representations that others make of us. Thus, feedback from other people and social feedback can also encourage change.

The *Schema Inversion* technique was created to optimize this reverse communication process and acts on two levels (specific and general). Through comparative analysis between the neurobiological processes of human and other mammalian stress responses and emotions, which was followed by a phase of clinical research, we have identified a series of postural modifications that are particularly effective in sending a bio-signal reverse feedback from the emotion that generated them. Below are some specific factors for each emotion and others more transversal and common to different activation processes.

Specific elements

In relation to the *emotional reactions* of *fear, anxiety, stress, anguish*, it is particularly effective to focus on:
• raised shoulders - lower;
• limb retraction - stretch;
• feet and legs converging - rotate outwards;
• high lordosis augmentation - stretch the back of the neck and rotate the head back to vertical position;
• low lordosis increases - rotation of the pelvis taking care to keep the rectus abdominis soft.

In relation to the *emotions* of *anger, aggression, rage:*
• limb rotation - open and expose open shoulders and hands;
• rotation of the central axis – taking a forward facing stance and exposing the neck;
• bite closure - relax the masseter muscles;
• hypertonicity of the leg muscles - do not lean forward and stretch. Especially important for the hamstring, calf and ilio-psoas muscles;
• increase in upper lordosis - relax the front muscles of the neck and move the head so that it is once again 'resting' on the shoulders;
• increase in lower lordosis - rotation of the pelvis starting from flexing of the legs.

General elements

There are some postures that are strongly linked to a state of good psychophysical activation and to our sense of security. These are attitudes that the so-called alpha specimens, the leaders of the pack, assume in herds of animals. Security in their own resources, the fact of not being afraid of possible attacks (out of awareness, not out of superficiality) and having clear goals and priorities of their own and of the pack, lead them to assume these postures. Neuro-anthropological research and comparative neurobiology studies have also demonstrated the universal validity of these schemes.

Let's see what postural elements man shares with other mammals in this area. The first concerns the tendency to show the jugular, viscera and genitals which represent the first point of attack by a predator, without issues. Making slow movements and holding your gaze even in tense situations are signs of good emotional stability and a high awareness of one's own resources. Even speaking slowly and in a low tone has the same meaning for humans (just as alphas rarely bark and tend to emit sounds that are lower than the other members). Raising your arms, spreading your legs, taking up space, are all gestures that indicate that you are not afraid of a possible dispute with other suitors and that you tend to satisfy your needs without inhibitions (this does not make you appear aggressive or arrogant, but conveys a sense of freedom of action and not of inhibition).

If we ask shy people, often anxious about the judgment of others and their own worth, to assume the postures typical of confident people, something changes both emotionally and neurobiologically. In our research centre we tried to carry out an experiment and we realized that it is essential to respect some key factors to obtain these results. The first concerns the type of postures. These are not those classically indicated as "open" or "closed" by basic non-verbal communication. As we have mentioned, it is rather a question of those which recall the leaders of the pack in the various species of mammals, what we call Non-Verbal Communication from the Pack: exposure of the solar plexus and of the genitals (even when we are dressed, it is the posture that counts, not the actual performance), legs crossed in a manner usually considered impolite, holding gaze longer than normal, leaning on support points for comfort, displaying socially unacceptable factors such as sweat stains or torn clothes without embarrassment (if it happens, not for provocation), walking with large body movements and rather slowly, maintaining good muscle tone but never excessively contracting, even during stressful situations.

Another factor that makes the transition from posture to personal safety effective concerns timing: most people obtain this benefit between 3 and 5 weeks of experimentation in which they assume these postures at least six times a day (even just for two or three minutes).

A final aspect concerns the naturalness of these postures. Since we will be offering this to people who are not used to taking these positions, when they do they might feel awkward and forced. A good way to avoid this is by imitating known models (from people they know to movie characters); initially they will try to assume their attitudes, and then gradually they will find their own way of doing something similar spontaneously.

Technique upgrade - Objective observations

It is a variant of the previous technique or a possible enhancement thereof. The idea is to use photos and videos in everyday contexts to monitor yourself in unfavourable conditions and compare what you can do in moments of calm.

Empirical observations can also be made. For example, as we found in one of our research trials, one can measure the distance of one's head from the headrest in a car. The measurement can be done at different times and must be measured in the number of fingers that we can place between the neck and the headrest. It is a very immediate figure, which allows for clear and motivating feedback, for example when you go from four fingers away under stress to one or two fingers away after relaxing or applying a technique. Other ways to encourage pattern reversals can be implemented thanks to correct posture criteria. For example, when we're standing, viewed in profile, our ear should be on the same vertical line where the centre of our shoulder and pelvis are. Or, more simply, you can analyse your own photos - perhaps using those taken by others and shared on social networks - to see how the position of the shoulders, the head, the exposure of the solar plexus or other factors that can vary depending on the context and situations.

MOVEMENT AND POSTURAL FLOWS

Movement and posture are strictly connected in a two-way relationship with our adaptation processes, emotional processes and various thought paths (self-referred, in relation to others, in trying to solve a problem, etc.)[9]. There are affective and emotional movements that have been catalogued in many different ways by different schools of thought. To make an evaluation free from theoretical constructs and subjective interpretation, the common trait on which we can focus is the reading of the muscle chains involved, of the stress axes and of emotional responses. Before categorizing a movement or posture as "sad", "angry", "melancholy", etc. it can be useful to observe its constituent components, such as the shape and direction of movement, the effort exerted, muscle tension, the general subjective value (e.g. is it pleasant or unpleasant for the person?). Below we analyse some of the most interesting mechanisms to understand the functioning of these flows and on which to act concretely.

THE STRUCTURE OF MOVEMENT, STRESS AND EMOTIONS

To move and adapt to the environment you don't just need muscles, so before proceeding we need to broaden our perspective a bit. Fascia is the connective tissue found throughout the body: it surrounds all muscles, bones, ligaments, tendons and organs. The fascia provides the support that transfers the elastic pull of the muscles and holds different parts and organs of the body in place. It also creates distinct layers of fabric with surfaces that can slide over each other, thus allowing different parts to move.

Fascia is made up of tight bundles of collagen fibres that are extremely resistant to stretching. When a person is young and healthy, the fibres, bundles and layers are well aligned and distinct. As a person ages and overall body tone deteriorates, these fibres can fray, get stuck together, and shorten significantly. Thus the very thing that once supported the movement becomes – on the contrary – a limitation and cause of problems. When we observe a person with locked or stiffened movements we have to ask ourselves whether it is a momentary condition, such as a strong interference of intense emotions at that moment or a blockage of the security system, or if it is a chronic condition. In this second case, in modern life the causes can be different and widespread: conditions of prolonged stress; long periods of mood alteration; too little physical activity; irregular sleep-wake rhythms; intense use of alcohol and/or drugs, even far below what is normally considered pathological; and so on.

When the fascia is out of physiology, the movements become limited and less spontaneous, negatively influencing the sense of self-efficacy and mastery, not only in the movements, but with respect to life in general and also modifying one's self-image. Furthermore, the interoceptive mechanisms are altered, negatively influencing the various networks analysed in the switch 3 area. Similarly, all pain, from an accidental sprain to pain in the sciatic nerve, increases and lasts longer than usual over time. Thus a vicious circle is created and sustained at an inflammatory level (switch 2), with repercussions on the immune system and altering sensory perceptions (amplifying some irrelevant ones and cutting out others to avoid overload, but with the risk of losing important information).

In addition to collagen, fascia is also made up of extracellular matrix (see Switch 1) and fibroblasts, which in turn create matrix and collagen. In the fascia there are myofibroblasts, present throughout the body with a fundamental function in repairing wounds. When the fascia is subjected to intense and continuous tensile forces (as happens when maintaining stress or trauma postures for a long time after the event has ended), new ones are created by the fibroblasts, myofibroblasts, also known as *stress fibres*. Myofibroblasts can create a new tensile force capable of altering the entire musculoskeletal system.

These myofibroblast tensions are unresponsive and not modifiable through classic muscle movement. On the other hand they can be remodelled thanks to good hydration, by reducing inflammatory levels, by stretching exercises with tension and release mechanisms in physiology (such as *Isometric Emotions* and *Psychosomatic Stretching*), massages combined with specific phases of breathing and focusing of thought and of the emotional state in synergy or contrast (as in different variations of *Psychosomatic Release* techniques).

FREEDOM OF MOVEMENT = EMOTIONAL AND MENTAL FREEDOM

There are some interesting connections between muscular activation and emotional responses. In particular, there are a series of connections and interactions between *stress responses* and certain types of movement or postures that are taken to adapt to an environment, or in response to danger. For example, if a person that is in a good or neutral mood thinks about something negative, even for an instant, that immediately weakens the strength of *isometric contractions* (when muscle length doesn't change, such as when pushing your arms against a wall or remaining immobile), while there is no effect on an isotonic push (i.e. doing push ups), in *free movement* or in *flexible postures*[10].

This understanding has helped us develop *specific techniques*, such as *Isometric Emotions* and some variations of *Interpersonal Accommodation*, that alternate isometric contractions and muscle lengthening in coordination with mental states and contextual clues, so as to bring muscle tone back to its physiological state (i.e. hypo or hyper-active in conditions of chronic stress, or further to trauma) and to the appropriate state of activation or deactivation depending on requirements[11].

The employment of high-concentration and intentionally slow micro-movements (more specifically of a *myofascial unwinding*[12]), enables the patient to feel free and to move with a series of advantages, with direct experience (ease of movement, reduction/disappearance of pain) and – even more importantly to anyone working on mind and behaviour – with *indirect experience*[13]. The feeling of myofascial unwinding in fact enables us to perceive more resources in unpredictable situations, triggers the working of the Salience Network (see switch group 3 for more on both these concepts), helps the insula in the production of new and more effective body images and self-images and enables the *release and reworking of emotional experiences* connected to that state of activation.

ISOMETRIC EMOTIONS TECHNIQUE

Isometric Emotions are techniques developed to include all the core elements connected to primary responses to emotions and adaptation processes; from muscular reflexes to protect (such as when we rapidly retract a hand that is wounded) or breathing blockage (such as when we stub our toe and in practically any trauma, right through to feelings of anger or impotence), to the alternation between sympathetic and parasympathetic systems, visual representations, body maps and identity.

To intervene on these levels IE set out a series of exercises developed and structured in different variations. In this regard, the Psychosomatic Stretching exercises seen in the previous chapters are just a sub-technique of EI with a specific goal. The fil rouge are isometric contractions; those that occur when the muscle is engaged but not shortening (i.e. when we try to push or pull something that is firmly attached to a wall). We chose isometric contractions because they have strong neurobiological implications at a muscular level (average tone, release etc.) and at an emotional-psychological level (enabling experimentation of both power and impotence, stimulating the alteration of body maps, helping perceive resources etc.).

This example shows an isometric contraction that aims to reactivate the protective and antalgic reflex of the foetal position. It is a starting example that is ideal to develop awareness and then exercise control of all the muscles active in stress responses.

Isometric Emotions can be declined in different ways, each with its own specific objectives:

- To favour muscle release of tension accumulated over long periods of time due to constant stressful events. It is thus possible to break vicious psychosomatic circles and bring the adaptation-recovery process back to physiology.
- To intervene on the alteration that takes place during trauma in which breathing obstruction and a feeling of impotence alter motor schemes supporting dysfunctions at identity and active self-regulation level.
- As an instrument to help the recovery of a correct alternation between the sympathetic and parasympathetic system, thus enabling active regulation that is contextually adequate and modulated while totally under our control.

The base mode requires a few repetitions (usually 3–4) of isometric contraction in conditions of forced physiology, or in other words exhaling in contraction for around 5–8 seconds and inhaling in recovery phase for 7–10 seconds.

During these contractions it is possible to analyse various issues; levels of active physical awareness, ability for fine motor control of every movement, de-activation of all the muscles engaged in stress responses that are not actually required, distinguishing between postural and emotional schemas, recovering mastery and control via micro-adjustments, etc.

Awareness, functional activation, the active ability to enter a recovery phase, can all be amplified and used in synergy with the various variations that aim to shift focus on different elements (the self, others, context) and by introducing the cognitive sphere as an element of fine-tuning (such as for example attributing a numerical, percentual or symbolic value to the variations introduced with a request such as 'now contract at exactly 60% of your maximum strength').

PROGRESSIVE DISTANCING

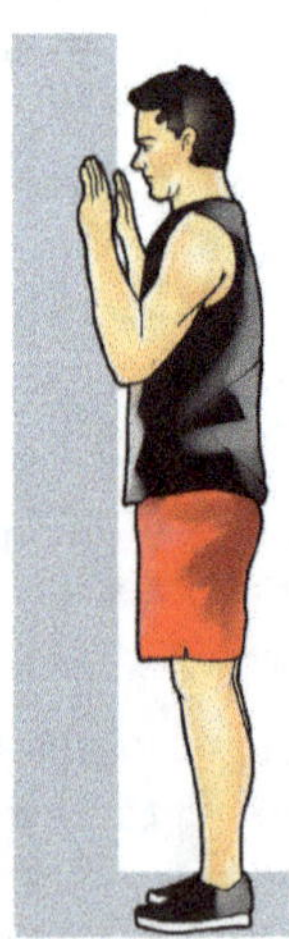

In this variant, isometric contraction progressively changes the distance from the obstacle/constraint, aiming for maximum control in every instance. The muscles

involved, the perceived spaces, the feeling of emotional and physical contrast are always different in each phase and can be explored to find well-being and mastery under any condition. In the second phase you may swap the wall with a person to work on interpersonal aggression experiences.

It is not just isometric contractions that can be used in change and transformation processes in synergy with cognitive and emotional variants. The use of slow micro-movements[14], for example, with great focus on attention and intentionality, enable the development of awareness of usually unaware adaptation processes in interpersonal dynamics such as, for example, a tensing of the neck muscles or shifting the barycentre when we perceive a challenge or an instance of social exclusion.

The targeted use of these *micro-movements*, in interaction with the therapist/facilitator who proposes different relational styles, allows us first of all to develop greater awareness and, secondly, mastery over these mechanisms, reinforcing the ability to centre and the sense of self-control in stressful interpersonal situations, learning to actively manage these forms of interpersonal adjustment.

A *simple interoceptive* test that I often propose can also become a tool to be used in everyday situations. It consists of alternating short moments (from 10 to 60 seconds) of total immobility with moments in which localized micro-movements are made. A typical example concerns the neck, which tends to stiffen during immobility, while movements of a few millimetres of the head give a sense of relief and control. You can also try to hint at muscle contraction, such as wanting to tilt the head, but without actually doing it. Just the stimulus to concretely think about starting the action (together with all the predictive games seen in Switch 3) offers a relevant signal that helps to go in the direction of physiology and allows you to regain awareness and mastery over the body and emotions.

Another interesting way of applying *micro-movements* concerns the possibility of doing them *with one part of the body while the others cannot move*. One case in point may be when you are at the dentist's; you have to keep your mouth open, the drill in your mouth is scary as well as triggering abundant salivation reflexes and, beyond possible phobias or subjective traumas, it is objectively dangerous to move your mouth suddenly in these conditions. The practical suggestion is applied by asking the person to concentrate their own possibility of movement in a finger (which they can raise or move sideways by a few millimetres, without anyone noticing), or in the movements of the abdomen which takes part in breathing (and which we feel to extend or inflate slightly more than usual), or in the rotation of the pelvis, thighs or feet (making slow micro-adjustments). In all these cases it is important to bring one's attention to that area and to the surrounding ones, leaving the rest of the body in the background, indirectly trying to leave it relaxed only in a passive way, i.e. without unnecessary contractions. Instead, where attention is directed, it is useful to listen carefully to what changes on a physical level and what effects are created on an emotional and mental level.

INTERPERSONAL ACCOMMODATION TECHNIQUE

Interpersonal Accommodation is a technique, or rather a series of techniques that intervene in a targeted way on mental, physical and emotional processes within interpersonal dynamics.

Daily experience and research confirm that in the management of relationships there are a series of contrasting processes; it is difficult to mediate between what we are and how we want to appear, between what we had planned to say or do and what actually comes naturally. There is also a series of switches between personal defence and being open to relationships, between wanting to be accepted a priori and having a special role, between bonds and freedom. In all these instances creative, motor, postural and emotional flows often do not flow freely and risk becoming dystonic and posing an obstacle to each other.

Interpersonal Accommodation techniques allow us to experiment with all these aspects and experience them with crystal clear awareness, to identify postural and motor schemas that sustain these dynamics and the way they interact and mutually influence each other in a two-way process with adaptation schemas, emotional responses and thought flows.

In the various exercises proposed you can transition from modes of nurture, protection, reciprocal nurture, cooperation, antagonism, creative play and much more. It is thus possible to explore new active modes of setting up interpersonal dynamics.

There are various ways to reach these objectives. The first one plays on physical interpersonal distance and analyses the involuntary alterations that are activated. To do this we use external objective elements such as photos or videos (when projected on a large screen it is possible to zoom in on details such as a raised shoulder, a shift backwards) or simple instruments to track heart beat variation or brain waves (using software that immediately highlights macro-categories such as focus, emotional engagement, stress etc.).

In this example of the application of Interpersonal Accommodation there is polyvalent contact that enables the controlled transition between different modes and experiences such as: interpersonal focus, nurture, trust, physical contact with mental detachment etc.

Another variation that is particularly effective involves the activation of the defence schema by giving someone a shove on the shoulder, for example, to help identify it. Once identified, the gesture can be replicated starting from the opposite position and magnifying strength each time. Forcing the schema this way makes it unnatural and it is thus possible to introduce new response modes.

In yet another version we work on the spontaneous ways of accommodating that many people implement on a daily basis. For example, there are people who put their legs under the chair and 'hook' the legs of the chair, often squeezing strongly, sometimes so much that they go red or even develop bruises when under stress. Then there are people who cannot lie on their backs peacefully when lying down (at home or on our bed) but tend to turn on one side, often without realizing it. Others find themselves pushing their head back against the pillow of the bed or the top of the chair. In a similar way we observe people who push with their arm against the office table, at lunch or against the steering wheel in the ca. When this type of modality is intercepted, an attempt is made to recreate the triggering situations and, when that protective behaviour is activated, the person's body is delicately adjusted (extending the legs, turning them, etc.), inviting them to remain in conditions of well-being in that scheme, with the help of breathing, mental techniques and any other strategy present in this book or in your current professional baggage.

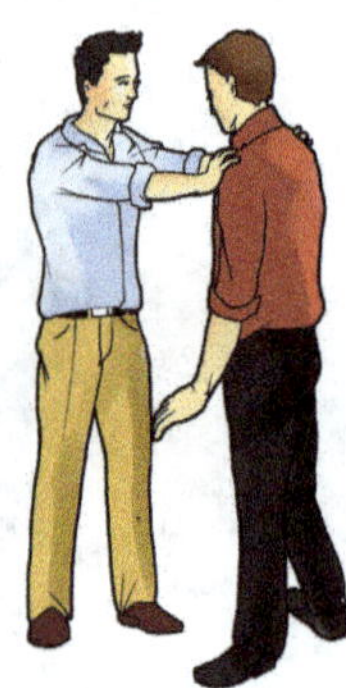

The image shows the initial trigger phase for a defensive mode that then enables us to intervene on the effectiveness and freedom of this pattern.

All this foundation work is, at first glance, very physical and focused on the physical level of lived experience. It is useful to explore the emotional experiences, the related self-images and all the factors of interest for that person in a second stage.

THE PHYSIOLOGY OF EMOTIONAL MOVEMENT: THE DEVIL IS IN THE DETAIL

When dealing with motor and postural flows it is important to devote particular focus to the physiology of movement. As brilliantly highlighted by Bessel van der Kolk, Peter Levine, Pat Ogden and others, it is important to regain the ability to move in a way that has emotional significance and that provides safety such as the gesture typically made to distance someone.

Fig. - Physical push exercises combined with images and thoughts of emotionally negative events, performed in a linear (A) or linear + rotational way, in accordance with muscular physiology (B). The difference in facial expression and muscle fluidity is immediately noticeable and is also confirmed by the patient's subjective experience and by biological parameters such as HRV and BIA.

These authors have focused on pushing away (to move an ill-intentioned person away), but it will be extremely interesting to work on the mirror movement as well. This movement is that of grabbing something or someone and bringing it or them closer. In fact, our body, expresses much more force in traction than in thrust due to the way it is built as we will see shortly. From an evolutionary point of view too we must consider that evolved mammals obtain maximum security not from the removal of the other (who could always return) but from their submission, which - as the name suggests - is the physical act of placing oneself below the other and remaining inert. In fact, even oriental martial arts, which take into consideration the physiology of the human body and the study of other animals during fights, attribute victory when an enemy is landed and blocked in that position. In daily life we don't have to go that far, but it is extremely useful to experience the sensation of keeping others under close control.

In any case, whether it is thrusts, tractions or other movements related to safety, protection or other affective and/or emotional dynamics, there is an interesting level that can be integrated and favoured even more. This is the biomechanical level which, precisely because it is rooted in the structure of bodily functioning, has a huge impact on the aspects that support the sense of mastery and efficacy in self-regulation from below.

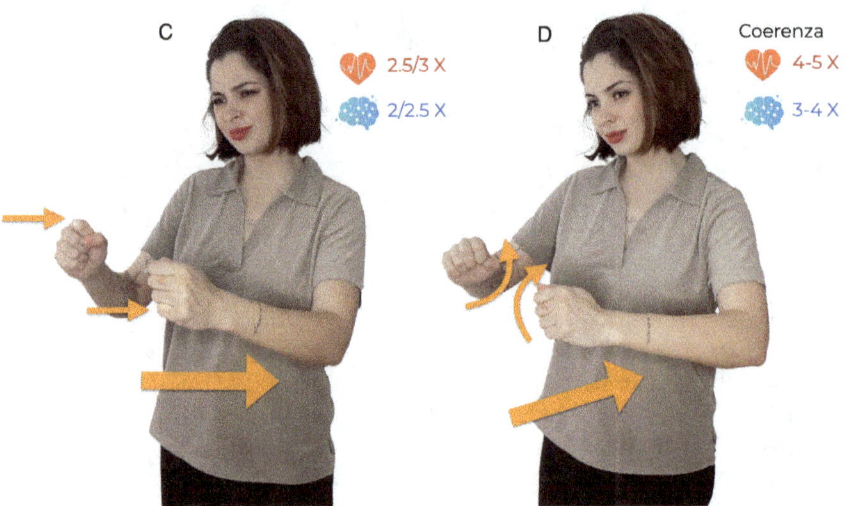

Fig. - Image similar to the previous one, but with pulling rather than pushing movements. From an anatomical and evolutionary point of view, tractions are even more effective in the sense of power and control that is developed.

Let us look at a practical example. We can try to delve into the fine details of what happens physically when we push someone away. As we distance the other person, our hands do not just enact an advancing movement; physiological movement also includes a rotation towards the inside (like the movement made to screw in a lightbulb). In addition to this, in conditions of total physiology, the motor schema includes the extension and rotation of the arm as well as the advancing of the shoulder[15].

Indeed, our body is built and developed to make spiral movements. If we look at the bones of arms and legs, such as a humerus or a femur, we immediately notice that the two heads at the ends of these bones are not aligned and formed to perform linear movements, but have a spiral structure around the bone itself. Even the insertion of the muscles is not on a straight line, but diagonal and it rotates around the joint, clearly demonstrating that the physiological movement of the limb is rotational on itself.

Furthermore, this type of movement should not be analysed in isolation, because it is now clear that muscles work by activation chains[16]. So the rotational movements are not limited to the arm only, but extend from one side to the hand and, in the opposite direction, can be traced back to the shoulder, back, buttocks, legs and feet. Returning to our exercise, in fact, there are also significant experiential differences if the movement is made with only one hand – rotating on the body's central axis, then moving the opposing shoulder backwards and rotating the hips correctly putting weight on both legs – compared to making the same movement with two arms[17].

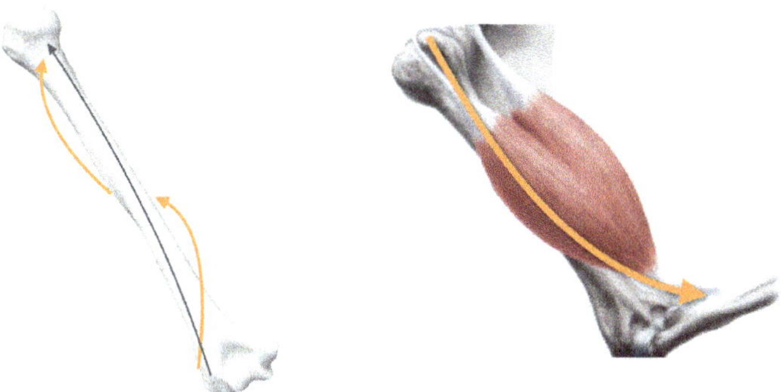

Fig. - The body is naturally structured to make circular and spiral movements. This is clearly seen by the twisting of the bones and the non-linear engagement of the muscles. Only by respecting this structure can you have fluid movements, a sense of mastery, emotional responses and adaptations that are perceived as they take shape. The sense of *agency* is embodied and works best if it respects the physiology of the body through which it manifests itself.

These are two totally different biomechanical processes, with very different repercussions on the sense of mastery and muscle power. The tensions kept in the body unnecessarily and which, as we have seen by analysing the Principle of minimum free energy, also impede thoughts and emotional experiences are thus released. In addition, an overall correct posture enables the release of a feeling of greater strength and a sense of security because it increases the protection of vital organs and lowers bodily alarm systems enabling a more powerful and complete cognitive reprocessing[18].

This recovery of innate rotation movements in the human body (i.e. the arm that rotates as we extend a hand and one shoulder advances while the other moves backwards as we distance or attack a person) enables the activation of greater power and sense of effectiveness. These are innate movement patterns that have been lost due to cultural influences. In fact, martial arts and yoga, for example, focus on recovering these modes of movement providing great physical value in self-regulation and power over emotional experience and in relationships. These devices can be introduced in interesting ways as value-add in psychophysical or sensorimotor techniques that are already in use, increasing their effects, but they can also be used as self-standing exercises for educational or preventive objectives such as actively managing bullying or developing effective public speaking.

BALANCE AND FLUIDITY OF CONTROL

Let us start from an important anatomical-functional thought before we analyse its practical implications on any intervention aimed at change; the active use of interoception and proprioception circuits project directly towards areas such as the nucleus of the solitary tract, the hypothalamus and the PAG. These structures govern the autonomous nervous system, so intervening on them means having a huge impact on sympathetic-vagal balance *at the heart of any stress, emotional or trauma response*. This happens far more effectively than through logical thought and dialogue, that certainly play a key role, but mainly in the following reorganisation phase. This type of stimulation can be achieved via: 1- *extremely slow physical activities or unusual movement* (such as focusing more on the positive phase of movement – when lifting a weight – than the negative phase – when lowering it); 2- *unnatural schemas* (i.e. walking backwards) or *highly complex coordination and balance movements* (from climbing to juggling as shown by Van der Kolk's research, right through to specifically developed techniques such as *Resource Balance*): 3- *by alternating partial and complete movement cycles* (so as to highlight that often habitual movement is incomplete); 4- and in many other ways that *subvert habits and drive a sensory, evaluation or executive reset.* These processes can also be managed in unison with physical disciplines such as Yoga and Tai Chi, learning to play a musical instrument, or via techniques developed ad hoc (see the Reboot Techniques and other strategies in this book).

An interesting way to bring this type of signal into daily life is to employ the principles of *Resource Balance* techniques (Switch 3) into different contexts and situations. For example, after doing some practice with the actual technique, the person can be invited to seek that kind of sensations and self-regulation in different situations of daily life: standing with knees bent during travel on the subway after returning from work; or making micro-adjustments of balance and verifying one's sensations while playing ping-pong or table tennis; paying attention to one's body modifications while witnessing a stressful scene (for example watching friends or family who play a sport and risk losing or getting hurt) and, in the meantime, seeking balance and physiology with all the strategies learnt in the Resource Balance technique or in others.

In addition to paying attention to the legs, in these situations it is also useful to pay attention to other important joints in our body, which serve balance and adjustment both on a physical, mental and emotional level. In particular, attention can be paid to keeping the pelvis mobile on the 3 axes, having a flexible neck and keeping the shoulders (in the broadest sense, also including the shoulder blades and other adjacent areas) unlocked and mobile, the wrists and fingers soft, not clenching the jaw.

EVEN MORE FLOWS

So far, we've looked at some of the main flows and ones that need to be worked on in many of the most common cases. As we saw in the initial part of this book, relating to the identification and analysis of flows, there are numerous other types of Flows which cover all levels of behaviour: *Communicative, Interpersonal, Creative, Logical, Mindset, Reading models,*

Power, Motivation, Posture and movement, Physical tone, Energy tone and many more. Let's look at some more *practical examples.*

Many people benefit greatly when they take weight and tension off their joints (spine, pelvis, knees, etc.) and put it back on the large muscle groups, so as to restore physical freedom and, at the same time, act on all subsequent emotional and motivational correlates (a sense of energy, a reduction in pain, greater expressive coherence, etc.). The easiest way to do this is to invite people to do simple bodyweight exercises looking for maximum flexibility of the body and to use only the large muscle groups such as legs and back.

Relational, communicative and power dynamics can be modified *by training different communication styles,* for example, starting from the linguistic register, but in such a way as to create new mental perspectives, change self-image and open up real possibilities for action.

2 COMMUNICATIVE-INTERPERSONAL TECHNIQUES

Technique - Style exercises

This technique helps to get out of habitual ways of responding to situations and communicating. Its name is borrowed from the exercises that aspiring writers and journalists are asked to do in which the same theme - for example a newspaper article on the opening of a painting exhibition - is rewritten several times in different styles: news, tabloid, humorous, promotional, etc.

We employ this method to increase the possibility of saying something or behaving differently the next time a certain event occurs, modifying one's reaction and, consequently, influencing the relationship with one's audience in a different way from usual. It is about trying to imagine behaviours and sentences in line with different styles of communication such as:

• with the utmost cold objectivity,

• in a calm and relaxed way,

• with an ironic attitude,

• with great passion for the topic but respecting the perspectives of others,

• boldly, as if there were no consequences,

- with the right level of aggression to be respected but without being destructive,
- with extreme faith in justice (from different points of view),
- and under any other perspective deemed interesting.

Technique - Role rotation

What creates problems in a communicative relationship is often the game of who is good and who is bad; who is the victim and who, on the other hand, benefits. Implicitly in the sentences we pronounce we suggest that we are the good guys and the others are the bad guys. With our words we transmit, in a more or less direct way, a relational concept. Take this exchange for example:

- boss: *I wish you would focus on work more*
- worker: *I'm sorry, I was a bit overburdened with things to do.*

The two are actually saying:

- boss: *I who am good, give you a job and you, who are bad, don't do it well.*
- worker: *You are bad and you don't give me, who am good, the tools to do this job well.*

As you well know from your own experience, this type of talk leads nowhere. It is an exchange that keeps both locked in their own positions and usually increases resentment and a sense of misunderstanding.

A similar pattern is that of the 'victim-perpetrator'. If a person drinks a bad cup of coffee and says to the barista "just what we needed today: bad coffee!", they project a message like: "I, *the poor victim, had to drink a bad coffee because you criminals don't know how to do it or you want to save money*". In this case the emphasis is shifted to the fact that one suffers the ignorance, the opportunistic advantages or the bad faith of the other.

On the other hand, creating free communication allows advantages for oneself and for the other. It doesn't make us feel and it doesn't reinforce the image of us as the disadvantaged, unfortunate one, of the victim that is good but always at a disadvantage, etc. Likewise, it does not make our counterpart feel attacked or accused, which allows space for open and constructive dialogue.

Let's see some useful tips for managing these communicative roles in an active way, not being subjected to them.

1. Do not position yourself as a victim of the event but as a potential good person who provides feedback that can give an advantage and help the

other be even better. Some people are used to playing the victim role. Others think it's effective, but it's not. Effectively playing the victim means manipulating others.

2. Do not position the other as a bad person, but as a good guy who unknowingly, involuntarily and for external causes found themselves in that situation. Positioning the counterpart as bad is a declaration of war and it leads to nothing constructive.

3. Don't compete to see who has suffered the most/is better or worse/etc. It's an endless, tiring game that leaves you unsatisfied in whatever way it goes, creates a new conflict in addition to the primary one but resolves none.

4. The potential victims to be identified are those who will be saved thanks to the agreement or clarification between the two (in the example of coffee, it is the other customers who are disappointed). Or it can highlight how our counterpart is also a victim of the situation (losing dissatisfied customers) but neither is portrayed as "the bad guy".

It is also possible to intervene on these registers by unhinging the normal processes of clustering (that is, the way in which we rapidly pigeonhole reality into reductive dichotomies, for example as soon as we see a person and evaluate them as nice vs. unpleasant).

In any case, it is a matter of identifying the neurobiological mechanisms so that change on each of these levels may represent a lasting, significant switch of behaviour and offer a retro-feedback which enhances change on all the other structural, metabolic and functional levels.

REFERENCES

[1] Quoidbach, Jordi, June Gruber, Moïra Mikolajczak, Alexsandr Kogan, Ilios Kotsou, and Michael I. Norton. 2014. "Emodiversity and the Emotional Ecosystem." Journal of Experimental Psychology: General 143 (6): 2057–2066.

[2] Fleming, S. M., & Dolan, R. J. (2012). The neural basis of metacognitive ability. Philosophical Transactions of the Royal Society B: Biological Sciences, 367(1594), 1338–1349.

[3] Carpenter, J., Sherman, M.T., Kievit, R.T., Seth, A., Hakwan, L., Fleming S. (2018). Domain-general enhancements of metacognitive ability through adaptive training. Journal of Experimental Psychology: General.

[4] Adams, R.A, Napier, G., Roiser, J.P., Mathys, C., Gilleen, J.. Attractor-like dynamics in belief updating in schizophrenia. Journal of Neuroscience 5 September 2018, 3163-17.

[5] Barrett, L. F., & Simmons, W. K. (2015). Interoceptive predictions in the brain. Nature reviews. Neuroscience, 16(7), 419–429.

[6] Benedetti F. Placebo effects: from the neurobiological paradigm to translational implications. Neuron2014;84:623–37

[7] Vives, M. L., & FeldmanHall, O. (2018). Tolerance to ambiguous uncertainty predicts prosocial behavior. Nature communications, 9(1), 2156.

[8] Fisher, Ronald Philip and Geiselman, R. Edward, The Cognitive Interview Method of Conducting Police Interviews: Eliciting Extensive Information and Promoting Therapeutic Jurisprudence (October 22, 2010). International Journal of Law and Psychiatry, 2010.

[9] Barsotti N. et al. (2018), La PNEI e le discipline corpo- ree, Milano: Edra.

[10] Hillman, C. H., Rosengren, K. S. & Smith, D. P. Emotion and motivated behavior: Postural adjustments to affective picture viewing. Biol. Psychol. 66, 51–62 (2004).

[11] Sinibaldi F., Achilli S. (2017) Evoluzione, Adattamento, Fisiologia - Recuperare le nostre abilità di base e sviluppare nuove potenzialità. Real Way of Life.

[12] Michalak, J., Aranmolate, L., Bonn, A., Grandin, K., Schleip, R., Schmiedtke, J., Quassowsky, S., & Teismann, T. (2022). Myofascial Tissue and Depression. Cognitive therapy and research, 46(3), 560–572.

[13] Pamukoff, D. N., Ryan, E. D., & Blackburn, J. T. (2014). The acute effects of local muscle vibration frequency on peak torque, rate of torque development, and EMG activity. Journal of electromyography and kinesiology : official journal of the International Society of Electrophysiological Kinesiology, 24(6), 888–894.

[14] Schleip, Robert. (2003). Fascial plasticity - A new neurobiological explanation: Part 1. Journal of Bodywork and Movement Therapies. 7. 11-19.

[15] Schleip, R., & Müller, D. G. (2013). Training principles for fascial connective tissues: scientific foundation and suggested practical applications. Journal of bodywork and movement therapies, 17(1), 103–115.

[16] Myers, Thomas W. (2011). Anatomy Trains. London: Urban & Fischer.

[17] Krause, F., Wilke, J., Vogt, L., & Banzer, W. (2016). Intermuscular force transmission along myofascial chains: a systematic review. Journal of anatomy, 228(6), 910–918.

---

[18] Sinibaldi F. (2018), Working with the body-mind unit to foster thoughts, emotions and personal development in: PNEI and the physical disciplines [orig. in Italian language: Lavorare con l'unità corpo-mente per favorire pensieri, emozioni e sviluppo personale in: La PNEI e le discipline corporee] (Barsotti N, Lanaro D, Chiera M, Bottaccioli F), Edra - Elsevier.

www.ingramcontent.com/pod-product-compliance
Lightning Source LLC
Chambersburg PA
CBHW071355150726
48000CB00001B/32